# CHILDREN'S HEARINGS
# IN SCOTLAND

AUSTRALIA
Law Book Co.
Sydney

CANADA and USA
Carswell
Toronto

HONG KONG
Sweet & Maxwell Asia

NEW ZEALAND
Brookers
Wellington

SINGAPORE and MALAYSIA
Sweet & Maxwell Asia
Singapore and Kuala Lumpur

# CHILDREN'S HEARINGS
# IN SCOTLAND

Kenneth McK. Norrie, LL.B., Ph.D., F.R.S.E.

*Professor of Law and Head of the Law School at the University of Strathclyde*

THOMSON

™

W. GREEN

First published 1997
Reprinted 2000

W. Green & Son Ltd
21 Alva Street
Edinburgh EH2 4PS

www.thomson.wgreen.com

*Typeset by LBJ Typesetting Ltd of Kingsclere*
*Printed and bound in Great Britain by TJ International*

No natural forests were destroyed to make this product;
only farmed timber was used and replanted.

A CIP catalogue record for this book is available from
the British Library.

ISBN 0414015878

# PREFACE

Part II of the Children (Scotland) Act 1995 came into force on April 1, 1997, which was the date at which I sought to state the law in the first edition of this book. In the eight years since then the new rules and procedures contained in the 1995 Act have settled well into the children's hearing system as it previously existed. There have been numerous important decisions from the Court of Session clarifying a variety of matters, all of which are dealt with in this second edition. Significantly more important and far-reaching, however, have been the legislative developments since 1997. The system itself has not undergone review or revision such as happened in 1995, but external events have led to legislation that has, by a sidewind, affected the operation of children's hearings. That legislation has not been primarily focused on children's hearings and is not, therefore, calibrated to the underpinning philosophies of the system. Barely a month after Part II came into force, a new Labour Government was elected, and great constitutional change quickly followed: devolution and the creation of a new Scottish Parliament, and the incorporation into domestic law of the European Convention on Human Rights. Human rights law affects every aspect of the children's hearing system, and has necessitated a different approach. In particular the European Convention focuses attention on all family members and not just the child, and it requires hearings to identify and protect children's rights to due process as well as their welfare. Other changes have come from the Scottish Parliament. Responding to public concerns about unruly behaviour, the Scottish Parliament has been active in promoting legislation designed to protect the public from such behaviour, as with the Antisocial Behaviour etc (Scotland) Act 2004. In so far as children's hearings are involved in antisocial behaviour orders, the Act refocuses attention away from the child to those who might be perceived as the victims of the child's behaviour. While even those who are totally child-centred in their approach to children's hearings are likely to support the application of human rights law to our system, the application of punitive and public protection measures as in the 2004 Act sits uneasily with the system as presently understood. It is all the more important, therefore, that we do not lose sight of the basic principles upon which the system is based and which still serve Scotland's children—and Scottish society—well today.

As always, thanks are due to a number of individuals who assisted, directly and indirectly, with the preparation of this new edition. In particular, the writings of, and personal discussions with, Sheriff Brian Kearney have allowed me to correct some misunderstandings which crept into the first edition. Personnel from the Scottish Children's Reporter Administration were again helpful in indicating their policies on numerous matters, especially in areas that had not come to the fore in 1997.

The law continues to develop and in places this book will be out of date even before it is published. I have attempted to state the law as at May 5, 2005.

*Kenneth McK. Norrie*

Howwood, May 2005

# CONTENTS

## CHAPTER TEN:   ADVICE AND REMIT HEARINGS IN OFFENCE-BASED CASES

## CHAPTER ELEVEN:   REVIEW HEARINGS

## CHAPTER TWELVE:   REVIEW OF THE ESTABLISHMENT OF THE GROUNDS OF REFERRAL

## CHAPTER THIRTEEN:   WARRANTS AND ORDERS TO APPREHEND AND DETAIN CHILD

## CHAPTER FOURTEEN:   APPEALS

## CHAPTER FIFTEEN: EMERGENCY PROTECTION OF CHILDREN

## APPENDICES

# TABLE OF CASES

# TABLE OF STATUTES

# TABLE OF STATUTORY INSTRUMENTS

**Scottish Statutory Instruments**

# TABLE OF CONVENTIONS

## CHAPTER ONE

# INTRODUCTION

## HISTORY

The children's hearing system is unique to Scotland. Its genesis is found in the Report of the Kilbrandon Committee,[1] which was appointed in 1961 to consider the provisions of the law of Scotland relating to the treatment of "juvenile delinquents and juveniles in need of care and protection or beyond parental control" and, in particular, the powers and procedures of the tribunals who deal with such juveniles. The Committee reported in 1964 and suggested a radical restructuring of the procedures for dealing with children with problems, a class which it defined widely. Its proposals, with some modifications, were adopted[2] and enacted in the Social Work (Scotland) Act 1968, which came into effect on April 15, 1971. For over 25 years thereafter, Part III of the 1968 Act was, together with the subsidiary legislation passed under it, the basic source of the law of Scotland in respect of child care and protection and juvenile justice. Though the system by and large worked well and attracted many supporters at home and admirers abroad, there were invariably certain difficulties with the operation of such a new and innovative system. In the late 1980s and early 1990s the system was subjected to rigorous scrutiny on various fronts, and a number of different reports about aspects of its operation were published.[3] In addition, a number of high profile cases, which were disastrous for the individuals concerned, brought some of the difficulties to the public attention. An increasing public awareness of the need for the highest calibre of provision for children, enhanced in part by the ratification of the UN Convention on the Rights of the Child, gave children's needs a higher political profile than they had ever had before. In 1995, Part III of the 1968 Act was repealed, and re-enacted in Part II of the Children (Scotland) Act 1995,[4] which is at least partly designed to rectify the flaws

---

[1] *Report on Children and Young Persons, Scotland,* Cmnd. 2306 (1964). An excellent summary of the conclusions of this Report can be found in *Stair Memorial Encyclopaedia of the Laws of Scotland, vol.* 3, paras 1278–1281.

[2] See the White Paper *Social Work and the Community,* Cmnd. 3065 (1966).

[3] See, for example, the *Report of the Inquiry into the Removal of Children From Orkney in February* 1991 (the Clyde Report, H.C. Papers 1992–1993, No. 195), the *Report of the Inquiry into Child Care Policies in Fife* (the Kearney Report, H.C. Papers 1992–1993 No. 191), *Reporters to the Children's Panel: Their Role, Function and Accountability* (the Finlayson Report, Scottish Office, 1992), *Review of Child Care Law in Scotland* (Scottish Office, 1990), and the White Paper, *Scotland's Children: Proposals for Child Care Policy and Law,* Cm. 2286 (1993).

[4] All statutory references in this book are, unless otherwise specified, to the Children (Scotland) Act 1995.

previously identified. The changes introduced by the 1995 Act, though important, were not fundamental and the basic philosophy behind the system remains as it was before. The system as governed by the 1995 Act and subsidiary legislation passed under it came into operation on April 1, 1997.

PHILOSOPHY OF THE SYSTEM

The Kilbrandon Committee Report and both the 1968 and the 1995 Acts are founded upon two basic premises, which together provide the philosophical underpinning of the children's hearing system in Scotland.

First, it is assumed that a child who has committed an offence, though culpable, is just as much in need of protection, guidance, treatment and control as is the child against whom an offence has been committed.[5] The commission of an offence by a child calls, in other words, for a caring response rather than a punitive response, just as the neglect of a child calls for a caring response. The welfare principle, which is today given practical effect by the rule in s.16(1) of the Children (Scotland) Act 1995 that "where . . . a children's hearing decide . . . any matter with respect to a child the welfare of that child throughout his childhood shall be their . . . paramount consideration", is perhaps not so substantial an innovation as is sometimes thought. It is certainly not the feature of the children's hearing system that makes the system unique. Since at least 1937, Scottish courts dealing with offences committed by children have been obliged to have regard to the welfare of the child,[6] and many foreign systems of criminal justice contain a similar provision. The unusual feature lies in the fact that it is the same tribunal, operating under the same procedural rules and having the same disposals available, that deals with all children identified as being in need of help, for whatever reason. Even more remarkable, perhaps, is the fact that Scotland retains this grasp on reality in the face of a near universal retreat from it elsewhere in the developed world.[7]

Secondly, it is recognised that a court of law, with its adversarial traditions, procedures and atmosphere, may well be an appropriate forum to resolve disputes of fact but is a singularly inappropriate forum for determining, in a welfare context, what if any form of protection, guidance, treatment or control an individual child needs. The child's needs can best be determined by a relatively[8] informal but carefully structured discussion involving the child and the child's primary carers. Twenty years before the United Kingdom ratified Article 12 of the UN Convention on the Rights of the Child[9] the children's hearing system

---

[5] Kilbrandon Report, paras 12–15.

[6] Children and Young Persons (Scotland) Act 1937, s.49(1).

[7] See C. Hallett, "Ahead of the Game or Behind the Times? The Scottish Children's Hearing System in International Perspective" (2000) 14 Int. J Law Pol & Fam 31.

[8] Relative to a court setting, that is.

[9] Which provides as follows: "States parties shall assure to the child who is capable of forming his or her own views the right to express those views freely in all matters affecting the child, the views of the child being given due weight in accordance with the age and maturity of the child. For this purpose, the child shall in particular be provided the opportunity to be heard in any judicial and administrative proceedings affecting the child, either directly, or through a representative or an appropriate body, in a manner consistent with the procedural rules of national law".

came into effect in Scotland with its central feature being a discussion with the child him or herself. The Kilbrandon Committee recognised that a court of law is not an environment which is likely to encourage a child to take an active or a helpful part in such a discussion, and for that reason the determination of what, if any, measures of care or supervision should be imposed lies with a lay tribunal, the children's hearing. This hearing is made up of three individuals whose only qualification beyond their training is their interest in, or knowledge of, the needs of children. They are locally recruited and serve, voluntarily and without payment, in their own local government areas. A court will still be involved if there is a dispute of fact as to the existence or otherwise of grounds of referral, for a court system designed to test evidence is accepted as the appropriate forum to find out the truth. It is far less appropriate a forum to determine how to react in the light of the discovered truth. It is this dichotomy between the role of the court and the role of the children's hearing that provides the defining characteristic of Scotland's system: its "genius", in the words of Lord President Hope.[10]

In addition to these two fundamental principles there are several other indigenous features of the system which serve to enhance the operation of these principles. First, the child is not looked at in isolation and is, rather, regarded as a member of a family unit. This recognises that a child's problems often stem from his or her home environment, or a failure in the normal upbringing processes, and can usually be effectively resolved only by affecting in some way that environment. So, though the children's hearing can impose compulsory measures of supervision over a child and not his or her parents, the parents do have an obligation to attend the hearing and have an obligation to co-operate with any social work involvement in the child's life that is deemed necessary. Secondly, each child is looked at as an individual.[11] There is no "tariff" for particular grounds of referral (as there might be in a criminal court) for it is the needs rather than the deeds of the child that is the primary consideration of the children's hearing. It follows from this that the hearing must have as much discretion as possible to structure whatever measures of supervision, whether orthodox or unorthodox, are deemed appropriate to the needs of the individual child. So any condition that the hearing consider necessary can be attached to a supervision requirement. And the supervision requirement has no fixed length (though it must be reviewed at stated intervals) and it can be either terminated or varied at any time to suit any changed circumstances. Thirdly, though the system contains some informality, that informality is seen only in the discussion of the case which lies at the heart of the procedure; other elements of the procedure are as formal and as mandatory as the procedure in a court of law. The children's hearing is a quasi-judicial tribunal which has many of the powers of a court and it must, therefore, for the protection of all those who appear before it, conform to the standards of procedural fairness required not only by natural justice but by international obligation. It is a fundamental misunderstanding to describe the whole procedure at a children's hearing as "informal".

---

[10] *Sloan v B* 1991 S.L.T. 530 at 548E.
[11] Kilbrandon Report, para.79.

Fourthly, the breadth of investigation and discussion is not bound by artificial limits. Once grounds of referral have been accepted or established it is open to the hearing to explore any aspect of the child's life that affects his or her welfare.[12] While the grounds of referral must receive some consideration, the outcome of the case depends upon what the hearing identify as the child's needs having had regard to all the circumstances and not just those contained in the grounds of referral. The hearing's powers of investigation are limited only by what might be relevant to the child's interests. Fifthly, the proceedings at a children's hearing are private and members of the public are not to be admitted. This principle is important not only because privacy will encourage a child to take part in the discussion, but also because children are less able than adults to cope with wide publicity of their personal affairs. Deterrence of others plays no part in either the hearing's deliberations or its outcomes.

As well as the features mentioned above, which have characterised both the structure and the operation of the children's hearing system since its inception, the influence of the European Convention on Human Rights (ECHR), particularly since its incorporation into domestic law by the Human Rights Act 1998, ensures that a number of other features are now central to the hearing system. Articles 6 (right to due process) and 8 (right to respect for family life) are particularly significant. Both the reporter and the hearing itself are "public authorities" for the purposes of the 1998 Act and are obliged, therefore, to act in a manner consistent with the ECHR[13]: it follows that both the process by which the child is referred and the process by which the outcome of the referral is decided must not infringe any ECHR requirement. The most important ECHR principle in this context is that of "proportionality". This is seen most explicitly in Art.8 (though the European Court of Human Rights has pointed out on various occasions that the proportionality principle is "inherent in the whole Convention").[14] Article 8(1) provides that everyone is entitled to respect for their private and family life. Any action to refer a child to a children's hearing, and any order made by a children's hearing, is an interference with, or limitation to, the child's and the parent's family life. As such it requires to be justified by the principle in Art.8(2) that there shall be no interference with a person's private and family life except when this is "necessary in a democratic society". The concept of "necessity" has been given a wide interpretation by the European Court of Human Rights. The Court requires that to be shown to be "necessary", the interference must be in accordance with the law, must pursue a legitimate aim, and the means adopted to achieve that aim must be "proportionate", that is to say the minimum that is necessary to achieve the aim.[15] It is not, for example, a proportionate response to a child's special educational needs to remove the child from

---

[12] Kilbrandon Report, para.77.
[13] Human Rights Act 1998, s.6.
[14] *Sporrong & Lönnroth v Sweden* (1982) 5 E.H.R.R. 35 at para.57; *Soering v United Kingdom* (1989) 11 E.H.R.R. 439 at para.89.
[15] See K. Norrie "A Child's Right to Care and Protection", Chap.8 in A. Cleland and E.E. Sutherland *Children's Rights in Scotland* (2nd ed., 2001).

his or her parents and prohibit contact;[16] it is not proportionate to remove a new-born child from its mother when its safety could be ensured by appropriate monitoring of the mother.[17] Within the children's hearing system there is seldom if ever any difficulty in identifying a legitimate aim: it is to protect or ensure or enhance the child's welfare. The more difficult issue is nearly always proving that the means adopted to achieve that aim are proportionate thereto. To a large extent this principle reflects the minimum intervention principle contained in s.16(3) of the Children (Scotland) Act 1995,[18] but it is in fact more focused in that it requires a clear identification of an aim, which is legitimate, and a clear and effective link between that aim and the means chosen to achieve it. But in itself the introduction by the Human Rights Act 1998 of the proportionality test did not require a change of mindset for any of the active participants in the children's hearing system. The Kilbrandon Report itself recognised[19] that a welfare-based approach might in fact and in practice "represent an appreciable inroad into personal and family life" which might be unacceptable and therefore could not be taken.

Article 6, on the other hand, can be argued to have required a change of mindset. Prior to the coming into force of the Human Rights Act 1998, the child's interests were considered paramount, which was often (perhaps wrongly) interpreted to mean that the child's interests were the exclusive concern of the hearing. Indeed Lord Justice-Clerk Ross may be found expressing the view that the child's welfare was more important than due process, and that procedural niceties must give way to the child's interests.[20] If this were ever truly the case it is certainly no longer so. Article 6 protects everyone's right to a fair hearing in the determination of their civil rights. One of these civil rights is family autonomy, or freedom from state interference (itself protected by Art.8). And this is a right that inheres in both child and parent. A system is not "fair" to one person if procedural niceties are bypassed in order to favour another person. And most importantly the right to a fair hearing inheres in the parents or relevant persons to the same extent as in the child: it follows that the active participants—the reporter and the panel members—may no longer ignore the interests of the parents but must protect them as well as the interests of the child. So the change of mindset required is for the hearing to operate in a way that balances sometimes competing interests, rather than simply holding the child's interests to be the paramount (by which was understood sole) consideration. The child's interests *are* paramount[21] but that does not prevent the reporter or hearing from balancing them with other considerations which they must also take into account.

## FLAWS IN THE SYSTEM

Though the children's hearing system in Scotland has many admirable qualities and is, it is submitted, hugely preferable to a court-based system

---

[16] *Kutzner v Germany* (2002) 35 E.H.R.R. 25.
[17] *P, C and S v United Kingdom* (2002) 35 E.H.R.R. 31.
[18] See pp.122–123 below.
[19] Kilbrandon Report, paras 79–80.
[20] *Kennedy v A* 1986 S.L.T. 358 at 362A.
[21] Children (Scotland) Act 1995, s.16(1)

of child care and protection and juvenile justice, our system is not perfect. It is operated by real men and women, who necessarily have the flaws of humanity. It also operates in the real world, where political and (especially) financial considerations play a large role in determining what resources are to be made available for the provision of services which can be called upon by the children's hearing. At the micro level, many panel members would be happier in requiring, say, an individual child to live in a residential establishment if that establishment had more resources than are, practically, available. The physical condition of many children's homes in Scotland is or ought to be a source of shame. At the macro level, hearings are frequently faced with having to make a decision as to what is the best resource available rather than the best resource for the child; and that often means that they have no effective choice at all.

As well as that practical flaw, which is unlikely to be resolved in the absence of a political willingness to invest substantially more heavily than at present in our child-care system, there were at least two legal flaws identified in the first edition of this book which have been or are being addressed. First, the unmarried father was for long not recognised as having a legal relationship with his child in Scots law.[22] Within the context of the children's hearing system, this meant that he (unlike the unmarried mother) had no automatic right (or duty) to attend a children's hearing, nor to appeal against their decisions, nor to call for a review of any supervision requirement they impose. A high percentage of the children who appear before a children's hearing have parents who are not married to each other, and the exclusion of the unmarried father discouraged men from playing a full role in the upbringing of their children. This was contrary both to the European Convention on Human Rights and to the UN Convention on the Rights of the Child. Article 14 of the European Convention prohibits unjustifiable discrimination based on sex[23]; Art.18 of the UN Convention requires that both parents are placed under common responsibilities for the upbringing and development of the child. There is presently a Bill before the Scottish Parliament to ameliorate this position and bring all fathers who are registered as such within the term "relevant person" for purposes of the children's hearing system (and for other purposes).[24]

Secondly, while the child and his or her parents are entitled to bring a representative to the hearing, there was no provision for paid legal representation at hearings. This was entirely unjustifiable. Children's hearings have huge, even draconian, powers over a child and his or her

---

[22] Except for the purposes of aliment and child support, succession, and the forbidden degrees for marriage and incest.

[23] *McMichael v UK* [1995] 20 E.H.R.R. 205, where the European Court of Human Rights held that the exclusion of the unmarried father from a children's hearing was justifiable, was argued on the basis that unmarried fathers are treated differently from married fathers. It ought to have been argued on the basis that male parents are treated differently from female parents. But in *Sahin v Germany* July 8, 2003 the European Court held that if a Member State wished to impose different rules for unmarried and married men then it needed to have very substantial grounds for doing so. None exists, it is submitted, in relation to entitlement to attend and take full part in a children's hearing.

[24] Family Law (Scotland) Bill 2005, presented to the Scottish Parliament on February 7, 2005.

family and can exercise these powers (which might, for example, include removing the child from his or her parents or authorising the locking up of the child in a secure unit) in the complete absence of legal representation. It is, of course, right that the child should be encouraged to speak at his or her own children's hearing, but few children have the confidence or the articulateness to argue why their welfare demands an approach different from that which the hearing are inclined to favour. The failure to allow paid legal representation amounted, it is submitted, to a breach of Article 40 of the UN Convention. This Article provides that children who are accused of a crime are to have legal assistance in preparing and presenting their defence. "Defence" means more than a denial of involvement and includes an explanation of that involvement. The children's hearing system encourages the child to give an explanation, but denied the child legal help in presenting that explanation. Yet, many who appear before the hearing have suffered from a lack of educational provision and are all the more in need of such assistance. Shortly after the coming into force of the Human Rights Act 1998 the Court of Session held that the failure of the state to provide paid legal representation to the child was a breach of Art.6 of the European Convention on Human Rights,[25] at least in certain circumstances, and it has now been provided by statutory instrument that such legal representation will be provided to the child in these circumstances.[26] These rules do not provide paid legal representation for the relevant persons (*i.e.* the child's parents) and it remains to be seen whether (for admittedly very different reasons) that gap is similarly found to be a breach of Article 6 which protects everyone's civil rights and not just those of children.

The children's hearing system continues to evolve, in light of better understandings and in response to political imperatives. Sometimes these political imperatives fit uneasily into the underpinning philosophy of the system. So for example in 2004 the Scottish Parliament, responding to public fears and pressures that in themselves were entirely legitimate, passed the Antisocial Behaviour etc (Scotland) Act 2004. The aim was to curb antisocial behaviour, primarily by the mechanism of antisocial behaviour orders granted by courts. If a child is to be the subject of the order, the children's hearing will have a role to play. But that role is not informed by hearing members' expertise in identifying the child's welfare: rather the purpose of the order is to protect others from actions of the child and this involves a small but dangerous shift in the focus of attention that hearing members are asked to give to individual cases. These orders are explicitly designed to deal with the deeds of the child and the needs of others. It was probably misconceived to involve children's hearings at all in the antisocial behaviour legislation.[27] The challenge remains therefore to ensure that legislators and policy-makers

---

[25] *S v Miller* 2001 S.L.T. 531 and 1304.

[26] See pp.91–93: below.

[27] In fairness it should be noted that there are some very valuable provisions contained in the Antisocial Behaviour etc. (Scotland) Act 2004, particularly in the strengthening of local authorities' duties to give effect to supervision requirements and the introduction of mechanisms to enforce these duties: see further at pp.22–23.

are fully aware of what it is that makes the hearing system successful, in order that that system can continue to build upon its experience as a means of identifying and addressing the issues of all children in need of protection, guidance, treatment or control.

## CHAPTER TWO

# THE PERSONNEL OF THE CHILDREN'S HEARING SYSTEM

## THE CHILDREN'S PANEL

In each of the 32 local government areas in Scotland there is a Children's Panel,[1] which is made up of members of the public who have been appointed to the Panel by the Scottish ministers; for each Panel there is also appointed a Chairman and a deputy chairman thereof.[2] While appointment is made by the Scottish ministers, they make appointments on the advice of the Children's Panel Advisory Committee (CPAC), which is a body formed by each local authority[3] to perform the following duties: (i) to submit names of possible panel members to the Scottish ministers; (ii) to advise Scottish ministers, in so far as they require advice, on the suitability of persons referred to them as potential panel members; and (iii) to advise the Scottish ministers on such matters relating to the general administration of the Panels as they may refer to the CPAC.[4] Members of the Children's Panel hold office for such period as is specified by the Scottish ministers and, though they can be removed from office by the Scottish ministers at any time,[5] their tenure of office is protected by the fact that they can be removed only with the consent of the Lord President.[6]

A list of the names and addresses of members of the Children's Panel for each local government area must be published by each local authority, and that list must be open to public inspection at the principal offices of the local authority, and at any place where an electors list for the local government area is available for inspection.[7]

It is from this Panel that members are chosen to constitute children's hearings to deal with the cases of individual children.[8] These hearings consist of three panel members, at least one of whom must be a woman

---

[1] Children (Scotland) Act 1995, s.39(1).
[2] Sch.1, para.1.
[3] Two or more local authorities can form between them a single CPAC, known as a joint advisory committee: Sch.1, para.8.
[4] Sch.1, para.6.
[5] Sch.1, para.2.
[6] Tribunals and Inquiries Act 1992, s.7(1)(e) and Sch.1, para.61(a).
[7] Children (Scotland) Act 1995, Sch.1, para.12.
[8] s.39(3).

and at least one of whom must be a man.[9] The selection of individual members of the panel to serve on any particular children's hearing is made either directly by the Chairman of the Children's Panel or his or her deputy, or by the operation of standing arrangements made by the Chairman. These arrangements may provide for the selection of members by members of the Panel appointed by the Chairman to do so[10]: this is the normal practice in large panel areas. It is to this lay tribunal[11] that the extensive decision-making powers over the lives of children and their families, described in the later chapters of this book, are given. Panel members are entitled to take time off work to sit on children's hearings.[12]

### The role of the chairman

One of the three members of the children's hearing will act as the chairman for each hearing. Every panel member is eligible to act as chairman and there is no special qualification required to do so, beyond membership of the Children's Panel and completion of training in the particular procedural responsibilities of chairmen. Selection of the chairman of a hearing lies with the Chairman of the Children's Panel or his or her deputy, or through the operation of standing arrangements made by the Chairman.[13] Though the chairman of the hearing has no greater say in the disposal of the case than either of the other members, he or she does have various statutory functions to perform, in four main areas: determining the procedure to be followed, deciding who may attend the hearing, giving explanations, and signing orders. How these functions are exercised will be discussed at the appropriate points later in this book, but for reference purposes it may be noted that the particular statutory functions of the chairman are as described below.

*Determining procedure*

- The procedure at any children's hearing shall be such as the chairman in his or her discretion determines.[14]
- The chairman of the hearing may at any time during the hearing adjourn the hearing, provided that the hearing can reconvene later on the same day.[15]

---

[9] s.39(5). Problems created by the law's ambivalence to transgender individuals, previously resolved in practice by ensuring that a transgendered panel member sat with another man and another woman, have now diminished. The Gender Recognition Act 2004 allows for a transgendered individual to be recognised for all legal purposes in their new sex; and even before the granting under that Act of a Gender Recognition Certificate, the law will accept that a person has changed sex if they have done so for all social reasons and the policy behind the gender specific rule in question is satisfied by such recognition: *A v Chief Constable of West Yorkshire Police* [2004] UKHL 21. The end result of this is that for the purposes of satisfying the gender-specific requirements for the makeup of an individual children's hearing a panel member will be recognised in his or her new sex if either (i) he or she has acquired a Gender Recognition Certificate under the 2004 Act to that effect or (ii) he or she has been living in the new gender and presents to the world (including the child and family attending the hearing) as a member of that gender.

[10] Children's Hearings (Scotland) Rules, 1996, r.10(1). These standing arrangements must be kept under review: r.10(2).

[11] Trained in accordance with Sch.1, paras 9 and 10.

[12] Employment Protection (Consolidation) Act 1978, s.29(1)(c).

[13] 1996 Rules, r.10(1).

[14] 1996 Rules, r.10(3).

[15] 1996 Rules, r.10(4).

*Attendances permitted*

- It is the responsibility of the chairman to take all reasonable steps to ensure that the number of persons present at a children's hearing at any one time is kept to a minimum.[16]
- The chairman may in his or her discretion permit the presence of certain specified persons who have no right or duty to attend a children's hearing.[17]

*Explanations to be given*

- The chairman shall, before the children's hearing proceed to consider the case, explain the purpose of the hearing to such persons as are present.[18]
- It is the duty of the chairman of the children's hearing to whom a child's case has been referred to explain to the child and the relevant person, at the opening of the proceedings on the referral, the grounds of the referral stated by the reporter, in order to ascertain whether these grounds are accepted in whole or in part by them.[19]
- The chairman must inform the child and any relevant person of the substance of any reports, documents and information made available to the children's hearing if it appears to the chairman that it is material to the decision and that its disclosure would not be detrimental to the interests of the child.[20]
- If the children's hearing have decided to exclude a journalist the chairman may, at the end of that exclusion, explain to the journalist the substance of what took place in his or her absence.[21]
- If the children's hearing have decided to exclude a relevant person the chairman must, at the end of that exclusion, explain to the relevant person the substance of what took place in his or her absence.[22]
- If the children's hearing have directed the reporter to apply to the sheriff for proof of the establishment of the grounds of referral, it is the duty of the chairman to explain to the child and to the relevant person the purpose of the application, and to inform the child that he or she has an obligation to attend the hearing before the sheriff.[23]
- Once a decision has been made on how to dispose of the case, but before the conclusion of the hearing at which the decision is made, the chairman must inform the child, any relevant person, any safeguarder, and any representative, if attending the hearing, of (a) the decision of the hearing, (b) the reasons for the

---

[16] s.43(2). See p.63.
[17] s.43(1) and 1996 Rules, r.13. See pp.63 and 76–78.
[18] 1996 Rules, r.20(2). See p.81.
[19] s.65(4). See pp.82–84.
[20] 1996 Rules, r.20(4) and r.22(4).
[21] s.43(5). See pp.75–76.
[22] s.46(2). See p.72.
[23] s.65(8). See p.86.

decision, (c) the right to appeal against the decision, and the right to apply for a suspension of the supervision requirement pending such appeal.[24]

- If the hearing was arranged to consider an application to suspend a supervision requirement pending an appeal, the chairman must inform the child and the relevant person of the decision of the hearing.[25]

*Stating the reasons for decision; signing*

- As soon as reasonably practicable after the end of the hearing the chairman shall make or cause to be made a report of the decision and a statement in writing of the reasons for the decision, and shall sign the report and statement.[26]
- In addition, it is for the chairman to sign all warrants, orders, supervision requirements, reports and statements of reasons (no matter who has drawn them up).[27]

## THE REPORTER

It is through the reporter that cases are referred to a children's hearing, and he or she has various investigative functions in relation to children.[28] A child cannot be referred to a children's hearing except at the instance of the reporter. It is the reporter who draws up the grounds of referral, and the reporter who seeks to have grounds which are not accepted or not understood established by proof in the sheriff court. It is tempting to regard the reporter in the way a prosecutor would be regarded in the criminal courts, but the analogy is not apt.[29] Though the reporter has a discretion whether or not to refer a case to a children's hearing (as a prosecutor has a discretion whether or not to bring a case to court), once he or she does so proceedings cannot be abandoned and the progression of the case thereafter lies in the hands of the hearing. The function of the reporter during the hearing is to keep a report of the proceedings of the hearing which must contain information on matters specified in the Rules.[30]

The Scottish ministers are empowered to prescribe the qualifications of reporters.[31] It is not a requirement that reporters be legally qualified, but if they are they are not to be regarded as practising solicitors for the purpose of being required to hold a practising certificate from the Law

---

[24] 1996 Rules, r.20(5). See p.124.

[25] 1996 Rules, r.23(4). See p.221.

[26] 1996 Rules, r.10(5). See p.124.

[27] 1996 Rules, r.29(1). If the chairman is unavailable, any member of the hearing can sign.

[28] See Chap.4.

[29] See the opinion of the Extra Division to this effect in *C v Miller*, 2003 S.L.T. 1379 at 1396C.

[30] 1996 Rules, r.31. On the reporter's legal immunities, see Kearney *Children's Hearings and the Sheriff Court* (2nd ed., 2000) at paras 2.07–2.10.

[31] s.40(1).

Society of Scotland.[32] Reporters are employed by the Scottish Children's Reporter Administration (SCRA)[33] and they are prohibited from being employed in any capacity at all by local authorities (though that prohibition can be removed in individual cases with the consent of SCRA[34]). The term "reporter" means the Principal Reporter and any officer of SCRA to whom he has delegated any of his functions under s.131(1) of the Local Government etc. (Scotland) Act 1994.[35] Throughout the Children (Scotland) Act 1995 the term "Principal Reporter" is used, but that is defined in s.93(1) in the same way as "reporter" is defined here. SCRA is responsible for the management of reporters, including their discipline and removal from office and their deployment throughout Scotland for the purposes of performing their duties.[36] Reporters (*i.e.* officers to whom the Principal Reporter has delegated his functions) must comply with any instructions or guidance given by the Principal Reporter.[37] If dismissed from office by SCRA, the Principal Reporter or any other reporter may appeal to the Scottish ministers against such dismissal.[38]

## THE CHILD

The child is the central figure at a children's hearing, even when he or she is not present. For the purposes of the children's hearing system, a child is a person who either (a) is less than 16 years of age, or (b) if currently subject to a supervision requirement, is less than 18 years of age, or (c) is a person who has been referred to a children's hearing, under regulations made under s.33, by a court in England and Wales or

---

[32] *Miller v Council of the Law Society of Scotland*, 2000 S.L.T. 513. The reasoning was that in the reporter's professional activities there was no person who can rationally be regarded as the reporter's "client". There remains some doubt (raised but not resolved in *Miller*) as to whether non-solicitor reporters have a right of audience before the sheriff principal: see the comments of Sheriff Principal Risk in *Templeton v E* 1998 SCLR 672 and his decision in *Nassaris v The Children's Hearing Reporter* November 5, 1998. In a note attached to the report of *Templeton*, I suggested that Sheriff Principal Risk was correct to hold that rights of audience on appeal to the sheriff principal are limited to solicitors. The passing of the Antisocial Behaviour etc (Scotland) Act 2004 addresses the point in its own particular context, by expressly providing (s.112) that Scottish ministers may empower a reporter (whether a solicitor or advocate or not) to conduct proceedings before either a sheriff or a sheriff principal on appeal against the making of a parenting order. The general point, however, could be argued either way. This rule, being expressly limited to parenting orders, might indicate that this is an exceptional power being conferred in limited circumstances on reporters who are not solicitors. On the other hand, it might indicate the legislature's lack of discomfort at non-solicitors having a right of audience before a sheriff principal. There is administrative convenience in not drawing unnecessary distinctions between different reporters. Sheriff Kearney has expressed the view that Sheriff Principal Risk's approach was unduly narrow: *Children's Hearings and the Sheriff Court* (2nd ed., 2000) at para.54.23. The matter awaits authoritative guidance from the legislature or the Court of Session.

[33] Local Government etc. (Scotland) Act 1994, s.128(4) and (5).

[34] Children (Scotland) Act 1995, s.40(2).

[35] s.40(5).

[36] Local Government etc. (Scotland) Act 1994, s.128(7).

[37] Local Government etc. (Scotland) Act 1994, s.131(2).

[38] Local Government etc. (Scotland) Act 1994, s.129(1).

in Northern Ireland, or (d) has been referred to a children's hearing on the basis of failure to attend school regularly[39] and, though over the age of 16, is not yet of school leaving age.[40] Hearings always commence with inquiries being made as to the age of the person referred[41] and the age declared, or determined by a children's hearing, to be the age of the person brought before them shall be deemed to be the true age of that person;[42] if that age later turns out to be incorrect then any decision the hearing have made remains valid.[43] If, however, in the course of the hearing it is discovered that the person is of a different age from that initially determined, the hearing may accept that different age and act accordingly[44] (*i.e.* if the person referred is found to be over 16 or 18 the proceedings must be terminated since the children's hearing will have no jurisdiction over him or her). If, however, in the course of proceedings commenced while the person referred is a child, that person ceases to be a child, the proceedings will not be terminated and the provisions in Chapter Two or Chapter Three of Part II of the Act will continue to apply as if the person had not ceased to be a child.[45]

## RELEVANT PERSONS

Every person who, in relation to the child, is a "relevant person" has a duty to attend at all stages of any children's hearing, a right to accept the grounds of referral stated by the reporter or to deny them and oblige the reporter to establish them by evidence before the sheriff, a right to appeal against any decision the hearing make in relation to the child, and a right to require a review of any supervision requirement. The relevant person is anyone who comes within one or more of the following three categories:

(a) A parent of the child who enjoys parental responsibilities or parental rights under Part I of the 1995 Act. This means (i) female parents,[46] (ii) male parents who are or were married to the female parent of the child at the time of the child's conception or subsequently,[47] or who are registered as the child's father,[48] (iii) male parents who have entered into a registered agreement with the female parent to share parental

---

[39] *i.e.* under s.52(2)(h).

[40] s.93(2)(b).

[41] s.47(1)(a).

[42] s.47(2).

[43] s.47(3).

[44] s.47(1)(b).

[45] s.93(3). But if the child attains the age of 18 during the proceedings, no supervision requirement can be imposed or continued.

[46] s.3(1)(a).

[47] s.3(1)(b). The marriage may be regular or irregular, valid, voidable or void (so long as, if void, it was believed in good faith by both parties to the marriage at the time it was entered into to be valid, whether as a result of error of law or error of fact).

[48] *ibid.*, as to be added by s.3(1)(b) of the Family Law (Scotland) Bill 2005, introduced to the Scottish Parliament on February 7, 2005 though not enacted as this book goes to press.

responsibilities and parental rights,[49] (iv) male parents who have been awarded parental responsibilities and parental rights by a court[50] and (v) male parents who have been appointed guardian to the child.[51] "Parent" includes persons presumed to be parent under s.5 of the Law Reform (Parent and Child) (Scotland) Act 1986, or deemed parent under s.27 or s.28 of the Human Fertilisation and Embryology Act 1990, or made parent either under s.30 of the 1990 Act or by means of an adoption order granted under s.12 of the Adoption (Scotland) Act 1978. It does not include any parent whose parental responsibilities and parental rights have been completely removed from them either under s.11 or s.86 of the Children (Scotland) Act 1995 or under the Adoption (Scotland) Act 1978 but, given that the paragraph refers to responsibilities "or" rights, this part of the definition will include a parent who holds some but not the full range of parental responsibilities and parental rights (for example the divorced father who possesses only the responsibility and right to maintain direct contact and personal relations with the child).

(b) Any person in whom parental responsibilities or rights are vested by, or by virtue of, any provision in the Children (Scotland) Act 1995. Parents with parental responsibilities and parental rights are covered by (a) above and this paragraph covers any other person, such as a person who has been given parental responsibilities and parental rights by a court in an action under s.11, or a guardian who acquires such responsibilities and rights on the death of a parent. "Person" is not limited for the purposes of Part II of the Act to natural persons[52] and will therefore include, it is submitted, a local authority to whom parental responsibilities and rights have been transferred under s.86. The fact that the paragraph refers to parental responsibilities "or" parental rights once again suggests that a person with one parental responsibility or parental right but not them all (such as a legal representative who does not have the right to determine the child's residence) will be a relevant person. In particular, a person with only the parental responsibility and right to maintain direct contact and personal relations with the child shall be a relevant person. It is important, however, to note that only an order under s.11(2)(b) will "vest parental responsibilities and parental rights" and so bring the person in whose favour the order is made within the definition of "relevant person". An order made under s.11(2)(d) merely regulating contact between the child and a person who does not otherwise have any parental responsibilities or parental rights (e.g. a sibling or a grandparent) does

---

[49] s.4.
[50] Under s.11(2)(b).
[51] By the court under s.11(2)(h) or by testamentary deed of a parent or guardian under s.7.
[52] As it is in Part 1: see s.15(4).

not in itself vest parental responsibilities and parental rights and so does not make the person a "relevant person".[53]

(c) Any person who appears to be a person who ordinarily (and other than by reason only of his or her employment) has charge of, or control over, the child. This is a matter of fact and not of law and so the ordinary and natural meaning is to be given to the words "ordinarily having charge of or control over the child". The aim of this provision is to identify persons who play a significant part in the child's upbringing and it will include, for example, an unregistered father who lives in family with the mother and the child and who takes a share in the upbringing of the child,[54] a grandparent or other relative who adopts the same role, and in some circumstances might include the spouse or cohabitant of the mother who has no genetic connection to the child but who treats the child as the child of the family and who is one of the child's primary carers. It also includes the foster carer who "ordinarily" has charge of or control over the child, that is to say the long-term foster carer.[55] Such a person is not "employed" to look after children, even when paid allowances to do so.[56] "Charge of or control over the child" does not require any legal relationship between the person and the child and is solely a question of fact. In relation to the previous legislation,[57] it was said that "the court or children's hearing which has to determine that question of fact has to consider all the circumstances disclosed to it that bear upon the issue as to whether or not the person claiming to be a [relevant person] had at the relative time the . . . charge of or control over the child. In most cases, the undisputed facts should show whether or not the person claiming to be a [relevant person] is

---

[53] See further, Wilkinson and Norrie *Parent and Child* (2nd ed., 1999) at para.9.11.

[54] See *C v Kennedy,* 1991 S.L.T. 755.

[55] See *S v N,* 2002 S.L.T. 589. An emergency foster carer who has charge of the child for only a short period would not be considered "ordinarily" to have charge or control. The difficult cases will be with carers who look after a child for a period of months rather than years.

[56] The essence of the employer-employee relationship is one of mutuality of obligation: an employee is obliged to perform services within the terms of the employment required by the employer: Craig and Miller, *Employment Law in Scotland* (3rd ed., 2004 paras 2.3–2.4). A foster carer is never legally obliged to take on the care of a child as required by a local authority and is not, therefore, "employed" by the local authority.

[57] Social Work (Scotland) Act 1968, s.94. That section defined "guardian" as a person who "has *for the time being* the custody or charge of or control over the child", which is more clearly a factual test than the current wording; but there was no parliamentary intent to change the test from a factual one to a legal one. The present definition is, however, more stable. So a neighbour, for example, looking after a child for two days would not be regarded as "ordinarily" caring for this child, although she could have been held to have been doing so "for the time being". If a child is removed from his or her family for a limited period of time under a child protection order (see Chap.15 below) the parent does not lose "relevant person" status under the present formulation although he or she would have done so under the 1968 provisions: see *S v Lynch,* 1997 S.L.T. 1377, in which a father lost title to attend the hearing simply because the mother snatched the child from his care and so he could not be said to have care of the child at the appropriate time. This decision would not be reached under the current legislation for the father could still then claim to be "ordinarily" having care and control.

entitled to be so described".[58] The current definition is in the present tense with the result, it is submitted, that the person claiming to be a relevant person must have charge of or control over the child at the date of the children's hearing or of the sheriff court hearing, and not at some time previously.[59] The Act does not state to whom it must appear that the person has charge of or control over the child[60] which suggests that, as a matter of fact, judgments made can be challenged as being factually wrong. So if the children's hearing or the sheriff fall into error as to who is or is not a relevant person for the purposes of proceedings before them any decision they make will be challengeable on the ground of procedural irregularity.[61]

There is a conflict of sheriff court authority as to whether a person can seek to become a relevant person by having the status conferred upon him by means of a specific issue order under s.11(2)(e) of the 1995 Act.[62] It is submitted that it is not incompetent for a person to seek a declarator as to whether or not he or she comes within the definition of "relevant person" as discussed above; but this would not be an action under s.11. Nor is it incompetent for a person to seek, by means of a s.11 order, to be conferred parental responsibilities and parental rights, with the inevitable consequence of becoming thereby a relevant person. But it is submitted that a person who is not a relevant person cannot be conferred parental responsibilities and parental rights if the only purpose is to bring the person within the definition. It would subvert the structure of the 1995 Act, with its two parts governing private law and public law procedures separately, were it otherwise. If there is some benefit to the child in the claimant being given parental responsibilities and parental rights then the order will be made but that benefit must, it is submitted, be something beyond the procedural benefit of the right to attend children's hearings and appeal their decisions.

<br>

SAFEGUARDERS

Safeguarders were introduced into the children's hearing system by s.66 of the Children Act 1975, coming into effect on June 30, 1985, with the insertion into the Social Work (Scotland) Act 1968 of a new s.34A thereof. That section was replaced by s.41 of the Children (Scotland) Act 1995, which provides that in any proceedings under Chapter Two or

---

[58] *per* Lord McCluskey in *C v Kennedy,* 1991 S.L.T. 755 at 757I–J.

[59] *cf. Kennedy v H,* 1988 S.L.T. 586, *per* Lord President Emslie at 590E–F. See also *T v A,* 2001 S.C.L.R. 647.

[60] Unlike the Social Work (Scotland) Act 1968, s.94.

[61] In *S v N,* 2002 S.L.T. 589 long-term foster carers attempted to oppose a mother's appeal from a decision of a children's hearing but the sheriff held that they had no title to do so as they were not (could not be) relevant persons. The Court of Session held the sheriff wrong on that score and his denial of the foster carers' right to be heard amounted, therefore, to a procedural irregularity.

[62] Compare *P v P,* 1999 S.C.L.R. 679 where this was held to be incompetent with *T v A,* 2001 S.C.L.R. 647 where it was not.

Chapter Three of Part II of the 1995 Act, either at a children's hearing or before the sheriff, the hearing or, as the case may be, the sheriff must give consideration to the question of whether it is necessary to appoint a person to safeguard the interests of the child in the proceedings and, if the hearing or the sheriff do so consider, they must make such an appointment, on such terms and conditions as appear appropriate. All local authorities will have a duty to maintain a panel of persons who may act as safeguarders[63] and the children's hearing or sheriff may only appoint as safeguarder a member of that panel. Before seeking nominations the local authority must determine the standard of any qualifications to be possessed by persons who may be appointed to the panel, and in both determining that standard and appointing members to the panel the local authority must consult the Sheriff Principal and the Chairman of the Children's Panel of the local authority area.[64] Appointment to the panel may not be made of a person who is a member of the local authority, a member of the children's panel or a member of the CPAC.[65] Appointment to the Panel is for a period not exceeding three years, though an existing appointee may be reappointed.[66] Membership of the panel may be terminated by the local authority where it is of the view (in agreement with the chairman of the children's panel and the sheriff principal) that the member is unable, unfit or unsuitable to carry out the functions of membership.[67] The local list must be kept under review by the local authority, in consultation with the Sheriff Principal and the local Chairman of the Children's Panel.[68]

Though s.41(1) in its terms permits appointment of a safeguarder by a children's hearing or a sheriff "in any proceedings" under Chapters Two or Three, there are some necessary limitations to this. Apart from "proceedings under section 57" when, expressly, safeguarders cannot be appointed,[69] appointment would be incompetent in any proceedings in which a dispositive decision were made. So, for example, a children's hearing who dispose of a case by discharging a referral or by imposing or continuing or terminating a supervision requirement cannot appoint a safeguarder, for the appointment is designed to assist the hearing in determining what the appropriate disposal should be. And a sheriff who finds grounds of referral not established or who dismisses an appeal from a decision of a children's hearing cannot appoint a safeguarder since the appointment then would serve no function. In other words, a safeguarder can be appointed only at a preliminary or intermediate stage in the process and not at the same time as a dispositive decision is made. Typically, a children's hearing may appoint a safeguarder when the grounds of referral are sent to the sheriff for proof or when a case is continued for further investigation, or when a warrant has been granted or continued; the sheriff may appoint a safeguarder before hearing

---

[63] Panel of Persons to Safeguard the Interests of Children (Scotland) Regulations 2001, SSI 2001/476, r.3.

[64] *ibid.*, r.4.

[65] *ibid.*, r.6(2).

[66] *ibid.*, r.7.

[67] *ibid.*, r.7(3).

[68] *ibid.*, r.8.

[69] s.41(2).

evidence of the existence of grounds of referral (whether under s.68 or s.85) or before hearing an appeal (or at any time during these proceedings).

**Term of appointment**

An appointment by a children's hearing lasts until a dispositive decision has been reached[70] or, if that decision is appealed against, until the appeal is disposed of. The person who was appointed to safeguard the child's interests therefore has no right or duty to attend a subsequent review hearing, until reappointed to the office of safeguarder by the review hearing. An appointment by a sheriff lasts until the sheriff has disposed of the issue in front of him (or, if his decision is appealed against, until the disposal of the appeal); if a safeguarder is considered necessary at a subsequent children's hearing, the appointment must be made by that children's hearing. It is unclear whether an appointment of a safeguarder can be terminated before a dispositive decision is made, and while this would normally be entirely unnecessary, extreme cases, such as when an appointee abuses his or her position, are not beyond the realms of imagination. A children's hearing may request that a particular individual be appointed as safeguarder, but they cannot require it. It has been held that there is no procedural irregularity if a hearing appoints separate safeguarders to two children in the same family and in the event only one safeguarder acts for both children.[71] Termination of membership of the panel from which safeguarders may be appointed[72] probably has the effect of terminating any particular appointment.

**Expenses**

The expenses of a person appointed as safeguarder, either by the sheriff or the children's hearing, shall, in so far as reasonably incurred by him or her in safeguarding the interests of the child in the proceedings, be borne by the local authority for whose area the children's panel from which the relevant children's hearing has been constituted is formed or (if the appointment is by the sheriff) within whose area the child resides.[73]

## LEGAL REPRESENTATIVES

The failure of the Children (Scotland) Act 1995, and before that of the Social Work (Scotland) Act 1968, to ensure that children appearing at children's hearings were afforded paid legal representation to assist them in presenting their case as they saw it was described in the first edition of this book as a fundamental flaw in the system. In 2000 the Human

---

[70] There is no explicit statutory provision to this effect, but it is certainly assumed by the Rules: see, *e.g.* 1996 Rules, r.14(3).

[71] *H v Kennedy,* 1999 S.C.L.R. 961.

[72] Panel of Persons to Safeguard the Interests of Children (Scotland) Regulations 2001, SSI 2001/476, r.7(3).

[73] s.41(4) and (5); Panel of Persons to Safeguard the Interests of Children (Scotland) Regulations, SSI 2001/476, r.10.

Rights Act 1998 came into force and it was no surprise that the first substantive challenge to the children's hearing system under that Act concerned this flaw. In *S v Miller*[74] the First Division held that a denial of legal representation to a child attending a children's hearing would be incompatible with Art.6 of the European Convention of Human Rights in two circumstances: when the complexity of the case is such as to prevent the child's effective participation, and when the child's liberty is at stake. In response, the Children's Hearings (Legal Representation) (Scotland) Rules 2002,[75] which came into effect on April 23, 2002, were passed, allowing either a business meeting or a children's hearing to appoint a legal representative to a child, even if a safeguarder has been appointed. The appointment is made from the list of either safeguarders, curators *ad litem* or reporting officers,[76] and it is to be noted that it is the hearing (or business meeting) that makes the appointment and not the child, family or the reporter (though in practice the identification of an individual legal representative will fall to the local authority). The appointment of a legal representative lasts until the time for appeal has passed from a dispositive decision.

## THE LOCAL AUTHORITY

While the local authority itself has no standing to attend the children's hearing and is in no sense a party to the proceedings, the local authority[77] does play a central role in the whole system. For one thing, there will nearly always be a local authority employee, in the form of a social worker, present.[78] Also, the local authority have various investigative duties in relation to children,[79] and must provide a social background report for every child whose case is referred to a children's hearing.[80] This report nearly always contains recommendations to the children's hearing, which are always to be given consideration by the hearing.

### Local authorities' duties to implement supervision requirement

In addition to the investigative and reporting duties mentioned above, the "relevant local authority" (that is to say the local authority for whose area the children's panel from which the children's hearing which imposed the supervision requirement was formed[81]) have the duty to implement any supervision requirement that is made in relation to the

---

[74] 2001 S.L.T. 531 and 1304.

[75] SSI 2002/63.

[76] Established under the Social Work (Panel of Persons to Safeguard the Interests of Children) (Scotland) Regs 2001 and the Curators *ad litem* and Reporting Officers (Panels) (Scotland) Regs 2001, SSI 2001/476 and 477.

[77] "Any reference in any enactment to a local authority ... shall be construed as a reference to a council constituted under section 2" of the Local Government etc. (Scotland) Act 1994: 1994 Act, s.183(2).

[78] See further, below at p.77.

[79] See below at pp.40–41.

[80] s.56(2).

[81] s.93(1).

child.[82] This will include fulfilling such duties as the hearing explicitly impose upon them in terms of the supervision requirement.[83] A child who is subject to a supervision requirement is regarded as being "looked after" by the local authority,[84] with the result that the duties owed by local authorities under Chapter One of Part II of the 1995 Act are owed to all children so subject.[85] Local authorities are therefore expressly obliged, for example, to safeguard and promote the child's welfare, and to take such steps as appear to them to be both practicable and appropriate to promote regular contact between the child and any person with parental responsibilities.[86] Additionally, local authorities have specified duties[87] in relation to the after-care of children who ceased to be subject to a supervision requirement but who were "looked after" by them at the time they ceased to be of school age or subsequently. And local authorities, being "public authorities" for the purposes of the Human Rights Act 1998, are required to fulfil the requirements of the European Convention on Human Rights, such as the duty to respect family life (in practice, to ensure that contact between child and family is maintained, and indeed encouraged, until such time as that contact is found to be positively detrimental to the child).

The primary duty of the local authority is to give effect to the supervision requirement. This duty is imposed on the local authority as a collective whole and not upon individual units or departments thereof. It follows that any condition contained within the supervision requirement can be one which is the responsibility of any department, such as social services, education, health, housing, or even recreation and leisure. A condition upon the child which requires some action by a local authority obliges the local authority to take that action. Though social services departments within local authorities are likely to be most commonly involved, a child's needs may require to be met through the facilities provided by other departments, and there is no reason why the children's hearing cannot require that such other facilities be provided. It is no excuse for a failure to give effect to a supervision requirement that the services to be provided are the responsibility of some department other than the social work department. So, for example, a condition that the child reside in a residential establishment obliges the local authority to provide a place in a residential establishment; a condition that the child attend some group work project obliges the local authority to provide a place at that project; a condition that the child attend a named public school obliges the local authority to allow the child to attend that school. If, for whatever reason, the local authority, in any of its guises, cannot provide the service to the child then they are obliged to seek a review of the supervision requirement and explain to the review hearing why the condition cannot be fulfilled: it is a breach of their statutory duty simply

---

[82] s.71.
[83] s.71(1A), as inserted by the Antisocial Behaviour etc (Scotland) Act 2004, s.136(2).
[84] s.17(6).
[85] See particularly the duties listed in s.17(1) and s.31, and the powers in s.26.
[86] s.17(1).
[87] See ss.29 and 30.

to fail to fulfil the requirement in the expectation of giving an explanation at the next scheduled review hearing.

In giving effect to a supervision requirement, the local authority may request help in the fulfilling of their duties from any other local authority, a health board or NHS trust, and any other person authorised by the Scottish ministers. On receipt of such a request for help, the person or body requested must comply with it provided it is compatible with their own statutory or other duties and obligations and does not unduly prejudice the discharge of any of their own functions.[88] This allows local authorities to access, for example, medical or psychological services for the child even when they do not themselves directly provide these services.

### Enforcing local authorities' duties

Prior to the passing of the Antisocial Behaviour etc (Scotland) Act 2004, the Children (Scotland) Act 1995 contained no provision relating to the enforcement of a local authority's duty under s.71 to give effect to the supervision requirement, though the normal procedure for enforcing statutory duties contained in s.45 of the Court of Session Act 1988 was theoretically available (though never utilised in practice). It was also possible, though exceptionally rare, for a person injured by a local authority's failure to fulfil its duties to sue for damages.[89] These were weak remedies and relied to a large extent on the very people who tended to resist local authorities' plans to seek them: the child and his or her family. Important amendments to the Children (Scotland) Act 1995 were made by the Antisocial Behaviour etc (Scotland) Act 2004, putting it in the hands of the hearing itself and the reporter to enforce local authority fulfilment of duties towards the child and family contained in the supervision requirement. A children's hearing reviewing a supervision requirement may come to the conclusion that the local authority has not fulfilled any of its duties, either the general duty to give effect to all supervision requirements[90] or the duties explicitly imposed on the local authority by the terms of the particular supervision requirement.[91] If so, the hearing may direct the reporter to give notice to the local authority of an intended application of enforcement to the sheriff principal, and if the hearing does so they must also require a further review 28 days after the giving of this notice.[92] If at that further review it appears to them that the local authority continues to be in breach of their duties, then the hearing may authorise the reporter to make an application to the sheriff principal.[93] An application by the reporter to the sheriff principal for an order requiring the local authority in breach of a duty imposed by a supervision requirement to fulfil its duty is competent only with the children's hearing's authorisation and only if the

---

[88] s.21.

[89] See *Barrett v Enfield London Borough Council* [2001] 2 A.C. 550; J. Murphy, "Children in Need: The Limits of Local Authority Accountability" (2003) 23 Leg. Stud. 103.

[90] s.71(1).

[91] s.71(1A), as inserted by the Antisocial Behaviour etc (Scotland) Act 2004, s.136(2).

[92] s.71(7A)–(7D), as so inserted.

[93] s.71(7E), as so inserted.

local authority have continued to fail to fulfil its duties.[94] But discretion lies with the reporter, who may decide not to make an application to the sheriff principal. The Act gives no guidance to reporters as to how to exercise their discretion, other than the important rule that they are to take no account of local authority resources: in other words it is no excuse that the local authority claims not to have the means to fulfil their duties. If the sheriff principal finds the local authority in breach, he may make an order requiring the local authority to fulfil their duty.[95] That order is final.[96]

This is an important new power, though it leaves much unsaid, in particular whether sheriffs principal are entitled to take account of claimed lack of resources in determining whether to make the order. And the Act is silent as to the consequences of the local authority's failure to follow the order—though presumably the normal remedies for contempt of court will be available.

---

[94] s.71A(2) and (3), as inserted by the Antisocial Behaviour etc. (Scotland) Act 2004, s.136(3).

[95] s.71A(1), as so inserted.

[96] s.71A(7), as so inserted.

## CHAPTER THREE

# THE GROUNDS OF REFERRAL

## INTRODUCTION

The question of whether compulsory measures of supervision are necessary in respect of a particular child arises if, but only if, one or more of the conditions listed in s.52(2) of the Children (Scotland) Act 1995 exists in relation to that child.[1] These conditions, together with the statement of facts the reporter is founding upon as evidence of the satisfaction of the conditions, are known as the grounds of referral, and it is common to refer to the satisfaction of the conditions as the establishment of the grounds of referral. The grounds founded upon by the reporter can be established either (i) by the child and such relevant persons as attend the hearing accepting that they exist,[2] (ii) by the sheriff finding established the grounds of referral,[3] (iii) by a court in certain specified proceedings being satisfied that the grounds exist,[4] (iv) by a criminal court, having found a person guilty of certain offences, certifying that grounds of referral in respect of a particular child shall be treated as having been established,[5] or (v) by a child pleading guilty to or being found guilty of an offence by a criminal court which remits the case to a children's hearing for disposal.[6] It is competent for the reporter to refer a child on the basis of a number of different grounds and, indeed, the same statement of facts can often indicate the satisfaction of more than one of the conditions in s.52(2).[7] At least part of the grounds of referral stated by the reporter must be established, and the hearing can consider the case whenever that is so, even if other parts are not established.

The effect of the establishment of the grounds of referral is two-fold. First, it raises the question of whether compulsory measures of supervision are necessary. The existence of the grounds is by no means conclusive of that necessity (though, conversely, the absence of any ground of referral is conclusive of the lack of a need for compulsory

---

[1] Children (Scotland) Act 1995, s.52(1).

[2] s.65(5). See further, below at pp.85–87.

[3] s.68(10) (on application by the reporter: see further, Chap.7) or s.85 (on application by the child or relevant person for review of the establishment of the grounds: see further, Chap.12).

[4] s.54. See further, below at pp.44–45.

[5] Criminal Procedure (Scotland) Act 1995, s.48. See further, below at pp.45–46.

[6] Criminal Procedure (Scotland) Act 1995, s.49. See further, below at p.47.

[7] As a simple example, the child's refusal to go to school can amount to grounds of referral based on school non-attendance and on being outwith parental control.

measures of supervision). Rather, the existence of the grounds merely raises the question, which can be answered either (in the negative) by the reporter exercising his or her discretion under s.56(4) not to refer the child to a children's hearing[8] or (in the negative or in the affirmative) by the children's hearing arranged by the reporter under s.65. Secondly, the establishment of the grounds of referral founds the jurisdiction of the children's hearing. If grounds of referral do not exist in relation to a child the children's hearing have no jurisdiction to consider the child's case; indeed there is no case for the hearing to consider. The children's hearing are not entitled, therefore, to discuss the child's situation or to make any dispositive decision at any time prior to the establishment (by whatever means) of the grounds of referral. (They do, however, have jurisdiction to grant warrants[9] to find and keep the child as soon as the child is referred to them by the reporter).

## THE GROUNDS

Section 52 sets out the grounds upon which a child can be referred to a children's hearing. The wording of the section is in many respects infelicitous, not least in the reference to "conditions" while all other parts of the Act refer to "grounds".[10] There is, however, little difference between conditions and grounds: what are commonly referred to as "the grounds of referral"[11] or, occasionally, the "grounds for referral"[12] are the conditions listed in s.52(2), together with the statement of facts which the reporter claims indicates the satisfaction of these conditions. It is the conditions and the statement of facts (together referred to as the grounds) that must be explained by the chairman at the commencement of the proceedings in accordance with s.65(4) and which must be established before the case can be considered. The conditions are as follows.

### (a) That the child is beyond the control of any relevant person

One of the major responsibilities adults owe to children in their care is the responsibility of providing them with control, in order that the child might learn how to fit in to the society of which he or she is a member. Appropriate control is an essential aspect of the growth and development of a child and if any person who has that responsibility is unable, for whatever reason, to exercise control the child shall be considered to be beyond the control of such a person; if the person is a "relevant person", the ground of referral exists. A "relevant person" is someone who has parental responsibilities or parental rights in relation to a child (however acquired), or who appears to be a person who ordinarily (other than by reason only of employment) has charge of or control over a child.[13] It does not matter why the relevant person is unable to exercise

---

[8] See below at pp.49–51.
[9] Under ss.45 and 66.
[10] See, for example, ss.65, 68 and 69.
[11] As in s.69(1).
[12] As in s.68(8).
[13] s.93(2)(b). See above at pp.14–17.

control, and it might be because of illness, incapacity or facility of the relevant person, instability or hyperactivity of the child, a breakdown of the relationship between the two, or for any other reason. The ground exists whenever the child is beyond the control of one of the relevant persons, even when not beyond the control of another relevant person. "Control" must, it is submitted, be interpreted in a manner appropriate to the particular child and its meaning and content will alter as the child grows up: the control required to be provided to a young child is very different from that to be afforded to a teenager who is nearing 16. Similarly, some children, due to their individual circumstances or due to their own (perhaps disturbed) personalities, will require greater control than others.[14] "Control" is to be interpreted according to the need of the particular child for protection, guidance, direction and advice. A child who defies the control appropriately sought to be exercised, and puts him or herself at risk thereby, is in need of compulsory measures of supervision, which might include measures of "control".[15]

**(b) That the child is falling into bad associations or is exposed to moral danger**

This condition is to be interpreted in the light of the harm that might befall the referred child. An association is "bad" when it threatens to interfere with the child's good health, sound development or appropriate welfare; moral danger is the exposure of the child to influences which subvert the generally accepted standards of society and thereby make the child less able to fit appropriately into society. The purpose of this condition is less to do with the child's present behaviour and more to do with the need to protect the child from influences which will colour his or her character in the future in a detrimental manner, such as those that encourage the child to a life of criminality, prostitution, corruption, or drug or alcohol abuse. It is often used when the child is allegedly exposed to sexual behaviour.[16] One must, however, be careful with this condition and, it is submitted, it must be interpreted in the light of dangers to the child of particular lifestyles rather than particular acts. The commission by a parent of a criminal offence does not indicate that the child is falling into bad associations, but the fact that the parent is a habitual criminal probably does: in the latter but not (necessarily) in the former case the danger is real that the child, under the influence of the parents, will follow their lead and adopt their attitudes to the criminal law, to the child's obvious and long-term detriment.

**(c) The child is likely (i) to suffer unnecessarily; or (ii) to be impaired seriously in his or her health or development, due to a lack of parental care**

"Parental care" is care provided by any person (whether a parent or not) who has the parental responsibility of safeguarding and promoting the child's health, development and welfare.[17] The reason for the lack of care

---

[14] As did the children in *D v Kelly*, 1995 S.L.T. 1220.

[15] s.52(3).

[16] As in, for example, *Sloan v B*, 1991 S.L.T. 530, *F v Kennedy* (No. 2), 1993 S.L.T. 1284 and *G v Scanlon*, 1999 SLT 707.

[17] It is unlikely to be held to include the care required to be shown by a *de facto* carer under the terms of s.5 of the Children (Scotland) Act 1995, though a parent who allows such a carer to fail in the responsibilities imposed by that section may thereby him or herself be guilty of a lack of parental care.

is irrelevant, whether it is incapacity, indolence, indifference or malice towards the child, and the ground will include a practical inability such as, for example, to provide suitable accommodation.[18] The important point is the effect that the lack of care has on the child rather than the reason for the lack of care. The test is an objective one, namely whether a reasonable person looking to the circumstances of the particular case would consider that the child is likely to be caused unnecessary suffering or serious impairment of health or development through lack of parental care.[19] This condition is not satisfied by showing that some other person than the parent or some other mode of caring might be better for the child.[20] Suffering, which may be physical or emotional, is "unnecessary" when it is avoidable through the exercise of proper care; an impairment of health or development is "serious" when it is not trivial or transient. A lack of parental care can be either a failure to protect the child or nurture him or her, or active treatment of or behaviour towards the child. It might cover, for example, failure to feed and clothe the child properly, maintaining a dirty and unhealthy living environment, allowing the child to wander the streets unsupervised late at night, allowing the child access to (or even providing) potentially harmful substances such as alcohol or pornography, failing to provide the emotional stability and social intercourse that is essential to the proper development of a child's character, allowing or even encouraging the child to enter into harmful relationships, acting in such a way as has the effect of lowering the child's self-esteem,[21] or any other act or omission which the reasonable parent would not have done or failed to do, including ill-treatment short of a criminal offence. It must be likely that the deprivation of reasonable care will continue and will harm the child materially in the future: the test is an objective one and it is prospective.[22]

It is the "likelihood" of the child suffering that raises the question of whether compulsory measures of supervision are necessary; in addition, a likelihood that there will be a lack of parental care can satisfy this condition.[23] This might be when there is a substantial or real, and not remote, chance that the lack of parental care will cause suffering to the child. Speculative injury is not sufficient, though the court accepts that it may be unrealistic to require precise specification of the harm that the child might suffer.[24] In the context of a criminal charge it has been held (and there will be no difference in the present context) that being intoxicated while looking after a child does not in itself create a likelihood of injury (though if it renders the person incapable of caring for the child it will inevitably amount to a lack of care)[25]; rather, there must be some evidence to support an inference that suffering is likely to

---

[18] *D v Kelly*, 1995 S.L.T. 1220 at 1223L. See also *Finlayson, Applicant*, 1989 S.C.L.R. 601.

[19] *M v McGregor*, 1982 S.L.T. 41, *per* Lord Justice-Clerk Wheatley at 43.

[20] *D v Kelly*, 1995 S.L.T. 1220; *H v Harkness*, 1998 S.L.T. 1431 at 1435J. This consists with E.C.H.R. jurisprudence: *Olsson v Sweden (No. 2)* (1994) 17 E.H.R.R. 134 at para. 72; *K.A. v Finland* Jan 14, 2003, at para. 92.

[21] As in *R v Grant*, 2000 S.L.T. 372.

[22] *D v Kelly*, 1995 S.L.T. 1220, *per* Lord Murray at 1224B.

[23] *McGregor v L*, 1981 S.L.T. 194; *M v McGregor*, 1982 S.L.T. 41.

[24] *H v Harkness* 1998 S.L.T. 1431, *per* Lord Coulsfield at 1435I.

[25] *H v Lees, D v Orr*, 1994 S.L.T. 908.

be caused such as, for example, the child needing fed or being left by an open fire and the parent being too intoxicated to notice the danger. Nor is the likelihood of suffering necessarily constituted by leaving even a very young child alone, though the length of time the child is left would be important, as would the circumstances and the potential sources of danger to which the child is thereby exposed.[26] The likelihood of suffering can be gleaned from the parents' past actions, such as their treatment of their other children, at least when the circumstances suggest that they are likely to treat the referred child in the same way. So this ground can exist even when the child has never in fact been in the care of the relevant person.[27] If it is proved that the habits and mode of life of the parents are such as to yield the reasonable inference that they are unlikely to care for the referred child in a manner likely to prevent unnecessary suffering or serious impairment of his or her health or development, the ground of referral is established.[28] A failure to provide or to consent to medical treatment considered necessary by sound medical opinion will constitute lack of parental care, even when the parents make their decision after careful consideration of the issue.[29] Parental good faith is nothing to the point: if their decision is not that which the reasonable parent would make, then they can be said to be showing a lack of parental care.[30]

**(d) That the child is a child in respect of whom any of the offences mentioned in Schedule 1 to the Criminal Procedure (Scotland) Act 1995 has been committed**

A child who has been the victim of any of the specified offences may be at risk of being offended against again or may be in need of direction and guidance in coming to terms with his or her experiences. The specified offences (usually known as "scheduled offences") are as follows:

(i) any offence under Part I of the Criminal Law (Consolidation) (Scotland) Act 1995 (*i.e.* sexual offences),

(ii) any offence under ss.12,[31] 15,[32] 22[33] or 33[34] of the Children and Young Persons (Scotland) Act 1937,

(iii) any other offence involving bodily injury[35] to a child under the age of 17 years, and

(iv) any offence involving the use of lewd, indecent or libidinous practice or behaviour towards a child under the age of 17 years.[36]

---

[26] *M v Normand*, 1995 S.L.T. 1284.

[27] *McGregor v L*, 1981 S.L.T. 194.

[28] *ibid.*, at 196.

[29] *Finlayson, Applicant*, 1989 S.C.L.R. 601.

[30] *D v Kelly*, 1995 S.L.T. 1220.

[31] Cruelty (including neglect and assault) to person under 16. This provision is often used when the parent exceeds the bounds of legitimate chastisement: see for example *G v Templeman,* 1998 S.C.L.R. 180.

[32] Causing or allowing person under 16 to be used for begging.

[33] Exposing child under seven to risk of burning.

[34] Causing or allowing person under 16 to take part in dangerous performance.

[35] "Bodily injury" requires physical injury or injury to the body of the child: *B v Kennedy*, 1987 S.L.T. 765; *F v Kennedy*, 1988 S.L.T. 404. Emotional injury is not covered here.

[36] For a discussion of the nature of this crime, see Gane, *Sexual Offences* (1992) at pp.74–77; Gordon, *Criminal Law* (3rd ed., by M.G.A. Christie, 2001) at para.36.09.

In addition, it is provided by s.52(7) of the Civic Government (Scotland) Act 1982 that references to offences mentioned in Schedule 1 to the Criminal Procedure (Scotland) Act 1975[37] shall include an offence under s.52(1)(a) of the 1982 Act, that is to say, taking, distributing, possessing or publishing indecent photographs of a person under the age of 16 years.

It is of no significance who perpetrated the offence, nor where the offence was perpetrated; these matters will, of course, be highly relevant to the final disposal of the child's case. Proof of this ground, despite being proof of a criminal offence, is on the civil standard,[38] and this standard can be met even in the absence of a conviction: the issue at stake (with this ground) is the harm to the child rather than how or by whom it was perpetrated. As such, there is no requirement that there be proved to have been a conviction before it can be established that this ground exists. Nor is there any requirement that the perpetrator be charged, or even identified.[39] Indeed, the ground might exist even when a prosecution results in an acquittal.[40] A conviction is evidence of the commission of the offence,[41] but it must be established that the child was a victim: the ground "is concerned with offences and not offenders".[42] The hearing may, of course, take into account the identity of the offender (if known to them) in making their disposal of the referral, but the sheriff is not entitled to make findings of fact beyond those necessary for the establishment of the ground.[43]

Though this ground, in its terms, refers to the commission of certain offences, it is not implicit that the actions which amount to the offences must have taken place in Scotland. In *S v Kennedy*[44] it was argued that since events which took place in Germany could not be tried as offences in Scotland they could not therefore amount to a ground of referral that the child was the victim of a Schedule 1 offence. This argument was, however, rejected on the basis that on a proper interpretation of the statute, the ground of referral is established when there is proved to have been conduct amounting to any of the Schedule 1 offences rather than the commission of a Schedule 1 offence. The result was that it did not matter where the conduct took place. This interpretation is justified by the purpose of the statute, which is to provide protection for children at risk from conduct rather than to provide punishment for crimes against the law of Scotland. There is nothing anomalous about this result when it is remembered that the condition in this paragraph can be established (on the balance of probabilities) even in the face of an acquittal by a criminal court (because of a failure to prove the crime beyond reason-

---

[37] This reference was not amended by the Criminal Procedure (Scotland) Act 1995 which replaced the 1975 Act, apparently by oversight. Either the oversight is overlooked or the offences in the 1982 Act no longer found a ground of referral: the court is highly unlikely to adopt the second alternative.

[38] *McGregor v D*, 1977 S.L.T. 182.

[39] *McGregor v K*, 1982 S.L.T. 293; *Kennedy v F*, 1985 S.L.T. 22.

[40] cf. *Kennedy v B*, 1992 S.C.L.R. 55.

[41] Law Reform (Miscellaneous Provisions) (Scotland) Act 1968, s.10.

[42] *S v Kennedy*, 1987 S.L.T. 667, *per* Lord Justice-Clerk Ross at 669I.

[43] *S v Kennedy*, 1987 S.L.T. 667.

[44] 1996 S.L.T. 1087.

able doubt). The reference to Schedule 1 is not a reference to particular crimes, but a means of identifying or characterising the conduct struck at.[45]

**(e) That the child is, or is likely to become, a member of the same household as a child in respect of whom a scheduled offence has been committed**

If the adults in a household, one child of which was the victim of a scheduled offence, were unable to protect that child, the question arises as to whether they will be able to protect other children in the same household and, consequently, if one child in a household has been the victim of a scheduled offence all the children who are members of that household may be referred to a children's hearing. In addition, children who are likely to become members of that household may also be referred[46]: this might include, for example, a child born to a woman in a hospital who is likely, on leaving hospital, to become a member of a household in which one of the members was the victim of a scheduled offence.

This paragraph covers both the case where an adult member of the household constitutes the threat and where the threat comes from outside the household. In the former case there is likely to be, in addition, a ground under paragraph (f) below. As with the ground in paragraph (d) above, it is not necessary for the satisfaction of this condition that the perpetrator be identified, or that any criminal charge be laid against anyone. The question is simply whether the child referred under this paragraph is, or is likely to become, a member of the same household as a child who could be referred to a children's hearing under paragraph (d) above. To establish this ground both the offence and membership of the household must be proved.[47] The identification of the victim will be a practical necessity for the satisfaction of this condition. If a referral has previously been made of the victim of the offence under paragraph (d) and the sheriff finds, after hearing evidence, that the ground is established, the production of a certified copy of the sheriff's interlocutor will be sufficient proof that that child was the victim of a scheduled offence,[48] and all that will need to be proved in relation to the child referred under the present paragraph is membership of the same household as the victim. If, on the other hand, the sheriff finds the ground under paragraph (d) not established in relation to the child victim, it will be difficult for a reporter to argue that other children in the same household are properly referred under the present paragraph, but it would not, it is submitted, be incompetent to attempt to do so. The investigation of the child referred under this paragraph may well reveal

---

[45] *per* Lord Murray at 1093H. This is very similar to the reasoning found in Lord Dunpark's dissenting judgment in *Merrin v S*, 1987 S.L.T. 193. *cf. Harris v E*, 1989 S.L.T. 42 in which a ground of referral was found established when the child was shown to be the victim of an offence which was not a scheduled offence at the time it was committed but had become a scheduled offence at the date of the referral.

[46] This is an addition to the predecessor ground as it appeared in s.32(2)(d) of the Social Work (Scotland) Act 1968. For a discussion of "likelihood" in this context, see *Templeton v E*, 1998 S.C.L.R. 672 (Sh Ct) at 678–679.

[47] *Ferguson v S*, 1992 S.C.L.R. 866.

[48] *McGregor v H*, 1983 S.L.T. 626.

information not available when the other child was referred under paragraph (d). It is open to a reporter to refer a child under this paragraph even after having taken the decision not to refer the victim of the scheduled offence under paragraph (d): though this would be unusual it might be appropriate, for example, if the victim is about to leave home or about to attain the age of 16 and is no longer in need of protection, guidance, treatment or control, while the child referred under this paragraph remains vulnerable. It is open to the relevant persons to deny the existence of the ground under the present paragraph even when, at the referral of the child victim under paragraph (d), they accepted the factual basis which now forms the basis of the referral of another child. Their acceptance in the previous referral is not sufficient proof before the sheriff that the present condition is satisfied.[49]

There have been a number of cases concerned with the meaning of "household" for the purposes of this condition and the conditions in paragraphs (f) and (g), both under the Social Work (Scotland) Act 1968 and the Children (Scotland) Act 1995.[50] It has been accepted that persons can be members of the same "household" even when they live apart: the word refers more to a continuing relationship than to physical proximity. So in *McGregor v H*[51] the First Division held that a child was a member of the same household as another child even although the other child had been removed from the family home as a compulsory measure of supervision. Lord President Emslie said: "The word 'household' in s.32[52] is plainly intended to connote a family unit or something akin to a family unit—a group of persons, held together by a particular kind of tie who normally live together, even if individual members of the group may be temporarily separated from it . . . The test is membership of the household and not whether a child is . . . 'living' in the same household as the victim of a relevant offence".[53] This dictum was applied in *Kennedy v R's Curator ad litem*,[54] in which a 13 year-old child had been subjected to lewd and indecent practices by her father and her one- and-a-half-year-old half sister was referred to the children's hearing, on the ground that she was a member of the same household as a person who has committed a scheduled offence.[55] Though the parents accepted this ground of referral, the hearing directed the reporter to make an application to the sheriff for the establishment of the ground, since the referred child was too young to understand. Shortly after the hearing, and before the case called before the sheriff, the child's mother removed herself and the child from the father and went to live with her own mother and claimed before the sheriff that the child was no longer a member of the same "household" as her father. That claim failed. Lord President Hope pointed out that, "the important question . . . is whether the ties of affection and regular contact which hold the parties together

---

[49] *M v Kennedy*, 1995 S.L.T. 123; *M v Constanda* 1999 SLT 494.

[50] For a discussion, see Norrie, "The Meaning of 'Household' in Referrals to the Children's Hearing" 1993 S.L.T. (News) 192.

[51] 1983 S.L.T. 626.

[52] The 1968 predecessor of s.52 of the Children (Scotland) Act 1995.

[53] 1983 S.L.T. 626 at 628.

[54] 1993 S.L.T. 295.

[55] *i.e.* a ground under what is now s.52(2)(f).

as a group of persons still continue. Since the criterion is that of relationship rather than locality, it is necessary to examine closely the reasons given for the suggestion that the relationship has broken down. A temporary separation will not do, especially as s.32(2)(dd) looks to the future as well as the present state of affairs".[56] There must be more than a mere physical separation, otherwise the policy of the Act could be frustrated by determined parents. It follows that a separation will not destroy a "household" when it is due only to the intervention of the authorities[57] or to a fear that steps may be taken by the authorities which might result in compulsory measures of supervision being imposed.[58]

So, a continuing relationship is important for the continuation of a household, but a relationship, even of blood and affection, will not in itself be sufficient. Nor will the mere fact that a person has parental responsibilities and parental rights in relation to the child, nor the fact that there exists between the two members of the asserted household "family life" within the meaning of Art.6 ECHR.[59] There is no presumption that a daughter lives in the same household as her father.[60] "Household" involves more than simply a relationship and requires, it is submitted, some living together either presently, or in the past with the possibility of re-establishing the cohabitation. If the child is at risk from a merely visiting father another ground could doubtless be used to refer him or her to the children's hearing (such as, for example, the "bad associations" ground in s.52(2)(b) or the lack of parental care ground in s.52(2)(c)).

A rather different aspect of the same point was raised in *A v Kennedy*,[61] in which a child born in June 1983 had died two months later as a result of being wilfully assaulted and ill-treated at his parents' home. Eight and a half years later the mother gave birth to another child and the reporter sought to refer this child to a children's hearing on the ground that the child was a member of the same household as a child who was the victim of certain specified offences. The parents disputed the ground of referral on the basis that the "household" into which the new baby had been born was different from that in which the previous child had lived.[62] They argued that the household had developed to such an extent that it could no longer be regarded as the same household: the previous child had died eight and a half years prior to the new baby entering the household, and an older sister, who had been removed after the death and sent to live with foster parents, had now returned to live with the parents under a supervision requirement. The parents argued that these substantial developments suggested that the household into which the baby was born was different from that in which the previous

---

[56] 1993 S.L.T. 295 at 300A–B.

[57] As in *McGregor v H*, 1983 S.L.T. 626.

[58] 1993 S.L.T. 295, *per* Lord President Hope at 300B.

[59] *Templeton v E*, 1998 S.C.L.R. 672 (Sh. Ct.)

[60] *Ferguson v S*, 1992 S.C.L.R. 866.

[61] 1993 S.L.T. 1188.

[62] The fact that the statute referred to a child who "is" a member of the same household as the child referred was not relied upon by counsel for the parents since the intention of the statute, as the Court put it, could clearly only be achieved by interpreting the word "is" to include "was".

child had lived. The Second Division disagreed and held that the "household" remained that which had existed when the baby died. Lord Justice-Clerk Ross pointed out that a household can continue even although there are changes in its membership. An older child may leave and a younger child may arrive, yet the "household" might remain intact. In *Cunningham v M*[63] Sheriff Principal Macphail summed up the authorities as follows:

> "The question whether people are members of the same household is a question of fact and degree; the concept of 'household' is of a group of persons and not the location in which they live; the fact that persons are living for the time being in separate houses is not decisive of the question whether they are members of the same household; the important question is whether ties of affection and regular contact which hold the parties together as a group still continue; the criterion is that of relationship rather than locality".

**(f) That the child is, or is likely to become, a member of the same household as a person who has committed a scheduled offence**

A child who lives with a scheduled offender may well not be in need of compulsory measures of supervision, but the very existence of the offence raises the question. The meaning of "household" will be the same as discussed under paragraph (e) above. The condition in this paragraph is satisfied whenever a scheduled offence has been committed, even when that offence was not committed against a child.[64] It will normally be essential to establish who the perpetrator is in order to establish that the child is a member of his or her household, though, rarely, it might be possible to establish that one of a number of adults in a household committed the offence without establishing precisely who. It is not, however, necessary that any charges have been laid against the perpetrator, and indeed the ground can be established even when a prosecution has been brought but has failed.[65] The onus of proof in establishing this ground is on the balance of probabilities (as it is for all the grounds except that in paragraph (i) below[66]). Proof of a conviction is sufficient evidence.[67]

**(g) That the child is, or is likely to become, a member of the same household as a person in respect of whom an offence amounting to incest or intercourse with a child by a step-parent or person in a position of trust has been committed by a member of that household**

Under s.32(2)(e) of the Social Work (Scotland) Act 1968 female children who were members of the same household as female victims of

---

[63] November 25, 2004, Edinburgh Sheriff Court, at para.26.

[64] Some of the sexual offences in Part I of the Criminal Law (Consolidation) (Scotland) Act 1995 can be committed against adults. See for example *G v Scanlon*, 1999 S.L.T. 707 where the offence (lewd and libidinous practices and underage sexual intercourse) was committed against the child's mother.

[65] *Kennedy v B*, 1992 S.C.L.R. 55.

[66] *Harris v F*, 1991 S.L.T. 242.

[67] Law Reform (Miscellaneous Provisions) (Scotland) Act 1968, s.10.

the crime of incest[68] could be referred to the children's hearing if both females were members of the same household as the perpetrator of that crime. This tortuous condition was rendered unnecessary in 1986, when incest became in all cases a scheduled offence, and while it has been slightly tidied up, the condition remains under the current legislation entirely otiose. The condition has been expanded by the 1995 Act so that boys as well as girls can be referred under this paragraph to a children's hearing, and it is further expanded to cover the offences related to incest[69] which were created by the Incest and Related Offences (Scotland) Act 1986 and which are now contained in the Criminal Law (Consolidation) (Scotland) Act 1995. However, since incest and the related offences are all offences listed in Sch.1 to the Criminal Procedure (Scotland) Act 1995, it follows that if the referred child lives in the same household as the perpetrator (a circumstance necessary for the existence of this ground) then he or she can also be referred to a children's hearing under paragraph (f) above. In practical terms, bearing in mind that the membership of both the victim[70] and the perpetrator of the referred child's household must be established under this paragraph, reporters may well be more inclined to refer the child under paragraph (f) where only the perpetrator's membership of the child's household is at issue. And from the point of view of the chairman of the hearing, who must explain the ground of referral to the child and the relevant person,[71] for the reporter to adopt that approach will invariably be better. If the nature of the offence under paragraph (f) is made plain to the hearing (as, invariably, it must be), there is no benefit to be obtained in referring also under paragraph (g), and reporters who do so achieve nothing but risk a delaying denial and impose upon the hearing the unnecessary burden of explaining this overly complicated condition. Reporters should avoid this paragraph like the plague.

### (h) That the child has failed to attend school regularly without reasonable excuse

Parents have a duty to educate their children,[72] and children have a right to be educated.[73] Most children receive their education by attending school and their failure to do so regularly, without reasonable excuse, whether as a result of their own failure to go or their parents' failure to

---

[68] Incest is penile penetration of the vagina between relatives in the following categories: mother-son, grandmother-grandson, great grandmother-great grandson, father-daughter, grandfather-granddaughter, great grandfather-great granddaughter, brother-sister, aunt-nephew, uncle-niece, adoptive or former adoptive mother-adopted or former adopted son, adoptive or former adoptive father-adopted or former adopted daughter: see Criminal Law (Consolidation) (Scotland) Act 1995, s.1.

[69] These are intercourse with a step-child or former step-child while that person is under the age of 21 (Criminal Law (Consolidation) (Scotland) Act 1995, s.2), and intercourse with a person over whom the accused stands in a position of trust or authority (Criminal Law (Consolidation) (Scotland) Act 1995, s.3).

[70] Technically, incest is a crime without a victim. If both participants do so willingly, they are both guilty: see Norrie, "Incest and the Forbidden Degrees of Marriage in Scots Law" (1992) 37 J.L.S.S. 216.

[71] s.65(4).

[72] Education (Scotland) Act 1980, s.30.

[73] Standards in Schools etc (Scotland) Act 2000, s.1.

send them, raises the question of whether compulsory measures of supervision are necessary in order to ensure that their right to education is enforced. The paragraph makes no specific exception for children who are educated by means other than attending school (which the law permits), but the providing to a child of an efficient education suitable to his or her age, ability and aptitude will clearly constitute a reasonable excuse for the child not attending school. In relation to the vast majority of children, who have attended a public school, this ground is one of the easiest to establish and an authorised record of attendance provided by the school will usually leave no room for argument.[74] Dispute is more likely to revolve around the question of whether the child has a reasonable excuse for non-attendance. Lack of reasonable excuse, though it is part of the ground of referral, does not require to be proved by the reporter[75]; rather, it is for the child or parent to show reasonable excuse once the reporter has proved non-attendance. (In practical terms, however, it is difficult to imagine a case in which the sheriff's decision would turn solely on the question of onus.) For the purposes of the parents' duty to secure the child's regular attendance at school under s.35 of the Education (Scotland) Act 1980, it is provided that there is a reasonable excuse for the parent's failure to ensure the child's attendance in the following circumstances:

(a) there is within two miles of the child's home, in the case of a child under eight, and within three miles in the case of any other child, measured in both cases by the nearest available route, no public or other school the managers of which are willing to receive the child and to provide him or her with free education, and either (i) no arrangements have been made by the education authority for enabling the child to attend an appropriate school, or for the provision of transport or the payment of travelling expenses, or (ii) any arrangements so made are such as to require the child to walk more than two miles (or three miles in the case of a child eight years of age or more) in the course of any journey between his or her home and school; or

(b) the child is being prevented by sickness from attending school or receiving education; or

(c) there are other circumstances which in the opinion of the education authority or the court afford a reasonable excuse.[76]

The existence of the circumstances in either (a) or (b) will almost certainly amount to reasonable excuse for the purpose of this paragraph; other than these, there will be few circumstances likely to be held to

---

[74] Education (Scotland) Act 1980, s.86: the head teacher's certification of attendance is presumed accurate until the contrary is proved.

[75] In *Kennedy v Clark*, 1970 S.L.T. 260 it was held that a prosecutor does not need to prove lack of reasonable excuse when prosecuting a parent for not ensuring the child's regular attendance. But see *O'Hagan v Rea* 2001 S.L.T. (Sh. Ct.) 30.

[76] Education (Scotland) Act 1980, s.42. See *Skeen v Tunnah*, 1970 S.L.T. (Sh. Ct.) 66 and *R v Devon County Council, ex parte G*, [1988] 3 W.L.R. 1386; J. Scott *Education Law in Scotland* (2003) at pp.203–206.

justify denying the child of his or her right to education.[77] It would not, it is submitted, be reasonable to keep a child off school in order to look after a sick parent[78] or to help with a disabled sibling, though the length of absence might sometimes be considered relevant. It would not be reasonable to keep a child off for even one day in order to assist in the parents' business, such as their shop; it might on the other hand not be unreasonable to take a child on a family holiday during the school term, on a single occasion. It will seldom, if ever, be reasonable for a child on his or her own initiative to stay away from school. An exclusion order issued due to the child's disruptive behaviour may not constitute a reasonable excuse for not attending school.[79]

The statute does not say so but it may be assumed that this paragraph can be used to refer a child to a children's hearing only when the child is within the ages of compulsory education (basically, 5 and 16); there is clearly a reasonable excuse for not attending when attendance is legally a matter of choice.

Isolated absences may not prevent the child from having attended school "regularly": the ground is designed to bring to a hearing children who are falling into a pattern of non-attendance and a single absence would not, it is submitted, satisfy this condition. However, reporters must strive to strike a difficult balance here, for sometimes isolated absences can be indicative of a real risk that they will become more frequent. There is little doubt that the earlier a potential school refuser is brought to a hearing the more likely it is that compulsory measures of supervision will be successful in returning the child to regular attendance.

### (i) That the child has committed an offence

One of the abiding principles upon which the Kilbrandon Report was based is the fact that the child who has committed a criminal offence is as much in need of care and supervision as the child who is the victim of abuse or neglect. This principle was given statutory recognition in the Social Work (Scotland) Act 1968 and it remains central to the thinking behind the current legislation. That the child has committed a criminal offence is one of the most common grounds under which children are referred to children's hearings,[80] though the consideration and disposal of a case brought on this ground are no different from cases brought on

---

[77] s.42 is designed to avoid punishment of parents where this is not appropriate, but considerations relevant to that question are not necessarily relevant to the question of whether the child who is not receiving an education is in need of compulsory measures of supervision.

[78] *cf. Jenkins v Howells* [1949] 2 K.B. 218.

[79] In *D v Kennedy*, 1988 S.L.T. 55 it was held that the ground of referral was not established when the child was excluded on the basis of an allegation of misconduct which was neither established in the evidence nor admitted by the child or parent. Though no concluded opinion were expressed by the court on what would be the case if misconduct was established, it would be sensible practice for reporters relying on this ground when the child has been excluded to lead evidence of the conduct which justified the child's exclusion.

[80] It is the single most common ground under which boys are referred to children's hearings. Girls are referred rather less frequently under this ground.

any other ground. The hearing considering the case are less concerned with the question of the child's guilt than with the question of whether compulsory measures of supervision may be necessary. The proceedings are not criminal proceedings since they are not concerned with prosecution and can lead to no conviction.[81] Nevertheless, this ground is slightly different from the other grounds in two major respects. First, proof, if an application has been made to the sheriff to establish the ground, is on the criminal rather than the civil standard[82] and the rules of evidence applicable to criminal rather than civil cases will be applied.[83] And secondly, the ground is applicable only to children who are older than eight years, which is currently the age of criminal responsibility.[84] A factual basis which would justify a child over the age of eight being referred under this paragraph will usually justify a referral under another paragraph if the child is under eight.

### (j) That the child has misused alcohol or any drug, whether or not a controlled drug within the meaning of the Misuse of Drugs Act 1971

This ground is designed to give effect to Art.33 of the UN Convention on the Rights of the Child, which obliges States to take all appropriate measures to protect children from the dangers of illicit use of drugs. Even without this paragraph[85] children who misuse drugs or alcohol could be referred under another ground in any case, such as being beyond parental control, or falling into bad associations, or lack of parental care. Drug and alcohol abuse is, however, a significant threat to the well-being of some children and the introduction of this ground serves to strengthen the concern rightly felt about the problem. Also, it may well be clearer as a condition in itself rather than evidence of another condition, and thus easier to establish.

The use of alcohol or drugs by the child is not sufficient: there must be "misuse".[86] A child may legitimately take a drug for medicinal purposes and may even, in some circumstances, drink alcohol without this being a misuse. If the child took alcohol without responsible adult supervision, or to such an extent as to become inebriated, then there is likely to have

---

[81] *per* Lord President Emslie in *McGregor v T*, 1975 S.L.T. 76 at 81. See also *S v Miller,* 2001 S.L.T. 531. Proceedings based on s.52(2)(i) do, however, result in the child being treated as an "offender" for the purposes, for example, of the Rehabilitation of Offenders Act 1974: see *Stair Memorial Encyclopaedia of the Laws of Scotland* vol.3, para.1337.

[82] s.68(3)(b). And the reporter cannot avoid this higher standard of proof by drawing up different grounds, such as exposure to moral danger, if the factual basis of the ground is the commission of an offence: *Constanda v M,* 1997 S.L.T. 1396.

[83] See below at pp.108–109.

[84] *Merrin v S*, 1987 S.L.T. 193. The age of criminal responsibility has recently been subject to much debate and there are presently proposals to restructure the law here. See *Report on the Age of Criminal Responsibility* (Scot. Law Com. No. 185, 2001), discussed by C. McDiarmid "Age of Criminal Responsibility: Raise it or Remove it?" 2001 J.R. 243 and E. Sutherland "The Age of Reason or the Reasons for an Age?" 2002 S.L.T. (News) 1.

[85] There was no equivalent in s.32 of the Social Work (Scotland) Act 1968.

[86] "Misuse" will frequently amount to an offence under the Misuse of Drugs Act 1971. Sheriff Kearney (*Children's Hearings and the Sheriff Court* (2nd ed., 2000) at para.46.22 suggests, on analogy with *Constanda v M,* 1997 S.L.T. 1396 that if the sole basis of the referral is that the child has committed an offence under the 1971 Act, reporters ought not to seek to avoid the higher standard of proof by relying on this ground rather than that contained in s.52(2)(i).

been a misuse. It must be the child who has misused the alcohol: it would not normally be considered to be a misuse by a young child to be plied with alcohol by an adult,[87] and that circumstance will appropriately be dealt with as a lack of parental care. The use by a child of drugs, for anything other than medicinal purposes, will clearly amount to misuse.

**(k) That the child has misused a volatile substance by deliberately inhaling its vapour, other than for medicinal purposes**

An identical ground was introduced into the Social Work (Scotland) Act 1968 by the Solvent Abuse (Scotland) Act 1983, which indicates that what is in mind here is "glue-sniffing", or the inhaling of the vapours from similar intoxicating substances. This dangerous practice has been the cause of death of a number of children, and a child who has indulged in the practice may well need help, advice and guidance to avoid doing so in the future; in addition the practice may be symptomatic of a more deep-seated problem in the child's life. In either case the question of whether compulsory measures of supervision are necessary clearly arises.

**(l) That the child is being provided with accommodation by a local authority under s.25, or is subject to a parental responsibilities order obtained under s.86, of the 1995 Act and, in either case, his or her behaviour is such that special measures are necessary for his or her adequate supervision in his or her interest or the interest of others**

The local authority have various duties as respects any child who is being accommodated by them under Chapter One of Part II of the Children (Scotland) Act 1995 or who is subject to a parental responsibilities order. In carrying out these duties it sometimes happens that special measures are necessary properly to supervise the child, and if so the child can be referred to a children's hearing in order that the children's hearing can give consideration to such measures as are deemed necessary. Most frequently this will involve some form of restraining measure in the child's own interests or in the interests of those to whom the child poses a threat. Or it might be that access to special resources, such as specialist accommodation, is more readily available than otherwise when it is a condition or authorisation under a supervision requirement that the child is given such access.

Under s.25 of the 1995 Act, a local authority is obliged to provide accommodation to any child (i) in respect of whom no-one has parental responsibility or (ii) who is lost or abandoned or (iii) who was being cared for by a person who is now prevented, whether or not permanently and for whatever reason, from providing the child with suitable accommodation or care.[88] In addition, the local authority is entitled, but not obliged, to provide accommodation for any child in their area if they consider that to do so would safeguard or promote the child's welfare.[89] Any such child may be referred to a children's hearing under this

---

[87] N.B. the offence under s.16 of the Children and Young Persons (Scotland) Act 1937 to give excisable liquor to a child under five except in case of sickness or emergency, or on medical advice.

[88] s.25(1).

[89] s.25(2).

paragraph. In addition, a child who is subject to a parental responsibilities order may be referred even when not being accommodated by a
local authority: such a child is always being "looked after" by the local
authority.[90]

**(m) That the child is not subject to a supervision requirement but the reporter
has been required to refer the case to a children's hearing under s.12(1) of the
Antisocial Behaviour etc (Scotland) Act 2004[91]**

On the face of it, this provision is entirely circular: there is a ground of
referral in respect of the child because the reporter has been obliged to
refer the child. The mischief is, however, clear: the behaviour that
justifies a sheriff in making an antisocial behaviour order over a child is
behaviour that raises the question whether the child is in need to
compulsory measures of supervision.[92] The reporter is deemed to believe
that question has an affirmative answer.[93] The 2004 Act describes the
behaviour that justifies the making of an antisocial behaviour order as
behaviour or the pursuance of a course of action that causes or is likely
to cause alarm or distress to at least one person not in the same
household[94] as the person so behaving.[95] It is to be noted that it is not
the behaviour that is the ground of referral but the requirement on the
reporter: so the behaviour itself is not open to challenge by the child or
relevant person at the hearing at which grounds of referral are put for
acceptance or denial. The hearing is not the place to challenge the
making of the antisocial behaviour order.

---

[90] s.17(6)(c).

[91] Inserted by the Antisocial Behaviour etc. (Scotland) Act 2004, s.12(3).

[92] See further, below at pp.46–47.

[93] Children (Scotland) Act 1995, 65(1A), as inserted by the Antisocial Behaviour etc.
(Scotland) Act 2004, s.12(4).

[94] "Household" is presumably to be defined as it is for the other parts of the 1995 Act:
see above at pp.31–33.

[95] Antisocial Behaviour etc. (Scotland) Act 2004, s.143(1).

## CHAPTER FOUR

# PRE-HEARING PROCEDURES

## INTRODUCTION

It is the reporter's responsibility to decide whether a child should be referred to a children's hearing and, having made that decision, to arrange the hearing and to ensure that proper notifications thereof are given and that appropriate documentation is supplied to those entitled to receive documents. The statute and Rules govern not only procedures at the hearing but also the reporter's duties and role leading up to any children's hearing.

## REFERRAL OF CHILD TO REPORTER

There are no means by which a child can be referred to a children's hearing otherwise than through the reporter and in the vast majority of cases the reporter has a discretion to refer or not to refer the child. The reporter must, however, be in possession of sufficient information concerning a child before he or she will be in a position to exercise that discretion. He or she is, therefore, dependent for the proper carrying out of his or her functions on receiving information concerning children from various sources, including local authorities, schools, welfare agencies, the courts and the police. There are different statutory provisions concerning the transmission of information to the reporter, according to whether the information comes from a local authority, from the police, the court or from any other person. Wherever the information comes from, the reporter must keep a record of the name and address of the person who provided it. [1]

### Referral from the local authority

Local authorities, through their social services and education departments, are uniquely well-placed to acquire information concerning children in their areas, and much of the information that a reporter relies upon comes ultimately from this source. Whenever information is received by a local authority[2] which suggests that a child may be in need

---

[1] Children's Hearings (Scotland) Rules 1996, r.3(1).

[2] Information is "received by a local authority" when any of their officers or agencies, or anyone acting on their behalf, comes to hold information of the appropriate nature. This will include social work departments, education departments and local authority medical services, but it is not limited to these agencies and the phrase is to be given wide scope.

of compulsory measures of supervision, the local authority must cause inquiries to be made, unless they are satisfied that no inquiries are necessary.[3] This information may be of any nature that raises concerns about the health, development or welfare of the child. The investigations to be carried out, usually by the local authority's social work department, are to be directed towards the question of whether grounds of referral exist in relation to the child, for it is only if they do exist that the question of whether compulsory measures of supervision are necessary arises. It is not for the local authority to determine that compulsory measures of supervision are necessary (just as it is not for the police to determine that an alleged offender is guilty) though invariably that question will be uppermost in the minds of the investigators: rather they must determine whether compulsory measures of supervision may be necessary. If the local authority are satisfied that investigations are unnecessary, for example because it is clear that grounds of referral do exist, or it is clear that none exists, then the local authority are not obliged to make inquiries. If the local authority's investigations are being frustrated by the unreasonable refusal of parents to allow them access to the child they may seek a child protection order from the sheriff court to allow them to carry out their statutory duty of investigation.[4] Making the threat of seeking such an order might well prove useful in encouraging co-operation with local authority investigations rather more often than it would be appropriate actually to carry out the threat.

Once the local authority have completed their investigations and they are able to say whether it appears to them that compulsory measures of supervision may be necessary, or they have so concluded without investigation, they must give to the reporter such information about the child as they have been able to discover if it appears to them that such measures may be necessary.[5] It has been said that "to the local authority is given the judgment, in cases in which it receives information, of whether there may be a need for compulsory measures but not of whether there is an actual need. Accordingly, it is obliged to transmit information whenever the view that compulsory measures of supervision are required could reasonably be entertained even if in its judgment alternative measures, or no action, would be preferable".[6]

Education authorities (which all local authorities are) are additionally entitled under s.36(3) of the Education (Scotland) Act 1980[7] to give information about a child of school age to the reporter where the child has failed to attend a public school regularly, though since the coming into force of the Children (Scotland) Act 1995 this entitlement has been limited to cases in which there is no requirement on the local authority under s.53(1) of the 1995 Act to give information to the reporter. This qualification would seem to have no effect other than to prevent an overlap of provisions and consequent confusion as to the statutory authority under which the local education authority are acting.

---

[3] s.53(1)(a).
[4] s.57(2): see further pp.229–230.
[5] s.53(1)(b).
[6] Wilkinson and Norrie, *Parent and Child* (2nd ed., 1999) at para.19.09.
[7] As amended by the Children (Scotland) Act 1995, Sch.4, para.28(2).

If a child is being looked after by a local authority under Chapter One or Chapter Four of Part II of the 1995 Act (*i.e.* is being provided accommodation without a supervision requirement, or is subject to a parental responsibilities order in the local authority's favour), and has been placed in secure accommodation, the local authority must forthwith and in any event not later than 24 hours from the time of the placement inform the reporter of the placement.[8] Within 72 hours of the placing of the child in secure accommodation the reporter must proceed in accordance with s.56 of the Act[9] (*i.e.* he or she must investigate the case and decide whether or not to arrange a children's hearing, as described below[10]).

### Referral from the police

The most common source of the reporter's information about children is the police. If a police officer has reasonable cause to believe that compulsory measures of supervision may be necessary in respect of a child, he or she is under a statutory duty to give to the reporter such information concerning the child as he or she has been able to discover.[11] In addition, police officers are also obliged to report to the appropriate prosecuting authorities the commission of offences that come to their attention,[12] and whenever that duty arises they are also obliged to make such a report to the reporter whenever their report is "in relation to a child".[13] This phrase is not limited to the situation of the child committing an offence, and will include cases in which the child is the victim, for such a report would, it is submitted, "relate to a child". If it were intended to limit this duty to cases involving alleged offences by children the statute could easily have said so.[14]

There is also an obligation on police officers to inform the reporter whenever a child who appears to have committed an offence has been detained in a place of safety[15] but it has been decided that charges are not to be proceeded with against the child.[16] In these circumstances the reporter must, unless he or she considers that compulsory measures of supervision are not required in relation to the child,[17] arrange a children's hearing to which he or she must refer the case.[18] A children's hearing arranged under this provision must decide whether to grant a warrant to keep the child in the place of safety[19] and also whether to

---

[8] Secure Accommodation (Scotland) Regulations 1996, reg.7.

[9] Secure Accommodation (Scotland) Regulations 1996, reg.8. In calculating the 72 hours, Sundays and public holidays are excluded: reg.2(2).

[10] At pp.48–52.

[11] s.53(2)(a).

[12] Police (Scotland) Act 1967, s.17(1)(b).

[13] s.53(3).

[14] *cf.* s.53(4) which clearly includes cases in which the child is a victim of an alleged offence.

[15] "Place of safety" is defined as in s.93 of the Children (Scotland) Act 1995, except that for present purposes it does not include a police station.

[16] Criminal Procedure (Scotland) Act 1995, s.43(5).

[17] In which case he or she must direct that the child shall no longer be kept in the place of safety: Children (Scotland) Act 1995, s.63(3).

[18] Children (Scotland) Act 1995, s.63(1).

[19] See below at pp.200–201.

direct the reporter to arrange a children's hearing for the purpose of putting grounds of referral to the child and the relevant person.[20]

If the child has absconded from a place of safety and been arrested and returned there,[21] but the occupier of the place of safety is unwilling or unable to receive the child back, this must be intimated to the reporter forthwith. If the child is presently subject to a supervision requirement, the reporter must bring the child before a children's hearing for that requirement to be reviewed[22]; if the child is not presently subject to a supervision requirement the reporter must then consider whether compulsory measures of supervision are required in respect of the child.[23]

### Referral from other persons

Any person other than a local authority or a police officer (both of whom have duties), is entitled to pass to the reporter such information as he or she has been able to discover which gives reasonable cause to believe that compulsory measures of supervision may be necessary in respect of a particular child.[24] There is no limitation on who has the right to pass information to the reporter, and it may be a medical practitioner, law enforcement officer, school teacher, group leader, neighbour, relative, child protection agency or even the child him or herself. The right or duty to give information exists only in so far as the person with the information has reasonable cause to believe that it indicates that compulsory measures of supervision may be necessary in relation to the child. This suggests that there is no right to give information when there is no reasonable cause for that belief. It is clearly not the aim of the Act to discourage the passing of information concerning children to the reporter, even when investigations are likely to show that there is no cause for concern,[25] but it is important that there be sanctions against persons who waste reporters' time and potentially traumatise children by passing on false information about them. A person acting maliciously in giving information concerning a child without any reasonable cause to believe that grounds of referral exist can be sued for damages. The transmission of information to the reporter is clearly an act which is protected by the defence of qualified privilege in the law of defamation, but it is not protected by absolute privilege and in order to establish civil liability for the wrongful transmission of information the pursuer would have to show both malice on the part of the defender and want of

---

[20] See below at p.201.

[21] Under s.82(1).

[22] s.82(5)(a). Curiously, s.73 does not list this circumstance as one in which a review must be held, and in its terms s.82(5)(a) merely says that a child can be kept in a place of safety until a review. But it would be against the interests of the child to be detained until the next scheduled review and the implication is clear that the reporter should arrange a review as soon as possible: see further, below at pp.166–167.

[23] s.82(5)(b).

[24] s.53(2)(b).

[25] See further *D v NSPCC* [1978] A.C. 171.

probable cause.[26] In addition, it might in some circumstances amount to a criminal offence knowingly to give false information to the reporter, at least when the information is to the effect that the child has committed an offence,[27] and possibly in any case in which the information suggests that grounds of referral exist.

### Referral or remit by the court

Another source from which the reporter may receive information is the court, for it frequently happens that in the course of other proceedings information comes to light which suggests to the court that grounds of referral exist in relation to a child. Both civil and criminal courts have the power to refer a child to the reporter but only in certain specified circumstances, and there are different rules depending upon the nature of the court proceedings. Even outwith the specified circumstances a judge or any other person involved in court proceedings can, of course, refer any child to the reporter under the provisions of s.53(2) as discussed above, but there are procedural advantages (at least for the reporter) if the reference comes formally from the court.

### Referral by the court: s.54

Under s.54 of the Children (Scotland) Act 1995 a court may refer a child to the reporter in any of the following proceedings:

(a) an action for divorce or judicial separation or for declarator of marriage, nullity of marriage, parentage or non-parentage;

(aa) an action for dissolution or declarator of nullity of a civil partnership or separation of civil partners;

(b) proceedings relating to parental responsibilities or parental rights within the meaning of Part I of the 1995 Act;

(c) proceedings for an adoption order under the Adoption (Scotland) Act 1978 or for an order under s.18 of that Act declaring a child free for adoption; and

(d) proceedings for an offence under s.35 (failure of parent to secure attendance of child at school), s.41 (failure to comply with attendance order) or s.42(3) (failure to permit examination of child) of the Education (Scotland) Act 1980.[28]

Where, in any such proceedings,[29] the court is satisfied that any of the grounds of referral (except that the child has committed an offence)

---

[26] See generally Norrie, *Defamation and Related Actions in Scots Law* (1995) at pp.123–124. In *W v Westminster City Council (No. 1)* [2004] E.W.H.C. 2866 and *(No. 2)* [2005] E.W.H.C. 102 it was held in England that absolute privilege, which applies in all judicial proceedings, does not extend to case conferences in child protection processes and that these are covered only by qualified privilege. These processes tend to be internal to local authorities but the same rule would apply to a meeting between a reporter and a reporter-manager. Proceedings at children's hearings, being quasi-judicial, are on the other hand protected by absolute privilege, with the result that active participants therein cannot be sued at all for any defamatory statement they may utter in the course of the hearing.

[27] See *Stair Memorial Encyclopaedia of the Laws of Scotland,* vol.7, paras 524–535.

[28] s.54(2), as amended by the Civil Partnership Act 2004 (c. 33), Sch.28, para.61.

[29] "Any proceedings" is not, it is submitted, limited to proceedings at first instance: an appeal court could competently make a referral under s.54.

exists, that court may refer the matter to the reporter, specifying which ground it has found to exist.[30] If it does so, the reporter's investigative duties and his or her discretion to refer, or not to refer, the case to a children's hearing are the same as in any other circumstance in which the reporter is given information.[31] However, if the reporter does decide to arrange a children's hearing, there will be no need for that hearing to seek acceptance of the grounds of referral from the child and relevant persons (though the grounds should nevertheless be explained by the chairman at the commencement of the hearing[32]), for it is provided[33] that the ground identified by the court will be treated as if it had been established by the sheriff in an application under s.68. The hearing can therefore move straight on to a consideration and disposal of the case under s.69 or s.70. Because of this provision, a court in the relevant proceedings must be careful to conclude that grounds of referral exist only when there is sufficient evidence to suggest it and also, it is submitted, only when sufficient opportunity has been afforded to the child and the relevant persons to challenge that evidence. The risk is that unless sufficient evidence is considered, and the opportunity afforded to challenge it, the fair trial requirement in Art.6 of the ECHR will be breached. For it is to be remembered that, unlike s.68 applications, the main purpose of the court proceedings will not have been directed towards establishing whether or not grounds of referral exist, but will concern a quite different matter (*e.g.* the resolution of a dispute as to where the child is to live, or whether he or she is to be adopted). The holding that grounds of referral exist will be a subsidiary matter to the main purpose of the proceedings and the possibility that the rights of the family will be overlooked is therefore greater than in a s.68 application. The wording of s.54(1) would appear to allow the court to refer any child to the reporter, and not only the child who is the subject of the relevant proceedings.[34]

### Referral by the court: s.48

Under s.48 of the Criminal Procedure (Scotland) Act 1995, a criminal court which has convicted a person of either a Sch.1 offence[35] or the offence of incest with a person aged 17 years or over,[36] or an offence under s.21 of the Children and Young Persons (Scotland) Act 1937[37]

---

[30] s.54(1). If the action is one for divorce, judicial separation, nullity of marriage or dissolution of civil partnership and the court does not consider itself in a position to make such a referral without further consideration, it must postpone its decision on the granting of the decree in the action until it is in such a position, so long as exceptional circumstances make it desirable to do so: s.12.

[31] So under s.54(3) the reporter must make such investigations as he or she thinks appropriate (*cf.* s.56(1), below at pp.47–48) and then arrange a children's hearing if he or she considers that compulsory measures of supervision are necessary (*cf.* s.56(6), below at pp.51–52).

[32] See 1996 Rules, r.20(2).

[33] s.54(3).

[34] *cf. McArdle v Orr*, 1994 S.L.T. 463. There may indeed be no child who is directly the subject of proceedings, as in, for example, a divorce action in which the child's residence is not in dispute.

[35] For scheduled offences, see above at pp.28–29.

[36] Which itself is a scheduled offence.

[37] Vagrants preventing children from receiving education.

may refer either the child victim of the Sch.1 offence or the s.21 offence, or any child who is or is likely to become a member of the same household as the offender of the Sch.1 offence or (tautologously) the offence of incest, to the reporter. If the court does so then it will certify that the offence is a ground established for the purpose of referral to the children's hearing.[38] This means that there will be no need for the hearing to seek acceptance of the grounds of referral from the child and relevant person (though the grounds should nevertheless be explained by the chairman at the commencement of the hearing[39]), and the hearing can move straight on to the consideration and disposal of the case. Certification that a ground of referral exists does not, however, oblige the reporter to arrange a children's hearing and he or she retains the discretion to decide against referring the case to a children's hearing.[40] The matter could have been expressed more clearly in the statute, but it has long been accepted that the reference by the court does not limit the reporter's discretion in this way.[41]

### Referral by the court under the Antisocial Behaviour etc (Scotland) Act 2004

One of the various amendments to the children's hearing system made by the Antisocial Behaviour etc (Scotland) Act 2004 which does deliberately limit the reporter's discretion is contained in s.12(1) of that Act. Whenever a sheriff makes an antisocial behaviour order (ASBO) or an interim ASBO in respect of a child, he may require the reporter to refer the child's case to a children's hearing. This is not a referral to the reporter in the way that the provision discussed in the paragraph immediately above is, entitling the reporter to decide whether to arrange a children's hearing, but is rather a requirement on the reporter to arrange a hearing, whether or not the reporter is of the view that the child is in need of compulsory measures of supervision. The only analogous provision to this detraction from the reporter's discretion is the anomalous rule contained in s.63 of the Children (Scotland) Act 1995[42] under which a children's hearing can require the reporter (in very limited and self-contained circumstances) to arrange a children's hearing, and this provision is virtually unused. For a sheriff to require the reporter to arrange a hearing will put the reporter in a very awkward position if he or she does not believe the child is in need of compulsory measures of supervision. The 2004 Act addresses this in law but not in reality by inserting a further provision into the 1995 Act to the effect that if the reporter is satisfied that he or she has been required to arrange a children's hearing then he or she is to be taken to be satisfied that compulsory measures of supervision are indeed necessary in respect of the child.[43] This provision may be compared with that relating to

---

[38] Criminal Procedure (Scotland) Act 1995, s.48(1).

[39] See 1996 Rules, r.20(2).

[40] For the conviction and imprisonment of the offender may have removed the source of danger from the child's life.

[41] See Kearney, *Children's Hearings and the Sheriff Court* (2nd ed., 2000) at para.3.15.

[42] For which see p.201 below.

[43] Children (Scotland) Act 1995, s.65(1A), as inserted by the Antisocial Behaviour etc. (Scotland) Act 2004, s.12(4).

parenting orders under the 2004 Act, where the court may merely require the reporter to consider whether to apply for such an order.[44] Section 12(1) of the 2004 Act does not oblige the sheriff who makes an ASBO to require the reporter to arrange a children's hearing, but merely permits him to do so, and it would be appropriate, it is submitted, for sheriffs to be reticent about exercising this power. It is to be remembered that the reporter is free to arrange a children's hearing in the absence of a direction that he or she does so, based upon the same grounds as led to the ASBO[45] and it is the reporter's belief that the child is in need of compulsory measures of supervision that ought to be the basis for the referral from the reporter to the children's hearing.

### Remit by the court: s.49

If the child him or herself has pled guilty to or been found guilty of an offence by a criminal court that court may remit the child's case to a children's hearing for consideration and disposal under the terms of s.49 of the Criminal Procedure (Scotland) Act 1995.[46] If it does so, a certificate signed by the clerk of the court stating that the child has pled guilty to or been found guilty of the offence to which the remit relates shall be conclusive evidence for the purposes of the remit that the offence has been committed by the child.[47] The result again is that the ground does not need to be put to the child and relevant person for acceptance. In this sort of case, however, which is technically a "remit" from the court of the child's case rather than a "reference" by the court of the child, the reporter is obliged to arrange a children's hearing to which the case shall stand referred for consideration and disposal and he or she cannot decide not to arrange a children's hearing.

INVESTIGATING THE CHILD'S CASE

Having received information concerning a child from any of the sources mentioned above, the reporter must decide, first, whether or not to make an initial investigation and then, secondly, whether or not to arrange a children's hearing.[48] The local authority may already have conducted investigations,[49] and further investigations by the reporter will be required only when he or she is not yet in possession of sufficient information to determine whether a children's hearing requires to be arranged (that is to say whether in his or her view compulsory measures of supervision are necessary); no investigation is necessary when the reporter is of the view that he or she already has sufficient information to make that decision. It is the question of whether compulsory measures of supervision are necessary that the reporter must investigate, rather

---

[44] Antisocial Behaviour etc (Scotland) Act 2004, s.114.

[45] No question of *res judicata* will arise since the two processes are designed to achieve quite separate aims.

[46] See below at Chap.10.

[47] Children (Scotland) Act 1995, s.50(1).

[48] s.56(1).

[49] Under s.53(1)(a).

than simply whether grounds of referral exist, though it is only if such grounds exist that the question of whether compulsory measures of supervision arises, and so often both questions must be addressed.

If the reporter decides that an initial investigation is required, the form of that investigation can be as the reporter thinks fit. It will normally include requesting the local authority to draw up a social background report, detailing any circumstances that he or she considers necessary,[50] including information additional to that given by the local authority under the terms of s.53.[51] The local authority are obliged to supply this report.[52] The report may contain such information, from any person whomsoever, as the reporter or the local authority thinks fit. The reporter may also seek reports from anyone else, such as the police or medical profession, though there is no obligation on anyone other than a local authority to supply a report. There is nothing to prevent the reporter from inviting for interview any person who may help the reporter come to the decision he or she has to make, and this might include, in appropriate cases, the child and his or her parents; there is, however, no power to enforce attendance at any such interview.

### DECIDING WHETHER TO ARRANGE A HEARING

Having made such investigation as he or she thinks necessary, the reporter must then make a decision whether a children's hearing requires to be arranged. This decision is not expressly governed by the overarching principles in s.16 of the 1995 Act[53] (which refers to decisions made by a court or a children's hearing only and not to decisions made by the reporter), but inevitably the reporter will be guided by his or her assessment of the child's welfare. In addition, being a "public authority" for the purposes of the Human Rights Act 1998, the reporter must act at all times, including making decisions, in a manner consistent with the ECHR. This means, in this context, that the reporter must bring to the decision-making process considerations of proportionality: is it, in other words, a proportionate response to the child's difficulties that a hearing be arranged? Whatever decision the reporter makes he or she must keep a record of it and, if the original information came from the police or the local authority, he or she must give notice of the decision to the chief constable or the local authority.[54]

As well as deciding whether to arrange a children's hearing, the reporter may, either at this stage or after any hearing, make an application to the sheriff for a parenting order under the Antisocial Behaviour etc (Scotland) Act 2004. The sheriff may make such an order if (i) the child has been engaged in anti-social behaviour or criminal conduct[55] and making the order is desirable in the interests of preventing

---

[50] s.56(2).
[51] s.56(3).
[52] s.56(2).
[53] See below at pp.121–123 for details.
[54] 1996 Rules, r.3(2).
[55] Or conduct that would have been criminal had the child been over the age of eight years: Antisocial Behaviour etc. (Scotland) Act 2004, s.102(7).

the child from engaging in such conduct, or (ii) it is desirable in the interests of improving the welfare of the child to make the order. Before applying for a parenting order, the reporter must consult the local authority for the area where the child ordinarily resides.[56] "Consult" is designed to encourage co-operation but does not inhibit the reporter's discretion in any way. On a request by the reporter for the purpose of determining whether to make an application for a parenting order, the local authority must supply a report on the parent and the child and such circumstances concerning each as appear to the reporter to be relevant.[57] Unlike any power vested in the children's hearing, a parenting order made by a court can require the relevant person to comply with requirements specified in the order,[58] and so this option is suitable when the reporter is of the view that an order over the child will achieve far less than an order over the relevant person. The 2004 Act is, therefore, a significant additional power in the reporter's armoury.[59] As well as making an application for a parenting order *ex proprio motu*, the reporter may be required to consider whether to make such an application, either by a court[60] or by a children's hearing.[61]

### Decision not to arrange a children's hearing

The reporter can decide not to arrange a children's hearing if he or she is satisfied either that no grounds of referral exist in relation to the child or that, even although such grounds do exist, no compulsory measures of supervision are necessary. "Necessity" here includes a consideration of "necessity" for interfering with family life in terms of Art.8(2) of the ECHR (*i.e.* would the interference pursue a legitimate aim and if so would the means adopted go beyond the minimum necessary to achieve that aim?). The question of whether compulsory measures of supervision are required, which arises only if grounds of referral exist,[62] can at this stage in the process (though only at this stage) be answered by the reporter him or herself deciding that no compulsory measures are necessary. This is an important power, giving to the reporter a vital role in sifting out cases in which grounds of referral clearly exist but in which, equally clearly, the child is not in need of any compulsory measures of supervision. The reporter has had this discretion since the children's hearing system was instituted and it has proved to be an essential part of the process, preventing the system from being clogged up with cases in which no reasonable panel member would impose a supervision requirement. There are many children who may be involved, for example, in an isolated incident of petty theft or of school truanting, for whom the shock of being investigated is sufficient persuasion not to repeat the

---

[56] *ibid.*, s.102(9), The local authority itself may apply for a parenting order, in which case it must consult with the reporter.

[57] *ibid.*, s.113(2).

[58] *ibid.*, s.103.

[59] For a critical view of the likely efficacy of parental orders, see E.E. Sutherland, "Parental Orders: A Culturally Alien Response of Questionable Efficacy" 2004 J.R. 105.

[60] Antisocial Behaviour etc (Scotland) Act 2004, s.114.

[61] Children (Scotland) Act 1995, s.75A, as inserted by the Antisocial Behaviour etc. (Scotland) Act 2004, s.116.

[62] s.52(1).

incident.[63] Or, the police may have reported that a child has been the victim of a Sch.1 offence by a stranger in circumstances which no caring parent could have prevented (the crazed gun-man scenario and the like). In such cases, the reporter is able to decide for him or herself that compulsory measures of supervision are not necessary and therefore that no children's hearing need be arranged.

Whenever the reporter decides that a children's hearing does not need to be arranged, this decision must be intimated to the child, any relevant person, and the person who brought the case to the reporter's notice, or any of those persons.[64] The words "or any of those persons" suggest a discretion on the part of the reporter to decide who is to be informed, but good practice would suggest that if the child and relevant person are aware of the investigation (as will normally be the case) they should be informed, and if they are unaware of the investigation, or none was considered necessary, the person who supplied the information should be informed. If the reference to the reporter was from a local authority or a police officer the reporter must give notice of the decision not to arrange a children's hearing to the local authority or, as the case may be, the chief constable of that decision.[65] In addition, if the reference to the reporter was from a local authority acting under reg.7 of the Secure Accommodation (Scotland) Regulations 1996,[66] the reporter must inform the local authority within 72 hours of his or her decision not to arrange a children's hearing, and the local authority must thereupon arrange for the child's discharge forthwith from secure accommodation and for any relevant person to be informed of the child's discharge.[67]

If the decision is taken not to arrange a children's hearing, the reporter has three separate powers, to be exercised when he or she considers it appropriate. First, he or she may refer the child's case to a local authority for the purpose of the authority providing advice, guidance and assistance to the child and family under Chapter One of Part II of the Children (Scotland) Act 1995.[68] Such a reference should be made only when the reporter has reason to believe (*e.g.* having talked to the family and the social work department) that any help offered is likely to be accepted and is likely to prove beneficial to either the child or his or her family, or both. If the reference to the reporter was under the Secure Accommodation (Scotland) Regulations, the reporter must refer the child back to the local authority within 72 hours.[69] Secondly, if it appears to the reporter that an education authority is not fulfilling its duties under the Education (Scotland) Act 1980 in relation to the child he or she may refer the matter to the Scottish Ministers.[70] Thirdly, as

---

[63] Some reporters adopt the useful practice of calling a child in and giving a verbal warning of what might happen if the theft or truanting continues, and some police officers are willing to assist by performing that role too.

[64] s.56(4)(a).

[65] 1996 Rules, r.3(2).

[66] See above, at p.42.

[67] Secure Accommodation (Scotland) Regulations 1996, reg.8(2)(a). The 72 hours do not include Sundays or public holidays: reg.2(2).

[68] s.56(4)(b).

[69] Secure Accommodation (Scotland) Regulations 1996, reg.8(2)(b).

[70] s.56(4)(c), as inserted by the Antisocial Behaviour etc. (Scotland) Act 2004, s.137(2).

described above,[71] the reporter has the power, even when deciding not to arrange a children's hearing, to apply to the sheriff for a parenting order under the Anti-Social Behaviour etc. (Scotland) Act 2004.

The decision not to refer the child to a children's hearing cannot be retracted by the reporter unless new circumstances, which are additional to those discovered in the course of the investigation to determine whether to arrange a children's hearing, come to the attention of the reporter.[72] These new circumstances might indicate quite different grounds of referral, or they may concern the same—for example, when the decision not to arrange a children's hearing was made on the basis of lack of evidence that has now come to light. It is unclear when the statute envisages that the reporter's decision is made and when, therefore, it becomes irrevocable. It is submitted that before the reporter's opinion can properly be characterised as a "decision", some step must be taken consequent upon it or pursuant to it. That step will normally be giving the intimation required under s.56(4)(a) or under the Rules: in other words, the decision not to refer the child to a children's hearing is irrevocable only once the reporter has informed the child, relevant person or person who brought the case to the reporter's attention of that decision.

### Decision to arrange a children's hearing

The reporter is obliged by s.65(1) to arrange a children's hearing when satisfied (i) that at least one of the grounds of referral exists *and* (ii) that compulsory measures of supervision are necessary.[73] The reporter can be satisfied that a ground of referral exists only when confident that he or she would be able to prove its existence before the sheriff if an application under s.68 were required to be made. If, in addition, it appears to the reporter that compulsory measures of supervision are necessary in respect of the child (and would be proportionate to the child's difficulties), he or she is statutorily obliged to arrange a children's hearing to which the case shall be referred for consideration and determination.[74] If the reporter decides to arrange a children's hearing, he or she must request a report on the child from the local authority unless he or she has already done so as part of an initial investigation,

---

[71] Above at pp.48–49.

[72] s.56(5).

[73] If the reference to the reporter was made under the Secure Accommodation (Scotland) Regulations 1996 (see above at p.42) the hearing must be arranged within 72 hours of the placing of the child in secure accommodation, or, if it is not reasonably practicable to arrange a hearing or to state grounds within 72 hours, within a further 24 hours from the end of the 72 hours: Secure Accommodation (Scotland) Regulations 1996, reg.8(3) and (4). The 72 hours do not include Sundays or public holidays: reg.2(2).

[74] s.56(6). This provision is to be compared with, and is probably tautologous in light of, s.65(1). The later provision obliges the reporter to arrange a children's hearing when he or she is satisfied that compulsory measures of supervision are necessary *and* when at least one of the grounds of referral exists; the present provision obliges the reporter to arrange a children's hearing when it appears to him or her that compulsory measures of supervision are necessary. The question of whether compulsory measures of supervision are necessary arises only if at least one of these grounds exists (s.52(1)), with the result that both s.65(1) and this provision amount to exactly the same thing.

and he or she may request any supplementary information.[75] The local authority must provide such reports and information, and any other information concerning the child or his or her circumstances that they consider to be relevant. The reporter is not obliged to wait until the children's hearing is arranged before requesting such a report, and it will normally be sensible for him or her to make the request as soon as the decision to arrange a hearing has been made. Once the decision is made, and some action is taken consequent upon the decision, to refer the child to a children's hearing, the reporter has no power to abandon the case,[76] and its future progress lies in the hands of the children's hearing. If the reference to the reporter was from a local authority or a police officer the reporter must give notice of the decision to arrange a children's hearing to the local authority or, as the case may be, the chief constable.[77]

## BUSINESS MEETINGS

Procedure at a children's hearing lies in the hands of the hearing members, and in particular of the chairman.[78] It frequently happens, however, that the proper performance of the reporter's pre-hearing duties requires that he or she is made aware of some procedural decision before the date of the hearing which, in theory, will determine the procedure to be followed. For example, the hearing can release the child from the duty to attend the hearing,[79] but it is useful for the reporter to know this beforehand in order to determine whether or not to arrange for the bringing of the child to the hearing. Prior to the coming into force of the 1995 Act, matters such as these were determined, at least in some panel areas in Scotland, by informal preliminary meetings between the reporter and panel members. Under the 1968 Act, such meetings had no place in the statutory framework but, when the matter came to the attention of the court in *Sloan v B*[80] their validity received judicial sanction as involving no illegality or unfairness. That sanction was, however, expressly limited to such preliminary meetings doing no more than giving guidance to the reporter on such matters as who he or she should invite to the hearing, and the legally efficacious decision on attendance remained to be made and recorded by a properly constituted children's hearing[81] (that is the hearing considering the child's case). Section 64 of the 1995 Act puts such meetings on a statutory basis, and gives the child and the relevant person a chance to express their views. It permits—but, importantly, does not require—the reporter to arrange what is called a "business meeting" at which certain specified procedural and other matters can be discussed and determined before the start of

---

[75] s.56(7).
[76] Unless, if a s.68 application has been made, the reporter abandons the application due to inability to prove the ground of referral.
[77] 1996 Rules, r.3(2).
[78] 1996 Rules, r.10(3).
[79] s. 45(2): see below at pp.64–67.
[80] 1991 S.L.T. 530.
[81] per Lord President Hope at p.540.

the proper children's hearing.[82] The reporter is given no guidance as to when it would be appropriate to arrange such a meeting, though presumably he or she will do so whenever there is doubt about any of the matters, listed below, that are open to discussion by a business meeting or whenever, for the proper performance of his or her functions, the matter has to be resolved before the actual hearing.

The business meeting will be between the reporter and three members of the children's panel from which the children's hearing is to be constituted (not necessarily the same members as will constitute the actual children's hearing); there must be at least one male panel member and at least one female panel member.[83] It is common for business meetings to be scheduled to take place with three panel members who have previously been scheduled to attend unrelated children's hearings.

The prohibition on publication of proceedings at children's hearings,[84] and the appeal provisions,[85] apply to business meetings also.[86] Business meetings, not being children's hearings, cannot appoint safeguarders, though they can appoint legal representatives.

### Notification of business meetings

Unlike the informal meetings held before the commencement of the 1995 Act, business meetings require to be intimated by written notice to the child and any relevant person, not later than four working days before the date of the meeting.[87] That notice, given by the reporter, must include intimation of:

(a) the arrangement of the meeting and of the matters which may be considered and determined by the meeting;
(b) the child's and relevant person's right to make their views on those matters known to the reporter; and
(c) the duty of the reporter to present those views to the meeting.[88]

In addition, the child, any relevant person and any existing safeguarder must be advised by the reporter of their entitlement to make their views on the matters to be considered by the business meeting known to the reporter, and that any such views will be presented by the reporter to the business meeting.[89] The reporter must record in writing any views given to him or her other than in writing, for the purposes of presenting these views to the business meeting, and he or she must as soon as reasonably practicable after receiving them give a copy of those views in writing to the panel members who will attend the business meeting and any other person who received notice of the meeting.[90] Any views expressed must be considered by the business meeting before making a determination or

---

[82] s.64(1).
[83] 1996 Rules, r.4(1). See p.10 n.9 above.
[84] Contained in s.44: see below at pp.78–80.
[85] Contained in s.51: see below at Chap.14.
[86] s.64(5).
[87] 1995 Act, s.64(2) and 1996 Rules, r.4(3).
[88] s.64(2).
[89] 1996 Rules, r.4(4).
[90] 1996 Rules, r.4(5) and (6).

giving guidance or direction to the reporter.[91] In addition, not later than four working days before the date of the meeting the reporter must:[92]

(a) give notice in writing to the members of the panel who will attend the meeting of the date, time and place of the meeting;

(b) give notice in writing to the child, any relevant person[93] and any safeguarder that the meeting has been arranged and of the date on which it is to be held; and

(c) give to the members of the panel and to the child, any relevant person and any safeguarder (i) notice of the matters referred to the business meeting for determination or for direction and guidance, (ii) a copy of any documents or information relevant to these matters and (iii) a copy of the grounds of referral of the case of the child prepared in terms of s.65 of the Act.[94]

**Matters to be considered at a business meeting**

The matters which are open to be discussed and determined by the business meeting are listed in the 1996 Rules[95] and the Legal Representation Rules.[96] Though mostly the matters concern guidance that is to be given to the reporter and therefore do not give cause for appeal, there is at least one substantive (and therefore appealable) decision that a business meeting can make under the 1996 Rules and potentially another under the Legal Representation Rules. It lies with the reporter to determine whether or not he or she needs guidance on the matters listed in the 1996 Rules. The matters that are open to decision and guidance at business meetings are as follows:

(i) Whether notice of the children's hearing is to be given by the reporter to a person as a "relevant person". In effect, the business meeting asked to give guidance and direction to the reporter on this matter will be determining whether a person is a relevant person, within the meaning of s.93(2),[97] for the

---

[91] 1995 Act, s.64(4) and 1996 Rules, r.4(7).

[92] 1996 Rules, r.4(3).

[93] One of the issues which the business meeting may decide is who is a relevant person. Reporters are therefore faced with the interesting duty of notifying an individual of a meeting which will determine whether that individual should be notified. To avoid a procedural irregularity in failing to notify someone who ought to have been notified, reporters should err on the side of caution. They are not prohibited from notifying a business meeting to someone not strictly entitled to notification, and in cases of doubt notification should always be given to the person the business meeting is considering whether he or she should be regarded as a relevant person.

[94] If the business meeting is preliminary to a review hearing a copy of the original grounds of referral need not be given to the stated individuals, since there will, for the purposes of that hearing, be no grounds of referral prepared in terms of s.65.

[95] 1996 Rules, r.4(2).

[96] Children's Hearings (Legal Representation) (Scotland) Rules 2002, SSI 2002/63, r.3.

[97] See further, above at pp.14–17.

purposes of the duty and right to attend a children's hearing.[98] If a person is regarded as a relevant person by the business meeting, then the reporter will be obliged to intimate the hearing to that person in terms of r.7 of the 1996 Rules. However, it remains open to the actual children's hearing to determine that the person is not a relevant person (or that a person is, contrary to the view of the business meeting, a relevant person).[99] Since this decision of the business meeting will have immediate substantive effect (in requiring or not the reporter to notify the person of the children's hearing) it would appear that the decision is appealable in terms of s.51.[1]

(ii) Whether notice is to be given that the child is released from the obligation to attend the children's hearing. In other words, the business meeting may decide that the child should be informed by the reporter that he or she need not attend the hearing. It should be noted that it is not the business meeting that releases the child from the obligation to attend, but the children's hearing themselves in terms of s.45(2)[2] and the basis of the business meeting's decision must therefore be the likelihood that the children's hearing will so release the child. The business meeting's decision does not bind the children's hearing, which should make their decision even after the child has been informed that he or she need not attend: if, as is open to them, the hearing come to a different decision from that reached by the business meeting then the hearing will have to be continued in order to allow for the child's presence. It would be good practice, therefore, for reporters to intimate to the child (at least when the child is of an age to understand) that while the business meeting has concluded that he or she need not attend, an actual children's hearing may call upon the child to attend. This decision of the business meeting is for the reporter's guidance only and, being without immediate substantive effect, is not appealable.

(iii) Whether notice is to be given to a relevant person that the hearing are satisfied that it would be unreasonable to require his or her attendance or that his or her attendance is unnecess-

---

[98] It should be remembered that even when a person is determined not to be a relevant person, he or she may be permitted to attend a children's hearing if the chairman considers that he or she will have something relevant to contribute (see below at pp.76–77). It is open to a business meeting to suggest to the reporter that such a person be invited to attend, though there is no legal obligation on the reporter to follow the suggestion. But nor is there any legal prohibition on the reporter notifying the hearing to others than those who must receive notification.

[99] Either because they disagree with the decision of the business meeting or because circumstances have changed since the date of the business meeting.

[1] A person deemed by a business meeting not to be a relevant person may not be given notification and will thereby lose the opportunity to influence the course of the hearing. That will be sufficient interest to give such a person title to appeal and there is no need, it is submitted, to wait until a substantive decision is made and to appeal against that.

[2] s.45(2) says that the children's hearing can release the child from the obligation to attend. Rule 4(2) does not say that the business meeting can release the child, but merely that the child should be so informed.

ary for the proper consideration of the case.[3] In other words, the business meeting may conclude that the children's hearing is likely to go ahead even in the absence of a relevant person who has a duty to attend. Again, however, it is only the actual children's hearing and not the business meeting who have the power to make that determination and the business meeting's function is limited to requiring the reporter to give notice to the relevant person that he or she need not attend. Again, the notice should, it is submitted, contain intimation that the actual children's hearing may not agree with the business meeting. This decision of the business meeting is for the reporter's guidance only and, being without immediate substantive effect, is not appealable.

(iv) Whether to appoint a legal representative to the child. The business meeting's powers here are the same as those of a children's hearings and are discussed more fully in that context.[4] It may be noted here however that a positive decision on the part of the business meeting not to appoint a legal representative to the child may well be appealable by that child.[5]

Once a determination has been made by a business meeting, or they have given guidance or direction to the reporter, the reporter must, as soon as reasonably practicable, give written notice of the determination, guidance or direction to the child, the relevant person and any safeguarder.[6]

## Notification of Children's Hearings and Supply of Documents

Where the reporter arranges any children's hearing (whether after an initial investigation, or to review a current supervision requirement, or for any other reason required or permitted under the 1995 Act), he or she must notify various individuals and, in order to allow them to prepare properly for the hearing, he or she must also supply various documents to them at some time before the hearing takes place. If, when supplying these documents, the reporter considers that the disclosure of the whereabouts of the child or of any relevant person may place the child or the relevant person at risk of serious harm (whether or not physical harm) he or she may withhold such information as is necessary to prevent such disclosure and indicate the address of the person as that of the Principal Reporter.[7] Any notice in writing or other document and any oral notification which may or must be given by the reporter may be given or issued by the Principal Reporter or by a person duly authorised

---

[3] Under s.45(8).
[4] See pp.91–93 below.
[5] See Norrie "Legal Representation at Children's Hearings: The Interim Scheme" (2002) 7 S.L.P.Q. 131.
[6] 1996 Rules, r.4(8).
[7] 1996 Rules, r.9.

by him or by any constable.[8] Such notice or document to be given to a child or relevant person may be:

(a) delivered to him or her in person;
(b) left for him or her at his or her dwelling-house or place of business or, where he has no known dwelling-house or place of business, at any other place in which he or she may at the time be resident;
(c) where he or she is the master of, or a seaman or other person employed in, a vessel, left with a person on board thereof and connected therewith; or
(d) sent by post in a registered or first class service recorded delivery letter to his or her dwelling-house or place of business.[9] If posted, the notice shall be deemed to have been given on the day following the date of posting.[10]

### Notification to panel members

The individual panel members who will constitute any particular hearing are chosen by the chairman of the relevant children's panel. Once they have been chosen the reporter must give them notification of the time and place of the hearing. This must be done wherever practicable at least seven days before the date of the hearing.[11] In order that panel members be familiar with the child's case before the start of the hearing, it is also provided that they should be supplied with certain documents and information relevant to the consideration they must give to the case at the hearing. So, as soon as reasonably practicable, but wherever practicable not later than three days before the date of the hearing, the reporter must give to each of the members of the children's hearing a copy of any of the following documents that are relevant to the child's case:

(a) a report of a local authority on the child and his or her social background (a "social background report");
(b) a statement of the grounds of referral;
(c) any judicial remit or reference or any reference by a local authority;
(d) any supervision requirement to which the child is subject;
(e) any report prepared by any safeguarder appointed in the case; and
(f) any views of the child given in writing to the reporter.[12]

In addition, any information or any document other than those mentioned above which is material to the consideration of the case must be

---

[8] 1996 Rules, r.30(1).
[9] 1996 Rules, r.30(2). It is not notification to send notice to an address at which the reporter is aware the person is not living: per Lord President Hope in *Sloan v B*, 1991 S.L.T. 530 at 540I.
[10] 1996 Rules, r.30(4).
[11] 1996 Rules, r.5(1).
[12] 1996 Rules, r.5(1).

made available by the reporter to the members of the children's hearing before the hearing.[13]

The decision of which of the above are relevant or material in any particular case would seem to lie with the reporter, though if a children's hearing are of the view that they cannot make an informed decision without a particular document they can call for that document to be supplied to them. The reporter's decision on relevancy is not unchallengeable and it is a ground of appeal, based on procedural irregularity, that appropriate documentation has not been supplied to the hearing.[14]

Any documents made available to the members of the children's hearing must be kept securely in their custody, and members may not cause or permit any information contained therein or disclosed during the hearing to be made known to any person.[15] Immediately after the conclusion of the children's hearing the chairman and members must return to the reporter any documents which have been made available to them.[16] It is a criminal offence for any person to "publish" information which is intended to, or is likely to, identify the child concerned in, or any other child connected with, the case, his or her address or his or her school[17] and in this context "any person" clearly includes members of the children's hearing.

### Notification to the child

The reporter must give to the child not less than seven days before the hearing written notification of the fact that a children's hearing has been arranged to consider his or her case and in that notice the child must be informed of his or her right and obligation to attend the hearing and of the date, time and place of the hearing.[18] The child must also be informed of the entitlement to indicate whether or not he or she wishes to express views, of the entitlement to express views, and of the fact that if views are expressed to the reporter before the hearing the reporter will convey these views to the members of the children's hearing, to any relevant person and to any safeguarder.[19] Hearings arranged to consider the case of a child kept in a place of safety or secure accommodation or

---

[13] 1996 Rules, r.5(2). Any information or document which has been made available to panel members must also be made available, if requested, to any member of the Scottish Committee of the Council on Tribunals who is attending the hearing (*ibid.*, r.5(6)) and to any member of the Children's Panel Advisory Committee or to any member of a sub-committee of the Advisory Committee who has given notice of his or her intention to attend the hearing as an observer (*ibid.*, r.5(7)). Papers must be returned to the reporter at the end of the hearing.

[14] See for example *D v Sinclair*, 1973 S.L.T. (Sh. Ct.) 47.

[15] 1996 Rules, r.5(4). This rule is qualified to the extent necessary for the fulfilment of the obligation to reveal the substance of reports to the child and relevant person. An implicit qualification is that such substance will thereby be revealed to other persons attending the hearing.

[16] 1996 Rules, r.5(5).

[17] s.44, as amended by the Criminal Justice (Scotland) Act 2003, s.52. See further, below at pp.78–80.

[18] 1996 Rules, r.6(1). Notification of the right to attend must be given even when the child has been relieved of the obligation to do so under s.45(2): r.6(3).

[19] 1996 Rules, r.6(4).

to deal with an application to suspend a supervision requirement or to review the case of a child transferred on an emergency basis (*i.e.* basically, emergency hearings arranged at short notice) must be notified to the child as soon as reasonably practicable in writing or, if written notice is not possible, orally.[20]

Not less than seven days before the date of a hearing at which grounds of referral are to be explained, the child must be given a copy of a statement of the grounds of referral.[21] This statement must be signed by the reporter and must (i) specify which of the s.52(2) conditions the reporter is relying upon and (ii) state the facts on the basis of which it is sought to show that any condition is satisfied.[22] There is no statutory requirement to provide any other information to children, which would leave them as the only active participants without foreknowledge of information contained in the hearing papers. This position was challenged in *S v Miller*.[23] The Principal Reporter (the defender in the case) conceded that non-provision of papers was indefensible in ECHR terms, with the result that s.6 of the Human Rights Act 1998 (the requirement on public authorities to act consistently with the ECHR) imposed an obligation on reporters to provide children with papers (reporters having much discretion to act in ways that are not explicitly prohibited). The scheme introduced by SCRA to regulate provision of papers to children is contained in their Practice Guidance Note 24. Children over 12 are, under this scheme, sent the same documents as are sent to panel members and relevant persons, though certain information may be withheld if (i) it is likely to cause significant distress or harm to the child if disclosed to him/her because he/she is unaware of the information, (ii) it is likely to cause significant distress or harm to the child if he/she is made aware that others are aware of the information, (iii) it is likely to cause significant distress or harm to a relevant person or any other person if the child is made aware of the information; or (iv) it is likely significantly to prejudice the prevention or detection of crime or the apprehension or prosecution of an offender. Children under 12 will not be sent hearing papers, unless either the child or his or her representative requests papers or the writer of the report expresses the view that it is in the child's interests to receive the report (in either case subject to the withholding of certain information on the same basis as for children over 12).

### Notification to relevant persons and certain parents

Where a relevant person has a right and an obligation to attend the children's hearing, the reporter must give him or her written notice, if his

---

[20] 1996 Rules, r.6(2).

[21] 1996 Rules, r.18(1)(b). In cases where before the children's hearing the child is being kept in a place of safety or secure accommodation, the period of seven days does not apply, and the child must be given a copy of the grounds of referral as soon as reasonably practicable: r.18(2).

[22] 1996 Rules, r.17(1). In cases in which the ground is that the child has committed an offence the statement of facts must have the same degree of specification as is required by s.138(4) of the Criminal Procedure (Scotland) Act 1995 in a charge in a complaint and the statement must also specify the nature of the offence in question: r.17(2).

[23] 2001 S.L.T. 507.

or her whereabouts are known,[24] of that person's right and obligation to attend, and of the date, time and place of the hearing.[25] This notice must be given not later than seven days before the date of the hearing,[26] except that with hearings arranged on an emergency basis the notice must be given as soon as reasonably practicable and if notice of an emergency hearing cannot be given in writing it may be given orally.[27] Any document given to or information made available to the chairman and members of the children's hearing must at the same time (unless previously supplied) be given to or made available to each relevant person.[28] Notification of the right to attend must also be sent, together with copies of the documents and information panel members and relevant persons receive, to any genetic father of the child who is not a relevant person but who is living with the genetic mother of the child,[29] on the same timescale. The relevant person whose whereabouts are known (but not the genetic father living with the genetic mother[30]) must also be given a copy of the statement of the grounds of referral not less than seven days before the hearing or, if the child is being kept in a place of safety or in secure accommodation, as soon as reasonably practicable before the date of the hearing.[31]

It is not immediately clear whether the Rules require the relevant person and the genetic father who has a right to attend to return the documents they received back to the reporter at the conclusion of the hearing. The clear implication from the proviso at the end of r.5(3) is that they do not have to, at least when the hearing's decision is to continue the case to a subsequent hearing.[32] However, the last sentence in r.5(7) provides as follows: "Any person provided with papers under this rule . . . shall return to the Principal Reporter at the end of the hearing any document which has been made available to him". On first reading this sentence seems to apply only to the persons provided with reports under r.5(7).[33] But the 1996 Rules consistently use "rule" to mean the whole rule and "paragraph" to mean the numbered paragraphs within each rule. This can be seen clearly, for example, in r.5(5)

---

[24] The reporter has no statutory obligation to make inquiries as to the whereabouts of the relevant person.

[25] 1996 Rules, r.7(1). Notice of the right to attend must be given even when the relevant person has no duty to attend (*i.e.* after the hearing have relieved that person of the obligation to attend under s.45(8)(b)): 1996 Rules, r.7(2).

[26] 1996 Rules, r.7(4).

[27] 1996 Rules, r.7(5).

[28] 1996 Rules, r.5(3). Individual copies must be sent to each individual relevant person.

[29] 1996 Rules, r.5(3) and r.7(3).

[30] Because he has no right to accept or deny grounds of referral.

[31] 1996 Rules, r.18(1) and (2). The relevant person need not be given a copy of the grounds of referral more than once, even although grounds are to be explained at more than one hearing: r.18(4).

[32] 1996 Rules, r.5(3) imposes an obligation on reporters to give copies of documents to each relevant person, and continues: " . . . except that where a children's hearing is arranged to continue consideration of the case of the child by virtue of s.69(2) of the Act, this obligation of the Principal Reporter shall apply only in respect of any information or document which has not already been made available to the person concerned".

[33] *i.e.* members of the CPAC or any sub-committee thereof.

and (6) where the words "this rule" make sense only if they refer to the whole of r.5. It must follow that the last sentence in r.5(7) also applies to the whole of r.5, with the result that each relevant person and genetic father supplied with documents must return these documents at the end of the hearing. Rule 5(3) seems to give an implicit exception, so that documents can be kept until a dispositive decision is reached. It would be good practice for reporters to warn relevant persons in advance of making documents available to them that they will be required to return them to the reporter once the dispositive decision has been reached.

### Notification to safeguarder

Any safeguarder who has been appointed by a children's hearing must be given notice of the date, time and place of the hearing at the same time and in the same manner as notice is given to a relevant person; he or she must also receive the statement of the reasons for his or her appointment.[34] Any information or documentation made available to the members of the children's hearing must also be made available to any safeguarder regardless of the date of his or her appointment in the proceedings.[35] The safeguarder must keep securely in his or her custody any documents made available to him or her and must return them to the reporter when he or she has completed the performance of all the duties associated with his or her appointment as safeguarder; he or she must not cause or permit any information contained in the documents or otherwise disclosed during the hearing to be made known to any person, other than may be necessary for the performance of his or her own duties.[36]

### Notification to Legal Representative

If a business meeting or a children's hearing have appointed a legal representative to a child the reporter must notify the legal representative of the time and place of the hearing at least seven days before the date of the hearing and must, at least three days before the date of the hearing, give to the legal representative a copy of the documents which are relevant to the case of the child being considered.[37] Any document, information or copies of any document provided to panel members must be made available to the legal representative.[38]

### Notification to chief social work officer

Where the reporter arranges any children's hearing he or she must notify the chief social work officer of the appropriate local authority of the date, time and place of the hearing, and of the name, date of birth and address, so far as is known, of the child whose case is to be considered at

---

[34] 1996 Rules, r.14(2).
[35] 1996 Rules, r.14(5).
[36] 1996 Rules, r.14(6).
[37] Children's Hearings (Legal Representation) (Scotland) Rules 2002, SSI 2002/63, r.4(2).
[38] *ibid.*, r.4(1).

the hearing.[39] This is to allow for the attendance at the hearing of a social worker.

---

[39] 1996 Rules, r.8.

# CHAPTER FIVE

# ATTENDANCE AT AND PRIVACY OF THE HEARING

## INTRODUCTION

It has long been recognised that a child is more likely to feel able to take part in a discussion in a private rather than in a public forum, and it has always been the rule, now embodied in s.43(1) of the Children (Scotland) Act 1995, that a children's hearing is to be conducted in private and that members of the public are not permitted to attend. In addition, publication of the proceedings is an offence.[1] There are, however, some individuals who are obliged to be present, some who have a right to choose to be present and some who may, at the discretion of the chairman, be allowed to be present. It is only those persons whose presence is necessary for the proper consideration of the case that is being heard, or whose presence is permitted by the chairman, who can attend at a children's hearing.[2] The presence of those who have an obligation or a right to attend is normally (but not always) necessary for a proper consideration of the case. The discretion to permit the presence of individuals who have no statutory right to attend a children's hearing rests solely with the chairman, who is guided in the exercise of that discretion by s.43(2), under which he or she must take all reasonable steps to ensure that the number of persons present at a children's hearing at any one time is kept to a minimum. This does not entitle the chairman to exclude any person who has a right to attend, except for a reason specified in any statutory provision which permits such exclusion[3]; rather, it does no more than exhort the chairman to minimise the number of those persons whose presence can be permitted on a discretionary basis. These will be, for the most part, observers rather than active participants, but individuals such as foster carers, members of the household who are not "relevant persons", or other relatives may well have some role to play in helping the consideration of the case. Even when a hearing is limited to those who have a right to be present, the numbers will frequently reach double figures: there may be present three panel members, the reporter, the child, two parents, a representative, a safeguarder and a social worker. The chairman can sanction an arrangement whereby parts only of the hearing take place in the presence of particular individuals.

---

[1] Children (Scotland) Act 1995, s.44: see below at pp.78–80.
[2] s.43(1).
[3] As in s.43(4) in relation to journalists or s.46 in relation to relevant persons.

## The Child

The most important person at the hearing is the child. It is the child's hearing, and it is the child's case that is being considered. The child's right to participate in proceedings concerning his or her private and family life is a central element of both Art.6 (right to a fair hearing)[4] and Art.8 (right to respect for private and family life).[5] It follows that in most cases the child ought to be present at all stages of the procedure.[6] Under the 1995 Act, the child who has been notified of the fact that a children's hearing has been arranged,[7] whether to put grounds of referral or to discuss established grounds and make a disposal or for a review of an existing supervision requirement or to consider a warrant, is granted the right and placed under an obligation to attend all stages of the hearing, together with any continuations thereof.[8] This is a significant change from the pre-1995 position, under which the child had a duty but not the right to attend. The practical result of that was that a child could be excluded against his or her wishes from a consideration of his or her own case.[9] The present legislation is more Convention-compliant, for the child has both the duty and the right to attend, and while the hearing can release the child from his or her duty,[10] they can never remove the child's right. It follows that if the child insists on attending, he or she cannot be excluded from any part of the hearing and that is so even after a hearing have released the child from the obligation to attend. In the absence of any release, the child has a duty to attend his or her own children's hearing, and while breach of that duty is not a criminal offence[11] it may justify the children's hearing in granting a warrant to detain the child.[12]

### Releasing the child from the duty to attend

Notwithstanding the child's obligation to attend at all stages of the children's hearing considering his or her case, the children's hearing may decide to release the child from that obligation. This will permit the children's hearing to consider the child's case in his or her absence if he or she then decides not to exercise the right to attend. The decision to release the child can only be made on one or other of the following two grounds, and in making the decision the welfare of the child must be the hearing's paramount consideration.[13]

(a) In a case concerned with a Sch.1 offence, the child may be released from the obligation to attend if the children's hearing

---

[4] *L v Finland* (2001) 31 E.H.R.R. 30.

[5] *TP & KM v United Kingdom* (2000) 34 E.H.R.R. 2.

[6] This does not include any business meeting arranged under the terms of s.64, for such a meeting determines merely procedural matters.

[7] On notification, see above at pp.58–59.

[8] s.45(1).

[9] The competency of excluding a child was one of the major issues in *Sloan v B*, 1991 S.L.T. 530: see Norrie, "Excluding Children from Children's Hearings", 1993 S.L.T. (News) 67.

[10] See below at pp.64–67.

[11] As it may be for a relevant person: see below at p.68.

[12] See below at pp.190–191.

[13] s.16(1) applies to such a decision.

are satisfied that the attendance of the child is not necessary for a just hearing of that case.[14] The aim here is to avoid the possibility of the child being inhibited or influenced in what he or she says by the presence of another person, and also to avoid distress to the child caused by being in the presence of an alleged or actual abuser. However, a "just hearing" is one that is just to all parties who may be affected by the outcome and, it is submitted, the children's hearing must consider the interests of more than simply the child (though the child's interests are paramount). A just hearing will often require that a Sch.1 offender (whose Art.6 and Art.8 rights must also be respected) be given the chance to answer any point expressed by the child, and it is only when no such issue arises that the child's presence can be said to be unnecessary for a just hearing of the case.

(b) In any case, the child may be released from the obligation to attend if the children's hearing are satisfied that it would be detrimental to the interests of the child for him or her to be present at the hearing of the case.[15] It would appear that the primary aim of this paragraph is to avoid distress to the child, but since it would clearly be detrimental to his or her interests to be influenced by the presence of another person it must also be an important purpose to prevent such influence from being exercised. There must be shown to be a detriment to the interests of the child and it is not sufficient that the child simply wishes not to attend.

The decision to excuse a child from attendance is not appealable by a relevant person who is insisting that the child be present.[16]

The power to release the child from the duty of attending is expressly "without prejudice" to the child's right to attend: this is important as an emphasis that all this provision does is to release the child from the obligation to attend and it does not remove the child's right to attend. The hearing cannot "exclude" the child in the way that they can "exclude" a journalist under s.43(4)[17] or relevant person under s.46(1).[18] The hearing ought, therefore, to inquire as to the child's wishes in relation to attendance before making their decision one way or the other,[19] and there would be little point in granting the release if the child expresses a wish and an intention to attend. Release is more likely to be appropriate in the case of a child who is too young to choose to exercise the right to attend. The child's right to attend is further protected by the provision in the Rules[20] that where the hearing are satisfied that the child need not attend he or she must be informed by the reporter, in

---

[14] s.45(2)(a).

[15] s.45(2)(b).

[16] The question of appeal by the child does not arise since the child may choose to exercise his or her right to attend even after having been excused of the duty to attend.

[17] See below at pp.74–76.

[18] See below at pp.70–72.

[19] The opportunity to express views is afforded the child at business meetings: see above at pp.53–54.

[20] Children's Hearings (Scotland) Rules 1996, r.6(3).

writing, that although he or she has been released from the obligation to attend, he or she still has the right to do so if he or she wishes. Otherwise a notice of authority not to attend might be misinterpreted as a prohibition from attending.

Releasing the child from the obligation to attend does not release the chairman from the obligation in s.65(4) to explain the grounds to the child.[21] In other words, while the child may be released from the obligation to attend, the chairman must still explain to the child the grounds of referral. Allowing the child not to attend the part of the hearing at which the grounds are explained would deny the chairman of the opportunity to fulfil his or her obligation to explain and would, therefore, be incompetent unless the child were too young to understand and reference to the sheriff is required in any case under s.65(9)(a). It follows that the power to release the understanding child from the obligation to attend can be exercised only in relation to the other stages of the hearing, that is to say the consideration of the case and its disposal, and any review subsequent to the imposition of a supervision requirement, or in relation to the granting or continuing of a warrant.

It is, in any case, a power that should be used only sparingly. Hearing members can learn a great deal from the demeanour and appearance of even a very young child, and his or her interactions with those around him or her. Taking the words of the statute literally, a just hearing of the case of a child too young to take part in the discussion will never require that child's presence, but there was no intent on the part of the legislature that it become common practice for young children not to be present and mere age does not in itself justify the child's non-attendance: the hearing must in all cases remember that every child, of whatever age, possesses a right to attend. A children's hearing should therefore start with the presumption that the child should attend, until they are persuaded that one or other of the circumstances in s.45(2) exists and, in addition, that it is in the best interests of the child not to be obliged to attend.

There are some matters that remain unclear from the terms of the statute, in particular the questions (i) how long does the release last and (ii) can one children's hearing release the child from the obligation to attend a future children's hearing? The answer to both these questions turns on the interpretation of the words "all stages of the hearing", as they appear in s.45(1). A children's hearing can release the child from his or her obligation to attend all stages of the hearing: this could mean either (i) all stages conducted on that day by the hearing granting the release, or (ii) all stages of all hearings, including continuations, until a dispositive decision is made, or (iii) all hearings until the child leaves the system. The last-mentioned interpretation is clearly wrong. The difficulty with adopting the second interpretation is that the disposal of the case will commonly be done by a hearing composed of different members from the hearing at which the grounds were explained to the child, and they may disagree with the former hearing's granting of a release. There is much to be said for the view that all s.45(2) does is to allow a children's hearing to release the child from the obligation to attend that

---

[21] s.45(2) is expressly stated to be "without prejudice to . . . s.65(4)".

particular hearing: this obviates the possibility of a preliminary hearing (such as the one at which grounds are put) making an important decision which the disposing hearing might not agree with. However, there is practical awkwardness in adopting this intepretation, since it would require the reporter to arrange for the child's presence in every case until the hearing on the day decides to allow the child to go home again[22]: in some cases this will serve no purpose at all and might even be harmful to the child's interests. It is submitted, therefore, that a release granted by a hearing which is satisfied that the conditions exist for releasing the child of his or her obligation can remain effective until the case has been disposed of by the making of a dispositive decision. A child will not then be obliged to attend at the consideration of his or her case or continuations thereof but would be obliged to attend at a review of any supervision requirement imposed or continued as the disposal (unless a review hearing subsequently decides otherwise). Any hearing arranged after the release has been granted but before the referral is disposed of may still, of course, come to the view that the child's presence is necessary for them to make a properly informed decision—in which case they can withdraw the release and continue the case to allow the child to attend. In other words, the release lasts until the case has been disposed of or, if earlier, until a subsequent hearing withdraws the release. In practice it will be rare for one hearing to disagree with another on this matter, but the child's circumstances might have changed sufficiently to render the previously granted release inappropriate. For example, the hearing at which grounds, involving a Sch.1 offence, are to be put to the child and relevant person might decide that the child's presence is not necessary for a just hearing of the case due to the risk of the child being intimidated by an alleged abuser; yet when the case comes back to a hearing for disposal after the grounds are found established by a sheriff, the abuser might have indicated that he or she will not attend the hearing and the risk to the child thereby alleviated. In such circumstances if the child has not exercised his or her right to attend, the hearing may well consider it appropriate to continue the case and withdraw the release of the obligation to attend.

**Ensuring the attendance of the child**

It is the reporter who is responsible for ensuring that the child is properly notified of the hearing[23] and for securing the attendance of the child at any hearing or continuation thereof.[24] In order to allow the reporter to fulfil that obligation the children's hearing can issue a warrant to find the child, keep him or her in a place of safety, and bring him or her before a children's hearing. Such a warrant can be issued either prospectively, when it is likely that the child will not attend, or retrospectively, when the child has in fact breached his or her obligation to attend. These warrants are discussed in Chapter 13.[25]

---

[22] Unless, following the instructions of a business meeting, he or she has notified the child that the child need not attend.

[23] 1996 Rules, r.18.

[24] s.45(3).

[25] Below at pp.188–192.

## THE RELEVANT PERSON

Participation in the decision-making process has long been seen by the European Court of Human Rights as a crucial element in the protection of family members' right to a fair hearing and right to respect for their private and family life.[26] The children's hearing system has always encouraged relevant persons to participate fully. Under the 1995 Act, every relevant person has a right to attend the children's hearing and is indeed obliged so to attend.[27] Failure to attend in breach of this obligation is a criminal offence which renders the offender liable on summary conviction to a fine not exceeding level 3 on the standard scale.[28] In most cases there will be either one or two adults who, in relation to a child, are "relevant persons", but there might be more and in theory, indeed, there is no limit to the number. In arranging attendance at the hearing it is the reporter who must, it is submitted, make the decision of whether it appears to him or her that any particular individual ordinarily has charge of or control over the child, though if a business meeting so directs, he or she must treat a person as a relevant person. Any such person requires to be given notice of the hearing by the reporter and must be allowed by the chairman to attend the hearing, and must be given the opportunity to accept or deny the grounds of referral.

The relevant person's right and obligation to attend the children's hearing extends to all stages of the hearing, that is to say the explanation of the grounds, the consideration of the case, and the making of the decision by the hearing, as well as any other part of the procedure, whether at an initial hearing, a dispositive hearing or at a review hearing (though it should be remembered that who satisfies the description of relevant person may change through time and the matter should be considered afresh by each hearing: recognition as a relevant person at one hearing does not imply such recognition at the next hearing[29]). There is no right to attend a business meeting arranged under s.64.

### Relieving the relevant person of the obligation to attend

The relevant person has an obligation to attend at all stages of the hearing, unless the children's hearing are satisfied that it would be unreasonable to require his or her attendance or that his or her attendance is unnecessary for the proper consideration of the case.[30] It would be unreasonable to require attendance when the cost and inconvenience of attending outweighs the contribution that the person is

---

[26] *B v United Kingdom* (1987) 10 E.H.R.R. 87; *W v United Kingdom* (1988) 10 E.H.R.R. 29; *Venema v Netherlands* [2003] F.L.R. 552; *TP & KM v United Kingdom* (2002) 32 E.H.R.R. 2.

[27] s.45(8).

[28] s.45(9).

[29] This proposition is not inconsistent with *Kennedy v H,* 1988 S.C. 114, 1988 S.L.T. 586 where it was held that title to appeal against a decision of a children's hearing inhered only in a person who was a relevant person (then called guardian) at the time of the decision being appealed against. Title to appeal against a decision requires an interest at the time the decision was made.

[30] s.45(8)(b).

likely to make to the hearing; this is more likely to be accepted by the hearing when another relevant person is attending than when the only relevant person seeks, or all the relevant persons each seek, not to attend. It will seldom be unreasonable to require attendance when the child would otherwise be left to attend alone.[31] Attendance would be unnecessary when the relevant person has nothing at all to contribute to the hearing's consideration, for example, when that person has had no contact with the child for some years and has nothing to offer the child. The children's hearing can proceed in the absence of a relevant person even at a hearing at which grounds of referral are to be put and the relevant person's absence does not prevent them from moving on to a consideration of the case if the child and any other relevant person who is present accepts the grounds.[32] Since failure to attend without a dispensation is a criminal offence,[33] the hearing ought to make a positive (and recorded) decision to this effect with reasons and ought not simply to proceed in the absence of the relevant person. A decision to proceed in the absence of the relevant person does no more than take away the legal obligation to attend: it does not take away the right to do so (unless, in addition, a decision to exclude the relevant person under s.46 has been made) and a relevant person can still attend if he or she chooses to do so even after the hearing have decided to proceed in his or her absence.[34] Such a decision will most commonly be made when the relevant person has failed to attend the hearing, the members of which are of the view that they can proceed satisfactorily without the relevant person, but it would be competent for a children's hearing to decide that it would be unreasonable or unnecessary to require the relevant person's attendance at a subsequent hearing, such as a continued hearing.

**Ensuring the attendance of the relevant person**

A children's hearing have no power to issue a warrant to find and keep and bring before the hearing any person other than the referred child. There is no way, therefore, that they can directly ensure that the relevant person fulfils his or her obligation to attend. However, it is open to the hearing to direct the reporter to bring the relevant person's non-attendance to the attention of the procurator fiscal, because a failure to attend in the absence of any dispensation granted by the hearing is a criminal offence.[35] Alternatively, if the relevant person is also keeping the child away from a hearing, a warrant can be issued to bring the child to a hearing; this will often encourage the unwilling relevant person to attend. However, it is to be remembered that such a warrant can only be issued when it is in the interests of the child to do so: but it is clearly against the interests of any child for a relevant person to act in such a way as denies the child the right, granted by s.45(1)(a), to attend his or her own children's hearing.

---

[31] One circumstance in which it might be unreasonable would be when the child is over 16 and no longer living with, and without any continuing relationship in fact with, the relevant person.

[32] s.65(10).

[33] s.45(9).

[34] And the relevant person must be so informed by the reporter: 1996 Rules, r.7(2).

[35] s.45(9).

The reporter has no responsibility under the 1995 Act to ensure the attendance of the relevant person, as he or she does in relation to the child.[36] However, the reporter does have a means of ensuring the relevant person's attendance if this can be shown to be desirable in the interests of improving the welfare of the child. The Anti-Social Behaviour (etc) (Scotland) Act 2004 permits the reporter to apply for a "parenting order" in these circumstances and this order can require a specified person to comply with any requirement specified in the order[37]: this might include a requirement to attend a children's hearing. However, though the obligation to attend is thereby reinforced, the penalty for failure to comply with the order is the same as that for failure to attend in any case.[38] However, it may well be that a person is more likely to obey a court order specifically directed to him or her than to a statutory provision directed to all parents and it may be that this order can be used by reporters acting in the interests of children.

**Exclusion of the relevant person**

It sometimes happens that it will be against the interests of the child to be in the same room as the relevant person, or one of the relevant persons. This might be because the child is afraid of that person, or is likely to be influenced in what he or she says, or because it would be upsetting and unsettling for the child to have any contact with a parent from whom he or she has been removed in traumatic circumstances. Under the pre-1995 legislation, the only way to protect the child from such harmful contact was by excluding the child from all or part of the hearing. This did, however, have the serious drawback that the child was thereby denied the chance of contributing to the discussion; in addition it suggested that the parent had a stronger right to attend the children's hearing than the child had. Under the present legislation a child may still be released from the obligation to attend the hearing, in similar circumstances,[39] but in addition the 1995 Act permits the children's hearing to exclude the relevant person from any part or parts of the hearing for so long as is necessary in the interests of the child, where they are satisfied of either of the following conditions.

    (a) That they must do so in order to obtain the views of the child in relation to the case before the hearing.[40] This deals with the situation where there is a risk that the child will be influenced in what he or she says (or does not say) by the presence of the relevant person. This may be because there is a conflict of interest between the relevant person and the child, or because the child is embarrassed to talk about certain personal matters in front of the relevant person, or because the child is afraid to speak truthfully (or at all) in front of the relevant person. In

---

[36] s.45(3). See above at p.67.
[37] Antisocial Behaviour etc (Scotland) Act 2004, ss.102(3) and 103(1).
[38] *ibid.*, s.107. The welfare of any child of the relevant person is to be taken into account in determining the penalty.
[39] See above at pp.64–67.
[40] s.46(1)(a).

addition, this ground might also be used if the relevant person is disrupting the hearing or, due to the person insisting on answering for the child, the child is being deprived of the chance to speak for him or herself.

(b) That the presence of the person or persons in question is causing, or is likely to cause, significant distress to the child.[41] This will commonly be because the parent has abused the child and the child is afraid of the parent, but it might also be, for example, when the child is settled in an environment away from the parent and the security of that settlement would be threatened by disturbing contact with the parent. In addition, it might also cover the situation in which the relevant person's behaviour towards the hearing is so disruptive that the child is distressed as a consequence.

The children's hearing are not obliged to exclude a person even when one of the grounds for exclusion exists. It is a matter within their discretion. The power to exclude rests with the hearing as a whole and not solely with the chairman. As usual, decisions are made on a majority basis and the paramount consideration in making the decision is the welfare of the child,[42] but given that the parents' as well as the child's family life is being interfered with, the relevant person's right to a fair trial (including in particular their right to be part of the decision-making process[43]) must be taken into account. The hearing must, therefore, balance the benefit to the hearing process in excluding the relevant person with the compromising of the relevant person's ECHR rights that exclusion necessarily (but sometimes legitimately) involves. The decision to exclude a relevant person is not in itself appealable,[44] but it will always be good practice to specify in the statement of reasons why the decision was made. It is a power that must be used with sensitivity. Many parents will not like the thought of leaving their child alone at a hearing and some will refuse to leave, or refuse to leave without the child. The legal power to bring a child before a hearing ought to be explained to such a parent, as well as their right to be informed of what happens in their absence. It will, however, often be better to allow a relevant person to stay if they insist rather than to risk them effectively bringing the hearing to a premature end by removing the child.

Though s.46(1) says that a relevant person can be excluded from "any part or parts of the hearing", this is not, in fact, the case. The power to exclude exists only "where a children's hearing are considering the case of a child". A children's hearing cannot proceed to a consideration of the child's case until the grounds of referral have been accepted or established[45] and it follows that the power to exclude a relevant person under this provision cannot be used to exclude a relevant person from

---

[41] s.46(1)(b).

[42] s.16(1).

[43] See n.26 above.

[44] Though the subsequent dispositive decision might be appealable on the ground that there was a procedural irregularity in excluding the person when no reasonable hearing would have come to the view that one of the grounds for exclusion exists.

[45] See wording of s.69(1).

that part of the hearing at which grounds are put. The need for a relevant person's acceptance of the grounds cannot, therefore, be avoided by excluding that person before the grounds are put and relying on s.65(10).[46] It is competent, however, for grounds of referral to be put to the child and the relevant person separately. In addition, as will be seen in the next paragraph, the excluded person must be brought back into the room to be informed of the decision and what happened while he or she was absent.

If a relevant person is excluded under s.46(1), the chairman is obliged, at the end of the exclusion, to explain to such a person the substance of what took place in his or her absence.[47] The "substance" is the generality of the discussion and the procedure and not the detail. The chairman's explanation must be such as to allow the relevant person to understand the issues that were discussed in his or her absence, and their relative importance. There will usually be little point in excluding a parent solely in order to allow a child to speak freely on matters he or she does not want his or her parents to know about and good practice would require that it be made plain to both relevant person and child that the substance of what takes place must be revealed. It is not possible, therefore, to use the exclusion as a means of protecting the child's confidentiality against a relevant person. The exclusion of the relevant person is likely to be most useful as a means of avoiding distress to the child rather than as a means of encouraging him or her to speak. The difficulty in achieving that aim is that the relevant person must be present at the start of the hearing and at the end, and in order to avoid the possibility of harmful contact the chairman may sanction an arrangement in which the child is excused while the relevant person is present. There is no requirement that the grounds of referral be put, or the decision explained, to the child and the relevant person at the same time.

### REPRESENTATIVES AND LEGAL REPRESENTATIVES

The 1995 Act itself does not give any right to the child or relevant person to be accompanied at the hearing by a "representative" or a legal representative (though curiously the Act does allow "representatives" to be excluded[48]). The right of representatives to attend children's hearings is contained in the Rules. Rule 11(1) of the 1996 Rules permits the child and the relevant person to be accompanied by one person each for the purpose of representing the child and the relevant person, or by one person who will represent them both.[49] Each relevant person (and there will often be two and sometimes more) is entitled to bring a representa-

---

[46] Which allows a hearing to go on to a consideration of the case without the relevant person's acceptance if the relevant person does not attend.

[47] s.46(2). It will be a procedural irregularity for the chairman to fail to or refuse to give an explanation, or not to explain sufficiently, and will therefore be a ground of appeal since it would deny the relevant person the chance to respond and the chance, therefore, to influence the hearing's decision.

[48] This does not, it is submitted, cover "legal representatives" appointed under the 2002 Rules.

[49] 1996 Rules, r.11(3).

tive. The role of this (non-legal) representative is to assist the person represented in the discussion of the child's case.[50] The relevant person's representative, but not (if different[51]) the child's representative, can be excluded by the children's hearing[52] on the same terms and conditions as the relevant person can be excluded[53]; if such a representative is excluded the substance of what has taken place must be explained to him or her after the exclusion has ended.[54] It would seem that a representative can attend even when the person he or she is representing does not (either because of exclusion or because of failure to turn up).

There is no limitation on who can act as a representative and it might include, for example, a sibling, a cohabitant, a close family friend, a teacher, another member of the child's household who does not qualify as a relevant person, or a solicitor. If the child or relevant person chooses to employ a solicitor to attend the hearing as a representative, they must pay for that themselves as legal aid is not available. However, since 2002 it has been possible for a legal representative to be appointed to the child by the hearing[55] and, if this happens, the legal representative will be paid for by the local authority[56] and he or she has an entitlement to attend the hearing.[57] The role that the legal representative is to adopt is not explicitly set out in the rules, though the basis for the appointment gives some indication of that role. The appointment is made if the child is not otherwise able to present his or her case effectively or if secure accommodation is being considered as an outcome.[58] It might be taken from this that if appointed for the former reason the legal representative's primary role is to assist the child in presenting the child's case, though this role would be somewhat otiose if a (non-legal) representative is present and effectively performing that function. It is submitted, rather, that the legal representative ought to adopt the normal role of legal representative in an adversarial[59] forum: that is to say taking instructions from the client (in this case the child) and acting upon them. This will involve acting as the child's advocate and adviser, and also acting as "procedural watchdog".[60] In this way both due process and the child's rights of appeal are effectively protected.

SAFEGUARDERS

If a safeguarder has been appointed by a children's hearing under s.41,[61] he or she is entitled to receive notice of the date, time and place of the

---

[50] 1996 Rules, r.11(2).

[51] The issue of who the person is representing ought to be clarified at the start of the hearing.

[52] s.46(1).

[53] For which, see above at pp.70–72.

[54] s.46(2).

[55] Children's Hearings (Legal Representation) (Scotland) Rules 2002, SSI 2002/63.

[56] Though local authorities are reimbursed by the Scottish Executive.

[57] This is not actually specified in the rules, but is a necessary implication thereof.

[58] See pp.91–93 below.

[59] This is not to suggest that solicitors ought to adopt an adversarial approach to their role. Rather, they should act as they would if privately employed by the child to attend, say, a child welfare hearing in the sheriff court.

[60] The phrase used by the European Commission of Human Rights to describe why legal representatives are necessary to ensure a fair trial in *Ensslin v Federal Republic of Germany* (1978) 14 D.R. 64 at para.114.

[61] See below at pp.89–91.

children's hearing, and he or she is also entitled to be present throughout the duration of any hearing until the disposal of the case.[62] A safeguarder appointed by a sheriff (*e.g.* in an application to find established the grounds of referral under s.68[63]) is not entitled to attend the hearing though he or she may be permitted to attend by the chairman if his or her presence is justified by special circumstances,[64] such as his or her particular knowledge of the case acquired in the performance of the duties of safeguarder before the sheriff. In *Catto v Pearson*[65] it was held that a hearing who permitted a safeguarder appointed by a sheriff to attend and take a full part in the discussion of the case had impliedly appointed that person as safeguarder for the purposes of the hearing. It may well be that this aspect of that decision has not survived the coming into force of the 1995 Act, since the provision in s.41(3) requiring a children's hearing who appoints a safeguarder to state the reasons for their decision to do so[66] would seem to preclude implied appointments. If a safeguarder appointed by a sheriff is allowed to be present and no decision to appoint him or her safeguarder, nor reason for doing so, is recorded, then the right to attend the hearing is found in r.13(d) rather than in implied appointment.[67]

JOURNALISTS

Though it very seldom happens that journalists attend hearings (for nothing can be published that is either intended to or likely to identify any child concerned in or connected with a hearing, the child's address or the child's school[68]) *bona fide* representatives of a newspaper or news agency do have the right to attend any children's hearing.[69] They probably also have a right to take notes during the proceedings, but they certainly do not have the right to make audio or visual recordings of what is happening. The right to attend is subject to the power vested in the children's hearing to exclude a journalist from part or all of the hearing if they are satisfied that either of the following two conditions is satisfied.

> (a) That it is necessary to do so, in the interests of the child, in order to obtain the child's views in relation to the case before the hearing.[70] This covers the case of the child who is unwilling

---

[62] 1996 Rules, r.14(2) and (3).

[63] See below at pp.101–103.

[64] 1996 Rules, r.13(d).

[65] 1990 S.L.T. (Sh. Ct.) 77.

[66] A provision which had no precedent in the 1968 Act, under which *Catto* was decided.

[67] The practical difference, which was the issue in *Catto v Pearson,* is that a safeguarder properly appointed is entitled to appeal the hearing's decision, while a person permitted to be present is not. Hearings should therefore make themselves aware at the commencement of any hearing of the standing of any person who attends.

[68] s.44(1), as amended by the Criminal Justice (Scotland) Act 2003, s.52: see further, below at pp.78–80.

[69] s.43(3)(b).

[70] s.43(4)(a).

to speak while the journalist is present, either because he or she is inhibited due to the large number of people present at the hearing, or is afraid that the journalist will report his or her views, or because the matters being discussed are of a particularly personal nature. This provision might, in addition, be used to limit the number of journalists present at any one time. "Necessity" should not, it is submitted, be construed too strictly to mean that the journalist can be excluded only when the child will definitely remain silent if the journalist were to be present. Rather, it will be necessary in the interests of the child to exclude a journalist whenever this is likely to make it easier for the child to speak openly, for it is always necessary for the hearing's proper consideration of the case that they be able to hear as much as possible from the child.

(b) That the presence of the journalist is causing, or is likely to cause, significant distress to the child.[71] Attention must be paid to the word "significant", though again it should not be construed too strictly. There is probably no requirement that the distress be of a long lasting nature, so long as it is genuine and severe at the moment. A mere preference on the part of the child is not sufficient and the journalist cannot be excluded simply because the child objects to his or her presence.[72]

Since both of the stated grounds for exclusion are directed towards the effect on the child, neither would seem to be capable of permitting the exclusion of a journalist when the child is not present. The decision to exclude a journalist lies with the whole hearing and not solely with the chairman. It is not an appealable decision, if for no other reason than that there is no one with an interest to appeal. Even if a stateable interest could be identified, the presence or otherwise of journalists would not have affected the disposal of the case.[73]

If a journalist has been excluded from a children's hearing under the terms of s.43(4), the substance of what has taken place may be explained to the journalist by the chairman, after the exclusion has ended.[74] While it is for the chairman to give the explanation, it is probably for the hearing as a whole to decide whether any explanation should be given. They might decide that no explanation should be given if, for example, the matters discussed were particularly personal. If the journalist has been excluded because he or she has deliberately distressed the child, the hearing might quite properly take the view that the journalist has forfeited the right to an explanation. Indeed it is difficult to imagine a situation in which it would be appropriate to reveal to a journalist what occurred during his absence, given that there is so little that can be reported in any case. If the exclusion is to allow the child to speak freely,

---

[71] s.43(4)(b).

[72] Though there is nothing to stop the hearing requesting that the journalist voluntarily leaves in these circumstances.

[73] Sheriff Kearney points out (*Children's Hearings and the Sheriff Court*, (2nd ed., 2000) at para.49.07) that an appeal can be successful only if the procedural irregularity was "material".

[74] s.43(5).

that aim could hardly be achieved if matters were subsequently to be revealed; and if the exclusion was because of the child's distress at the journalist's presence, the child's welfare is unlikely to be enhanced by giving information concerning the child. It should be remembered that the decision whether to reveal to a journalist the substance of what occurred is to be determined by having regard to the welfare of the child as the paramount consideration[75] and should not be influenced by considerations of "freedom of the press" or "the public's right to know". This is entirely consistent with Art.6(1) of the ECHR, which explicitly provides that "the press and public may be excluded . . . where the interests of juveniles . . . so require". It may be that in most cases it is only procedural information that should be revealed, such as "the grounds of referral were denied and the reporter was directed to make an application to the sheriff for proof of the grounds", or "the hearing has been continued for further investigation". If any information is to be given to a journalist previously excluded, then this must be done in the presence of the child and the relevant person, since they have a right to attend all parts of the hearing.

### OBSERVERS

Observers may exceptionally be permitted by the chairman to be present, though the chairman must always bear in mind his or her duty to take all reasonable steps to ensure that the number of persons present at any one time be kept to a minimum.[76] It is considered essential that trainee panel members have the opportunity to witness hearings before they themselves sit and in cases in which there is a small number of active participants it will be appropriate for the chairman to permit them and their instructors to do so.[77] In addition, trainee reporters, trainee social workers, students and others with a legitimate interest in learning about the children's hearing system may be permitted to attend. Observers take no active part in the hearing, though rules relating to confidentiality apply to them as to the participants. It is a courtesy to introduce any observers to the child and the relevant person and, though the decision ultimately rests with the chairman, it is good practice to ask the child and relevant person whether they have any objection to the observer's presence and to disallow that presence if an objection is expressed. The only observers who have a right to be present, whether or not the chairman wishes, are journalists (for which see above) and members of the Council on Tribunals, or of the Scottish Committee of that Council, in their capacity as such[78]: objections from the child and relevant persons do not take away these people's right and should not, therefore be invited by the chairman.

### OTHER PERSONS

The chairman of the hearing, taking account of the rules in s.43(1)–(3) of the 1995 Act concerning the privacy of the hearing and the require-

---

[75] s.16(1).
[76] s.43(2).
[77] Rule 13(b) of the 1996 Rules allows them, at the discretion of the chairman, to attend.
[78] s.43(3).

ment to keep the numbers present to a minimum, may permit the following persons to be present:

(a) the chairman and members of the CPAC for the local authority area of the children's hearing and the clerk to the CPAC of the local authority;
(b) any members or possible members of children's panels whose attendance is required at children's hearings for the purpose of their training as members of children's hearings, and their instructors;
(c) any student engaged in formal education or training in social work or any person engaged in research relating to children who may be in need of compulsory measures of supervision; and
(d) any other person whose presence at the hearing may in the opinion of the chairman be justified by special circumstances.[79]

Paragraphs (a) to (c) refer to passive observers who will take no part in the hearing but this is not so for paragraph (d). Under paragraph (d) the chairman ought to permit the attendance of any person who has a significant interest in the child's well-being or has something relevant to contribute to the discussion. In *L v H*[80] Lord Justice-Clerk Ross expressed the hope that the chairman would permit the attendance of an unmarried father who had, and who exercised rights of, access to the child. Though it is not legally mandatory for a social worker to be present, a hearing at which the child's case is to be considered is unlikely to be able to come to a satisfactory and fully informed decision unless the social worker allocated to the child's case, or a senior social worker with overseeing responsibility for that case, attends. This is because the social worker represents the local authority, whose duty it is to implement any supervision requirement. Other persons who can assist in the determination of where the child's interests lie can be permitted to be present as active participants, such as school teachers, key workers, groupwork leaders, and relatives and short-term foster carers. Translators may sometimes need to be present. In addition constables, prison officers or other duly authorised persons who have in their lawful custody a person who has to[81] attend a children's hearing shall be entitled to be present at the hearing for the purposes of escorting that person.[82]

### Genetic fathers

Genetic fathers who are not relevant persons have at the time of writing no right to attend a children's hearing considering the case of their child, for the law encourages unmarried fathers to turn their backs on their responsibilities. There is one exception. If the genetic father is living

---

[79] 1996 Rules, r.13.
[80] 1996 S.L.T 612.
[81] This means, has a duty to attend, and is therefore limited to the child or a relevant person.
[82] 1996 Rules, r.12(2).

with the genetic mother[83] then he will be entitled to attend at all stages of the children's hearing while the hearing are considering the case of his child.[84] He can be excluded on the same basis as the relevant person can be excluded.[85] The reporter must provide him with notification of the children's hearing[86] and also make available to him any information or document made available to the members of the children's hearing.[87] It is important to note that this bizarre little provision does no more than give the right to attend the hearing and to receive papers. It does not make the genetic father a relevant person. So he has no right to accept or deny the grounds of referral, no right to appeal any decision made, nor right to call for a review. The chairman of the hearing must take care, in performing his or her duties of explanation, to ensure that the attending father is made aware of his invidious lack of rights.

In the vast majority of cases in which the father is living with the mother, the father will be a relevant person in any case and will not need to rely on r.12(1) for his right to attend. Rule 12(1) is effectively limited to cases in which the parents live together but the child lives somewhere else. It may be that the provision is designed to avoid children's hearings having to worry about whether an unmarried father (who lives with the mother) should be allowed to attend, but his status is so limited within the system that the provision is likely to cause more confusion, and resentment, than it can ever hope to resolve. It would be wrong to assume that Art.8 of the ECHR requires "relevant persons" to be interpreted to include all fathers who have some vestige of what could be called "family life" with their children,[88] but the obligation to respect family life certainly has to be taken into account in determining whether a particular person comes within the definition of relevant person. The issue will be resolved by the granting of parental responsibilities to unmarried fathers on registration of paternity.

## REPORTERS

There is nothing in the Children (Scotland) Act 1995 or in the Rules which requires the reporter to be present at the children's hearing, but this is the invariable practice, and the only way in which the reporter can fulfil his or her duty to make a record of the hearing.[89] Though it is hardly conceivable that the issue would arise, it will be within the powers of the chairman to exclude the reporter from at least part of the proceedings.

## PROHIBITION ON PUBLICATION OF PROCEEDINGS

It is a criminal offence for any person to publish any matter either intended to or likely to identify any child concerned in, or any child

---

[83] N.B. not necessarily living with her "as husband and wife". It would seem sufficient that he is sharing accommodation with the mother.
[84] 1996 Rules, r.12(1).
[85] See above at pp.70–72.
[86] 1996 Rules, r.7(3).
[87] 1996 Rules, r.5(3).
[88] *T v A*, 2001 S.C.L.R. 647.
[89] 1996 Rules, r.31.

connected in any way with, the case, the proceedings or the appeal, or his or her address or school: this prohibition applies to proceedings at a children's hearing or before a sheriff in relation to child protection orders, exclusion orders, referrals from a children's hearing, rehearing of evidence, or any appeal.[90] This is designed to preserve the confidentiality of the child, and to give content to the rule contained in s.43(1) that children's hearings are to be conducted in private. The prohibition against publication applies in England and Wales and in Northern Ireland as well as in Scotland.[91] The rule protects not only the referred child or child who is the subject of the proceedings but also any other child who becomes concerned in the proceedings, such as a sibling of the referred child or a child witness.[92] Any person who contravenes the prohibition will, subject to the defence mentioned below, be guilty of an offence and will be liable on summary conviction to a fine not exceeding level 4 on the standard scale in respect of each such contravention.[93]

The prohibition is not limited to representatives of the media[94] or publishers and distributors of material containing the information but includes individuals who take an active or professional part in the hearing, such as reporters, social workers, panel members, parents and relatives. The extension of the offence to cover such individuals provides an important protection to children's confidentiality, given the fact that copies of documents and information are given to relevant persons as of right.[95]

An exception to this prohibition is contained in s.53 of the Criminal Justice (Scotland) Act 2003, under which the reporter may inform the victim of an offence of what action he or she has taken in the case, and of any disposal of the case.

### Meaning of "publish"

To publish includes (a) to publish matter in a programme service, as defined by s.201 of the Broadcasting Act 1990 and (b) to cause matter to be published.[96] The meaning of "publish" is wider than this, and the word has to be interpreted in the light of its clear aim, which is to protect the privacy of children. However, it is likely that for one person to inform another person is not to "publish", which probably requires a more general communication, though it is not necessary that the communication be to a large number of individuals. "Publish" means, it is submitted, put into the public domain. So it is not a publication for a relevant person to show the documents he or she receives from the reporter to a legal adviser, but it may well be publication to show them to a representative of the press. There is likely to be a large grey area

---

[90] s.44(1), as amended by the Criminal Justice (Scotland) Act 2003, s.52. Similar rules apply to proceedings relating to parenting orders made under the Antisocial Behaviour etc (Scotland) Act 2004, s.111, but no such rules apply to proceedings under that Act relating to ASBOs.

[91] s.105(8).

[92] *McArdle v Orr*, 1994 S.L.T. 463.

[93] s.44(2).

[94] As was a similar prohibition contained in s.58 of the Social Work (Scotland) Act 1968.

[95] 1996 Rules, r.5(3). See above at pp.59–61.

[96] s.44(4).

here in which it is unclear whether a sharing of information is or is not a publication, and it is submitted that both the motivation with which the information is passed and the legitimacy of the interest in the child's case that the receiver of the information has are both relevant to the question of whether there is "publication".

### Defence

It is a defence in proceedings relating to this offence for the accused to prove that he did not know, and had no reason to suspect, that the published matter was intended, or was likely, to identify the child or the address or the school.[97] The defence will be available, for example, to a distributor of a newspaper which, unknown to him, carries the prohibited material. Those responsible for the contents of the material, such as newspaper editors, will not be able to rely on this defence since they are or should be in a position to know the effect of what they publish. The onus is on the accused to prove his own ignorance.

### Permitting publication

The sheriff, in relation to proceedings before him, the Court of Session in relation to appeal proceedings before them, and the Scottish ministers in relation to proceedings at a children's hearing are empowered to dispense with the requirement that there be no publication of the child's identity or address or school.[98] The children's hearing themselves have no power to grant such a dispensation. Dispensation can be given only in the interests of justice. In making their decision, however, sheriffs and the Court of Session must regard the child's welfare as their paramount consideration,[99] and this has the result, it is submitted, that the publication ban can be lifted only when this is in the interests of justice *to the child;* circumstances in which this will be so are difficult to visualise but might, for example, cover the case of a child who wishes publicly to clear his or her name from a misrepresentation made in a previous, unauthorised, publication. The Scottish ministers are not governed by s.16, but the welfare of the child will in any case be a heavy consideration in their balancing of the interests of justice. If they do decide to lift the publication ban this should be only in the most exceptional circumstances and only to the extent that is absolutely necessary to achieve the particular interests of justice that have been identified. The interests of persons other than the child may well be taken into account by the Scottish ministers, but again it is difficult to visualise circumstances in which this would be appropriate. No dispensation was ever given by the Secretary of State (the pre-devolutionary predecessor of the Scottish ministers) under the equivalent provision in the 1968 Act.[1]

---

[97] s.44(3).
[98] s.44(5).
[99] s.16(1) applies here as to any other decision affecting the child.
[1] According to the Earl of Lindsay, speaking for the Government in the House of Lords Committee of the Whole House, June 7, 1995, col.95.

## CHAPTER SIX

# PRELIMINARY PROCEDURE AT THE HEARING

## INTRODUCTION

Procedure at a children's hearing is governed by a combination of (i) the statutory rules contained in the Children (Scotland) Act 1995 and the rules and regulations made under it, and (ii) good practice which has been developed over the years by panel members. The format for most hearings is the same, being (basically) introductions and explanations, consideration through discussion, and decision. However, the procedural steps to be taken within that format depend upon the decisions that are open to the hearing and the stage that the child's case has reached.

## OPENING THE PROCEEDINGS

A children's hearing ought always to open with the chairman introducing the three members of the hearing, by name, to those who are attending. If the reporter has not already made clear to the hearing members who any individual person attending the hearing is, the chairman ought to require the individual to identify him or herself, for this is the only way that the chairman can fulfil his or her duty to ensure that only those who have a right or a duty to attend at the hearing do so. Hearing members should be aware from the start of the status of each attending person. The child, or if too young the relevant person, or if no relevant person is present some other participant who can speak to these matters, should then be asked to give the child's name and address. The hearing is expressly required to make inquiry as to the child's age and they can proceed only when either (i) the child gives as his or her age an age at which, for the purposes of the hearing system, the child will be considered "a child" or (ii) the hearing determines that the child is "a child".[1] It is also good practice for the chairman to check that the relevant person has received such documentation and information before the hearing as he or she is entitled to receive in terms of the Rules.[2]

Once these introductions and determinations have been made, the chairman must then explain to such persons as are present what the purpose of that particular hearing is.[3] Once this has been done the

---

[1] Children (Scotland) Act 1995, s.47(1). "Child" is defined in s.93(2)(b): see above at pp.13–14.

[2] Children's Hearings (Scotland) Rules 1996, r.5(3): see above at pp.59–61.

[3] 1996 Rules, r.20(2) and r.22(2).

hearing proper can commence. At any point during any type of hearing, the chairman may adjourn the hearing, but only in circumstances in which the hearing can sit again on the same day.[4] If the hearing requires adjourning until another day, for whatever reason, then it must be continued rather than adjourned.[5]

The procedure to be followed after the introductions and explanations depends upon the nature of the hearing. If grounds of referral have not yet been accepted or established, the chairman must now explain these grounds in order to determine whether they are accepted or not by the child and relevant person. The procedure for doing so shall be described in this chapter. If the grounds of referral have previously been accepted or established the hearing can move straight on to a consideration of the case, as it may do if the hearing has been arranged to review the case of a child currently subject to compulsory measures of supervision. Consideration of the case in any of these circumstances will be examined in Chapter 8.

## EXPLAINING THE GROUNDS OF REFERRRAL

A children's hearing can consider the case of a child referred to them only when either the grounds of referral have been accepted in whole or in part by the child and all the relevant persons who attend the hearing, or the grounds have been found established by the sheriff on an application under s.68.[6] It follows that, whenever the reporter has stated grounds of referral in accordance with the rules, the chairman of the children's hearing must put those grounds to the child and relevant person and ask them whether or not they accept the grounds of referral.[7] This must be done at the opening of the proceedings on the referral,[8] that is to say before any discussion on any substantive matter takes place (though after the child's identity and age have been established). At this stage in the proceedings, the only question that is relevant is whether the grounds of referral are accepted or not.

Putting the grounds of referral to the child and relevant person serves two purposes. First, it allows the children's hearing to determine whether the grounds of referral stated by the reporter are accepted in whole or in part by the child and the relevant persons[9] and thus determines which of two different courses of proceeding the hearing must thereafter take. And secondly, it establishes the basis of fact upon which the children's hearing must found their consideration, if the grounds are accepted.[10]

---

[4] 1996 Rules, r.10(4).

[5] For continuations of hearings, see below at pp.127–130.

[6] s.69(1). On s.68 applications, see Chap.7.

[7] This is unnecessary in certain circumstances, that is to say when a court in other proceedings has found that a ground of referral exists in relation to a child: see s.54 of the Children (Scotland) Act 1995, discussed above at pp.44–45; s.48 of the Criminal Procedure (Scotland) Act 1995, discussed above at pp.45–46; s.49 of the Criminal Procedure (Scotland) Act 1995, discussed above at p.47; and the Antisocial Behaviour etc. (Scotland) Act 2004, discussed above at pp.46–47.

[8] s.65 (4)

[9] s.65 (4)

[10] The children's hearing are expressly obliged to consider the grounds, accepted or established, under s.69(1).

The chairman ought to explain to the child and relevant person, before reading the grounds to them, that it is not open to the hearing, at this stage of the proceedings, to enter into any discussion of the grounds, and that all the hearing can do is (i) explain the grounds and (ii) determine whether they are accepted or denied. It is often difficult to distinguish an explanation from a discussion, but it must be done. Parents frequently attempt, in response to the chairman's explanation, to enter into a discussion of how they see the situation, but the hearing are unable, at this point, to give any consideration to what is said. All that should be sought at this point is, effectively, a yes or no answer from the child and relevant person, and it may sometimes be appropriate for the chairman to inform them that all they are required to do is to give such a one word answer. (It should also be explained, of course, that there can be full discussion at a later stage.) If the child or relevant person is unable to give a one word answer then the chairman should attempt a further explanation, unless it is clear that no explanation will be sufficient to allow the child or relevant person to give a definite answer. The chairman must be careful not to appear to put pressure on either the child or the relevant person to secure an acceptance of the grounds of referral: at this stage in the proceedings, the children's hearing are entirely disinterested in whether or not grounds of referral exist, for it is as much in the interests of a child in respect of whom grounds do not exist to have this established as it is in the interests of a child in respect of whom grounds do exist to have that established. The child and relevant person must be as free from pressure as possible to give one answer rather than another—except pressure to be truthful.[11]

### To whom the explanation must be given

The duty to explain the grounds of referral falls on the chairman of the children's hearing to whom the child's case has been referred,[12] and the explanation must be given to both the child and those relevant persons who are attending. The obligation to explain to the child does not apply where the children's hearing are satisfied that the child will not be capable of understanding,[13] and the obligation to explain to the relevant person will not apply where the relevant person is not attending the hearing.[14] Though all the relevant persons have a duty to attend at all stages of a children's hearing and failure to do so can be a criminal offence, it often happens that relevant persons do not attend and there is no power under the 1995 Act or anywhere else to bring them before a hearing.[15] This does not, however, prevent the hearing from proceeding with the child's case, for failure of a relevant person to attend results in the forfeiture of that person's right to deny the grounds of referral and so ensure an application to the sheriff for proof. It should be noted,

---

[11] The child and relevant person are not, of course, on oath so they have no legal obligation to be truthful. But it should be explained to them that it will *always and without exception* be in the child's interests for truthful answers to be given.

[12] s.65(4).

[13] s.65(9). See further, below at pp.87–88.

[14] s.65(10).

[15] See further, above at p.69.

however, that this provision is limited in its terms to "the relevant person", and the requirement of the child's acceptance of the grounds before the hearing can proceed is not affected by the absence of the child. If the child is not present, for whatever reason, there can be no acceptance and either the reporter must be directed to apply to the sheriff as under s.65(7), or the hearing must be rescheduled to allow for the child's attendance (with or without a warrant). It should also be noted that the power of the children's hearing to proceed in the absence of the relevant person cannot justify not putting the grounds to the relevant person who has been excluded from the hearing under the terms of s.46. The power to exclude applies only to the part of the proceedings at which the children's hearing have moved on to a consideration of the child's case, and not to the part at which grounds are being put in order to establish whether or not there is any case to be considered.[16]

**What must be explained**

The chairman is obliged to explain "the grounds stated by the reporter for the referral"[17]: this includes more than a reference to whichever paragraph in s.52(2) the reporter is founding upon, and includes in particular the statement of facts upon which the reporter is alleging the conditions in that paragraph are based. Though the various paragraphs in s.52(2) are commonly referred to as the "grounds of referral", that section itself refers to "conditions". The obligation under s.65(4) is to explain "the grounds", which includes both the conditions specified in s.52(2) and the statement of facts that the reporter alleges points to the satisfaction of these conditions. The duty of the chairman is not simply to read out the grounds as specified by the reporter, but to explain what these grounds mean. Explaining the grounds of referral is sometimes the most difficult task that faces the chairman of the children's hearing, for it may involve an explanation of the law, for example the concept of art and part guilt, or the meaning of "reasonable excuse" for not attending school regularly, or the crime of lewd and libidinous conduct. It is, however, worth spending some time on explaining what the grounds of referral mean since this will very directly protect the right of the child and the relevant person to deny the stated grounds and to have them tested by evidence in a court. And it is also likely to help the discussion when the children's hearing move on to a consideration of the case that the child and family understand precisely what it is that has concerned the reporter sufficiently for him or her to decide to refer the case to a children's hearing. It is to the detriment of a child who may be in need of compulsory measures of supervision to have a consideration of the case delayed by applying to the sheriff for proof when, with a careful explanation, the child could have been brought to an understanding of the grounds of referral. The chairman should, therefore, seek advice from the reporter before the hearing if the grounds contain references to legal concepts with which he or she is unfamiliar.

---

[16] See further, above at pp.71–72.
[17] s.65(4).

### ACCEPTANCE OR DENIAL OF THE GROUNDS OF REFERRAL

Once the chairman has explained the grounds of referral to the child and the relevant person, and the children's hearing are satisfied that the explanation has been understood,[18] the chairman must then ask the child and the relevant person to indicate whether they accept the grounds stated by the reporter as true or not, for it is the very purpose of the explanation to put the child and the relevant person in a position to answer that question. There are three possible responses that the child and the relevant person can give, and how the children's hearing can proceed thereafter depends upon which response is given: (1) they may all accept the grounds of referral as stated by the reporter, (2) one or more of them may deny completely the grounds as stated by the reporter, or (3) one or more of them may accept the grounds in part and deny them in part.

#### Acceptance of the whole grounds

Where the child and all the relevant persons who attend the children's hearing have understood the explanation given by the chairman and accept the grounds of referral as stated by the reporter, the hearing can then move on to the next stage of the proceedings, which is a consideration of the case under s.69(1).[19]

#### Denial of the whole grounds

Where either the child or the relevant person or both deny the grounds of referral stated by the reporter, the hearing has two options: they may either discharge the referral in whole, or they may direct the reporter to apply to the sheriff[20] for a finding as to whether the grounds of referral are established.[21] The choice of which option to adopt is governed by the welfare principle,[22] but one of the difficulties facing children's hearings is that this decision has to be made only on the basis of the reports already presented to them. No discussion is permitted with the family or the social worker or anyone else in order to assist the hearing in determining which option is more appropriate, and the hearing will often not be in a position, without such a discussion, to determine wherein the child's interests lie. The choice, therefore, is usually made by having regard to the seriousness of the allegations made in the grounds of referral. Unless the allegations are considered to be obviously trivial, few hearings are willing to make the dispositive decision of discharging the referral. It is submitted that this is appropriate. Referrals should be discharged after a denial of the grounds only when the children's hearing are of the view, on the information they have, that even if the grounds of referral are found established, the referral would likely be discharged after a consideration of the case. This will occur most often with referrals of

---

[18] On lack of understanding, see below at pp.87–89.
[19] See Chap.8.
[20] Under s.68: see Chapter 7.
[21] s.65(7)(a).
[22] s.16(1).

children currently under supervision with whom it is felt that the establishment of further grounds would serve no useful purpose, but it could occur with new referrals too, though more rarely since few hearings will be in a position to make that judgment in the absence of a full discussion (which is not permitted).

If the children's hearing decide to direct the reporter to apply to the sheriff for proof of the denied grounds, the chairman of the hearing must explain to the child and the relevant person the purpose of the sheriff court hearing; it must also be explained to the child that he or she has an obligation to attend the hearing before the sheriff.[23] There is no obligation to do so but it is good practice for the chairman to advise the child and relevant person to seek legal advice, and to inform them that legal aid may be available for the proof hearing. The reporter is obliged to give notice in writing to the child and relevant person of the fact that he or she has been directed to make a s.68 application.[24] This will ensure that the child and relevant person are kept informed of their rights and duties whether or not they attended the children's hearing.

### Acceptance in part

If either the child or the relevant person or both accept the grounds in part and deny them in part, the children's hearing may either proceed with the hearing in respect of the grounds that have been accepted,[25] or direct the reporter to make an application to the sheriff for proof as if the grounds had been denied in whole.[26] The children's hearing are not permitted, at this stage, to discharge the whole referral,[27] nor are they able to proceed in respect of the parts of the grounds accepted and at the same time refer the other parts to the sheriff, for the power to refer the case to the sheriff[28] is expressly stated to exist only when the hearing do not consider it appropriate to proceed in respect of the accepted grounds. The decision to direct the reporter to apply to the sheriff brings the proceedings at this particular hearing to an end.

Acceptance of part of the grounds of referral is common when there are numerous grounds some of which are not accepted, or when some of the statements of fact are not accepted. So long as there is enough left in the accepted portion to satisfy one of the conditions in s.52(2) the hearing may proceed to a consideration of the case.[29] So it is an acceptance in part if the child accepts that he or she has not attended school regularly without reasonable excuse, but denies that it is to the extent specified in the statement of facts; it is also an acceptance in part

---

[23] s.65(8).

[24] 1996 Rules, r.19. The reporter ought also to send to the child and relevant person a copy of the statement of reasons which in practice will be drawn up by the hearing: see further, below at p.124.

[25] s.65(6).

[26] s.65(7)(b).

[27] Although they may do so after having considered the case (*i.e.* the grounds that have been accepted).

[28] Contained in s.65(7).

[29] The children's hearing do not "discharge" the denied grounds, but simply proceed in respect of the accepted grounds. It is the referral as a whole that can be "discharged" (though it is common to talk, inaccurately, of "discharging" denied grounds).

if the child admits one offence when the reporter has specified another (at least when the two offences can be justified by the same set of facts[30]). The decision whether to proceed to a consideration of the accepted grounds, or alternatively to direct the reporter to make an application to the sheriff for proof, is to be made by the hearing in the light of the welfare principle contained in s.16(1) and will normally turn on whether the hearing consider the denied parts of the grounds will affect the eventual outcome of the referral. This is not, however, the only consideration. It may be considered detrimental to the child to delay a consideration of his or her case, in which case it would be proper to proceed with the hearing in respect of the grounds which have been accepted, so long as there is enough of a basis of fact in the accepted grounds to allow the children's hearing to conduct a proper discussion of the child's needs. Conversely, there are situations in which it would inhibit a proper consideration of the child's case (and therefore be detrimental to the child's welfare) to proceed to a consideration of the accepted parts while there are far more serious parts which, if established, would fundamentally affect that consideration and the likely outcome. If the children's hearing decide to proceed in respect of the grounds that are accepted, they cannot consider in their discussion those grounds or parts thereof that have not been accepted, nor can they allow the denied grounds to influence their dispositive decision.

Difficult questions of emphasis may arise if the children's hearing decide to proceed, for they are permitted to consider the whole of the child's "case", which might well include the fact that allegations have been made but are denied. The proper approach is to treat any ground or part thereof that is denied as not established fact. For example, a child may be referred to a children's hearing on the ground that he is beyond parental control and this may be accepted; in addition, there may be a number of offences specified as grounds which the child denies on the basis that while he was present he did not take part in the offences. If the hearing proceed on the basis that the child is beyond parental control they cannot take into account the allegation that offences have been committed, but they can, it is submitted, take into account the fact that the child is associating with persons who lead the child to the attention of the police. A discussion of these matters is not a discussion of the denied "grounds", but of circumstances in the child's life which might or might not help the children's hearing to determine the best way forward.

### Lack of Understanding

Where a children's hearing are satisfied that the child either will not be capable of understanding an explanation of the grounds of referral or

---

[30] It would be denial of the grounds of referral if, say, the reporter specified a ground of theft and the child admits an assault. *cf.* Act of Sederunt (Child Care and Maintenance Rules) 1997, r.3.50, under which the sheriff in an application under s.68 can find proved any offence the evidence establishes, whether or not it is the offence specified by the reporter. Rule 3.50 does not apply to children's hearings, but only to sheriffs.

has not understood the explanation that has been given, their options are the same as when the grounds have been denied in whole, that is to say they must either discharge the referral or direct the reporter to apply to the sheriff court for proof.[31] The decision of which option to adopt is, of course, governed by the welfare principle.[32] Whenever an application is made to the sheriff on the basis of lack of understanding it should be made plain which paragraph of s.65(9) the children's hearing are relying upon to justify the application (that is to say whether the child (a) will not be capable of understanding an explanation or (b) has not understood the explanation given).[33] Though the obligation to explain the grounds of referral rests with the chairman of the children's hearing,[34] the assessment that the child will not understand or has not understood the explanation is one to be made by the hearing as a whole, and in the unlikely event of disagreement amongst the hearing members a majority decision is, as always, sufficient. The question is one of fact and not, therefore, one to which the welfare test in s.16(1) applies. And not being a dispositive decision, it is not appealable under s.51.[35] To understand a ground of referral the child must be capable of understanding not only the words used by the chairman but also why the alleged facts are giving cause for concern: it is not sufficient, for example, that a child understands that he or she was left alone in an empty and unheated house but does not understand that this ought not to have happened.

The reason for the child's lack of understanding is irrelevant, and the hearing should take account of any proferred reason only in so far as it assists the question of whether the child has understood or not. In many cases, the age of the child will make it quite obvious that the child will not be capable of understanding any explanation: a baby or toddler, for example, will clearly not understand, however straightforward the grounds of referral are. The chairman is under no obligation to attempt an explanation in these circumstances. It should be noted that it is not a ground in itself for relieving a child of the obligation under s.45(2) to attend the hearing that the child will not understand an explanation of the grounds of referral, though this, in addition to some other factor, may well indicate that it would be detrimental to the child's interests to attend.[36]

**The relevant person's understanding**

There is no provision dealing with the relevant person's lack of understanding but it seems clear that a relevant person who does not understand an explanation of the ground cannot give an acceptance thereof, and if there is no acceptance by an attending relevant person this must be treated as a denial of the whole grounds. The chairman ought in all cases to attempt to explain the grounds of referral to any relevant person who attends the hearing.

---

[31] s.65(9).
[32] s.16(1).
[33] *cf. Sloan v B*, 1991 S.L.T. 530.
[34] s.65(4).
[35] See below at pp.211–213.
[36] See further, above at pp.64–67.

## WARRANTS

If the reporter has been directed to apply to the sheriff for a finding as to whether the grounds of referral are established, the children's hearing must also give consideration to the welfare of the child in the meantime. If they feel that, for some reason, there is a risk to the child they may grant a warrant to keep the child in a place of safety.[37] A discussion of the child's present circumstances is permitted at this stage, even although grounds of referral have not been accepted, and often the decision will have to be made on the basis of facts which are vehemently disputed. The hearing members must do their best to judge credibility in assessing disputed allegations and they must, of course, make their decision by having regard to the child's welfare as their paramount consideration, as well as taking account of the proportionality requirement from the European Convention on Human Rights.[38] The details of such a warrant are described fully in Chapter 13.

## APPOINTING A SAFEGUARDER

In any proceedings under Chapter Two or Chapter Three of Part II of the 1995 Act, and not just those at which grounds of referral are put to the child and relevant person, the children's hearing must consider whether it is necessary to appoint a person to safeguard the interests of the child in the proceedings at the hearing and, if they do consider it so necessary, they must appoint a safeguarder on such terms and conditions as appear appropriate.[39] The question of appointment of a safeguarder is one for the children's hearing as a whole[40] to decide and, as always in relation to decisions of a children's hearing, a majority decision is sufficient. The decision is governed by the welfare principle in s.16(1), but not the other two overarching principles in s.16(2)[41] or (3).[42] Nevertheless, it will often be appropriate to discuss the possible appointment of a safeguarder with a child, and invariably so with an older child. The chairman should always explain to the child and the relevant person the purpose of the appointment and the role the safeguarder will perform, and as part of that explanation it is good practice to stress the independence of the safeguarder from both the local authority and the children's panel. Considerations of proportionality would seem to have no place in the decision to appoint a safeguarder.

A children's hearing is required under the rules[43] to state the reasons for any decision that they make. In addition, they must also state why

---

[37] Under s.66.

[38] On proportionality, See above at pp.4–5.

[39] s.41(1).

[40] Under the 1968 Act the question was (for no good reason) one for the chairman alone. Curiously, the current court rules still refer to appointment "by the chairman of the children's hearing": see Act of Sederunt (Child Care and Maintenance Rules) 1997, r.3.45(2), and r.3.54(1)(d). The Children's Hearings Rules, like the statute itself, refer to safeguarders "appointed by a children's hearing": see 1996 Rules, r.14.

[41] Taking appropriate account of the child's views.

[42] The minimum intervention principle.

[43] 1996 Rules, r.10(5).

they felt it necessary in the interests of the child to appoint a safe-guarder.[44] This serves the useful purpose of indicating to the safeguarder the issues that he or she ought to address.[45]

Section 41 of the 1995 Act does not specify the circumstances in which the appointment of a safeguarder might be appropriate, except that it must be necessary to safeguard the interests of the child in the proceedings. This might be, for example, because there is a conflict of interests between the relevant person and the child, or because there is a conflict of views between the family and the Social Work Department, or because this is the best way of allowing the child to express his or her view of the proceedings or to explain how the child sees the situation, or because it is felt that a safeguarder might be able to identify the real cause of the child's difficulties, or because it is felt that the child needs independent (though not necessarily legal) advice in the course of the proceedings.

### The role of the safeguarder

The role of the safeguarder is not specified in either the 1995 Act or in the associated Rules and Regulations, except that the appointment is of a person "to safeguard the interests of the child in the proceedings". The expectation is that the safeguarder will meet with the child, the child's family (which is wider than simply the relevant persons) and any other significant person; and he or she is obliged to draw up a report in writing on the case of the child.[46] It is not specified what should be in this report, but in the normal case it will attempt to identify the relevant issues and make a recommendation as to what disposal available to the hearing would best serve the child's interests. It must be given to the reporter, who must then make it available to the hearing members and the relevant persons.[47] In addition, the safeguarder is entitled to be present throughout the duration of any hearing of the case until the disposal of that case,[48] and is entitled to play an active role in the discussion of the case. The children's hearing are obliged to endeavour, during the hearing, to obtain the views of any safeguarder who attends on what arrangements would be in the best interests of the child.[49] But the very fact that the safeguarder's role is not delimited by statute means that the safeguarder is entitled to interpret his or her role in a wide sense. It may be appropriate, for example, for the safeguarder to do little more than to find out what the child thinks and to articulate the child's views on his or her behalf, on the ground that it is in the interests of the child to have

---

[44] s.41(3) and 1996 Rules, r.14(1). Although these provisions are in their terms limited to decisions to appoint a safeguarder, it is good practice for hearings to state reasons why they did not appoint a safeguarder, if for no other reason than to indicate that they fulfilled their statutory obligation to give the matter consideration.

[45] It is, of course, for the safeguarder him or herself to decide what issues he or she will explore, but it will always be helpful for the safeguarder to know what issues concerned the children's hearing.

[46] 1996 Rules, r.14(4).

[47] 1996 Rules, r.5(1)(e) and r.5(3).

[48] 1996 Rules, r.14(3).

[49] 1996 Rules, r.20(3)(d) (disposal hearings), r.22(3)(c) (advice hearings) and r.26(1) (warrant hearings).

his or her views properly presented. Or, the safeguarder might consider it appropriate to do little more than explain to the child the process that the child has found him or herself involved in—again it is in the interests of any child to be helped to a full awareness of a process which to many will be alien, baffling and frightening: knowledge empowers and for a safeguarder to adopt a purely educative, informative or advisory role will in some cases satisfactorily safeguard the child's interests.

To assist in the performance of the safeguarder's function, the reporter is obliged to make available to the safeguarder, regardless of the date of his or her appointment in the proceedings, any information or document which he or she has made available to the members of the children's hearing.[50] After the hearing, the safeguarder is entitled to be given written notification of the decision, the reasons for the decision, and the right of the child and relevant person to appeal against the decision.[51] The safeguarder may appeal against the decision of the children's hearing on the child's behalf. On the completion of the performance of his or her duties, the safeguarder must return to the reporter all documents made available to him or her, and until he or she does so these documents must be kept securely in the safeguarder's custody and their contents not made known to any person, other than may be necessary for the performance of the safeguarder's duties.[52] The safeguarder, like everyone else, is subject to the prohibition on publication of any matter which may identify any child involved in the hearing or his or her address or school.[53]

## APPOINTING A LEGAL REPRESENTATIVE

A children's hearing may appoint a legal representative to any child, notwithstanding that a previous hearing or business meeting has considered the issue, and notwithstanding that a safeguarder has been appointed.[54] The reporter is required to inform the local authority of the making of the appointment.[55] It is the local authority that makes the arrangements for the legal representative to attend the hearing, and the appointee must be a member of either the Panel of Persons to Safeguard the Interests of Children or the Panel of Curators *ad litem* and Reporting Officers[56] as well as being the holder of a current practising certificate issued by the Law Society of Scotland. The local authority must notify the reporter of the name of the person appointed. There are two grounds upon which the appointment may be made.[57]

First, the appointment may be made when legal representation is required to allow the child to participate effectively at the hearing.

---

[50] 1996 Rules, r.14(5).

[51] 1996 Rules, r.21(1) (disposal hearings), r.22(7) (advice hearings), and r.26(1) (warrant hearings).

[52] 1996 Rules, r.14(6).

[53] s.44, as amended by the Criminal Justice (Scotland) Act 2003, s.52: see above at pp.78–80.

[54] Children's Hearings (Legal Representation) (Scotland) Rules 2002 SSI 2002/63, r.3.

[55] *ibid.*, r.3(3).

[56] *ibid.*, r.5.

[57] *ibid.*, r.3(2).

"Effective participation" is to be assessed in light of the First Division's decision in *S v Miller*,[58] which led to the provision. It is to be remembered that there are already various provisions designed to ensure the child's effective participation, not least the appointment of a safeguarder, as considered above. It follows that legal representation is designed to achieve more than the sort of participation that a safe-guarder might effect. Participation in this context means being able to put across the child's point of view, whether or not directed to the child's best interests; this might involve the expression of the child's views as to where these interests lie but will seldom involve the expression of the legal representative's own view on that matter. Participation also means being able to take part in the discussion of legal complexities, such as for example the meaning of particular grounds of referral or the effect of the Rehabilitation of Offenders Act 1974.

The second circumstance in which an appointment of a legal repre-sentative might be made is when it may be necessary to make a supervision requirement (or to continue a supervision requirement) which includes a requirement that the child reside in a named residential establishment and the child is likely to meet the criteria specified in s.70(10) of the 1995 Act and the Secure Accommodation (Scotland) Regulations 1996. It must be a serious possibility being genuinely considered that the child will be required to reside in secure accommo-dation before the hearing is obliged to appoint a legal representative. If this arises unexpectedly and the appointment was not made by an earlier hearing or a business meeting then the hearing that now realises it must consider the matter may well have to be continued in order to allow the appointment to be made. A hearing that continues its consideration of the case for the appointment of a legal representative may in the interim grant a warrant to keep the child in a place of safety, which itself contains a secure accommodation authorisation. The fact that no legal representative could have been present when that decision was made does not render the decision contrary to the ECHR demands for a fair trial, since legal representation will in any case be available at the sheriff court if the warrant is appealed against.[59] In the case cited the First Division said this:[60]

> "Two points may be noted. First, where a children's hearing has to be arranged as a matter of urgency it may well be impracticable for a solicitor to be instructed and attend before the hearing. Secondly, the appointment by the children's hearing of a solicitor for a child is not mandatory. For example, it is not necessary if the child is already advised by a solicitor who will appear on his or her behalf. Having regard to the age of the child it may be necessary or preferable that a safeguarder is appointed instead of a solicitor. However, where the child is able to give instructions to a solicitor and the detention of the child in secure accommodation is in question, it would be normal for a solicitor to represent the child".

---

[58] 2001 S.L.T. 531 and 1304.
[59] *Martin v N,* 2004 S.L.T. 249.
[60] *ibid.*, para.16.

It would be wrong, however, to interpret this as a requirement that the child has capacity to instruct a solicitor before the appointment of a legal representative is appropriate. There is no such limitation in the Rules and to imply it would be inconsistent with the thinking behind *S v Miller* itself, which set out the client's inability to participate as one of the circumstances in which legal representation would be appropriate. The First Division in *Martin v N* cannot be taken to have meant more than they said, which is that sometimes there will be other ways than the appointment of a solicitor that the aim sought can be achieved.

CHAPTER SEVEN

# APPLICATION TO THE SHERIFF UNDER SECTION 68

INTRODUCTION

One of the defining characteristics of the children's hearing system is the clear separation of roles between the body that determines what, if any, measures of supervision are necessary to meet the child's needs, and the body that determines whether, if the matter is disputed, any one or more of the grounds of referral exists. It is only when there is no dispute, or any dispute has been resolved by a finding that grounds of referral do exist, that the question arises as to whether compulsory measures of supervision are necessary.[1] The sheriff court is the appropriate forum for resolving disputes of fact relating to the existence or otherwise of grounds of referral, for in that forum evidence can be taken on oath and can be challenged by cross-examination; the children's hearing is the appropriate forum for identifying what, if any, measures of supervision would best meet the child's needs, because the hearing is designed to foster discussion with the child and his or her family of the grounds of referral, other relevant circumstances, and possible ways forward.

> "It was this separation between the issues of adjudication of the allegations in the grounds for the referral and the consideration of the measures to be applied which lay at the heart of the recommendations of the Kilbrandon *Report on Children and Young Persons, Scotland* (Cmnd. 2306) of April 1964 which were in due course implemented by the Social Work (Scotland) Act 1968. The genius of this reform, which has earned it so much praise which the misfortunes of this case should not be allowed in any way to diminish, was that the responsibility for the consideration of the measures to be applied was to lie with what was essentially a lay body while disputed questions of fact as to the allegations made were to be resolved by the sheriff sitting in chambers as a court of law".[2]

The reporter may be directed to make an application under s.68 to the sheriff to establish grounds of referral in any of a number of different circumstances: (i) where either the child or any one or more of the relevant persons do not accept the grounds as put to them by the chairman of the children's hearing,[3] (ii) where only part of the grounds is

---

[1] Children (Scotland) Act 1995, s.52(1).
[2] *Sloan v B*, 1991 S.L.T. 530, *per* Lord President Hope at 548D–E.
[3] s.65(7)(a).

accepted and the hearing do not consider it appropriate to proceed in respect of the accepted part,[4] (iii) where the children's hearing are satisfied that the child will not be capable of understanding an explanation of the grounds[5]; or (iv) where the children's hearing are satisfied that the child has not understood the explanation given by the chairman.[6] In any of these circumstances the children's hearing may direct the reporter to apply to the sheriff for a finding as to whether the stated grounds of referral are established (unless they decide to discharge the referral[7]). It is open to the reporter to abandon the application, either in whole or in part, at any stage in the proceedings before the application is determined,[8] though it would appear that an application must be made before it can be abandoned, and the reporter has no authority to ignore the hearing's direction to apply for proof. It would be appropriate to abandon an application when the reporter comes to be of the view[9] that he or she will not be able to establish in court that the grounds of referral exist, due for example to the death or disappearance of a vital witness, or because the emergence of new information has put a different light on the circumstances, persuading the reporter that the child is definitely not in need of compulsory measures of supervision. The reporter must notify abandonment to the child,[10] any relevant person whose whereabouts are known to the reporter, and any safeguarder appointed by the sheriff.[11] If the application is abandoned in whole, the sheriff must dismiss the application and discharge the referral.[12]

### Time-scale

The application must be made within seven days of the children's hearing at which the direction to the reporter was made, the day of the hearing counting as the first day.[13] If the application is not made timeously, the referral falls, though there would seem to be nothing to prevent the reporter in that case founding upon the same facts and the same grounds to make a new referral to the children's hearing.[14] As the delay inherent in such a proceeding would clearly be contrary to the interests of a child who may be in need of compulsory measures of supervision, reporters should make every effort to ensure that applications are made in time. Once the application is lodged, it must be

---

[4] s.65(7)(b).

[5] s.65(9)(a).

[6] s.65(9)(b).

[7] See above at pp.85–86.

[8] Act of Sederunt (Child Care and Maintenance Rules) 1997 (hereinafter AS 1997), r.3.46(1).

[9] *After* the original hearing. It would be extremely bad practice for the reporter to arrange a children's hearing while he or she is of the view that the grounds could not be proved, and in the hope that they will simply be accepted.

[10] Unless service on the child had previously been dispensed with.

[11] AS 1997, r.3.46(2).

[12] AS 1997, r.3.46(3).

[13] AS 1997, r.3.45(1). If a safeguarder was appointed by the children's hearing, the reporter must intimate this to the sheriff clerk and lodge along with the application any report made by the safeguarder: r.3.45(2).

[14] See *McGregor v L,* 1983 S.L.T. (Sh. Ct.) 7.

heard by the sheriff within 28 days thereof[15] and if it is not the referral falls though, again, the reporter can found upon the same facts to make a fresh referral.[16] An application is "heard" timeously so long as some substantive step in the process is taken by the sheriff within that period,[17] but the application does not need to be disposed of within that period.[18] So the sheriff may continue the case beyond the 28 days,[19] either to give more time for the preparation of the case, or because the presentation of the evidence is taking a long time. Likewise, if the child fails to attend, the granting of a warrant under s.68(6) will amount to a substantive step in the process and the application is not rendered out of time even although the child is not found until after the end of the 28–day period. The decision to continue the case is subject to the welfare principle in s.16(1), and it is never in the interests of a child who may be in need of compulsory measures of supervision for that question to be left unanswered for longer than is necessary: this suggests that cases ought not to be continued for mere administrative convenience but only when it is necessary for the proper conduct of the hearing of the application.

## JURISDICTION

It is expressly provided that in relation to referrals on the basis that the child has committed a criminal offence (*i.e.* referrals under s.52(2)(i)) the application under s.68 must be made to the sheriff who would have jurisdiction to try the case if the child were being prosecuted for the offence that founds the referral.[20] That does not mean that a referral cannot be made if the ground founded upon is an offence which cannot be tried before a sheriff, like murder or rape. Section 68(3)(a) is to be taken to refer to the sheriff's territorial rather than procedural jurisdiction,[21] for otherwise reporters would be tempted to ensure the sheriff's jurisdiction by presenting serious allegations in a way that diminished their true import (such as, for example, alleging lewd and libidinous conduct, or assault, when the reality was the much more serious offence of rape). In cases other than referrals under s.52(2)(i) it will be appropriate to make the application to a sheriff court situated in the local authority area within which the children's hearing took place. In *Sloan v B*[22] Lord President Hope, referring to *Sloan, Petitioner*,[23] said that "the view which was taken by the court is that an application under s.42[24] cannot competently be dealt with outside the area of the local

---

[15] s.68(2).

[16] *McGregor v L*, 1983 S.L.T. (Sh. Ct.) 7.

[17] *H v Mearns*, 1974 S.L.T. 184.

[18] *H v McGregor*, 1973 S.L.T. 110, *per* Lord Wheatley at 115. *cf.* s.60(8) under which an application to set aside or vary a child protection order must be "determined", *i.e.* disposed of, within three working days; and s.51(8) under which an appeal against a warrant must be disposed of within three days of lodging the appeal.

[19] AS 1997, r.3.49.

[20] s.68(3)(a).

[21] *Walker v C (No. 2)*, 2003 S.L.T. 293.

[22] 1991 S.L.T. 530.

[23] 1991 S.L.T. 527.

[24] The 1968 predecessor of s.68.

authority from which it originates".[25] So if the children's hearing was constituted from the Children's Panel for, say, Orkney, the application can be made only to the sheriff court in Orkney. If the local authority area covers more than one sheriff court district, then the reporter would seem to have a choice of court, though it may be open to the hearing to direct the reporter to apply to a particular sheriff court if they consider that it is in the interests of the child to do so, and the reporter is probably obliged to follow any such direction.[26] It has been suggested that the sheriff probably has power to refuse jurisdiction if the choice of his court amounts to an abuse of process, such as when the forum has been deliberately chosen to make it difficult for the child or relevant person to attend.[27] It is competent for the reporter to apply to the *nobile officium* for a direction that the hearing of the application be held outside the sheriff court district within which is situated the sheriff court to which the application has been made. The Court of Session, while recognising the competency of the petition, refused to make such an order in *Sloan, Petitioner*[28] when the reporter had argued that it would be appropriate to hear the application for proof elsewhere in the Sheriffdom of Grampian, Highland and Islands, to avoid the necessity of certain child witnesses (not the children referred) having to travel to Orkney (though an order was pronounced requiring the sheriff to hear the evidence of the child witnesses in another location within the sheriffdom). Such a petition might be granted if, taking account of all the circumstances of the case, it was convenient to all parties, and particularly the child, for the application to be heard in another sheriff court district. The sheriff has no jurisdiction to hear an application for the establishment of grounds of referral in relation to a child who is not present in Scotland at the relevant time.[29] Clearly there is no jurisdiction if the child has never been in Scotland, but there is jurisdiction if the child is present in Scotland at the relevant time, regardless of where the child was at the time of the conduct which gave rise to the need for the referral.[30] It is presence at the relevant time, rather than habitual or normal residence, that is important.[31] And the relevant time is the moment at which the reporter refers the child to the children's hearing, for this is a distinct statutory step which requires him or her to state grounds (as opposed to the moment at which he or she receives information, which may or may not lead to a referral). Thereafter a children's hearing (and the sheriff) do not lose jurisdiction merely because the child is removed from Scotland, but removal from Scotland after the reporter has started an investigation but before a referral to the hearing will have exactly that effect.[32] Though this decision is clear to the

---

[25] 1991 S.L.T. 530 at 542J–K.

[26] Just as he or she is obliged to make the application, when directed to do so.

[27] Wilkinson and Norrie, *Parent and Child* (2nd ed., 1999) at para.19.63.

[28] 1991 S.L.T. 527.

[29] *Mitchell v S,* 2000 S.L.T. 524.

[30] *ibid.,* at 527G, founding on *S v Kennedy,* 1996 S.L.T. 1087, where it was held there was jurisdiction even when the offence committed against the child had been committed abroad.

[31] *ibid.,* at 527H.

[32] *ibid.,* at 528D–E.

effect that there is jurisdiction if the child is present in Scotland at the time of the referral from the reporter to the children's hearing, it was subsequently held by Sheriff Principal Young that the converse (there is never jurisdiction if the child is not present at that time) does not apply.[33] In that case a child was already subject to a supervision requirement and it was held that since he was already subject to the jurisdiction of the children's hearing (and therefore the sheriff) a new referral to the sheriff was competent. Sheriff Principal Young made the powerful point that to hold presence in Scotland on the date of referral essential would mean that a referral in respect of a child being brought up in Scotland would be incompetent if on the date the reporter made the decision so to refer the child happened to be on a family holiday abroad.[34] It would be an odder result still if the reason the child was outwith Scotland was to satisfy the terms of an existing supervision requirement (as in the present case).[35]

ATTENDANCE AT THE PROOF HEARING

**The child and relevant person**

Reflecting the right and obligation to attend his or her own children's hearing, the child has both the right and the obligation to attend the hearing of the application before the sheriff.[36] There is, however, no provision imposing an obligation on the relevant person to attend.[37] Indeed, the statute does not expressly grant the relevant person a right to be present, though the provision entitling both the relevant person and the child to be legally represented[38] can be taken to imply such a right. Each may be represented by a person other than a legally qualified person[39]: this gives them an equal right to the reporter, who has a right of audience even when not legally qualified.[40]

**Removing the right and the duty to attend**

The sheriff may relieve the child of the obligation to attend the hearing of the s.68 application where he is satisfied that it would be detrimental to the interests of the child for him or her to be present at the hearing of the application[41]; if the application relates to any of the grounds involving the commission of a Sch.1 offence by someone other than the child,[42] the sheriff must *in addition* be satisfied that the obligation on the

---

[33] *Walker v C (No 1)*, 2003 S.L.T. (Sh. Ct.) 31.

[34] *ibid.*, at 33I.

[35] *ibid.*, at 33J. The sheriff principal did go on to interpret *Mitchell v S* as requiring that the child be ordinarily resident outwith Scotland before jurisdiction was lost (at 34C), though that is contrary to an express statement of the Lord Justice Clerk in *Mitchell*.

[36] s.68(4).

[37] *cf.* s.45(8) and (9) in relation to the relevant person's obligation to attend the children's hearing.

[38] s.68(4). See also AS 1997, r.3.47(6), which assumes that the relevant person will be present.

[39] s.68(4) and AS 1997, r.3.21.

[40] s.40(4).

[41] s.68(5)(b).

[42] *i.e.* grounds under s.52(2)(d), (e), (f) or (g).

child to attend is not necessary for the just hearing of the application.[43] It would be detrimental to the interests of the child to have to attend at the sheriff court if, for example, that attendance is likely to prove unduly traumatic, or if the child is too young to contribute in any way to the hearing and for some reason he or she should not be brought. Age alone does not make it detrimental to the child's interests to attend, but if the child is too young to take any realistic part little more is needed, it is submitted, to allow the sheriff to excuse attendance. It may be detrimental to the child's interests, for example, to miss a day's schooling or to cause the child distress. This must, however, be balanced against the fact that the child's interests are undoubtedly best served by the sheriff being able to determine the truth of the matter, and very much more will be required to justify the child's absence when his or her presence is likely to assist the sheriff in that quest, for example by acting as a vital witness. It is difficult to imagine a situation in which it would be proper to relieve the child of the obligation to attend when the ground of referral is that he or she has committed an offence. If the case involves a Sch.1 offence the child can be allowed to be absent only when this does not interfere with the just hearing of the application, and a "just hearing" refers, it is submitted, not only to justice to the child. Justice may sometimes require that an alleged abuser has the opportunity directly to challenge his or her accuser, and if the child is the accuser a just hearing will normally require the child's presence. In these cases the sheriff must be persuaded of the concurrent satisfaction of both paragraphs in s.68(5).[44] It is possible to envisage a case in which the child might properly be excused from attending the hearing of the evidence before the sheriff but not from the consideration of his or her case by a children's hearing (or vice versa). It is competent to relieve the child from attending part only of the proceedings.

In addition to relieving the child of his or her obligation to attend, the Rules permit the sheriff to exclude the child from any stage of the proceedings (that is to say, the sheriff may take away the child's right to attend granted by s.68(4)(a)). This may be done where the nature of the case or of any evidence to be given is such that the sheriff is satisfied that it is in the interests of the child that he or she should not be present at any stage of the proceedings; in that event any safeguarder and the relevant person or[45] representative of the child must be permitted to remain during the absence of the child.[46] The sheriff may also exclude any person, including the relevant person (and, presumably, including the referred child) when any child[47] is giving evidence if the sheriff is

---

[43] s.68(5)(a).

[44] *cf.* s.45(2) where the similar paras (a) and (b) are conjoined with "or", while in s.68(5) the paragraphs are conjoined with "and".

[45] The use of the word "or" suggests that the child's representative cannot remain if the relevant person insists on remaining. Since applications are heard in chambers, however, the sheriff will have a discretion and unless there is good reason why the representative should not remain, in most cases it will be appropriate for the sheriff to allow him or her to do so.

[46] AS 1997, r.3.47(5).

[47] Under the previous law, only a parent of the referred child could be excluded, and only from evidence given by the referred child: AS (Social Work) (Sheriff Court Procedure Rules) 1971, r.8(4): see *T v Watson*, 1995 S.L.T. 1062, the decision in which is no longer good law.

satisfied that this is necessary in the interests of the child giving evidence *and* either (a) he must do so in order to obtain the evidence of the child, or (b) the presence of the person in question is causing or is likely to cause significant distress to the child.[48] Where it is a relevant person who was excluded and that person is not legally represented, the sheriff must inform that person of the substance of any evidence given during the exclusion and must give that person an opportunity to respond by leading evidence or otherwise.[49]

**Ensuring the child's presence**

If the child breaches his or her obligation to attend the hearing of the s.68 application the sheriff may grant an order to find the child and keep him or her in a place of safety until the sheriff can hear the application.[50] The effect of this order is discussed more fully in Chapter 13.[51]

**Journalists**

The hearing of the s.68 application will be in the sheriff's chambers,[52] which means that members of the public are not admitted, and journalists have no right to be present.[53] However,

> "it is in the discretion of the judge or sheriff to permit anyone including the press to attend the proceedings which are being conducted in his chambers. This is because there is no general rule which prevents this from being done . . . By providing that the proceedings are to be in chambers, Parliament has done what was necessary to allow the sheriff to decide this matter as he thinks fit. It is a matter for his discretion and thus subject entirely to his control as to who, other than those who have a duty or right to be there, may attend and for how long they may remain".[54]

In the case cited, the sheriff had permitted journalists to be present, and Lord President Hope said this:

> "We have no criticism to make . . . of the sheriff's decision to allow the journalists to attend . . . The sheriff had to deal with the situation as he found it when he opened the proceedings for which he was responsible in the sheriff court. The press had been present at the proceedings before the children's hearing, and the case had already received a great deal of publicity which was likely to continue. It was suggested that he was wrong to allow the journalists to attend at their request, not on the motion of any party, and to do so when the debate on competency had reached such a stage that they could not get a balanced view of it. But these were matters for

---

[48] AS 1997, r.3.47(6).
[49] AS 1997, r.3.47(7).
[50] s.68(6).
[51] At pp.204–205.
[52] s.93(5).
[53] *cf.* s.43(3) in relation to journalists' presence at children's hearings.
[54] *Sloan v B*, 1991 S.L.T. 530, *per* Lord President Hope at 551D–E, G.

the sheriff, and for what it is worth we think that he was right to exercise his discretion as he did in the exceptional circumstances of this case".[55]

It would be wrong to interpret these dicta as indicating that journalists should be permitted to be present only in exceptional circumstances. Given the limitations on what may be reported[56] it may be that sheriffs ought usually to permit journalists who wish to be present to be so unless there is good reason why they should not be.[57] It is difficult to imagine who, other than journalists and those directly connected to the child or the application, should ever be permitted to be present in the sheriff's chambers.

## Preliminary Matters

The sheriff ought always to start the proceedings in a s.68 application by inquiring as to whether the child and the relevant persons accept or deny the grounds of referral. Although he is not expressly obliged to do so under the statute or the Rules, this is the only means by which he can secure certain rights and determine how he is to proceed in the conduct of the application. If the child and relevant person now accept the grounds of referral which either or both denied at the children's hearing then the sheriff is obliged to dispense with hearing evidence, unless he is satisfied that in all the circumstances of the case the evidence should be heard[58]: this imposes upon the sheriff, it is submitted, a duty to inquire after the matter, otherwise he will not know whether the obligation to dispense with the evidence applies or not. It is the right of the child and relevant person to withdraw at the s.68 hearing any acceptance of the grounds of referral previously given at the children's hearing.[59]

### Appointing a safeguarder

As soon as reasonably practicable after the lodging of the s.68 application, the sheriff must give consideration to the question of whether it is necessary to appoint a person to safeguard the interests of the child in the proceedings, and if he considers this to be necessary he must make such an appointment (either immediately or at any later stage of the application[60]) on such terms and conditions as appear to him to be appropriate.[61] He may make the appointment whenever he thinks it is necessary and may do so either on his own initiative or on being

---

[55] 1991 S.L.T. 530 at 551H–1.

[56] See s.44 and discussion thereof above at pp.78–80.

[57] See, however, the more cautiously expressed view of Sheriff Kearney in *Children's Hearings and the Sheriff Court* (2nd ed., 2000) at para.28.07.

[58] s.68(8). See further, below at p.111.

[59] *Kennedy v R's Curator ad litem*, 1993 S.L.T. 295.

[60] Though if the necessity for a safeguarder becomes apparent at a later stage, this will invariably delay the process since the hearing would need to be adjourned to allow the safeguarder time to prepare.

[61] s.41(1) and AS 1997, r.3.7(1). See McGhie, "The Role of the Safeguarder" (1994) 39 J.L. S.S. 26.

requested to do so. The decision to appoint a safeguarder is one in which the welfare of the child is the sheriff's paramount consideration,[62] though, perhaps anomalously, it is not one with which he is obliged to have regard to the views of the child. There is no further indication in the legislation as to the circumstances in which it would be appropriate for a sheriff to appoint a safeguarder: a safeguarder can be appointed by the sheriff whenever this is necessary to protect the child's interests. This might be because, for example, there is a risk that the relevant persons or their representatives will not or cannot look after the child's interests properly, or because the sheriff considers that the appointment is the best way to find out the child's views on the matter at issue (it always being in the child's interests to have his or her views properly expressed). But it should be emphasised that the power to appoint a safeguarder under the 1995 Act is deliberately expressed in wider and vaguer terms than under the previous legislation,[63] with the result, it is submitted, that the sheriff need identify no reason for the appointment of a safeguarder other than that he considers it necessary to protect the interests of the child. It is, however, of great use to the safeguarder to be given some indication beyond that general reason why his or her appointment was considered by the sheriff to be necessary. The child's interests may be safeguarded by the child's receiving advice from a safeguarder as to whether to accept the grounds of referral sent for proof. The safeguarder may also be in a position to advise the sheriff whether it is in the child's interests that he exercise his power to dispense with hearing evidence,[64] or to relieve the child of the obligation to attend,[65] or to exclude any person while the child is giving evidence.[66] An educative, informative or advisory role will always be appropriate and often sufficient.

Sometimes a safeguarder will already have been appointed by the children's hearing which directed the reporter to make a s.68 application or by the sheriff in related proceedings. In that situation (if the sheriff decides to appoint a safeguarder) the same person must be appointed safeguarder for the purposes of the s.68 application, unless the sheriff, on his own motion or on cause shown by a party, directs otherwise.[67] Safeguarders appointed by the sheriff in a s.68 application have the powers and duties at common law of a curator *ad litem* in respect of the child and are entitled to receive from the reporter copies of the application, all productions, and any papers which were before the children's hearing.[68] He or she must determine whether the child wishes to express views in relation to the application and, if the child does so wish, transmit these views to the sheriff; in addition he or she must make such enquiries so far as relevant to the application as he or she thinks appropriate.[69] The safeguarder is entitled to become a party to the

---

[62] s.16(1).

[63] s.34A of the Social Work (Scotland) Act 1968 permitted such an appointment only when there was a risk of a conflict of interests between the child and the parent.

[64] Under s.68(8).

[65] Under s.68(5).

[66] Under AS 1997, r.3.47(6).

[67] AS 1997, r.3.7(2).

[68] AS 1997, r.3.8.

[69] *ibid.*

proceedings and is obliged to intimate to the sheriff clerk without delay and in any event before the hearing of the application whether or not he or she intends to do so.[70] As a party, the safeguarder may appear personally in the proceedings or instruct an advocate or solicitor to appear on his or her behalf.[71] If the safeguarder does not become a party, he or she must report in writing to the sheriff on the extent of his or her enquiries and his or her conclusions as to the interests of the child.[72] Any report submitted to the sheriff is not evidence as to the existence or otherwise of a ground of referral, but it may be used by the sheriff as a "check on the view which he had formed on the evidence".[73]

The role and interest of the safeguarder appointed by a sheriff comes to an end at the termination of the proceedings before the sheriff, but there is nothing to prevent the chairman of the children's hearing who subsequently consider the child's case (if the grounds of referral are established) from permitting the safeguarder appointed by the sheriff to be present at the hearing, or to prevent the reporter circulating to all three members of the hearing any report the safeguarder has drawn up for the sheriff. If (but only if) the children's hearing appoint the sheriff's appointee as a safeguarder, then that safeguarder will have title to appeal against any decision made by the children's hearing.[74]

**Pleas to the competency of the application**

An application to the sheriff cannot be dismissed before the hearing of the evidence on the ground that it is irrelevant,[75] because the proceedings before the sheriff are designed not to establish guilt or innocence but to determine whether the child may be in need of compulsory measures of supervision; and it follows that technical rules designed to protect accused persons are not appropriate in s.68 applications. He can, however, disqualify himself from hearing evidence and put the case out for hearing before another sheriff if it is appropriate to do so to avoid, say, perceptions of bias.[76] The sheriff is normally obliged to hear the evidence tendered by or on behalf of the reporter[77] and if, after considering the evidence, he is of the view that the grounds of referral

---

[70] *ibid.*

[71] AS 1997, r.3.9(1). If the safeguarder is him or herself an advocate or solicitor, he or she must not also act as advocate or solicitor for the child: r.3.9(2).

[72] AS 1997, r.3.10(1). A safeguarder who intimated an intention not to become a party to the proceedings may subsequently seek leave to do so (r.3.10(3)) and if evidence has already been heard in part the sheriff may order the evidence to be reheard in whole or in part (r.3.47(8)).

[73] *Kennedy v M*, 1989 S.L.T. 687, *per* Lord Brand at 689D.

[74] See *Catto v Pearson*, 1990 S.L.T. (Sh. Ct.) 77 and comments thereupon, above at p.74. Safeguarders appointed by the sheriff do not have the right to appeal from decisions of the children's hearing: AS 1997, r.3.53(3) is expressly limited to appointees of the children's hearing.

[75] *McGregor v D*, 1977 S.L.T. 182, in which the child's solicitor had argued that the statement of fact did not amount to the crime allegedly committed by the child which the reporter sought to establish as a ground of referral.

[76] *F v Constanda*, 1999 S.L.T. 421.

[77] AS 1997, r.3.47(1). And see *Kennedy v B*, 1973 S.L.T. 38; *McGregor v D*, 1977 S.L.T. 182; *McGregor v D*, 1981 S.L.T. (Notes) 97; *Kennedy v S*, 1986 S.L.T. 679. The sheriff may dispense with hearing evidence under s.68(8).

have not been established, so he will hold.[78] Sometimes, however, the application can be dismissed on the ground of incompetency, although only when the incompetency is radical. An application which is not heard within 28 days of being lodged must, it is submitted, be dismissed by the sheriff as incompetent (and it is not open to the parties to agree that the proof should go ahead). So must an application that purports to be based on a need for compulsory measures of supervision without reference to any of the extant grounds of referral in s.52.[79] Applications which are made timeously and which are otherwise procedurally unchallengeable can be dismissed as incompetent even before evidence is led only when the incompetency cannot be put right and the sheriff would be unable, whatever the evidence, to hold the ground of referral established.[80] So in *Merrin v S*[81] a child under the age of eight was referred on the ground of having committed an offence, but no matter what the evidence presented, that particular child could not be guilty of any offence because he was below the age of criminal responsibility[82]: the sheriff was able, therefore, to dismiss the application as incompetent.[83] Similarly, if the sheriff has no jurisdiction, say because the child has never been in Scotland, then dismissal of the application as incompetent would be appropriate.[84]

## LEADING THE EVIDENCE

The onus lies with the reporter to lead evidence sufficient to persuade the sheriff that the grounds of referral have been established,[85] and the sheriff must hear the evidence tendered by or on behalf of the reporter.[86] Much of this evidence will already have been obtained by the reporter during the preliminary investigations that he or she is normally obliged to make.[87] In addition, once an application has been made to the sheriff, either in terms of s.68 or in terms of s.85,[88] the reporter is entitled to request any prosecutor[89] to supply him or her with any evidence lawfully

---

[78] See below at pp.112–113.

[79] *cf. McGregor v A*, 1982 S.L.T. 45.

[80] *Sloan v B*, 1991 S.L.T. 530, *per* Lord President Hope at 546E–G.

[81] 1987 S.L.T. 193.

[82] Criminal Procedure (Scotland) Act 1995, s.41.

[83] The fact that the child had performed acts which would have amounted to a criminal offence had they been performed by a person over the age of eight did not indicate that the child was in need of compulsory measures of supervision, because that need arises with child offenders due to their possessing *mens rea* which, given the age of this child, was necessarily entirely lacking.

[84] *Mitchell v S*, 2000 S.L.T. 524.

[85] *Ferguson v S*, 1992 S.C.L.R. 866.

[86] AS 1997, r.3.47(1).

[87] See further, above at pp.47–48.

[88] *i.e.* an application for proof of the grounds of referral or an application to review an earlier establishment of the grounds.

[89] Defined in s.307 of the Criminal Procedure (Scotland) Act 1995 as follows: " (b) for the purposes of summary proceedings, includes procurator fiscal, and any other person prosecuting in the public interest and complainer and any person duly authorised to represent or act for any public prosecutor". This definition applies for the purposes of s.53: s.53(7).

obtained in the course of, and held by the prosecutor in connection with, the investigation of a crime or suspected crime, whenever the evidence is such that it might assist the sheriff in determining the s.68 or s.85 application.[90] The evidence may relate to a crime or suspected crime committed by the child or against the child or by or against another member of the child's household. If such a request is made, the prosecutor is obliged to comply with it, unless he or she reasonably believes that it is necessary to retain the evidence for the purposes of the proceedings in respect of the crime, whether these proceedings have commenced or not.[91] In these circumstances, however, the prosecutor may nevertheless be able to comply with the reporter's request for co-operation, and such a request should be refused only when it is essential to the criminal proceedings that the evidence be retained by the prosecutor.[92]

Once evidence is in the reporter's possession, the leading of that evidence before the sheriff is not restricted or excluded on the basis that it would prejudice a fair trial of criminal charges arising from the same facts,[93] for there is no presumption that criminal proceedings take precedence over s.68 applications. The standard of proof required, in all cases except one, is the balance of probabilities, even when to establish the ground would require proof of the commission of a criminal offence (by a person other than the child referred)[94]: the statute imposes a higher standard only for the s.52(2)(i) ground, that is that the child has committed an offence, and this has been held to mean that the normal civil standard applies in all other cases.[95] If the grounds of referral are based on s.52(2)(i), then the sheriff must be satisfied beyond reasonable doubt that the grounds exist.[96] The sheriff does not, of course, make a finding of guilt, but holds, as with all the other grounds, that the facts indicate that grounds of referral exist and therefore that the child may be in need of compulsory measures of supervision. The only difference is that the sheriff must be satisfied of this to a greater degree of certainty than with the other grounds. With the other grounds, even when the sheriff is in no doubt whatsoever of their existence, the findings should not state that the reporter's case has been proved beyond reasonable doubt.[97]

The evidence is to be considered as at the date the sheriff sits and not as at the time of the original referral to the children's hearing. The

---

[90] s.53(4).

[91] s.53(4) and (5).

[92] The Lord Advocate may direct that in any specified case or class of cases any evidence lawfully obtained in the course of an investigation of a crime or suspected crime shall be supplied, without the need for a request under s.53(4), to the Principal Reporter: s.53(6).

[93] *Ferguson v P,* 1989 S.L.T. 681, *P v Kennedy,* 1995 S.L.T. 476.

[94] *i.e.* a ground under s.52(2)(d), (e), (f) or (g).

[95] *Harris v F,* 1991 S.L.T. 242; *B v Kennedy,* 1987 S.L.T. 765. See also *KA v Finland* Jan 14, 2003 at para.119.

[96] s.68(3)(b). See *Constanda v M,* 1997 S.L.T. 1396 where it was held that the reporter may not avoid the higher standard by using the same facts to found a different ground.

[97] *P v Kennedy,* 1995 S.L.T. 476 at 482E.

sheriff is therefore obliged to take account of any changes in the child's circumstances since then.[98]

In offence cases, once the reporter has led his or her evidence, the sheriff must decide whether that evidence is sufficient to establish the alleged grounds of referral, and he must give all the parties an opportunity to be heard on the question of whether the evidence is sufficient for that purpose.[99] If he thinks that the evidence is insufficient he must make a finding to that effect[1] and proceed in accordance with s.68(9).[2] If he thinks that the evidence tendered by the reporter is sufficient to establish the grounds of referral, then the child, the relevant person, and any safeguarder may give evidence and call witnesses with regard to the grounds of referral.[3]

### Rules of evidence

The proceedings, though essentially *sui generis* and governed by a self-contained code of procedure contained in the Act and the Rules,[4] will follow the normal principles of evidence in summary[5] civil proceedings,[6] except that the interests of the child are not to be thwarted by an over-rigid application of the rules of evidence or procedure.[7] But the interests of the child will always require that the truth be established and rules of evidence and procedure which are designed to achieve that end will be followed. So evidence will be led by the reporter, in the way that a pursuer in a civil suit would lead evidence, and his or her witnesses can be cross-examined by the other parties, and then re-examined. If the sheriff finds that a *prima facie* case has been established by the reporter, the child and relevant person and, if a party, the safeguarder can then call witnesses who in turn can be cross-examined by the reporter. The relevant person is both competent and compellable as a witness,[8] even when it is alleged that the relevant person has committed an offence against the child. The child, if of an age to be competent to give

---

[98] *Kennedy v B*, 1973 S.L.T. 38. See also *Harris v E*, 1989 S.L.T. 42 in which a change in the law was taken into account. A ground of referral was made out that the child had been the victim of a Sch.1 offence even although the offence was not scheduled at the time of its commission, but had become so by the date of the referral.

[99] AS 1997, r.3.47(2). This applies only to offence cases.

[1] AS 1997, r.3.47(3).

[2] See below at pp.112–113.

[3] AS 1997, r.3.47(4). The predecessor of this provision, r.8(2) of the Social Work (Sheriff Court Procedure Rules) 1971, imposed a positive obligation on the sheriff to tell the child, etc., that they may give evidence. Though the present provision is not worded in that way it would clearly be good practice for sheriffs to continue so to inform these parties—and it would of course be a procedural irregularity (and thus a ground of appeal) if a failure to do so effectively denied these parties the opportunity to lead evidence.

[4] *McGregor v D*, 1977 S.L.T. 182, *per* Lord President Emslie at 185.

[5] AS 1997, r.3.20.

[6] Even when the ground of referral is that the child has committed an offence: *McGregor v D*, 1977 S.L.T. 182.

[7] *W v Kennedy*, 1988 S.L.T. 583. See also *Kennedy v A*, 1986 S.L.T. 358, in which Lord Justice-Clerk Ross stated, at 362A–B, "The principles of natural justice must yield to the best interests of the child, and in any event the principles of natural justice cannot be invoked to produce a result which would be contrary to the clear provisions of a statutory instrument".

[8] *McGregor v T*, 1975 S.L.T. 76.

evidence,[9] will also be compellable, except that in a case in which the ground of referral is that the child has committed an offence the child will be neither compellable nor competent as a witness for the reporter.[10]

Except in cases in which the ground of referral is that the child has committed an offence,[11] the presentation of the evidence will be subject to the rules in the Civil Evidence (Scotland) Act 1988.[12] So the sheriff can find a fact proved if satisfied that there is sufficient evidence to do so, even although the evidence is not corroborated.[13] Uncorroborated evidence must, however, be credible and reliable before a sheriff is entitled to hold that it founds a ground of referral[14]; the practical result of this is that the reporter should always be in a position to lead corroborating evidence in case the primary witness turns out to be less reliable than expected. Indeed failure to lead corroborating evidence of a fact when that evidence is available might be material to whether the court is satisfied that the fact had been proved by the evidence led.[15] The sheriff is not entitled to hold that a child has committed a criminal offence on the basis of uncorroborated evidence, however credible, for the rule allowing uncorroborated evidence to be sufficient is expressly limited to s.68 applications other than those based on s.52(2)(i).[16]

The Civil Evidence (Scotland) Act 1988 also provides that evidence is not to be excluded solely on the basis that it is hearsay evidence,[17] and it follows that any party in a s.68 application can lead evidence of statements made which are not repeated or are even denied in court. This is particularly pertinent in relation to statements made by the child to social workers or investigators concerning how he or she has been treated. Evidence can be led that the child made a statement, for example that he or she has been abused, even when the child is unwilling to repeat the statement in court. Indeed, such evidence can be led even when it contradicts the evidence directly given by the child, and if more credible can be preferred by the sheriff.[18] It does not breach the "best evidence" rule[19] for the reporter to lead evidence that the child had

---

[9] See below at pp.109–110.

[10] Renton & Brown, *Criminal Procedure* at para.19.73 say that "there seems no reason why" the child should not be compellable and competent, but they give no authority for this and, since the Rehabilitation of Offenders Act 1974 applies to children found to have committed an offence, it would appear to be contrary both to natural justice and to the interests of the child to compel the child to give evidence against himself or herself.

[11] For which, see below at pp.108–109.

[12] "Civil proceedings" governed by the 1988 Act are defined in s.9 thereof to include s.68 applications except those based on s.52(2)(i), that the child has committed a criminal offence.

[13] Civil Evidence (Scotland) Act 1988, s.1.

[14] *M v Kennedy,* 1993 S.C.L.R. 69.

[15] *L v L,* 1996 S.L.T. 767; *McGowan v Lord Advocate,* 1972 S.C. 68.

[16] *F v Kennedy (No. 2),* 1993 S.L.T. 1284, *per* Lord Justice Clerk Ross at 1287.

[17] Civil Evidence (Scotland) Act 1988, s.2.

[18] *K v Kennedy,* 1993 S.L.T. 1281. Here the sheriff found a ground of referral, that the child had been subjected to a Sch.1 offence, established on the basis of evidence that she had made a statement to that effect, even although she retracted the statement and denied it in her own evidence.

[19] The normal rule in civil proceedings that a party must lead the best evidence available and that any other evidence cannot be led while better evidence is available: see Walker and Walker *Evidence* (2nd ed., by M. Ross, 2000) at para.20.1–20.2.

earlier made such a statement rather than calling the child to give direct evidence as a witness.[20] There may well be situations in which calling the child causes him or her harm or distress, and if the reporter feels able to establish the grounds of referral without calling the child, it is not incompetent for him or her to attempt to do so. Reporters do, however, have a difficult balance to strike between the short-term protection from distress that not calling the child might provide and the child's longer term interests which are always served by the proof of grounds of referral whenever such grounds exist.

It used to be thought that a qualification to the rule permitting hearsay evidence of what the child has said was that the child (or other person whose hearsay statements are being relied upon[21]) must be admissible as a witness, at the date of the proof hearing.[22] So the statements of a child who was too young to give any evidence could not be led as hearsay evidence.[23] The cases referred to were, however, overruled in the decision of a Court of Five Judges in *T v T*[24] where it was held that hearsay evidence may be led even when the maker of the statement would not have been an admissible witness.[25]

### Evidence in cases based on section 52(2)(i)

If the ground of referral is that the child has committed an offence, the rules in the Civil Evidence (Scotland) Act 1988 do not apply[26] and the normal rules concerning corroboration and hearsay evidence apply instead. How far these rules can be departed from in the interests of the child is open to some doubt. In *W v Kennedy*[27] it was held that the rule against hearsay (which then still applied in all civil proceedings) could not be used to frustrate the search for truth in a case which would now be governed by the 1988 Act; and it might be argued that the same principle should apply in a case today not governed by the 1988 Act (*i.e.* a case in which the ground of referral is that the child has committed an offence). In support of that it might be argued that one of the important principles underlying the Children (Scotland) Act 1995 is that alleged child offenders are to be treated in the same way as other children who may be in need of compulsory measures of supervision and that in all cases the purpose of a s.68 application is to identify whether that need might exist rather than to allocate blame. However, it is submitted that the better view is that the rules on corroboration and hearsay apply in s.68 applications based on s.52(2)(i) as they do in criminal trials. To hold otherwise would be inconsistent with the terms of the Civil Evidence (Scotland) Act 1988, which expressly exclude child offender cases from the rules contained therein. Also, proof being beyond reasonable doubt in child offender cases,[28] there is more of a need for corroboration and

---

[20] *F v Kennedy (No. 2)*, 1993 S.L.T. 1284.
[21] As in *Ferguson v S*, 1993 S.C.L.R. 712.
[22] *L v L* 1996 S.L.T. 767, *per* Lord Hamilton at 770H.
[23] *F v Kennedy (No. 1)*, 1993 S.L.T. 1277. See further, below at pp.109–110.
[24] 2000 S.L.T. 1442.
[25] *Per* Lord President Rodger at para.37.
[26] Civil Evidence (Scotland) Act 1988, s.9.
[27] 1988 S.L.T. 583.
[28] s.68(3)(b).

more of a need to avoid placing reliance on hearsay evidence. The reasoning in *W* v *Kennedy* should not be applied to child offender cases, for the court there was careful to emphasise that they were not laying down a rule that hearsay evidence is always admissible in s.68 applications, and they described the result in the case as only a "marginal relaxation" of the normal rule.[29] In addition, the fact that special rules relating to hearsay in child offender cases are now laid down by statute means that there is no room for arguing that any rules other than these can be applied. The Criminal Procedure (Scotland) Act 1995 sets down circumstances in which, in criminal proceedings, hearsay evidence will be admissible, and the phrase "criminal proceedings" is defined to include s.68 applications to find established a ground of referral under s.52(2)(i).[30] Under s.259(1) of the Criminal Procedure (Scotland) Act 1995, hearsay is admissible if the sheriff is satisfied that the maker of the statement is unavailable for reasons set out in s.259(2),[31] that the evidence would be admissible if the person were available, that the maker of the statement would have been a competent witness, and that there is documentary or oral evidence to the effect that the statement was made. Anyone causing the unavailability of a witness cannot lead hearsay evidence of statements the witness is alleged to have made[32]; evidence of the maker's credibility is competent[33]; notice in writing is normally needed if hearsay evidence is to be led.[34] In addition, s.260 permits the introduction of prior statements by a witness (but not the accused[35]) as evidence of any matter of which direct oral evidence by him would be admissible.

### Child witnesses

It frequently happens, and not only in cases involving Sch.1 offences, that the reporter or another party will wish to call the referred child as a witness. This raises the sometimes difficult question of the competency of the child to be a witness. Children, particularly younger children, are often too immature to understand the importance of being truthful while giving evidence. Reflecting the reality that different children acquire sufficient maturity at different times, the law of Scotland has never laid down a strict numerical age limit below which the child is considered incompetent as a witness. Each child must be judged individually, and a child is legally competent to be a witness whenever he or she is adjudged capable of telling the difference between truth and falsehood. The sheriff must therefore carry out a preliminary examination of the child, and if

---

[29] 1988 S.L.T. 583 at 586E.

[30] Criminal Procedure (Scotland) Act 1995, s.262(3).

[31] *i.e.* the person (a) is dead or unfit, (b) is outwith the UK, (c) cannot be found, (d) refuses to give evidence on the ground that it might incriminate him, or (e) having been called as a witness refuses to take the oath or to affirm or to accept an admonishment to tell the truth, or refuses to give evidence.

[32] s.259(3).

[33] s.259(4).

[34] s.259(5)–(7).

[35] s.261: this presumably includes the child referred.

that is inconclusive the sheriff may hear other evidence on the point,[36] to determine whether the child is mentally mature enough to understand the difference between telling the truth and telling lies[37]: if the sheriff is persuaded on the point the child must be admonished to tell the truth.[38] Though as a matter of logic and of function the distinction between the examination and the admonition is clear, there does not always have to be a strict temporal line between the two, so long as the different functions are borne in mind.[39] The sheriff cannot reserve judgment on the child's capacity to tell the difference between truth and falsehood until after the child has given evidence, for the very competency of the child to be called as a witness hangs on the question.[40] If the sheriff cannot determine whether the child knows the difference between telling the truth and telling lies, or he concludes that the child does not know the difference, that child is incompetent as a witness. But it does not follow from this that any hearsay evidence of the child's previous statements cannot be led: rather, the sheriff must use his common sense in deciding what weight to place on such evidence.[41] Indeed, if the intention of a party is only to rely on hearsay, it is not appropriate to subject a young child to a preliminary examination.

The general (but not universal) rule in Scots law is that a witness who is competent is also compellable. One important exception to that rule is that a person may not be called as a witness to give evidence against him- or herself. This would certainly apply in relation to a child for whom the ground of referral is that he or she has committed a criminal offence, notwithstanding the civil nature of the proceedings.[42] Another qualification to the general rules of evidence is found in ss.68A–68B of the 1995 Act,[43] which introduces restrictions on the types of questions that may be asked of a child in cases involving sexual abuse. These restrictions are not absolute and the sheriff may, at his discretion, permit the questioning for the proper administration of justice.

---

[36] It may be doubted whether the sheriff can make his judgment solely on the basis of other evidence without an examination of the child and the authorities suggest that other evidence can only supplement such an examination which cannot therefore be entirely dispensed with: see the authorities cited by Lord President Hope in *M v Kennedy*, 1993 S.C.L.R. 69 at 78C–E; *M v Ferguson*, 1994 S.C.L.R. 487, *per* Lord President Hope at 492C–D; *L v L*, 1996 S.L.T. 767, *per* Lord Hamilton at 772B. There are some difficulties with this approach, as explained by Sheldon in "Children's Evidence, Competency and the New Hearsay Provisions" 1997 S.L.T. (News) 1. See also *R v Walker*, 1999 S.L.T. 1233

[37] In exceptional circumstances, a sheriff is able to be so persuaded even when the child is unable to talk: see *M v Kennedy*, 1993 S.C.L.R. 69.

[38] *Rees v Lowe*, 1990 S.L.T. 507, *Kelly v Docherty*, 1991 S.L.T. 419.

[39] *R v Walker*, 1999 S.L.T. 1233, *per* Lord Prosser at 1236F.

[40] See *S v Kennedy*, 1996 S.C.L.R. 34, *per* Lord Justice-Clerk Ross at 40–41.

[41] *Per* Lord President Rodger in *T v T*, 2000 S.L.T. 1442 at para.38 (overruling *F v Kennedy (No 1)*, 1993 S.L.T. 1277).

[42] Though often said to be "civil proceedings *sui generis*", there are some criminal aspects, such as the Rehabilitation of Offenders Act 1974, and the rule against self-incrimination should be regarded as another such aspect. It is to be noted that the rule against self-incrimination, though not explicitly mentioned in Art.6 of the European Convention on Human Rights, has been recognised to lie at the heart of the notion of a fair procedure under Art.6: *Murray v United Kingdom* (1996) 22 E.H.R.R. 29; *Saunders v United Kingdom* (1996) 23 E.H.R.R. 313.

[43] As inserted by the Vulnerable Witnesses (Scotland) Act 2004 (asp. 3), s.23.

**Dispensing with the evidence**

The sheriff has the power to dispense with the hearing of evidence as to whether the ground is established and, instead of making a finding to that effect from the evidence, he is entitled to deem the ground to be established.[44] The sheriff is *obliged* to dispense with hearing evidence where the child and the relevant person who at the children's hearing denied the grounds of referral now accept them, for then there is no conflict for the sheriff to resolve; he *may* dispense with hearing evidence if the child could not or did not understand the explanation of the ground and the relevant person accepts the grounds, and it appears reasonable to the sheriff to dispense with hearing the evidence. In either case he may hear evidence if in all the circumstances of the case he is satisfied that evidence should be heard. This would be appropriate if, for example, the sheriff were not convinced that the child or the relevant person really understood what they were accepting, or were not convinced that the statement of facts is sufficient to found the grounds of referral, or were of the view that a risk existed that grounds were being accepted for ulterior motives.[45] The wording of s.68(8) does not permit the sheriff to dispense with the hearing of evidence and then hold the grounds not to be established.

The sheriff can make his determination to dispense with evidence at any time, whether before any evidence is led or while evidence is being led. A relevant person who denied grounds before the hearing may, for example, accept the grounds when it is explained by the sheriff what it is that is being accepted or when he or she realises that the evidence is incontrovertible. The decision whether to dispense with evidence or to hear it is a decision governed by the welfare principle in s.16(1). If the child could not or did not understand the explanation of the grounds of referral it may be reasonable to dispense with evidence when all the parties who can accept are accepting and there is no-one denying or disputing the grounds, though in fact this is a rather odd provision in that often nothing will have changed since the hearing which sent the matter to the sheriff: an application to the sheriff which ends in the grounds being found established without hearing any evidence will have amounted to a procedural delay with no obvious substantive benefit.

## THE SHERIFF'S DECISION

After having heard the evidence presented by all the parties, and having considered the closing submissions made by them, together with any safeguarder's report that has been submitted,[46] the sheriff must then

---

[44] s.68(8).

[45] It is not beyond the realms of imagination that an ill-intentioned mother could allege that her partner had sexually abused the child not to protect the child but to get rid of the partner from her life. If such an allegation is made and the child is too young to understand, the sheriff ought, it is submitted, never dispense with the evidence if all there is to suggest sexual or other abuse is the mother's acceptance of the grounds of referral. *cf. A v G,* 1996 S.C.L.R. 787.

[46] See *Kennedy v M,* 1989 S.L.T. 687.

decide whether or not the grounds of referral have been established. The Rules require that the sheriff give his decision orally at the conclusion of the hearing and he may at that time or within seven days thereafter issue a note of the reasons for his decision.[47] The decision is limited to the question of whether or not the grounds of referral have been made out. The sheriff is not entitled to go any further and he cannot, for example, express any view as to whether, and if so what, compulsory measures of supervision are required for the child, for that would be to usurp the function of the children's hearing, in whose remit such questions solely lie. Indeed, the sheriff is not entitled to indicate to the children's hearing factors in the case which he considers that they ought to take into account in their consideration of the case.[48] However, he is obliged to make findings on all the grounds that the reporter has attempted to prove established. It is not sufficient for the sheriff to hold one stated ground established and then send the case back to the children's hearing, for the hearing have a statutory obligation to consider all the established grounds.[49]

### Grounds found established

Where the sheriff has found the grounds of referral or any of them established, or has deemed them to be established under the terms of s.68(8), he is obliged to remit the case back to the reporter for the arranging of a children's hearing to consider the child's case under s.66.[50] In addition, if he is satisfied that the child's best interests require that he or she be kept in a place of safety or that there is reason to believe that the child will run away before the sitting of the children's hearing, the sheriff may issue an order requiring that the child be kept in a place of safety.[51] If the conditions for keeping the child in secure accommo-dation[52] are satisfied, the sheriff may attach to the order that the child be kept in a place of safety an authorisation to keep the child in secure accommodation: as with such authorisations granted by children's hear-ings, this does not require that the child be kept there, but authorises it if in addition the chief social work officer considers it necessary.[53]

### Grounds found not established

If the sheriff finds that none of the grounds of referral is established he must discharge the referral and release the child from any order, warrant or direction the child is subject to which relates to those grounds.[54] The sheriff has no option in this case and cannot, for example, find that other grounds than those relating to the application have been established.[55] If

---

[47] AS 1997, r.3.51.
[48] *Kennedy v A*, 1986 S.L.T. 358.
[49] *Harris v F*, 1991 S.L.T. 242 at 246F–G, *per* Lord Justice Clerk Ross.
[50] s.68(10)(a).
[51] s.68(10)(b). See further, below at pp.204–205.
[52] Specified in s.70(10).
[53] s.68(11).
[54] s.68(9).
[55] *cf.* the power of the sheriff in an application under s.85 to find established different grounds from those previously established and challenged in that application: see below at pp.182–183.

the evidence suggests the existence of other grounds the reporter may state these new grounds and arrange a children's hearing under s.65(1). If the sheriff finds that some of the grounds are not established and some are established he must remit the case back to the reporter in respect of the grounds that are established. In that case the children's hearing who consider the case must accept as fact that the grounds not established do not exist and cannot base their decision on them or take them into account in any way.

### Amending the grounds or statement of facts

In an early case, *McGregor v D*,[56] it was held that once the grounds have been put to the child and relevant persons, they could not thereafter be amended either by the reporter or by the sheriff. The rule now is that the sheriff may at any time, on the application of any party or of his own motion, allow amendment of any statement supporting the conditions of the grounds of referral.[57] In addition, it is provided that where in a ground of referral it is alleged that an offence has been committed by or against any child, the sheriff may find that any other offence established by the facts has been committed.[58] The sheriff should, however, be careful in exercising these powers to ensure that the grounds of referral found established do not indicate a case so substantially different from that which was originally put to the child and relevant person at the previous children's hearing that in effect a case has been found against them that they were not asked to answer. The power to amend a statement of fact does not, it is submitted, include the power to change the ground of referral the statement of facts is designed to support.

---

[56] 1977 S.L.T. 182. See also *S v Kennedy*, 1996 S.L.T. 1087.

[57] AS 1997, r.3.48.

[58] AS 1997, r.3.50. See *McGregor v D,* 1977 S.C. 330; S.L.T. 182 and *M v Kennedy,* 1996 S.L.T. 434 (on the similar rule contained in the Social Work (Sheriff Court Procedure Rules) 1971, r.10).

CHAPTER EIGHT

# CONSIDERATION OF THE CASE

## INTRODUCTION

The establishment of the grounds of referral, whether by the child and the relevant person accepting that they exist[1] or by the sheriff finding on the evidence that they exist,[2] or a court specifying them to exist[3] does no more than raise the question of whether compulsory measures of supervision are necessary in respect of the child,[4] and it neither answers that question nor indicates what protection, guidance, treatment or control the child might need. That determination lies in the hands of the children's hearing who, once the grounds of referral have been accepted or established, must move on to a consideration of those grounds, together with any report obtained from the local authority by the reporter, and any other relevant information available to them.[5] The two questions that are before the children's hearing at this stage in the proceedings are (i) whether the child is in need of compulsory measures of supervision and (ii) if so, what measures would best serve the child's needs.

Unless the hearing are going to consider the case in the absence of the child, any relevant person and any representative, the chairman must, before the hearing proceed to consider the case, explain the purpose of the hearing to such persons as are present.[6] This applies to all hearings and not just those at which the child's case is to be considered. Once that explanation has been given and the hearing are satisfied that, in general terms, it has been understood, the hearing can then move on to consider the case.

## DISCUSSING THE CHILD'S CASE

The consideration of the child's case takes the form of a discussion, led by the members of the hearing, with the child, the relevant persons who attend the hearing, any representative, legal representative, safeguarder, the social worker allocated to the case, and anyone else permitted to

---

[1] Under the Children (Scotland) Act 1995, s.65(5).
[2] On an application under either s.68 or s.85.
[3] Under s.54 of the 1995 Act or s.48 of the Criminal Procedure (Scotland) Act 1995.
[4] s.52(1).
[5] s.69(1).
[6] Children's Hearings (Scotland) Rules 1996, r.20(2) (disposal hearings) and r.22(2) (advice hearings).

attend by the chairman[7] who might be able to make a contribution to the determination of where the child's interests lie.[8] The reporter will not usually take part in the discussion, but it will sometimes be appropriate to ask the reporter questions, such as why he or she considered the case significant enough to bring before a children's hearing, or whether he or she holds any other information that might be relevant. As part of the discussion, the hearing must give consideration to the social background report submitted by the local authority, any judicial remit or other relevant document and any other relevant information available to them and any report submitted by the manager of any residential establishment in which the child is required to reside.[9]

This discussion is the central feature of the whole of the children's hearing system, and its aim is to allow the members of the hearing properly to determine wherein the child's interests lie, and properly to identify what is the best of the available options for the child's future. The principle underlying the system is that these matters can best be dealt with by an open discussion in which everyone present may take part and at which a consensus as to the best way forward for the child can emerge.

> "If there is informality in the procedure at hearings, it is manifested at the discussion stage when panel members must exercise very considerable skills in questioning and listening (and being aware of non-verbal communication signals). In meeting their legal obligations, the hearing must try to open up discussion with what may well be very reluctant family members: there is on-going concern about the 'silent child' phenomenon and the not uncommon problem of ascertaining what the child's view of the situation is".[10]

The child, if old enough, should be the central person in the discussion, though hearings must be sensitive to the fact that children attending hearings are likely to be apprehensive and nervous (which can sometimes come across as boorishness and bellicosity). While everyone who can make a contribution must be given the opportunity to do so, this should not be allowed to drown out the child's voice. There is an express statutory obligation[11] on the children's hearing to give the child an opportunity to indicate whether he or she wishes to express views, if he or she does so wish to give him or her an opportunity to express them and, taking account of the age and maturity of the child, to have regard to such views as he or she may express. The child should be strongly

---

[7] See above at pp.76–77.

[8] 1996 Rules, r.20(3) and r.22(3)(b) expressly require a discussion with the child, any relevant person, any safeguarder and any representative who attend the hearing.

[9] 1996 Rules, r.20(3)(a) and (b). At some point during the hearing the substance of these reports must be revealed by the chairman to the child and any relevant person if it appears to him or her that this is material to the manner in which the case should be disposed of and that its disclosure would not be detrimental to the interests of the child: r.20(4). The relevant person will, of course, have received copies of these reports under r.5(3) and the importance of r.20(4) is that it requires the substance to be revealed to the child. On whether the child receives reports, see p.59 above.

[10] *Stair Memorial Encyclopaedia of the Laws of Scotland,* vol.3 (1994), para.1344.

[11] s.16(2) and s.16(4)(a); 1996 Rules, r.15, r.20(3)(d) and r.22(3)(c).

encouraged to take a full part in the discussion but, at the end of the day, must be permitted to remain silent if he or she so wishes.[12] It is good practice to ask the child at various points throughout the discussion whether he or she agrees with what is being said about him or her by the surrounding adults and to give him or her an opportunity to comment. It is always courteous and usually helpful to allow every other person who attends in an active capacity a chance to say what they think, though it should be made plain that the discussion must be directed towards the child's interests, and the chairman of the hearing has the responsibility to ensure that the discussion is not diverted away from that topic. It frequently happens, for example, that members of the child's family attempt to revive old sources of dispute, or attempt to allocate blame for the problems which have arisen. These issues are usually entirely irrelevant to the task at hand. Or it may be that the grounds of referral are again denied: if so it should be made plain that while the grounds must be discussed, they will be treated as established fact at all times. Though consensus may be aimed at, this is, of course, not always achieved and the child and relevant person, or the social worker or the legal representative or the safeguarder, may radically disagree with some or all of the options that the hearing are considering. It should always be remembered that the sole decision-making power lies in the hands of the children's hearing, and the other participants in the discussion will sometimes need to be made aware that the discussion is designed to allow the three members of the children's hearing to make what they consider to be the best and most appropriate decision for the child.

**Extent of the discussion**

There was previously some dispute as to the extent to which the children's hearing could take account of matters not directly connected to the grounds of referral. In *K v Finlayson*[13] the sheriff held that the children's hearing could look no further than the facts established by the acceptance or establishment of the grounds of referral and that they could not, therefore, base their decision on other facts which came to their attention in the course of the hearing. This decision was, however, overruled by the First Division in the important case of *O v Rae*.[14] In this case, it was held that the children's hearing are entitled to take into account all relevant factors and that the test of relevancy of the hearing's consideration is whether the matter is relevant to the question of what course should be taken in the child's best interests.[15] The children's

---

[12] There is no obligation, however, on the chairman to indicate to the child that he or she has a " right to be silent", and it would normally be unhelpful to do so.

[13] 1974 S.L.T. (Sh. Ct.) 51.

[14] 1993 S.L.T. 570.

[15] *O v Rae*, 1993 S.L.T. 570, *per* Lord President Hope at 574. This case was followed in *M v Kennedy*, 1996 S.L.T. 434, in which the evidence was unclear as to whether the child had been the victim of an offence under s.3 of the Sexual Offences (Scotland) Act 1976 (sexual intercourse with a girl under the age of 13) or under s.4 thereof (sexual intercourse with a girl between the ages of 13 and 16). Because another ground of referral was established, the hearing were held entitled to take account of the undisputed fact that the girl had been subject to unlawful sexual intercourse, even although there was a dispute as to which particular crime she had been the victim of.

hearing are not, therefore, limited to a narrow consideration of the grounds alone but are entitled to ask for and consider information across a wide range and from a variety of different people.[16] The grounds upon which the child has been referred to the hearing are central to the discussion of the child's case, are always relevant, and must be considered,[17] but there may well be many other additional factors relevant to a determination of what, if any, measures of supervision are in the child's best interests. While the grounds of referral are central to the hearing's original consideration of the case,[18] they are not necessarily central to the disposal. A child may competently be subject to compulsory measures of supervision which would not be justified simply because of the existence of a ground of referral when there are other significant concerns that do justify them. Conversely, even the most serious and horrible offences against the child, such as his or her being shot at in a classroom and seriously wounded by a crazed gunman, or being kidnapped and raped by a stranger, might amount to a ground of referral but not go anywhere near justifying the imposition of compulsory measures of supervision. It is one of the strengths of the system that the existence of a ground of referral merely raises the question of whether compulsory measures of supervision are necessary[19] but does not determine their nature; it is that question that must be considered and answered by the children's hearing, and they are permitted to do so by having regard to any relevant matter that comes to their attention. The policy of the Act is clearly to leave the children's hearing free from artificial restraint in their exploration of what may be in the interests of the child.

An apparent anomaly resulting from this position is that the children's hearing might make their decision on the basis of alleged facts which are disputed by the child or relevant person and which have never been established by proof in a court of law. This raised concerns in *O v Rae*[20] in which a hearing took into account an unproven allegation of sexual abuse against her father made by a sibling of children referred on the basis of lack of parental care. It is, however, a misunderstanding of the system to assume that the children's hearing have no power to resolve disputes of fact.[21] The sheriff is empowered to resolve only disputes as to the existence of the grounds of referral (and any findings of fact made in the course of resolving such disputes must be accepted by the children's hearing[22]). However, disputes of fact can arise as to very many other circumstances, such as how often the child attends school, whether the parents have co-operated with social workers, or whether a parent's ex-

---

[16] *R, Petitioner*, 1993 S.L.T. 910, *per* Lord President Hope at 915C.

[17] At least at hearings when the grounds are being considered in order to determine whether or not to impose a supervision requirement: s.69(1). They are less important and may indeed be irrelevant to hearings at which a supervision requirement is being reviewed.

[18] They are "the hard core of the material upon which [the hearing's] decision is based", *per* Lord Justice-Clerk Grant in *Kennedy v B*, 1973 S.L.T. 38 at 40.

[19] s.52(1).

[20] 1993 S.L.T. 570. Mitchell described this as "the most fundamental flaw in our chidren's hearing system," 1997 Scolag 9 at p.11.

[21] See further, Norrie, "In Defence of *O v Rae*", 1995 S.L.T. (News) 353.

[22] *M v Kennedy*, 1993 S.L.T. 431.

cohabitant continues to have contact with the child. These issues may all significantly affect the outcome of a case, yet there is no mechanism to have them resolved by a court of law, and it rests with the children's hearing to resolve these disputes, by themselves assessing the credibility of statements which are not made on oath.[23] The theory underpinning this approach is that resolution of a dispute is less important than identifying the child's needs, and that if that identification requires dispute resolution, this is best achieved by a non-adversarial discussion in which every participant is able freely to express his or her view and is given an opportunity to challenge the views of the others. Many disputes are easily resolved by accepting the more credible story (*e.g.* when a teacher says that the child does not attend school and the child says that he or she does[24]); other disputes are entirely judgmental and therefore clearly rest with the hearing (such as, for example, whether the child has benefited from compulsory measures of supervision). Disputes of fact which might themselves amount to a ground of referral will, and should, normally be resolved by the reporter referring the child on the basis of new grounds which, if then denied, can be tested in court. Most other disputes of fact do not need to be resolved by the children's hearing, who are often entitled to take the very existence of a dispute as evidence of some problem that compulsory measures of supervision might be able to address. It is only in very rare cases that a disputed fact will clearly and fundamentally affect the outcome. In these cases, the children's hearing must make their judgment of credibility as best they can, and if their judgment is wrong this can be established on appeal to the sheriff, before whom evidence can be led on oath.[25] If the children's hearing are shown to have made a mistaken assessment of fact then their decision may be challenged as being not justified in all the circumstances of the case, and this ability for the system itself to be recalibrated protects it (and the case of *O v Rae*) from ECHR challenge.[26] The system would very rapidly break down if every dispute of fact that could influence the hearing's decision required that the hearing be brought to an end so that the matter could be sent off to the sheriff for resolution. A child ought not to be able to postpone a dispositive decision, for example in a case relating to school non-attendance, by denying that there is continued non-attendance since the date the grounds were established, even when that could amount to a new ground of referral.

**Discussing adoption**

One area of discussion that has for long caused problems is the local authority's plans for the adoption of the child. In *R. v Children's Hearing*

---

[23] A process not dissimilar from a court assessing the worth of hearsay evidence.

[24] This is not to suggest that any particular category of person, such as teachers, should always be believed by hearings. The present writer has had experience of a teacher at a special school denying a child's allegation that the teacher continually called him by a highly pejorative name—and finding the child more credible than the teacher.

[25] s.51(3). See further, below at pp.208–211.

[26] It may also be noted that the European Court has accepted that to take account of factors other than those which brought a party before a tribunal, in determining outcome, is not in itself an infringement of Art.6: *Engel v Netherlands* (1976) 1 E.H.R.R. 647 at para.90.

*for the Borders Region*[27] a children's hearing purported to exercise their power to specify the child's place of residence by ordering that the child "should reside in a preadoptive home chosen by the local authority". The Court of Session held that this was *ultra vires* of the children's hearing since a condition of residence must specify precisely where the child is to reside. In addition, the opinion was expressed, though *obiter*, that the challenged condition breached the statutory provision in the adoption legislation[28] prohibiting anyone other than an adoption agency from placing a child for adoption or making arrangements for the adoption of a child. Legislation quickly followed to reverse this opinion[29] and it is now provided[30] that the making under s.70 of the Children (Scotland) Act 1995 by a children's hearing of a supervision requirement which requires the child to reside at a particular place shall not constitute the making of arrangements for the adoption of a child. This means that a children's hearing can name as a child's residence the home of prospective adopters, knowing and intending that this will facilitate the adoption process in relation to that child.

However, there have been later sheriff court decisions[31] in which it has been held that while a children's hearing can require a child to reside with prospective adopters they cannot make any other decision which will facilitate adoption, and in particular they cannot terminate contact between the child and the genetic parent for any reason connected with the proposed adoption. The reasoning was that this would amount to "making arrangements" for adoption, which the amended legislation allows children's hearings to do only to the extent of requiring a child to live with prospective adopters. This approach would cause immense difficulties for hearings who, in the full knowledge of the adoption plans, would have to attempt to cast these plans from their minds and make a decision without reference to a factor vitally important in the child's future. It runs the severe risk of misrepresenting the true reasons for a decision if hearings are to skew their stated grounds for decision to avoid all mention of a factor which may have been uppermost in everyone's minds. And it is inconsistent with the proposition of the Inner House in *O v Rae*[32] that "any information which is relevant to the making of a supervision requirement . . . will be relevant information to which the children's hearing may have regard".

The assumption upon which the approach is predicated, that children's hearings must take a short-term view of the child's welfare, has never been correct, and there is no Court of Session authority for the proposition that a children's hearing is entitled or obliged to ignore important and influential facts. And indeed it is doubtful whether the sheriff court decisions mentioned above have survived (if they were ever

---

[27] 1984 S.L.T. 65.
[28] Now s.11(1) of the Adoption (Scotland) Act 1978.
[29] s.27 of the Law Reform (Miscellaneous Provisions) (Scotland) Act 1985.
[30] Adoption (Scotland) Act 1978, s.65(3).
[31] *A v Children's Hearing for Tayside Region*, 1987 S.L.T. (Sh. Ct.) 126, *M v Children's Hearing for Strathclyde Region*, 1988 S.C.L.R. 592. See also the sheriff's decision appealed against on other grounds in *Kennedy v M*, 1995 S.L.T. 717 (the issue was not discussed in the Inner House).
[32] 1993 S.L.T. 570 at 574.

good law) the passing of the Children (Scotland) Act 1995. Under
s.73(4), whenever the local authority intend to apply for a freeing order
or to place a child for adoption, or become aware of an adoption
application, they must refer the case of the child (if subject to a
supervision requirement) to the reporter for a review by the children's
hearing of that supervision requirement. The children's hearing must do
two things at this review: they must review the current supervision
requirement and they must draw up a report providing advice to the
court as to the proposed adoption.[33] It would be entirely unrealistic to
expect a children's hearing to ignore the adoption plans for the purposes
of the review and at the same time to give advice about these plans for
the purposes of the report to be sent to the court. Also, s.16(1) requires
the children's hearing to regard the welfare of the child *throughout his or
her childhood* as their paramount consideration, and this prevents them
from taking only a short-term view. It is submitted that a children's
hearing can and must take account of the local authority's plans for the
future of the child, even when these plans involve possible adoption, in
determining what terms and conditions should be attached to any
supervision requirement; and if they believe that adoption plans are best
for the child they can and must make whatever decision will, in their
view, further the child's best interests. It is only by doing so that the
children's hearing can fulfil their statutory obligation to give paramountcy to the welfare of the child throughout his or her childhood.

## MAKING THE DECISION

Once the hearing members have given consideration to all the issues that
they consider relevant, it is good practice for the chairman to inquire of
all those present whether there are any other issues that ought to be
raised. Then, after having given consideration, through discussion, to all
the circumstances of the child's case which have been put before them,
the children's hearing must make a decision of which of three options
most appropriately meets the child's needs. "The hearing should have
attempted to ascertain the family's views and discussed the range of
options on offer. The decision should not, therefore, come as a surprise
to anyone."[34] The hearing must do one or other of three things[35]: they
may decide to continue the case for further investigation on the basis
that they do not have enough information to come to a proper
decision[36]; they may decide to discharge the referral[37]; or they may
impose a supervision requirement on the child.[38]

Decisions are, as always, made on a majority basis,[39] and no decision
will have been made unless it attracts the support of at least two

---

[33] See below at pp.172–173.

[34] *Stair Memorial Encyclopaedia of the Laws of Scotland,* vol.3 (1994), para.1353.

[35] s.69(1) says that after considering the grounds and other information the hearing
"shall . . . " see p.282.

[36] s.69(2).

[37] s.69(12).

[38] s.70(1).

[39] Curiously, there is no statutory provision to this effect but it has been the universal
and accepted practice since the instigation of the children's hearing system in 1971.

members of the hearing. It is possible that each member of the hearing will decide upon a different one of the three possibilities listed, in which case no decision can be said to have been made. Unless one of the hearing members then wishes to reconsider his or her decision (which is competent if the chairman so permits), the only option is to continue the hearing: there is no provision for the hearing failing to come to a decision and such failure due to disagreement amounts, it is submitted, to an agreement that the hearing must be continued.

Making the decision is as much a part of the hearing as the consideration of the case, and it follows that those who have a right and a duty to attend the children's hearing (*i.e.* the child and the relevant person) must be present when the decision is being made.[40] The members of the children's hearing are not permitted to go into a closed session to discuss matters outwith the hearing or presence of the child and relevant person, though there is nothing to prevent them from discussing amongst themselves, in the presence of the child and relevant person, what the decision should be. It is not common practice for an individual member of the hearing to attempt to persuade his or her colleagues as to what the decision should be and while this would not be contrary to the terms of the statute or the Rules it is unlikely to prove terribly helpful. The three members of the hearing have an equal vote and are entitled to make their own decision without reference to the reasoning of their colleagues. Hearings should not be afraid of majority decisions rather than unanimous decisions, for they sometimes serve useful symbolic purposes for the child and the relevant person (as well as informative purposes for future hearings). It is one of the strengths of the system that there are three members of the hearing who may come from a very wide cross-section of the community and who may bring to the decision-making process very different perspectives and, indeed, attitudes. While the decision is that of the hearing as a whole, that decision is made up of the contributions of all three members.

### The overarching principles

The children's hearing are given statutory guidance as to how they should come to their decisions, in the form of a statement of three overarching principles, which must be given effect to in determining which option to choose. These are as follows.

First, the children's hearing must regard the child's welfare throughout his or her childhood as paramount.[41] This applies to all discretionary decisions made by the children's hearing concerning any matter with respect to a child, except that the hearing are entitled to make a decision which is not consistent with their affording paramountcy to the welfare of the child if such a decision is made for the purpose of protecting members of the public from serious harm (whether or not physical harm).[42] The principle does not apply to procedural or jurisdictional decisions, nor to matters of law.[43] The reference to the whole of the

---

[40] s.45(1)(a) confers upon the child and s.45(8)(a) confers upon the relevant person the right to be present "at all stages of the hearing".

[41] s.16(1).

[42] s.16(5).

[43] *S v Proudfoot*, 2002 S.L.T. 743.

child's childhood, an innovation in the 1995 Act, requires that children's hearings take a long-term view. Often it is difficult to predict what is in the child's interests beyond the immediate future, and the provision probably requires little more than that the hearing at least give consideration to the child's long-term future. Short-term gains are not, of course, to be dismissed as unimportant, especially since a child's perception of time-scale is very different from an adult's, but nor are long-term gains to be sacrificed for some immediate benefit. The balance is very difficult to strike correctly every time, and children's hearings are not to be criticised (nor their decisions overruled) if, with hindsight, it becomes obvious that a decision other than the one they have reached would have been preferable.

The second overarching principle governing the children's hearing's decision is that they must give the child an opportunity to indicate whether he or she wishes to express views, if he or she does so wish, to give him or her an opportunity to express these views, and to have regard so far as practicable to these views, taking account of the age and maturity of the child concerned.[44] Where the child has indicated that he or she wishes to express views the children's hearing may not make any decision unless an opportunity has been given for the views of the child to be obtained or heard.[45] The child's views may be conveyed to the children's hearing (a) by the child, or his or her representative, in person, (b) by the child in writing, on audio or video tape or through an interpreter, or (c) by any safeguarder appointed by the hearing.[46] It is presumed that a child of 12 years of age or more shall be of sufficient age and maturity to form a view.[47] These rules are to be applied whenever the children's hearing are considering whether to make, or are reviewing, a supervision requirement; when they are considering whether to grant or continue a warrant; when they are engaged in providing advice to a sheriff considering whether to continue a child protection order; and when they are drawing up a report for a court considering the adoption of the child.[48] Additionally, the 1996 Rules provide that they are to be applied where the children's hearing are considering whether to continue a child protection order, are considering whether to require the child to undergo assessment and are considering whether to issue a warrant under the Secure Accommodation (Scotland) Regulations 1996.[49]

The third overarching principle is that the children's hearing may not make an order imposing or continuing a supervision requirement or granting or continuing a warrant unless they consider that it would be

---

[44] s.16(2) and 1996 Rules, r.15(1).

[45] 1996 Rules, r.15(3).

[46] 1996 Rules, r.15(4).

[47] s.16(2) and 1996 Rules, r.15(5). It must not, however, be taken from this that a child under the age of 12 years is presumed insufficiently mature. Such presumptions, which may have some place in court proceedings, are inappropriate within the context of the children's hearing where each child is dealt with as an individual and the part they are to play in the discussion depending upon the hearing's own assessment of the child's capabilities.

[48] s.16(4)(a).

[49] 1996 Rules, r.15(2).

better for the child to do so than to make no such requirement or order at all.[50] This is the "minimum intervention principle". It is based on the premise that the state should get involved in the upbringing of children only when this is necessary, and that if it does get so involved it should do so only to the minimum extent necessary to achieve the desired purpose.[51] To apply this principle to the children's hearing would suggest that they should start off with the presumption that no supervision requirement will be made or continued, and that the onus is on those seeking the imposition or continuation of such a requirement to persuade the hearing that this is necessary. However, to analyse the principle in terms of onus of proof does not sit easily with the children's hearing system since no proof is led before the hearing, and the principle probably amounts, in this case, to little more than an injunction on children's hearings not to impose or continue a supervision requirement unless in the course of the discussion they have come to be of the view that it is likely to do more good than not imposing or continuing such a requirement.

The terminology of "minimum intervention" has been criticised.[52] However, this terminology captures, it is submitted, the flavour of the "proportionality" principle of ECHR law.[53] In essence this requires that an interference in the Art.8 right to family life (which any supervision requirement, or continuation thereof, involves) is proportionate to the legitimate aim it is designed to achieve, in the sense that it goes no further than is required for the achievement of that aim. The legitimate aim is easy to identify: making the child's life better. More difficult is ensuring that the means adopted to achieve that aim do not interfere any further than is necessary with the child's—and the parents'—right to family life. Clearly the more serious the grounds of referral the more serious the interference might be, but it is to be remembered that proportionality must exist between the child's needs (the legitimate aim) and the outcome, rather than between the grounds and the outcome. So even very minor grounds may justify a serious outcome if that is the only way—and the minimal way—to achieve the identified goal. The minimum intervention principle and the proportionality principle coalesce within the idea that the action of the state must be "necessary", which thus takes on a double meaning: a supervision requirement, or a warrant, or any other order over a child that interferes with his or her private or family life must be necessary in the domestic sense of being better for the child than not making the order, and it must be necessary in the ECHR sense of being a proportionate response to the child's needs: this is, however, a single rather than a double hurdle and in many respects is different ways of saying the same thing.

## STATING THE DECISION

The final stage in the proceedings at a children's hearing is the announcement by the chairman of the decision that the hearing make,

---

[50] s.16(3).

[51] The first leg of the principle as given here follows from the words of the Act, the second leg from its spirit.

[52] See Kearney, *Children's Hearings and the Sheriff Court* (2nd ed., 2000) at paras 2.20 and 25.12.

[53] See pp.4–5 above.

plus the reasons for that decision.[54] How the decision is announced is a matter for the chairman to determine, but the common practice is to invite each member of the hearing to state his or her decision and reasons, and for the chairman to sum up the conclusion of all three and to explain the meaning and effect of the decision to the child and relevant person. It is good practice to inquire whether the child and relevant person understand the decision and whether they want to ask anything about it. They must then be informed of their right of appeal and, where the appeal is against a decision imposing, varying or continuing a supervision requirement, of their right to apply to the children's hearing for a suspension of the requirement pending the appeal.[55] It is good practice for the chairman also to explain to the child and the relevant person the nature of the supervision requirement, how long it will last and when it might be reviewed. These explanations bring the hearing to an end.

At the conclusion of the children's hearing the chairman must write or cause to be written[56] a statement of the reasons for the decision to which the hearing have come.[57] This statement is necessary for the purpose of maintaining an accurate record of what has been decided, and also of explaining what has been done. Those affected by the decision are entitled to an explanation of the basis on which it has been reached.[58] The statement should therefore be a clear statement of the material considerations to which the children's hearing had regard in their decision and it must be intelligible to the persons to whom it is addressed—including those who were not present at the hearing—and it must deal with all the substantial questions which were the subject of the decision.[59] The decision is that of the hearing as a whole, even when made on the basis of a majority. There is no requirement that it be noted that the decision was a majority decision, but nor is there any prohibition on the chairman doing so and if the decision of the majority is to make or continue a supervision requirement it is often helpful to the subsequent review hearing to know that there was a dissent, and why. It is good practice for the chairman to consult with the other members of the hearing and, sometimes, the reporter as to how to present the statement of reasons, though the responsibility for doing so remains that of the chairman alone.[60]

---

[54] 1996 Rules, r.20(5) (disposal hearings) and r.22(5) (advice hearings).

[55] 1996 Rules, r.20(5)(c).

[56] There is no limitation on who the chairman might delegate the task of writing reasons to, but it is submitted that it is bad practice to delegate that task to anyone other than another member of the hearing.

[57] 1996 Rules, r.10(5).

[58] *per* Lord President Hope in *DH & JH v Kennedy,* December 20, 1991, unreported.

[59] *per* Lord President Hope in *Kennedy v M,* 1995 S.L.T. 717 at 723H, citing his own comments in *DH & JH v Kennedy,* December 20, 1991 unreported. A failure to make the reasons intelligible is a ground of appeal to the sheriff: see for example *D v Strathclyde Regional Council,* 1991 S.C.L.R. 185. And see also *H v Kennedy,* 1999 S.C.L.R. 961.

[60] It is suggested that it is also good practice for reasons to be written immediately the hearing is ended and not to delay until all the hearings in a particular session have been concluded. It is better that the next case suffers a short delay than that the reasons in the present case be put to the back of hearing members' minds, hopefully to be recalled

In terms of the Rules[61] the obligation to write a statement of the reasons applies only when some dispositive decision is being made, secure authorisation is being given, or a decision relating to a warrant is being made[62] : there is no statutory obligation to write reasons when the hearing is continued or when the reporter is directed to apply to the sheriff for a finding as to whether the grounds of referral are established.[63] However, it is universal, and good, practice for reasons to be written at the end of every hearing, no matter the outcome. It is good discipline for panel members and it assists both families and later hearings in understanding why the case has taken a particular procedural turn.

### NOTIFICATION OF THE DECISION

As soon as reasonably practicable after the children's hearing have made a decision disposing of the case,[64] the reporter must send to the child, any relevant person, any safeguarder and the local authority, the following:[65]

(a) notice of the decision and a copy of any supervision requirement or continuation thereof;

(b) a copy of the statement of reasons for the decision; and

(c) notice of the right to appeal.[66]

These notices must be in writing.[67] In addition, notice of a decision disposing of a case must be sent to any person with whom the child is residing[68] and, if the original information came from the police, to the

---

accurately after the next case. Some panel areas in Scotland avoid this completely by writing reasons while the child and relevant persons are still present and then reading them back. This is generally a good practice, so long as the family are made aware that it is not an opportunity to reopen the discussion or challenge any decision the hearing members have made.

[61] 1996 Rules, r.10(5).

[62] In addition, if a safeguarder is appointed, reasons for that decision must be stated: s.41(3) and r.14(1).

[63] The technical reason for this is that reasons are needed only for appealable decisions, while continuations and applications to the sheriff are not: see further, below at pp.211–213.

[64] In its terms this rule applies only to hearings which dispose of the case (and from which, therefore, an appeal can be taken). It will be good practice, however, for reporters to send details of procedural decisions, together with the statement of reasons which will invariably (though not compulsorily) have been drawn up in respect of those decisions.

[65] 1996 Rules, r.21(1).

[66] Unless the right to appeal has been limited by s.51(7) (frivolous appeals). And of course this notice should not be sent in relation to non-dispositive decisions (which are not appealable).

[67] On receipt of notice by a local authority, they must give to any person responsible for the child in terms of the supervision requirement a copy of any social background report that would assist that person in the care and supervision of the child, together with any information that will so assist that person: Children's Hearings (Transmission of Information etc.) (Scotland) Regulations 1996, reg.3.

[68] Taken literally, this means any person living in the same house (or possibly household) as the child and would include the child's siblings. It is probably intended to be limited to persons who have some responsibility for the care and well-being of the child.

chief constable of the appropriate police area.[69] If the decision was to make a supervision requirement in relation to a person over 16 or to terminate a supervision requirement over a person over 16, the reporter must give notice of that fact to the chief constable of the area where the child resides.[70]

---

[69] 1996 Rules, r.21(2).
[70] 1996 Rules, r.21(3).

## Chapter Nine

# DISPOSAL OF THE REFERRAL

## Introduction

Having considered the case in accordance with the rules and procedures discussed in the previous chapter, there are four decisions that are open to a children's hearing to make: they may (i) transfer the case to a children's hearing in a different local authority area, (ii) continue the case, (iii) discharge the referral, or (iv) make or continue (with or without variation) a supervision requirement.

## Transferring the Case

If the children's hearing are satisfied that the case they are hearing could be better considered by a children's hearing in a different local authority area, they may request the reporter to arrange for such a children's hearing to dispose of the case.[1] This can be done at any time during the course of the hearing, and the request will bring the hearing to an end. At the subsequent hearing arranged in the different local authority area any accepted or established grounds of referral do not need to be accepted or established again.[2] Transfer will be appropriate when the child is ordinarily resident in the area of a different local authority and when, therefore, the resources of that local authority will require to be called upon if the child is to be subjected to compulsory measures of supervision. For a children's hearing in making a supervision requirement can thereby impose obligations only on the local authority for whose area the children's panel from which the children's hearing which imposed the supervision requirement was formed.[3] So, for example, if a children's hearing for the City of Glasgow impose a supervision requirement upon a child before it, it will be the City of Glasgow Council which has the obligation to give effect to it[4]; but if the child lives outwith the City of Glasgow it may be practically impossible for that local authority to fulfil its obligations. In these circumstances it would invariably be better for the child's case to be transferred to a children's hearing elsewhere.

## Continuing the Hearing

Of the three options other than transfer available to the children's hearing after the discussion of the child's case, two are dispositive (*i.e.*

---

[1] Children (Scotland) Act 1995, s.48(1).
[2] s.48(2).
[3] s.93(1): definition of "relevant local authority".
[4] s.71(1).

they dispose of the referral one way or the other) and are appealable, and one, continuation, is not dispositive and therefore not appealable.[5] The hearing's consideration of the case is completed only when the members are in a position to make a decision as to what course of action is in the best interests of the child. It follows that a continuation is the proper course when the children's hearing are not in possession of sufficient information, and cannot obtain that information in the course of the current hearing, to make a dispositive decision. A continuation is appropriate, therefore, when the children's hearing are satisfied that in order to complete their consideration of the child's case, it is necessary to have further investigation of that case.[6] It is not laid down how long the continuation is to be for and the children's hearing have no power to specify the date on which the continued hearing is to sit. It rests with the reporter to arrange a continued hearing at a date sufficiently distant in time to allow the further investigations which have been identified as necessary to be carried out, but sufficiently close to the original hearing that the child is not left in limbo longer than is necessary. It should, in addition, be remembered that the requirements and warrants that can be made or granted by a hearing who choose the option of continuation[7] do have strict time-limits attached. A continued hearing can, again, continue the hearing and indeed there is no limit on the number of times this can be done (though the longer the delay in making a dispositive decision, the more likely it is that the child's interests will be prejudiced).

Hearings who continue a case ought to be clear, and ought to specify in their statement of reasons, why they consider that further investigations are necessary and what it is that is hoped to be learned in the course of these investigations. Continuation might be considered appropriate, for example:

- because a particular report has not been completed in time, or
- because the hearing has been convened on an emergency basis after a warrant has been implemented or surrendered to and the members of the hearing are not in possession of, or have not had time to digest, the various reports, or
- because an in-depth residential or community-based assessment is considered essential in order to identify the child's needs or the source of his or her difficulties, or
- because the accuracy of a report is being challenged and the hearing feel that further investigation is necessary to help them resolve a consequent dispute of fact, or
- because a particular resource which the members of the hearing consider might be appropriate has not been investigated and considered by the local authority, or
- because it is felt that a safeguarder might be able to identify significant features of the child's case that the social background report from the local authority has been unable to investigate or will be able to comment on the desirability of

---

[5] See below at pp.211–213.
[6] s.69(2).
[7] See below at pp.197–199.

increasing or decreasing contact between the child and another person or the efficacy of some other condition that the hearing are minded to attach to the supervision requirement, or

- because it is felt that the child is unable to contribute to the discussion properly, or secure accommodation is under active consideration, and a legal representative is therefore required to be appointed to the child.

Continuation is not appropriate when the hearing are of the view that, whatever the further investigation shows, the dispositive decision is likely to be the same (except where, for due process reasons, a legal representative requires to be appointed[8]), nor when the members of the hearing simply cannot make up their minds. The decision to continue should be made only when the children's hearing feel either that they do not have enough information to make a proper decision in the child's interests, or that some other piece of information might change the decision they would otherwise be inclined to make. Nor are continuations appropriate simply in order to see whether things will improve in the child's life (*e.g.* to see whether he or she can keep out of trouble with the police or can attend school on a regular basis, or to see whether the child's parents can look after the child properly). A referral, once made, should not be used as a sword of Damocles hanging over the child: children appreciate, above all else, certainty and security and such continuing uncertainty is invariably against any child's welfare. If there is a fear that short-term improvements in the child's position might not be long-lasting, the correct approach, it is submitted, is to make or continue a supervision requirement but to set an early review date under s.70(7).[9]

### Warrants on continuation

Whenever a children's hearing decide to continue the case for further investigation, with or without a requirement on the child to attend or reside at a clinic, hospital or other establishment, that hearing can grant a warrant requiring the child to be taken to, and kept in, a place of safety until the subsequent hearing begins or, if earlier, the expiry of 22 days.[10] This type of warrant is discussed more fully in Chapter 13.[11]

### Requirement to attend a clinic or hospital

A children's hearing who continue a case under s.69(2) may require the child to attend or reside at a clinic, hospital or other establishment during a period of not more than 22 days.[12] As explained above, continuation will be appropriate when further information is required and such a requirement can be made only for the purpose of gathering

---

[8] And it should never be thought that this appointment is procedural only. A hearing that appoints a legal representative may well be of the view that only one outcome is likely but the very existence of a legal representative may well allow them to consider other options.

[9] For which, see below at p.142.

[10] s.69(7) and (8).

[11] At pp.197–199.

[12] s.69(3).

this information. A child may, for example, be required to reside in an assessment centre, or to attend an educational psychologist, or even to undergo medical examination during the period of continuation, in order to give the continued hearing a fuller picture of his or her circumstances and needs. Before making such a requirement, the children's hearing must give the child the opportunity to express views on the question of whether the requirement should be made, and must take appropriate account of any views expressed; the requirement may not be made unless such an opportunity has been given.[13]

A requirement made under s.69(3) does not have the effect of a warrant, with the result that the child has significantly more freedom of movement than a child required to reside in the same place and for the same purpose under a warrant granted under s.69(4).[14] Nor does such a requirement take away the child's right to consent or refuse consent to any medical, surgical or dental procedure or treatment granted by s.2(4) of the Age of Legal Capacity (Scotland) Act 1991 to persons under the age of 16 who understand the nature and consequences of the procedure or treatment.[15] When the child is required to reside somewhere then he or she cannot be kept there for longer than the period of 22 days, which starts running on the day the investigation commences. This will usually be the day of the hearing which continues the case but if a place at, say, an assessment centre is not available immediately, the 22 days will start running the day the child first resides there. There is no requirement that the 22 days be consecutive. If the requirement is that the child attend at a clinic or hospital for assessment then the period of 22 days starts running when the child first attends and not the date of the hearing which imposed the requirement. This means that if an appointment (say, with an educational psychologist) cannot be had until 20 days after the hearing, the child can be required to attend for another appointment up to 22 days after the first appointment, but cannot be required to attend thereafter. Though the statute could have expressed the matter more clearly, the requirement to attend does not, it is submitted, amount to a requirement to attend up to 22 times of less than a day each with no limitation on the period between the dates of attendance.

If a child fails to attend or reside for investigation as required under s.69(3), a warrant may be granted under s.69(4) by the children's hearing, with or without an application to that effect by the reporter. Details of this type of warrant are given in Chapter 13.[16]

DISCHARGING THE REFERRAL

A children's hearing can make a supervision requirement under s.70 only when they are satisfied that compulsory measures of supervision are necessary in the interests of the child. If, after a sufficient consideration

---

[13] 1996 Rules, r.15.
[14] For which, see below at pp.198–199.
[15] s.90.
[16] At pp.198–199.

of the child's case, the grounds and the reports, and being guided in that consideration by the three overarching principles in s.16, they are not so satisfied their decision must be to make no supervision requirement and they are obliged to discharge the referral.[17]

The power to discharge the referral, even when grounds of referral exist, is important in emphasising that it is the children's hearing alone who decide, once a case has been referred to them, whether a child is in need of compulsory measures of supervision, and that such need is not conclusively proved by the mere establishment of the grounds of referral. There are many circumstances in which it might be considered appropriate to discharge a referral. The discussion when the grounds are being considered might have indicated to the members of the hearing that the event which led to the referral (*e.g.* an incident of petty theft) is unlikely to be repeated. Or the problem that led to the referral may have resolved itself (*e.g.* school attendance may no longer be a problem due to the removal from the school of a bully or because the child has lawfully left school). Or the threat to the child's well-being may have been removed from the child's environment (*e.g.* by the imprisonment of an abuser or the departure of an anti-educationalist). Or the hearing may consider that the grounds of referral are simply not serious enough to raise any real concerns for the welfare of the child, or that compulsory measures of supervision simply have nothing to offer the particular child. In a case in which members of the hearing are thinking of discharging the referral without imposing any compulsory measures of supervision, it will usually be good practice to inquire of the reporter why he or she referred the case to the hearing, for the reporter will previously have investigated the case and made a positive decision that the circumstances merited the imposition of compulsory measures of supervision.[18] The reporter's original concerns are always worth taking into account.

### Effect of discharge

When a referral is discharged, all warrants to find and keep the child, orders as to assessments and investigations, directions as to contact, and any other order or requirement made under ss.39—85 of the 1995 Act in respect of the case based on the referral that is discharged, will cease to have effect.[19] If the ground of referral was that the child had committed an offence, the discharge of the referral will entitle the child to a six-month rehabilitation period[20] rather than the normal period of a year when a supervision requirement is imposed.[21] The period runs from the date of the acceptance or establishment of the ground of referral.[22] A

---

[17] s.69(1)(c) and s.69(12).

[18] The reporter must arrange a children's hearing under s.56(4) whenever it appears to him or her that compulsory measures of supervision *are* necessary, and a decision of the children's hearing to discharge is, therefore, a decision to disagree with the reporter.

[19] s.69(13).

[20] Rehabilitation of Offenders Act 1974, s.5(3). After rehabilitation the child need not reveal the offence, except in the specified exceptions.

[21] 1974 Act, s.5(5)(f): see below at pp.132–133.

[22] Rehabilitation of Offenders Act 1974, s.3. It is submitted that "acceptance" refers to acceptance by the child, for otherwise the accepting child might have to wait longer for rehabilitation if his or her parent denies the grounds and they are subsequently established before the sheriff.

reporter cannot found upon the same facts as the sole or primary basis of a new ground of referral after an earlier referral has been discharged since this would, in effect, be the reporter seeking a review of a children's hearing's decision, which he or she has no legitimate interest to do. However, the facts of a previous referral can be used as part of the statement of facts with which the reporter seeks to establish new grounds, so long as there is sufficient new material to suggest that there is, in essence, a new case for the subsequent children's hearing to consider.[23]

### MAKING A SUPERVISION REQUIREMENT

If, after considering the case, the children's hearing are of the view that compulsory measures of supervision are necessary in the interests of the child, they may make a supervision requirement.[24] The wording of the statute is to be noted. If compulsory measures of supervision are deemed "necessary", the hearing "may" make a supervision requirement. There are no compulsory measures available to the children's hearing other than a supervision requirement, and the use of the permissive "may" as a response to a determination that compulsory measures of supervision are "necessary" might appear odd at first sight. However, this terminology allows the children's hearing to decide not to impose a supervision requirement in circumstances in which, even although such a requirement is considered "necessary" they are of the opinion that it will not, in fact, succeed in achieving any good (for example in the case of a child nearing 16 who refuses to co-operate with any help offered). Compulsory measures of supervision are necessary when the hearing are of the view that the child would not receive, or would not accept, protection, guidance, treatment or control without the imposition of the supervision requirement. If the local authority offer appropriate help and the child is willing to receive it, supervision will seldom need to be compulsory.

The Social Work (Scotland) Act 1968 contained a provision permitting the children's hearing to postpone the operation of a supervision requirement,[25] though the power was very seldom used. The 1995 Act contains no such provision, and though the hearing's powers to attach conditions to a supervision requirement[26] are wide, the wording of the relevant section[27] is inept to include a condition as to when the supervision requirement is to come into effect. It is submitted, therefore, that a supervision requirement in all cases comes into effect immediately at the end of the hearing that imposes it.

When the ground of referral is that the child has committed an offence, the period of rehabilitation[28] under the Rehabilitation of

---

[23] And rehabilitation under the Rehabilitation of Offenders Act 1974 does not prevent the hearing referring to or discussing, or the reporter using, a ground which founded a discharged referral even more than six months later: 1974 Act, s.7(2)(cc). See further, Kearney *Children's Hearings and the Sheriff Court* (2nd ed., 2000) at para.25.20.

[24] s.70(1).

[25] Social Work (Scotland) Act 1968, s.44(3).

[26] See below at pp.136–137.

[27] 1995 Act, s.70(3)(b).

[28] Rehabilitation means that the child does not have to reveal the offence, except in specified exceptions. See the Rehabilitation of Offenders Act 1974 (Exclusions and Exceptions) (Scotland) Order 2003 SSI 2003/231.

Offenders Act 1974 is one year from the date of the acceptance or establishment of the grounds of referral or, if longer, the period beginning with that date and ending when the supervision requirement ceases or ceased to have effect.[29] Most children will be rehabilitated, therefore, as soon as their supervision requirements are terminated.

### Requiring the child to reside in a specified place

There is no distinction, as there was under the previous law, between what used to be called a "residential" and a "non-residential supervision requirement", and the supervision requirement made under s.70(1) may or may not require the child to reside at a specified place or at specified places.[30] So the hearing might require the child to reside in a residential establishment, or with foster carers,[31] or with relatives, or with one parent, or in any other place deemed to be in the best interests of the child. Any such requirement supersedes, during its currency, any other court order regulating the child's residence (such as an order under s.11 of the Children (Scotland) Act 1995) to the extent that the requirement is inconsistent with the court order[32]; likewise it necessarily supersedes any general right of a parent to determine the child's residence under s.2 of the 1995 Act, or it temporarily prevents the exercise of such rights.[33] It is an important principle of human rights law that any requirement on the child to reside outwith the family home ought normally to be regarded as a temporary measure, to be discontinued as soon as circumstances permit, and any measures implementing such a requirement should be consistent with the ultimate aim of reuniting the relevant person and the child.[34]

If the children's hearing make a supervision requirement with a requirement that the child reside somewhere, that place must be expressly named. The requirement cannot be to the effect that the child is to reside, say, "otherwise than with the parents", or "in an establishment chosen by the local authority", or "with foster carers selected by the local authority".[35] If the specified place requires that the child will be under the charge of someone who is not a relevant person, the children's hearing must first receive and consider a social background report with recommendations from the local authority on the needs of the child and the suitability to meet those needs of the place to be named and the person to be in charge of the child; in addition, the local authority must confirm that the rules contained in the Fostering of Children (Scotland)

---

[29] Rehabilitation of Offenders Act 1974, s.5(5)(f). The incompatibility between this Act and the philosophy underpinning the hearing system is explored in *Stair Memorial Encyclopaedia of the Laws of Scotland*, vol.3 (1994), para.1337.

[30] s.70(3)(a).

[31] As in, for example, *Kennedy v H*, 1988 S.L.T. 586, *Catto v Pearson*, 1990 S.L.T. (Sh. Ct.) 77, *M v Kennedy*, 1993 S.L.T. 431, and *Kennedy v M*, 1995 S.L.T. 717.

[32] *Aitken v Aitken*, 1978 S.L.T. 183; *P v P*, 2000 S.L.T. 781.

[33] *ibid., per* Lord President Emslie at 185. The supervision requirement does not, however, make it incompetent for a court to make a residence order whose effect will be suspended until the residence requirement in the supervision requirement is terminated: *W v Glasgow Corporation*, 1974 S.L.T. (Notes) 5. See also s.3(4) of the 1995 Act.

[34] *Johansen v Norway* (1997) 23 E.H.R.R. 33 at para.78.

[35] *R v Children's Hearing for Borders Region*, 1984 S.L.T. 65.

Regulations 1996 have been adhered to.[36] A supervision requirement that specifies the place of residence of the child may specify a place in England or Wales, and if it does specify a place in England or Wales, it shall be authority for the person in charge of that place to restrict the child's liberty to such extent as is appropriate given the terms of the supervision requirement. [37]

If the child is required to reside in accommodation other than that provided by a local authority, the local authority must from time to time investigate whether, while the child is so resident, any conditions imposed by the supervision requirement are being fulfilled, and they must take such steps as they consider reasonable if they find that these conditions are not being fulfilled.[38] If the child is required to reside with a named individual who does not have parental responsibilities and parental rights in relation to the child, that individual will be obliged to do what is reasonable in all the circumstances to safeguard the child's health, development and welfare and in fulfilling that obligation will be entitled to consent to any surgical, medical or dental treatment or procedure.[39]

The power of the children's hearing to specify a place for the child's residence is unlimited, except in so far as the Fostering of Children (Scotland) Regulations 1996 must be satisfied. It is, however, almost certainly incompetent to require a child to reside outwith the United Kingdom as a condition in a supervision requirement, for there would be no way that the appropriate local authority could carry out their supervisory duties under s.71.[40] A requirement to reside in a residential establishment will normally be made only when the hearing are informed that there is a place for the child in such an establishment, but there is no prohibition on the hearing naming an establishment even in the absence of such a place. The hearing must make their decision in the child's best interests, and while that in practice will normally mean the best that is actually available to the child there is sometimes merit in making a decision knowing that the residential condition cannot be satisfied. This may indicate to the local authority that greater efforts should be made to find a suitable place. If the child has been required to reside in a residential establishment or other specified place but the local authority are unable to make immediate arrangements for the child's reception in that establishment or place, they may arrange for the child to be temporarily accommodated in some other suitable place for any period not exceeding 22 days commencing on the date the children's hearing make, continue or vary the requirement to reside.[41] If the local authority cannot ensure that the child will be received into the named

---

[36] Children's Hearings (Scotland) Rules 1996, r.20(6)

[37] s.70(4).

[38] s.71(2) and (3).

[39] s.5(1).

[40] Though a supervision requirement which does not specify a place of residence does not in itself prohibit the removal of the child from Scotland or the U.K. *cf.* s.73(7) which envisages that a child can be taken to live outwith Scotland without infringing the terms of a supervision requirement.

[41] Children's Hearings (Transmission of Information etc.) (Scotland) Regulations 1996, reg.4(1).

establishment or place within the 22–day period, they must refer the child's case to the reporter on the ground that the supervision requirement ought to be reviewed.[42] This hearing must be arranged by the reporter as soon as is reasonably practicable and in any event within seven days of receiving the reference from the local authority.[43] The children's hearing are not obliged to vary the supervision requirement if they remain of the view that the place originally named remains the best for the child, but if there is no realistic possibility of that place being available the hearing may be forced to make their decision on the basis of the best available option.

### Non-disclosure of child's whereabouts

If the supervision requirement requires the child to reside in a named place, the children's hearing may further require when making the supervision requirement that the named place shall not be disclosed to any person or class of person specified by the hearing.[44] The children's hearing must name the person or persons who are not to be told of the child's address, and they should specify in their statement of reasons why they have so ordered. The statute gives no indication as to when it would be appropriate for the children's hearing to exercise the power to make a non-disclosure requirement, and there is nothing to prevent them from doing so for the benefit of someone other than the child, such as foster carers or prospective adopters with whom the child has been placed. A requirement that the child's address be kept secret would, however, normally be considered appropriate when contact between the child and the named person is likely to be harmful to the child, and when it is believed that there is a risk that the named person will attempt to make contact. Both elements must be present if a requirement under this provision is not to breach the minimum intervention principle.[45] A requirement of non-disclosure is likely to be effective in achieving that end only when the child is being moved to a new address: there would be no point in making such a requirement when the named person knows the child's current address and the child is remaining there. And it is incompetent to make a non-disclosure requirement when the supervision requirement does not include within its terms a requirement that the child reside at a named place (which can, of course, be the place where the child is already residing[46]). The hearing are not expressly obliged by

---

[42] *ibid.*, reg.4(2).

[43] *ibid.*, reg.4(3). If the children's hearing is arranged to sit after the expiry of the 22 days—and this can never be more than seven days after such expiry—the child may be kept at the place he or she is being accommodated during these extra days.

[44] s.70(6).

[45] s.16(4)(a) does not in its terms refer to a requirement under s.70(6), but it can be argued that such a requirement is a part of the process of "making" a supervision requirement, with the result that the minimum intervention principle is to be applied. In any case it is a clear interference with the enjoyment of family life and thus justified only if necessary in ECHR terms, which brings in the proportionality test, described above at pp.4–5.

[46] With the result that, if the child is to remain at home or is to be returned home but the hearing wishes to keep this information secret from a named person, they must first name the child's residence as a requirement in the order.

s.16 to take account of the views of the child in deciding whether to make a non-disclosure requirement under this subsection, but it would be good practice to do so if the child is of an age to be capable of expressing a view, and if the requirement is part of the making of a supervision requirement then such an obligation does exist.

If the person from whom details of the child's residence are to be kept is present at the hearing,[47] care must be taken to ensure that the address is not mentioned and this might require that the person be excluded from part of the hearing.[48] In addition, the person may be entitled to receive a statement of the decision and the reasons for the decision,[49] and care should be taken to ensure that the address is not specified (though it must be specified in the actual supervision requirement).

## CONDITIONS ATTACHED TO THE SUPERVISION REQUIREMENT

The supervision requirement may require the child to comply with any condition contained in the requirement,[50] and may also require the relevant local authority to fulfil such duties as are necessary for the purpose of enabling the child to comply with the supervision requirement, including the duty to secure or facilitate the provision for the child of services of a kind other than that provided by the relevant local authority.[51] The discretion of the children's hearing is very wide here and they may impose any condition that they consider to be in the best interests of the child. A condition on the child might be that he or she lives at a named place (considered above), or attends school regularly, or attends some group-work or training project, or meets with a social worker on a stated basis, or co-operates with the plans drawn up by the social work department, or attends at a drug or alcohol rehabilitation unit, or any other condition. The only limitation is that the condition must require something of the child.[52] A children's hearing have no power to impose conditions on any other person[53] (other than a local authority), such as a relevant person (though the relevant person's responsibilities and rights cannot be exercised during the currency of the supervision requirement in any way which would be incompatible with the supervision requirement[54]). In relation to the local authority, the

---

[47] If a relevant person, he or she may have a right to be present.

[48] Though such a reason for excluding a person does not fit into either of the grounds of exclusion under s.46(1).

[49] 1996 Rules. r.21(1).

[50] s.70(3)(b).

[51] s.70(3A) and (3B), as inserted by the Antisocial Behaviour etc (Scotland) Act 2004, s.136(1)(a).

[52] Kearney points out *(Children's Hearings and the Sheriff Court* (2nd ed., 2000) at para.25.41) that theoretically this is so wide that the condition could be to the effect that an offending child make reparation to his or her victim, or undertake some form of community service but that such conditions would not be "in the spirit of the Act". This is undoubtedly so. The condition must, it is submitted, be clearly designed to protect, guide, treat or control the child. There is a huge difference between teaching the child how to fit properly into society and teaching the child a lesson. The former is a right and proper, the latter an illegitimate, basis for decision.

[53] *P v P,* 2000 S.L.T. 781 at 786D.

[54] s.3(4).

placing of the child under supervision necessarily imposes the duty upon the local authority to "look after" the child in terms of s.17 and to give effect to the supervision requirement under s.71,[55] this in addition to those duties explicitly imposed on the local authority as part of the supervision requirement. If the children's hearing decide to impose a condition on the child they must do so expressly and it must be specified in the relevant form: a passage in the statement of reasons issued by the hearing is not a condition attached to the supervision requirement.[56] And the condition must be expressed in clear and unambiguous terms.[57] The same will apply to duties imposed on local authorities.

The decision whether to attach a condition to the supervision requirement is one to which all three overarching principles in s.16 apply, even although s.16(4)(a)(i) (which lists decisions governed by the two overarching principles other than the paramountcy of the child's welfare) refers only to the making or reviewing of supervision requirements, for the terms upon which the supervision requirement is made are, it is submitted, part of the consideration of whether to make it. There is no reason to deny an obligation to have regard to the child's views in relation to conditions when there is such an obligation in relation to the supervision requirement itself; and it consists with the principle of minimum intervention, especially when read in light of the ECHR principle of proportionality, to allow the children's hearing to impose conditions only when they consider that to do so would be better than imposing no conditions. Conditions should be imposed only to achieve significant ends which are required in the child's interests and which are unlikely to be achieved without the condition being imposed.

Though the hearing are able to suspend supervision requirements that they make pending an appeal against the making of the requirement,[58] they are not entitled to suspend conditions attached thereto even if the child or relevant person wishes to appeal against a condition without challenging the need for a supervision requirement.[59]

### Conditions as to contact

In every case in which a children's hearing decide to make a supervision requirement[60] they are expressly obliged to consider whether to impose one particular type of condition onto the supervision requirement, that is to say a condition regulating contact between the child and any specified person or class of persons.[61] There is no obligation to impose such a condition, but merely to consider whether it would be in the interests of the child to impose such a condition.[62] The matter can be left in the hands of the social work department who will have the right to regulate contact whenever the child is being looked after by them in accommo-

---

[55] See above at pp.20–23.
[56] *Kennedy v M,* 1995 S.L.T. 717.
[57] *D v Strathclyde Regional Council,* 1991 S.C.L.R. 185 at 186F.
[58] s.51(9).
[59] *S v Proudfoot,* 2002 S.L.T. 743.
[60] Or, it is submitted, to continue a supervision requirement: see below at pp.171–173.
[61] s.70(2) and (5)(b).
[62] *Kennedy v M,* 1995 S.L.T. 717.

dation provided by the local authority[63]; but if the children's hearing consider it best to leave the matter in the hands of the social work department this is not properly regarded as a condition and should not appear as such.[64] That decision would not, however, be appropriate in circumstances in which the local authority are likely to respond by applying a policy rather than making individual decisions, such as when the child is being freed for adoption and the local authority policy is to reduce contact: in these and similar circumstances the hearing should make their own decision in relation to the particular child before them.[65] In many cases, for example when contact is not an issue, the consideration that must be given to the question of contact can be dealt with speedily, though, in order to show that the statutory obligation has been satisfied, it would be good practice to record as a positive decision the hearing's determination that such a condition is not necessary.

If a condition regulating contact is to be made then it should be in clear and unambiguous terms. It would, perhaps, have been sensible for the statute to limit the obligation to consider the issue of contact to situations in which the child is required to reside somewhere,[66] but the obligation is more general and applies also when the child remains at home. A condition regulating contact will normally be appropriate when the child is required to live away from home and it is in his or her interests to maintain contact with his or her parents or guardians, but the condition may also be imposed when the child remains at home and the child's interests would be served by some other person, such as an absent unmarried father, or a previous foster carer to whom the child has become attached, having contact. Or, since the condition "regulates" contact, it can be used to require that no contact be permitted between the child and the stated person. This whole provision is, however, slightly peculiar since the condition is in a supervision requirement over the child and it is only the child, in terms of s.70(3), who can be required to comply with the condition. The condition imposed by the children's hearing may purport to "regulate" contact between the child and another person, but steps can be taken to enforce that condition only when it is the child who breaches it. A parent's failure to maintain contact with the child when the children's hearing have considered such contact to be in the interests of the child will not automatically activate a review under s.73(4)(b), but it may well indicate to the local authority that a review should be requested in any case under s.73(4)(a).[67] The real effect of a condition of contact will often be to remove from the local authority the power to determine with whom the child is to have contact.

A condition attached to a supervision requirement that regulates contact between the child and any specified person or class of person

---

[63] It is to be remembered that the local authority will have the duty to take such steps to promote, on a regular basis, personal relations and direct contact between the child and any person with parental responsibilities in relation to the child as appear to the local authority to be both practicable and reasonable, having regard to their duty to safeguard and promote the child's welfare: s.17(1)(c) and (6)(b).

[64] *Kennedy v M*, 1995 S.L.T. 717.

[65] *H v Petrie*, 2000 S.L.T. (Sh. Ct.) 145.

[66] As it did with the power to make a non-disclosure requirement under s.70(6): see above at pp.135–136.

[67] On reviews, see Chap.11.

supersedes any other legal right of contact, to the extent that such a right is inconsistent with the condition. So, for example, a person with the parental right to maintain personal relations and direct contact with the child under s.2 of the Children (Scotland) Act 1995 cannot exercise that right during the currency of the supervision requirement if a condition attached to it is to the effect that the child is to have no contact with the person with the s.2 right.[68] And any court order under s.11(2)(d) of the 1995 Act regulating the arrangements for maintaining personal relations and direct contact between the child and another person is put in suspension during the currency of the supervision requirement, in so far as the court order is inconsistent with the condition attached to the supervision requirement.[69] If no condition regulating contact is attached to the supervision requirement, pre-existing rights of contact (in so far as it is apt to refer to them as "rights") are unaffected. So a court decree[70] allowing or requiring contact at stated times should still be given effect to if the children's hearing do not consider it appropriate to attach any condition regulating contact. In the absence of a court decree, however, contact between the child and any other person is within the practical control of the person who has care and control of the child, which might well be the local authority. A relevant person who is dissatisfied with the level of contact with the child that he or she is being permitted by the local authority cannot ask the court to make an order under s.11 which has immediate effect different from the terms of the supervision requirement,[71] but must seek a review of the supervision requirement and ask the children's hearing to attach a condition regulating contact in more favourable terms. Since only a relevant person can require a review of the supervision requirement it would appear that there are no means by which any other person, such as a grandparent with whom the child is required to have contact, can seek a variation of contact provisions, whether through the court or the children's hearing.

The regulation of contact in a supervision requirement can be as prescriptive or as non-prescriptive as the children's hearing consider appropriate. So they might specify where contact is to take place, how often, and whether it is to be supervised or not.[72] They may specify particular days and particular hours during which contact is to take place, if this is considered necessary. In general, however, it is likely that a child's interests will best be served by laying down only the general parameters of contact without too much prescription of detail. Children's lives tend to change more rapidly than adults and prescribed times have a habit of interfering with new interests or new friendships that the child subsequently develops. It is competent for a condition to prohibit contact between a child and a specified person, but if any form of family

---

[68] s.3(4).

[69] *Dewar v Strathclyde Regional Council*, 1985 S.L.T. 114.

[70] Granted under s.11(2)(d).

[71] In *P v P*, 2000 S.L.T. 781 (at 788L) the Inner House accepted that it would be competent to seek a contact order, but inappropriate other than in exceptional circumstances for a court to make an order that at the time of its making would be inconsistent with a condition attached to a supervision requirement.

[72] So, for example, in *O v Rae*, 1993 S.L.T. 570 the father was allowed supervised access for one hour per fortnight with each of his children.

life exists between them the European Court will impose a stricter scrutiny on such limitations to the parties' Art.8 rights and the justification for prohibiting contact will require to be particularly cogent and persuasive.[73]

### Conditions as to medical treatment

It is expressly provided[74] that a condition imposed under s.70(3)(b) can be to the effect of requiring the child to submit to any medical or other examination or treatment.[75] Such a condition would ensure that legal authority is provided to carry out medical examinations of children when this is necessary to determine what medical treatment they might need, and to ensure that such treatment as is necessary is given. A condition that the child submit to medical or other examination or treatment would not authorise medical examination for the purpose of gaining evidence in order to establish a ground of referral[76] nor for the purpose of completing an investigation into the child's needs when a case is continued under s.69(2)[77]: this condition is, rather, attached to the disposal of the case and is imposed as one of the compulsory measures deemed necessary in the interests of the child.[78] In determining whether to attach a condition of medical treatment to a supervision requirement, the children's hearing must have regard to the three overarching principles in s.16. It would be an unusual case in which a condition of medical treatment is deemed necessary, but the terms of the statute, referring to "medical or other examination or treatment" are deliberately wide and would certainly cover things like drug rehabilitation treatment or psychiatric assessment and treatment. However, it would be open to a children's hearing to require that the child undergo medical treatment when he or she is, for example because of religious influences, minded to refuse consent for the treatment.[79]

It is unclear from the terms of the statute what the strict legal effect of the condition is, that is to say whether it grants to a doctor authority to provide medical or other examination or treatment in place of the otherwise necessary consent, or whether it merely requires that the child or his or her legal representative[80] give such consent. It is submitted that the latter interpretation is correct. If the child is too young to consent then consent must be given by a person with parental responsibilities and parental rights in relation to the child, and a condition imposed *upon the child* that the child submit to medical treatment is not habile to replace

---

[73] See *Olsson v Sweden (No. 2)* (1994) 17 E.H.R.R. 134; *Johansen v Norway* (1997) 23 E.H.R.R. 33 at para.64; *K & T v Finland* [2000] 2 F.L.R. 79 at para.139.

[74] Presumably for the avoidance of doubt.

[75] s.70(5)(a).

[76] That can be achieved by means of a child assessment order under s.55.

[77] Which can be achieved by means of a requirement under s.69(3).

[78] s.52(3) defines supervision under a supervision requirement to include "protection, guidance, *treatment* or control".

[79] *cf. Finlayson, Applicant*, 1989 S.C.L.R. 601.

[80] "Legal representative" is used here not in the sense of the person appointed to the child for the purposes of the children's hearing, but in the sense of the person with the responsibility and right (under ss.1 and 2 of the 1995 Act) to represent the child in transactions having legal effect.

that person's consent. A doctor, in other words, would not be able to rely on the condition in the supervision requirement in the face of parental refusal to grant consent to the child's medical treatment.[81] This is expressly so in the case of a refusing child. If the child is mature enough to understand the nature and consequences of the proposed medical examination or treatment then that child has capacity to consent or refuse consent, under the terms of s.2(4) of the Age of Legal Capacity (Scotland) Act 1991.[82] That provision is expressly preserved by s.90 of the Children (Scotland) Act 1995, and the imposing of a condition under s.70(5)(a) relating to medical treatment is expressly made subject to s.90, which is in these terms: " . . . where a condition contained, by virtue of . . . s.70(5)(a) of this Act in a supervision requirement requires a child to submit to any examination or treatment but the child has the capacity mentioned in the said s.2(4) [of the 1991 Act], the examination or treatment shall only be carried out if the child consents". In other words, the condition that the mature child submits to medical treatment is not authority for carrying out that treatment: the child's consent is that authority, and a doctor who carries out the treatment without the patient's consent may be guilty of assault. The condition is, therefore, little more than a request, or an unenforceable direction. The children's hearing are not barred from imposing a condition of medical treatment on a refusing child, but such a condition will not provide legal authority for carrying it out.[83] Rather, a child who refuses to submit in the face of such a condition will be regarded as having breached that condition, and treated in the same way as any child who breaches a condition in a supervision requirement, that is to say will be brought back to a children's hearing for a review under s.73(4)(b). A children's hearing, however, ought to give especially careful consideration to the appropriateness of imposing such a condition in a supervision requirement when they know that the child is refusing.

### Conditions restricting movement

The conditions specified in s.70(10) for justifying the hearing in authorising that the child be kept in secure accommodation[84] also justify the hearing in making a "movement restriction condition".[85] This is a condition attached to the supervision requirement restricting the child's movements in such a way as may be specified, and requiring the child to comply with such arrangements for monitoring compliance with the

---

[81] The terms of s.70(3) are to be noted: "A supervision requirement may *require the child* . . . to comply with any condition"; and s.70(5)(a): "a condition . . . may . . . *require the child* to submit" to medical or other examination or treatment.

[82] Though the 1991 Act is worded in terms of capacity to consent and not capacity to refuse, it is submitted that the one includes the other since the whole point of a doctor asking a patient for consent is to allow the patient the opportunity to refuse. A more difficult question is whether something like psychiatric or psychological assessment which is clearly covered by s.70(5)(a) of the 1995 Act is within the phrase "medical, dental or surgical treatment or procedure" as used in s.2(4) of the 1991 Act.

[83] Just as a requirement on a child to reside at a specified address is not authority to lock the child in.

[84] See below at pp.144–145.

[85] s.70(9A), as inserted by the Antisocial Behaviour etc (Scotland) Act 2004, s.135.

condition as may be specified.[86] It is for the hearing to determine the nature of the conditions but it is envisaged that they might include imposing a curfew on the child, or requiring him or her to avoid certain localities. Arrangements for monitoring compliance might include requiring the child to report his or her movements regularly, or to wear some form of electronic tracking device. Regulations will govern how such monitoring is to operate.[87]

## SPECIFYING WHEN A REVIEW SHOULD TAKE PLACE

The children's hearing who make a supervision requirement may determine that the requirement shall be reviewed at such time during the duration of the requirement as they determine.[88] So they can require that the supervision requirement be reviewed after a period short of a year. This might be appropriate when, for example, the child is over 16 and probably needs only a few months to settle down, or a child has been returned to a parent's care in an attempt at rehabilitation but it remains unclear whether rehabilitation will succeed. This useful provision allows the children's hearing to make long-term plans for the child's future, by taking account of, and making provision for, any foreseeable changes in the child's circumstances. It would, however, be a misuse for children's hearings to require a review under this provision for no reason other than to "keep their eye on the situation".[89] It would be a proper use of this provision to utilise it to further definite plans, such as changes in the child's residence which will foreseeably become appropriate within a few months, or to give an older child a shorter period to prove that he or she can live satisfactorily without local authority involvement, or to provide a short-term safety net during a difficult transitional period in the child's life. A circumstance in which this power can most usefully be employed is when the child is nearing school leaving age and the hearing are minded to terminate the supervision requirement. If the requirement is continued until shortly after the child attains school leaving age, this obliges the local authority to provide guidance and assistance (in cash or in kind) until the child is 19, under the after care provisions contained in s.29 of the 1995 Act. Maintaining supervision for a few months in order to obtain this benefit will be justified even when there is nothing else to indicate that compulsory measures of supervision are necessary: and requiring an early review will ensure that the supervision requirement is not continued after its purpose has been achieved.

## AUTHORISING SECURE ACCOMMODATION

It sometimes happens that it is in a child's welfare to have his or her movements physically restrained, by being required to reside in an

---

[86] s.70(11), as so inserted.
[87] s.70(14), as so inserted.
[88] s.70(7). See further, below at pp.162–163.
[89] It is sometimes forgotten how stressful hearings are for many children, and it cannot be doubted that too many unnecessary hearings are not conducive to the child's welfare.

establishment that has the ability to lock the child in. This is referred to in Scottish legislation as "secure accommodation". Other terms of a supervision requirement may well require the child to live at one place rather than another, but these do not in themselves carry a right of physical enforcement and they do not, therefore, engage Art.5 of the European Convention on Human Rights (the right to liberty and security of person).[90] But keeping a child in secure accommodation, which necessarily involves physical enforcement of any condition to reside there, does engage Art.5[91] and it follows that the procedures which lead to a child's detention in secure accommodation must satisfy not only Arts 6 (due process) and 8 (private and family life) but also the requirements in Art.5. The most important of these requirements is that everyone deprived of their liberty shall be entitled to take proceedings by which the lawfulness of the detention shall be decided speedily by a court and his or her release ordered if the detention is not lawful.[92] Possibly the single most common complaint taken to the European Court is the claim that detention has been too long before a case has been heard in a court, and for that reason alone it is important that our law lays down—and practice adheres to—strict time-limits when secure accommodation is authorised.

Where the children's hearing are satisfied that they must make a supervision requirement which includes a requirement that the child resides in a named residential establishment,[93] they may specify in that requirement that the child shall be liable to be placed and kept in secure accommodation in that establishment during such period as the person in charge of that establishment, with the agreement of the chief social work officer of the relevant local authority, considers necessary.[94] The children's hearing have no power to require that the child be kept in secure accommodation; rather they simply authorise the placing of the child there. The actual decision that the child is to be placed in secure accommodation rests with the person in charge of the establishment, who must obtain the agreement to do so of the chief social work officer. That decision might be made on the basis of law (whether the chief social work officer agrees with the hearing's assessment) or practicality (whether a place in secure accommodation is available). Whether that process can be described as a "fair hearing" for the purposes of Art.6 of the European Convention is open to some doubt.[95] It has been held by the First Division that since the child has the right to challenge the hearing's decision to authorise secure accommodation within 21 days, the requirements for speedy determination in Art.5(4) are satisfied.[96]

---

[90] *S v Miller*, 2001 S.L.T. 531.

[91] *Martin v N*, 2004 S.L.T. 249.

[92] European Convention on Human Rights, Art.5(4).

[93] Defined in s.93(1) to mean, in relation to a place in Scotland, "an establishment (whether managed by a local authority, by a voluntary organisation or by any other person) which provides residential accommodation for children for the purposes of" either the Children (Scotland) Act 1995 or the Social Work (Scotland) Act 1968.

[94] s.70(9) and (9A), as substituted by the Antisocial Behaviour etc. (Scotland) Act 2004, s.135.

[95] See K. Norrie "Human Rights Challenges to the Children's Hearing System" (2000) 45 J.L.S.S. 19.

[96] *Martin v N*, 2004 S.L.T. 249.

This may be so, but it does not address the Art.6 question of whether the making of the crucial decision (by the chief social work officer and the person in charge of the institution), rather than the hearing's authorisation, amounts to a "tribunal" determining the child's civil rights and obligations as required by Art.6. It is suggested that it is not and that this process is, therefore, vulnerable to challenge.[97]

Before granting such an authorisation, the children's hearing must be satisfied that one or other of the following circumstances exists:

(a) The child must have absconded from a residential establishment at least once before and is likely to do so again in circumstances in which it is likely that his or her physical, mental or moral welfare will be put at risk.[98] Risk to physical welfare is a risk that the child will be bodily injured; risk to mental welfare is a risk that the child's mind or emotional state will be damaged; risk to moral welfare is a risk that the child will be deprived of appropriate moral guidance and support. It would seem at first sight that this paragraph is not sufficiently broad to allow the children's hearing to authorise secure accommodation for no purpose other than to prevent the child making his or her position worse by continued offending.[99] However, allowing a child freedom to continue with habits of criminality can, it is submitted, be said to put the child at moral risk since it is likely to deny the child appropriate moral guidance and may well threaten to turn a child who offends into an habitual offender. It is in any child's interests to be protected from that risk.

(b) The child is likely to injure either him or herself or some other person.[1] The injuries referred to are physical or mental or, perhaps, moral injuries but do not include, it is submitted, economic injuries such as damage to property.[2] These "injuries"

---

[97] The Human Rights Act 1998, s.21(1) defines "tribunal" as a body before which legal proceedings may be brought. In *Benthem v Netherlands* (1986) 8 E.H.R.R. 1 and *Belilos v Switzerland* (1988) 10 E.H.R.R. 466 a "tribunal" was described as a body characterised by its judicial function, that is a body having the power to give a binding decision after determination of questions of fact and law within its competence, and which follows a prescribed procedure. In *T v United Kingdom* (1999) 30 E.H.R.R. 121 the fact that the Home Secretary could determine how long a child convicted of murder would remain in prison was held to breach Art.6. If the crucial decision lies with the chief social work officer and the person in charge of the institution rather than the children's hearing, there is far less protection in the system than the Inner House assumed in *Martin v N* for while there is an appeal against the hearing's authorisation there is no appeal against the actual decision to place the child in secure accommodation. If after procedurally correct and factually justified authorisation is granted by a hearing, the actual decision to place the child in secure accommodation is made for malign or unjustified reasons it would seem that there is no appeal and this would be contrary to both Arts 5 and 6.

[98] s.70(1)(a), as amended by the Antisocial Behaviour etc. (Scotland) Act 2004, s.135.

[99] cf. *Humphries v S*, 1986 S.L.T. 683 in which it was held that detention in a place of safety "in the child's own interests" (the wording in the 1968 Act) could be authorised for this reason and that it would be too narrow an interpretation of "the child's own interests" to limit that phrase to the child's mental, physical or moral well-being.

[1] s.70(10)(b), as amended by the Antisocial Behaviour etc. (Scotland) Act 2004, s.135.

[2] The paragraph does not refer to "some other person's interests", which would include economic injuries.

can be of the child him or herself, or of some other person. So a children's hearing are entitled to authorise secure accommodation when there is a risk that if the child is not kept in such accommodation he or she will assault someone else. That risk will usually only be considered to be present when the child has a history of physically injuring others.

In either case the supervision requirement must specify a residential establishment as the child's place of residence. The local authority can submit a report to the children's hearing recommending secure accommodation only if they are satisifed that it is in the best interests of the child to be subject to such condition or order.[3]

In English law, a decision to place a child in secure accommodation is not one in which the child's welfare is the paramount consideration. In *Re M (A Minor) (Secure Accommodation)*[4] it was held that welfare, though always relevant, was not paramount since s.1 of the (English) Children Act 1989 makes welfare paramount only in relation to questions with respect to "the upbringing of the child", which the decision to place the child in secure accommodation was held not to be. Section 16(1) of the Children (Scotland) Act 1995, however, is significantly wider and provides that the welfare of the child throughout his or her childhood shall be the children's hearing's paramount consideration whenever they have to make a decision on any matter "with respect to the child". This clearly includes a decision to authorise the placing of the child in secure accommodation. However, s.16(5) of the 1995 Act provides that where a children's hearing consider it necessary, for the purposes of protecting members of the public from serious harm (whether or not physical harm), to make a decision which does not give paramountcy to the child's welfare, they may do so. The interplay between this provision and s.70(9) and (10) is not clear, particularly since the reference to harm to others is wider (being physical or not) in s.16(5) than in s.70(10). The problem is perhaps best illustrated by the question of whether secure accommodation can be authorised to prevent the child causing serious economic injuries to others (such as destoying their property). It is suggested that the answer to that question is no. To authorise secure accommodation the conditions in s.70(9) and (10) must be satisfied, and these conditions (which, as suggested above, do not permit authorisation to protect economic interests) are not enlarged by s.16(5). That subsection merely permits the departure from the welfare principle in the specified circumstances, but does not in itself authorise the making of any decision that is not justified by another express provision in the statute. Section 16 contains the criteria according to which particular decisions must be made, not the conditions which have to be satisfied before they can be made. So a children's hearing can

---

[3] Secure Accommodation (Scotland) Regulations 1996, reg.10. It is to be noted that the local authority have the right to take the public interest into account in deciding whether to recommend secure accommodation and can exercise their powers in a manner inconsistent with their duties to safeguard and promote the child's welfare when to do so is necessary for the purpose of protecting members of the public from significant harm (whether or not physical harm): s.17(5). This acts as a qualification to reg.10.

[4] [1995] 2 W.L.R. 302.

authorise secure accommodation only if the conditions in s.70(9) and (10) are satisfied and if such a decision is contrary to the child's welfare it can be made only if, *in addition,* the criterion for decision in s.16(5) is also satisfied. It is unlikely, however, that reliance will often have to be placed on s.16(5) for there are many situations, as shown above, where it consists with giving paramountcy to the child's interests to authorise the placing of the child in secure accommodation. This decision, perhaps more than any other, must crucially take account of the proportionality test: is secure accommodation truly the least invasive method of achieving the legitimate aim of improving the child's life?

**Placement in secure accommodation without authority of a children's hearing**

The chief social work officer and the person in charge of the residential establishment providing secure accommodation can place a child who is subject to a supervision requirement in secure accommodation provided the criteria in s.70(10) are satisfied and in addition they are satisfied that it is in the child's best interests to be so placed.[5] The reporter must be informed forthwith and in any event not later than 24 hours after the placement, and he or she must arrange a children's hearing within 72 hours of the placement to review the child's case as if reviewing an emergency transfer under s.72(2).[6] The child may also be detained on the same grounds by an order under s.44 or s.51 of the Criminal Procedure (Scotland) Act 1995.[7]

**Duties towards children in secure accommodation**

If a child has been placed and kept in secure accommodation, it is the duty of the managers and person in charge of the residential establishment to ensure that the child's welfare is safeguarded and promoted, and that the child receives such provision for his or her development and control as is conducive to his or her best interests.[8] The child's case must be reviewed by the chief social work officer and the person in charge of the residential establishment within seven days of the child's placement in secure accommodation, and at such times as appear to them to be necessary or appropriate in the light of the child's progress, and in any event at intervals of not more than three months; the child shall continue to be detained in secure accommodation only when, upon such review, they are satisfied that it is in the best interests of the child.[9] In conducting the review, regard must be had to whether the s.70(10) criteria still apply, whether it is still in the best interests of the child to be kept in secure accommodation and, where practicable, to the opinion of the child and "his parents".[10]

## REFERRING THE CASE FOR FURTHER ACTION

The Antisocial Behaviour etc. (Scotland) Act 2004 is designed to control the behaviour of unruly persons, and to provide protection from such

---

[5] Secure Accommodation (Scotland) Regulations 1996, reg.6(1).
[6] *ibid.,* reg.6(2), (3) and (4).
[7] *ibid.,* reg.13 and reg.14.
[8] *ibid.,* reg.4.
[9] *ibid.,* reg.15(1).
[10] *ibid.,* reg.15(2).

behaviour to others. The processes created by the 2004 Act sit uneasily with the existing children's hearing system, though the Act attempts, not wholly successfully, to harmonise these processes with that system. It does, however, also attempt to make the existing system operate more effectively, by permitting the hearing to require the reporter to refer certain matters on for further action in other fora.

**Parenting orders**

Whenever a child's case has been referred to a children's hearing or a children's hearing has been arranged to review a supervision requirement, the hearing may require the reporter to consider whether to apply for a parenting order under s.102 of the Antisocial Behaviour etc (Scotland) Act 2004.[11] This power is available whenever it appears to the hearing "that it might be appropriate for a parenting order to be made", but the Act gives no indication of when it might be considered so appropriate, or the basis upon which a hearing can make that judgment. But a parenting order is an order that requires something of the parent (unlike a supervision requirement, which requires something of the child and the local authority) and when it is perceived that, for example, a change in behaviour of the parent is needed more than a change in behaviour of the child then it might well be considered that the child's welfare would be better served by the reporter obtaining a parenting order than the hearing making a supervision requirement. Indeed, a package of measures in the child's interests might suggest that both a supervision requirement and a parenting order is appropriate. The hearing may require the reporter to consider making an application to the sheriff for a parenting order, but they cannot require him or her to make the application. A requirement to consider making an application might normally be perceived as the "disposal" of a referral, but in fact the power can be exercised by a hearing even when grounds of referral are not established: the power is activated by the referral itself and not the establishment of grounds. The child's welfare is paramount in the hearing's decision whether to require the reporter to consider applying for a parenting order[12] but it would seem that the other two overarching principles are not applicable to this decision. However, a hearing's decision as to the appropriateness or otherwise of making such a requirement will be more easily justified if they discuss the matter first with both the child and the parent and for that reason it would be good practice, it is submitted, to do so.

**Educational referrals**

Whenever a child has been referred to a children's hearing (and not only when grounds of referral are accepted or established) and the children's hearing consider that an educational authority have duties under the Education (Scotland) Act 1980 to the child but are not complying with those duties, the hearing may require the reporter to refer the matter to

---

[11] Children (Scotland) Act 1995, s.75A, as inserted by the Antisocial Behaviour etc. (Scotland) Act 2004, s.116.
[12] s.16.

the Scottish ministers.[13] It is not stated what action the Scottish ministers may take against a local authority that they consider to be in breach of their duties under the 1980 Act.

---

[13] s.75B, as inserted by the Antisocial Behaviour etc. (Scotland) Act 2004, s.137(4).

## CHAPTER TEN

# ADVICE AND REMIT HEARINGS IN OFFENCE-BASED CASES

## INTRODUCTION

Though in the generality of cases a child who commits an offence will be dealt with by having his or her case referred to a children's hearing[1] instead of being prosecuted in a criminal court,[2] there will be some situations in which the Crown or the procurator fiscal takes the decision that the appropriate course is to prosecute the child for the offence in the normal criminal courts.[3] This might be, for example, because of the seriousness of the alleged offence,[4] or because the child has committed a large number of offences, or because the children's hearing system has exhausted the good it can realistically do for the particular child. If the child, on prosecution, pleads guilty to or after trial is found guilty of an offence, the criminal court (whether the High Court or the sheriff court[5]) has the power and sometimes the duty, under the Criminal Procedure (Scotland) Act 1995, to seek advice from a children's hearing as to how it should dispose of the case (*i.e.* what sentence, if any, is appropriate); in addition the court may remit the case of the child to the children's hearing for disposal by them. The court may neither seek advice from, nor remit a case to, a children's hearing when the offence is one the sentence for which is fixed by law.[6]

The rules governing when a criminal court can seek advice from a children's hearing or remit the case for disposal to a children's hearing

---

[1] The condition being that contained in the Children (Scotland) Act 1995, s.52(2)(i).

[2] Indeed no child under the age of 16 can be prosecuted for any offence except on the instructions of the Lord Advocate, or at his instance: Social Work (Scotland) Act 1968, s.31(1).

[3] There is nothing in the statute that says that if a child is prosecuted he or she cannot later be referred to a children's hearing in respect of the same offence, but it is likely that the principle of *res judicata* would render any such referral incompetent. It could be argued that the children's hearing system, being *sui generis* and designed to protect the child's welfare, remains open in appropriate cases. A criminal court, on conviction, might determine that the child does or does not require punishment; this is irrelevant to the question of whether the child's welfare requires compulsory measures of supervision. However, it is submitted that this line of reasoning is not good. The court's power to remit the child's case to a children's hearing should be taken to exclude the reporter's power to refer the child when the court decides not to do so.

[4] As in, for example, *Codona v H. M. Advocate,* 1996 S.L.T. 1100, where a 14-year-old girl had been charged and convicted of murder.

[5] It is only these two courts that have jurisdiction over children under the age of 16: Social Work (Scotland) Act 1968, s.31(1).

[6] Criminal Procedure (Scotland) Act 1995, s.49(5).

differ according to whether or not the child is currently under supervision (and for that reason any court in which a child is being prosecuted should take care to ascertain whether this is so or not).

### CHILD NOT CURRENTLY UNDER SUPERVISION

Where a child who is not subject to a supervision requirement[7] has been prosecuted in the criminal court and has pled guilty to or been found guilty of an offence, the court has three options: (i) it can dispose of the case itself according to its normal criminal jurisdiction; (ii) it can remit the case for disposal by a children's hearing[8]; or (iii) it can request the reporter to arrange a children's hearing for the purpose of obtaining their advice as to how the court should dispose of the case.[9] If the third option is chosen it is open to the hearing to advise the court to dispose of the case itself, suggesting which of the sentences that are available to the court is the most likely to serve the interests of the child, or they may advise the court to remit the case back to the children's hearing for disposal; in either case the terms of the advice ought to explain to the court why the hearing favours one disposal over another. Advice to the court to remit the case back to a children's hearing would be appropriate whenever the hearing consider that the welfare-based system still has something to offer the child in the way of protection, guidance, treatment or control; advice to the court to dispose of the case itself would be appropriate when the hearing consider that realistically they have nothing beneficial to offer the child. The court must consider the advice obtained and having done so may either dispose of the case itself or remit it back to the children's hearing for their disposal,[10] whether this is what the children's hearing have advised or not (though it would be unusual for a court to make a remit at this stage against the advice of the hearing[11]). If the case is remitted back to the children's hearing, a certificate signed by the clerk of court stating that the person concerned has pled guilty to or has been found guilty of the offence to which the remit relates shall be conclusive evidence for the purposes of the remit that the offence was committed by the person,[12] and there will be no need to seek acceptance or establishment of a ground of referral under s.52(2)(i).

### CHILD CURRENTLY UNDER SUPERVISION

Where a child who is currently subject to a supervision requirement[13] has been prosecuted in the High Court and has pled guilty to or been found

---

[7] "Child" being for this purpose a person under the age of 16: Children (Scotland) Act 1995, s.93(2)(b)(i).

[8] Criminal Procedure (Scotland) Act 1995, s.49(1)(a).

[9] Criminal Procedure (Scotland) Act 1995, s.49(1)(b). The reporter must, of course, comply with this "request".

[10] Criminal Procedure (Scotland) Act 1995, s.49(2).

[11] Indeed, in practice, it is unusual for criminal courts to remit cases to children's hearings for disposal in cases in which the child is not currently under supervision.

[12] Children (Scotland) Act 1995, s.50(1).

[13] "Child" being for this purpose a person under the age of 18: Children (Scotland) Act 1995, s.93(2)(b)(ii).

guilty of an offence, the court may either (i) dispose of the case itself according to its normal criminal jurisdiction or (ii) at its discretion, request the reporter to arrange a children's hearing for the purpose of obtaining their advice as to the treatment of the child[14]; the High Court may not, at this stage, remit the case for disposal by a children's hearing. If the prosecution was in the sheriff court, the sheriff (whether the procedure is solemn or summary) must refer the case to a children's hearing for such advice[15] (and may, at this stage, neither dispose of the case himself nor remit the case to a children's hearing for disposal[16]). On receiving advice, the court (whether High Court or sheriff court) must consider that advice and may now either dispose of the case itself or remit it back to the children's hearing for their disposal, whether this is what the children's hearing have advised or not. Since these provisions refer only to the High Court and the sheriff court, it would seem that a child over 16 who remains subject to a supervision requirement and who is prosecuted in the district court can never have his or her case considered at an advice hearing.

PERSON AGED 16 OR OVER NOT CURRENTLY UNDER SUPERVISION

When a person who is aged 16 years or over but who is more than six months short of his or her 18th birthday, is not currently subject to a supervision requirement, and has pled guilty to or been found guilty of an offence by a court in summary proceedings,[17] the court may either (i) dispose of the case itself according to its normal criminal jurisdiction or (ii) at its discretion, request the reporter to arrange a children's hearing for the purpose of obtaining their advice as to the treatment of the person.[18] If it does the latter, then, having considered the advice that the children's hearing give, the court may either dispose of the case itself (whether in accordance with the advice it receives or not) or (but in this case only if this is what the children's hearing recommend in their advice) remit the case back to the hearing for them to dispose of it.[19] If the case is remitted back to the children's hearing,[20] a certificate signed by the clerk of court stating that the person concerned has pled guilty to or has been found guilty of the offence to which the remit relates shall be conclusive evidence for the purposes of the remit that the offence was committed by the person,[21] and there will be no need to seek acceptance or establishment of a ground of referral under s.52(2)(i). This is the only circumstance in which a person who is not subject to a supervision

---

[14] Criminal Procedure (Scotland) Act 1995, s.49(3). The reporter must, of course, comply with this "request".

[15] Criminal Procedure (Scotland) Act 1995, s.49(3).

[16] *Anderson v McGlennan,* 1998 S.C.C.R. 552.

[17] This will include, since the person is over 16, the district court, but will not include the High Court which does not conduct summary trials.

[18] Criminal Procedure (Scotland) Act 1995, s.49(6). The reporter must, of course, comply with this "request".

[19] Criminal Procedure (Scotland) Act 1995, s.49(7).

[20] Which, in practice, is highly unusual.

[21] Children (Scotland) Act 1995, s.50(1).

requirement on his or her 16th birthday can be made subject to such a requirement thereafter.[22] If the person is less than six months short of his or her 18th birthday (or is over that age), the court cannot refer the case for advice and must therefore deal with the case itself.

PROCEDURE AT AND POWERS OF ADVICE AND REMIT HEARINGS

**Advice hearings**

When the reporter arranges a children's hearing at the behest of a criminal court seeking advice as to how it should dispose of the child's case, the procedure to be followed by the children's hearing is similar to that at a normal hearing, except that no grounds of referral are put to the child and relevant person, and there is no dispositive decision for the hearing to make. The provisions concerning attendance at children's hearings, and the warrants that may be issued to ensure attendance, apply with equal force. The children's hearing do not, however, review any current supervision requirement the child may be subject to, unless a review hearing is being held at the same time, and the sole purpose of an advice hearing is to examine the child's circumstances through a discussion with the persons present, and to draw up a report for the court containing such advice as the hearing think appropriate. The chairman of the hearing must, before the children's hearing proceed to consider the case, explain the purpose of the hearing,[23] and then the hearing proceed to a consideration of the case. During that consideration the hearing must consider the reference by the court, any supervision requirement the child is subject to, the social background report and any other relevant document or information available to them; they must discuss the case of the child and afford the child, any relevant person, safeguarder[24] or representative who is present, an opportunity of participating in the discussion and of being heard on the case; and they must take steps to obtain the views of the child, any relevant person and any safeguarder[25] on what arrangements with respect to the child would be in his or her best interests.[26] Though not explicitly covered in the Legal Representation Rules, there would seem to be no reason to suggest that a hearing arranged to give advice could not appoint a legal representative to the child in appropriate circumstances.[27]

After the discussion, the children's hearing must determine what advice they will give the court.[28] The hearing[29] must then inform the

---

[22] Such a person is not a "child" for the purposes of the Children (Scotland) Act 1995, but the terms of that Act will apply as if the person were a child whenever a court has remitted a case to the children's hearing for disposal under this provision: Children (Scotland) Act 1995, s.50(2).

[23] Children's Hearings (Scotland) Rules 1996, r.22(2).

[24] Rule 22 applies to other forms of advice hearings and this explains the reference to a safeguarder. It is difficult to envisage a case in which a safeguarder would be in office when the children's hearing are providing advice under the terms of the Criminal Procedure (Scotland) Act 1995.

[25] See n.24 above.

[26] 1996 Rules, r.22(3).

[27] See above at pp.91–93.

[28] *ibid.*

[29] N.B.: not necessarily the chairman.

child, relevant person, safeguarder and representative of what the advice will be.[30] Though there is no express statutory obligation to do so, it is good practice for the chairman, at the end of the hearing, to remind the child that the court is not legally bound to follow the advice. Thereafter the chairman must make or cause to be made[31] a report in writing providing the advice, including a statement of the reasons for that advice; and the chairman must sign the report and statement.[32] Within seven days following a determination by the children's hearing, the reporter must send a copy of the report containing the advice to the court, and to the child, relevant person and safeguarder.[33] Since no dispositive decision is made, there is no appeal against the terms of the hearing's advice.[34]

While an advice hearing may competently continue the case to a subsequent hearing (if, for example, an up-to-date social background report is not yet available or if a legal representative is appointed) it is submitted that an advice hearing may not make any requirement under s.69(3) that the child attends or resides at a clinic or hospital for investigation before the continued hearing convenes. Section 69 is limited in its terms to cases in which grounds of referral have been accepted or established in accordance with s.68[35] or s.85,[36] and a hearing convened for the purposes of giving advice does not have the powers granted by s.69 of the Children (Scotland) Act 1995. A hearing which feels unable to give fully reasoned advice because of a perceived need for further investigation must, it is submitted, give advice in these terms (perhaps advising that the case be remitted back to them for disposal, in which case they will then be able to require the further investigations). Likewise an advice hearing arranged under s.49 of the Criminal Procedure (Scotland) Act 1995 has no power to appoint a safeguarder.

The welfare of the child will remain the hearing's paramount consideration and the advice the hearing give to the court must be in terms of what, in the opinion of the hearing, would serve the child's interests.[37] The criminal court can make its decision on grounds other than the child's welfare (and can therefore ignore the hearing's advice) but members of the children's hearing have neither training nor competence to give advice about any matter other than the child's welfare, such as the need for exemplary punishment or the need to deter others. The role of the children's hearing, in advice hearings, is to advise the court as to what would be in the interests of the child.

---

[30] 1996 Rules, r.22(5).

[31] This form of wording suggests that someone other than a hearing member can draw up the report, and in many panel areas this function is left to reporters. It is suggested that this is not a practice which should be encouraged. The advice is the hearing's advice and in the normal case it should be a hearing member who draws up the report containing that advice.

[32] 1996 Rules, r.22(6).

[33] 1996 Rules, r.22(7).

[34] Which explains the dearth of reported decisions on advice hearings.

[35] Application to the sheriff for proof of the original grounds: see Chap.7.

[36] Application to the sheriff to re-examine the original grounds: see Chap.12.

[37] The terms of the rules suggest this: see 1996 Rules, r.22(3) under which the hearing must seek the views of the child, relevant person and others as to what would be in the child's interests.

**Remit Hearings**

The procedure in cases remitted to the children's hearing from a criminal court for disposal is quite different from the procedure in advice hearings, for in remitted cases the role of the children's hearing is not to give advice but to make a dispositive decision under s.69 or s.70 of the Children (Scotland) Act 1995. If a case is remitted to the children's hearing from the court for disposal, the jurisdiction of the court in respect of the child ceases and the child's case stands referred to the children's hearing.[38] The powers and duties of the children's hearing are the same as if the case had been referred to them by the reporter under s.65,[39] and the procedure to be adopted is also the same. So the children's hearing must consider the case, taking account of the ground of referral, any reports and any other information that they have, and they can discharge the referral, continue the case, appoint a safeguarder or legal representative, or impose or continue a supervision requirement subject to such conditions as they think fit. Rules of attendance apply as in normal hearings, warrants may be granted, requirements to attend or reside at a clinic or hospital for further investigation can be made, secure accommodation authorisation can be given, and if the child is already subject to a supervision requirement that requirement must be reviewed at the same time in terms of s.65(3).[40]

It is not immediately clear from the wording of the statutory provisions whether the proceedings in remit hearings should open with the chairman seeking acceptance of the grounds of referral from the child and relevant person. Section 50(1) of the Children (Scotland) Act 1995 provides that a certificate signed by the clerk of the court stating that the child concerned has pled guilty to or has been found guilty of the offence to which the remit relates shall be conclusive evidence for the purposes of the remit that the offence has been committed by the child. This does not, however, quite say that the pleading or finding of guilt shall be treated as if a ground of referral has been established, for the children's hearing does not in any sense hear evidence. It is relevant to note that words which do have this effect appear in both s.54 of the Children (Scotland) Act 1995[41] and s.48 of the Criminal Procedure (Scotland) Act 1995.[42] There is a difference between, on the one hand, cases coming to

---

[38] Criminal Procedure (Scotland) Act 1995, s.49(4).

[39] Sheriff Kearney, *Children's Hearings and the Sheriff Court* (2nd ed., 2000) at para.24.19 suggests a constraint on the powers of a hearing when a previous hearing has advised a remit back to the hearing, to follow the advice. But there is no rule to this effect and two differently constituted hearings may well come to opposing conclusions, both reasonable and both justified in all the circumstances of the case. Most fact scenarios faced by hearings allow judgment to be exercised in determining welfare (the paradigm "judgment case") and judgment, by definition, contains a margin of appreciation. Just as one hearing is not to be criticised because another hearing (or a sheriff) would have decided differently, so too one hearing giving advice cannot be taken to bind another hearing called upon to make the dispositive decision.

[40] See below at pp.163–166.

[41] Where, in certain civil proceedings, the sheriff can specify that a condition has been satisfied and if he does so s.69(1) applies as if the condition were a ground of referral established in accordance with s.68.

[42] Where in certain criminal proceedings in which a child was the victim of an offence the court can "certify that the offence shall be a ground established" for the purposes of Part II of the Children (Scotland) Act 1995.

a hearing via s.54 of the Children (Scotland) Act 1995 or s.48 of the Criminal Procedure (Scotland) Act 1995 and, on the other hand, cases coming via s.49 of the Criminal Procedure (Scotland) Act 1995, for in the former but not in the latter the reporter retains a discretion whether to arrange a children's hearing or not.[43] If grounds of referral need not be put to the child and relevant person when the reporter has, in his or her discretion, decided to arrange a children's hearing, it is difficult to see why grounds of referral would have to be put when the reporter has no discretion and is obliged to arrange a children's hearing—for otherwise the reporter might find him or herself in the position of seeking to establish grounds in a case where he or she does not believe that compulsory measures of supervision are necessary. In addition, it would be a procedural waste of time (and not, therefore, in the interests of the child) to insist on a s.68 application when proof in the form of the clerk of court's certificate granted under s.50(1) is unchallengeable. It follows, it is submitted, that a children's hearing which is empowered by a remit under s.49 of the Criminal Procedure (Scotland) Act 1995 to dispose of the case can move straight on to a consideration of the case and disposal thereof as if a ground of referral under s.52(2)(1) had previously been established on an application by the reporter under s.68.

## Antisocial Behaviour Orders

Though not technically offence-based cases, it is convenient to deal here with the duty on courts considering making an antisocial behaviour order (ASBO) to take advice from children's hearings before determining whether or not to make such an order.[44] The sheriff must require the reporter to arrange a children's hearing for the purpose of obtaining advice, but it is not advice as to whether it is in the child's welfare to make an ASBO (as would be the case for any other form of advice hearing). Rather, it is advice as to whether the conditions for the making of such an order exist. These conditions are:

(a) that the child is at least 12 years of age,
(b) that the child has engaged in antisocial behaviour[45] towards a "relevant person",[46] and
(c) that an ASBO is necessary for the purpose of protecting relevant persons from further antisocial behaviour by the child.

This form of advice hearing is unique and will be difficult for hearings since their major expertise, identifying what is in the welfare of the child, is not called upon at all. Conditions (a) and (b) are matters of fact which the sheriff, hearing evidence, is far better placed than a children's

---

[43] See further above at, pp.44–47.
[44] Antisocial Behaviour etc (Scotland) Act 2004, s.4(4).
[45] Defined in s.143 of the 2004 Act as acting in a manner or pursuing a course of conduct that causes or is likely to cause alarm or distress to at least one person who is not in the same household as the child.
[46] N.B.: *not* defined as in the 1995 Act but as a person within the local authority's area.

hearing to determine and so their advice is not needed. Condition (c) is a matter of judgment not upon the child's welfare but upon the likely efficacy—from a third party's point of view—of the order. Children's hearings are unlikely to be able to make that judgment any better than a sheriff and their advice, for the most part, will serve no real (as opposed to procedural) purpose in the ASBO process. This is especially so since there is no process by which the third party needing protection can come to the hearing to explain that necessity. It will be as open to a hearing to advise that they cannot make the judgment, as it is for the sheriff to ignore any more substantive advice the hearing feels able to give.

## Chapter Eleven

# REVIEW HEARINGS

## Introduction

One of the underlying principles of the whole children's hearing system is that a child who has been made the subject of a supervision requirement is to remain subject to that requirement only for so long as his or her interests require that he or she be so subject. Because the child's circumstances may change fairly rapidly, and his or her needs may develop (often very much more quickly than adults'), the Children (Scotland) Act 1995 provides that the supervision requirement must be reviewed at certain stated intervals. If not timeously reviewed, it will cease to have effect and to bring the child back into the system would then require new grounds of referral to be accepted or established. There are various circumstances in which the reporter will be obliged to arrange a children's hearing for the purpose of reviewing the case of a child subject to a supervision requirement; most, but not all, of these circumstances are specified in s.73 of the 1995 Act. A review must be arranged by the reporter when he or she has been requested to do so by certain people and also, in the absence of any such request, in certain specified circumstances. Having arranged a review hearing, the reporter must also make any arrangements incidental to that review,[1] such as notifying the family and panel members,[2] calling for reports into the child's present circumstances from the appropriate local authority and any other reports in relation to the child that will be relevant to the children's hearing's consideration of the case. The powers and duties of the children's hearing on review are, by and large, conterminous with the powers of a children's hearing arranged to consider the original grounds of referral that brought the child into the system in the first place.

## Circumstances in Which a Review Must be Arranged

### The elapse of a year or the child's 18th birthday

There are only two circumstances in which the reporter, without being required to do so by any other person or body, must arrange a review hearing. First, a supervision requirement, if it has not otherwise been reviewed within that time, will remain effective for one year and it

---

[1] Children (Scotland) Act 1995, s.73(8)(b).
[2] For notification, see above at pp.56–62.

cannot remain in force for a period longer than one year unless it has been continued, with or without variation, within a year of its imposition or last continuation.[3] If the reporter has not been required to arrange a review before then, he or she must do so not more than three months before the anniversary of its imposition or last continuation.[4] This review is commonly referred to as the annual review. Secondly, a person cannot be subject to a supervision requirement after reaching the age of 18 years, and any subsisting requirement automatically ceases to have effect on the person's 18th birthday, even without the meeting of a hearing to terminate it.[5] The reporter does, however, have an obligation to arrange a review within three months of the expiry of the supervision require-ment[6] and if expiry would be effected by the young person's 18th birthday, any continuation of the requirement would last only until that date.[7] In either of these cases, if the reporter fails to arrange a review hearing the supervision requirement will cease to have effect on the person's 18th birthday or on the anniversary of its being imposed or continued; but reporters who are of the view that compulsory measures of supervision are no longer necessary should not simply fail to arrange a hearing, for not only would that breach their statutory obligation but it would also usurp the function of the children's hearing, in whose sole remit the question of whether compulsory measures of supervision are necessary lies.

If a children's hearing is arranged because the supervision require-ment is about to expire and they decide not to continue the requirement, they must then go on to consider whether supervision or guidance is still nevertheless required for the child; if they do so determine, the local authority must offer such supervision or guidance to the child and supply it if the offer is accepted.[8] This is a slightly odd provision, not only in its limitation to review hearings arranged because the supervision require-ment is about to expire, but also because if the children's hearing consider that the child still requires compulsory supervision and guid-ance, then a continuation of the supervision requirement will nearly always be the correct decision. And it will have little practical effect at reviews held because the child is about to attain the age of 18, since once the child becomes 18 he or she is no longer a "child" to whom the local authority are obliged to provide guidance or supervision. The only circumstance in which this provision will have significance is if the supervision requirement is terminated because the child absolutely refuses to co-operate with compulsory measures of supervision but has indicated a willingness to co-operate on a voluntary basis.

**Local authority request for review**

The most common circumstance in which a review will be held (apart from the annual review) is when a local authority have requested it. The

---

[3] s.73(2).

[4] s.73(8)(a)(v).

[5] s.73(3).

[6] s.73(8)(a)(v).

[7] Though it will only be in very rare circumstances indeed that a supervision requirement will be continued so close to its subject's 18th birthday.

[8] s.73(12).

local authority that are responsible for giving effect to the supervision of the child may call for a review of the requirement by referring the child's case to the reporter[9] and if they do so the reporter then has an obligation to arrange a review hearing.[10] There are a number of different circumstances in which the local authority will be obliged to request a review. In each case, if the circumstances exist, the matter is one of obligation upon the local authority who cannot decide simply to let the matter lie until the annual review (unless, perhaps, the annual review is imminent in any case).

First, a review must be requested whenever the local authority are satisfied that the current supervision requirement ought to be varied or terminated.[11] They may come to this view because some change has taken place in the child's circumstances since the supervision requirement was made or last reviewed which indicates that its terms and conditions are no longer appropriate. It might be, for example, that the plans for the child have worked successfully, or the threat to the child's well-being has been lifted, and that compulsory supervision is therefore thought by the local authority to be no longer necessary. Or it might be that the plans are not working and some change in the terms of the supervision is considered necessary to give effect to new plans which the local authority have drawn up and which they believe would better serve the child's needs. Or the child's circumstances may be such that different terms in the supervision requirement are now needed, for example in relation to contact or where the child is to live. In particular, the local authority must refer the case of the child to the reporter on the ground that the supervision ought to be varied where, in terms of the supervision requirement, the child was required to reside in a residential establishment or other specified place but it appears that the local authority will be unable to make immediate arrangements for his or her reception in that establishment or place before the expiry of a period of 22 days.[12]

Secondly, a review must be requested whenever the local authority are satisfied that a condition in the supervision requirement is not being fulfilled.[13] It does not matter why the condition is not being fulfilled, whether it is because of a radical change in the child's circumstances, or non-co-operation by the child, or lack of resources by the local authority, or for any other reason. It is to be remembered that conditions are imposed upon the child,[14] and any breach of which the local authority are aware will require the local authority to request a review. The local authority must therefore keep a watchful eye on the situation to monitor whether or not all the conditions in the supervision requirement are being fulfilled. However, there is no sanction in the Act for the failure of a local authority to bring the case back to a hearing when conditions are

---

[9] s.73(4) and (5).
[10] s.73(8)(a)(i).
[11] s.73(4)(a).
[12] Children's Hearings (Transmission of Information etc.) (Scotland) Regulations 1996, reg.4(1) and (2). See further, above at pp.134–135.
[13] s.73(4)(b).
[14] See above at pp.136–137.

not fulfilled,[15] but it is no excuse for such a breach of a statutory obligation that those charged with implementing the supervision requirement do not consider the condition appropriate and would prefer to work with the child without the condition being attached. If that is considered to be the case, the local authority should call for a review[16] and explain to the children's hearing why it would be better for the child that the condition be removed.

Thirdly, a review must be requested whenever the local authority are satisfied that the best interests of the child would be served by their doing any of the following acts, and they intend to do so: (i) applying under s.86 of the 1995 Act for a parental responsibilities order, (ii) applying under s.18 of the Adoption (Scotland) Act 1978 for an order freeing the child for adoption, or (iii) placing the child for adoption.[17] All these acts are seen as things that will significantly change the child's circumstances, so making it necessary that a review of the child's case be held in order to determine whether it is appropriate to continue with the supervision requirement in its present form in light of these changed circumstances. A children's hearing arranged as a result of a referral for any of these reasons[18] must not only review the supervision requirement, but must also draw up a report as specified under s.73(13)[19] and indeed this will usually be the main purpose of the review hearing since the child's circumstances will not normally have changed by the time the hearing is held.[20]

Fourthly, a review must be requested whenever the local authority become aware that an adoption application has been or is about to be made in respect of the child under s.12 of the Adoption (Scotland) Act 1978.[21] At such a review, the children's hearing will be obliged both to review the current supervision requirement, and to draw up a report under s.73(13).[22] The statute requires a review each time one of the events mentioned in the previous paragraph or in this paragraph occurs, with the unfortunate result that the child might be brought before a children's hearing on two or even three occasions within a fairly short period of time to examine, effectively, the same question.

### Review required by child or relevant person

The child or relevant person can require a review at any time after three months from the imposition or last continuation of the supervision

---

[15] It is arguable that an action for breach of statutory duty might be possible at the instance of a child who suffers loss by being subject to a supervision requirement longer than his or her welfare requires, but such an argument is unlikely to be sustained in the light of *M (A Minor) v Newham London Borough Council* [1995] 2 A.C. 633. But it is not entirely impossible: see *Barrett v Enfield London Borough Council* [2001] 2 A.C. 550.

[16] Under s.73(4)(a).

[17] s.73(4)(c). See also s.22A of the Adoption (Scotland) Act 1978: below at pp.167–168. If the reporter is notified that agreement to the adoption or freeing application is unlikely to be forthcoming, this review must be held within 21 days of that notification: Children's Hearings (Scotland) Rules 1996, r.22(8), which should refer to s.73(8)(a)(i).

[18] Or under s.22A of the Adoption (Scotland) Act 1978.

[19] See below at pp.172–173.

[20] Note that the review must be arranged when an order is applied for rather than when it is granted.

[21] s.73(5).

[22] See below at pp.172–173.

requirement, whether varied then or not,[23] and if either or both do so the reporter is obliged to arrange a children's hearing.[24] The months are calendar months and three months after the date on which the requirement was made, continued or varied is the day after the expiry of the three months.[25] The call for a review can be made at a time before the expiry of the three months, but the children's hearing cannot consider the case until after that expiry.

The age at which a child has capacity to call for a review is not specified, nor has it been discussed in any reported case law. There would be acute awkwardness in attempting to apply the rules contained in the Age of Legal Capacity (Scotland) Act 1991 to this question. Requiring a review is clearly a "transaction having legal effect", the effect being to require the reporter to arrange the review; but if s.2(1) of the Age of Legal Capacity (Scotland) Act 1991 applies, this would mean that a review could be called for by a child only when the child is of an age at which it is "common" for persons of the child's age and circumstances to do so and on terms which are not unreasonable. It is, in fact, highly unusual for children to call for reviews of supervision requirements[26] and the requirement that the terms of the transaction be not unreasonable is redundant in this context. It is submitted that the 1991 Act is not designed to cover this situation and that the better view is that the terms of s.73(6), permitting "a child" to call for a review, implicitly confers capacity on all children subject to supervision requirements, however young, or alternatively that the right to call for a review is not a right the exercise of which requires any formal legal capacity at all.[27] In practice, reporters are likely to arrange a review called for by a child unless the child clearly has no understanding of what it means to do so.

The relevant person[28] who may call for a review under this provision will normally be the same person as is obliged under s.45(8) to attend the children's hearing considering the case of the child.[29] However, if a child's family circumstances have changed since the last children's hearing, it is possible that a different person will come within this category. Any person who has, ordinarily, charge of or control over the child can call for a review under this provision, and there is no requirement that that person was a relevant person at the time of the making of the supervision requirement or of its last review.[30] Although the statute does not say so, in this context the person must have charge of or control over the child *in the opinion of the reporter,* since it is to the reporter that the call for a review is directed.

---

[23] s.73(6).

[24] s.73(8)(a)(ii).

[25] For example, a supervision requirement made or continued on March 23, can be reviewed at the instance of the child or relevant person on or after June 24.

[26] Though "common", as used in the 1991 Act, refers not to numerical frequency but to the unexceptionality of the act. It would be unexceptional for a child of 14 to call for a review, and exceptional for a five-year-old to do so.

[27] Rather as the (admittedly more positive) right to attend one's own children's hearing is not a right the exercise of which requires formal legal capacity.

[28] Defined in s.93(2)(b).

[29] See above at pp.14–17, 68–69.

[30] *cf.* Title to appeal: see below at pp.206–207.

**Proposal to remove child from Scotland**

The jurisdiction of the children's hearing extends only to Scotland, and the removal of the child from Scotland will render it practically impossible for the relevant local authority, whose duty it is to implement the supervision requirement,[31] to fulfil that duty. In order that the efficacy of the supervision requirement is not frustrated by such removal, an obligation is imposed on any relevant person who intends to remove a child subject to a supervision requirement from Scotland to notify the reporter at least 28 days before that removal.[32] Such notice is required only when the proposal is that the child be taken to live outwith Scotland and not merely for a holiday. Extended holidays may well cause problems here, and the test is probably one of whether the intention is to change the child's habitual residence.[33] On receiving notice under this subsection, the reporter must then arrange a children's hearing to review the supervision requirement.[34] The children's hearing, by specifying a place of residence for the child within Scotland, may effectively prohibit the child's removal from the jurisdiction (if, as always, they consider that this is necessary in the interests of the child). Again, this provision is designed to ensure that a review takes place whenever there is, or is about to be, a significant change in the child's circumstances. However, it is noticeable that the statute lays down no sanction on a relevant person who fails to give the reporter the appropriate notification—or indeed any other person who breaches the condition by removing the child.

**Review required by children's hearing**

A children's hearing who make a supervision requirement may at the same time determine that the requirement shall be reviewed at such time during the duration of the requirement as they determine.[35] Such a determination cannot postpone a review that would be required by another provision in the statute, but it can require a review before one would otherwise be held. If the children's hearing make any such determination, the reporter is obliged to arrange a review within the time laid down.[36]

It is not clear from the wording of s.70(7) whether a children's hearing who are minded to utilise this power must specify an exact date before which[37] a review must be held, or whether they are entitled to require a review at an unspecified but certain time in the future.[38] It is submitted that the provision should be interpreted to permit maximum flexibility in

---

[31] s.71.

[32] s.73(7).

[33] On parental intention to change a child's habitual residence in relation to the Hague Convention on International Child Abduction, see *Findlay v Findlay* (No. 2), 1995 S.L.T. 49; *M, Petitioner* November 11, 2004.

[34] s.73(8)(a)(iv).

[35] s.70(7). See further, above at p.142.

[36] s.73(8)(a)(iii).

[37] Practicality would not permit the hearing to require a review on, rather than on or before, a specified date.

[38] s.70(7) says "A children's hearing who make a supervision requirement may determine that the requirement shall be reviewed at such time during the duration of the requirement as they determine". The difficulty lies in the words "at such time".

pursuit of the child's best interests. It may frequently happen that a children's hearing are of the view that once a certain event occurs compulsory measures of supervision will no longer be necessary or will become inappropriate in their present form, that it is likely the event will occur in far less than a year's hence, but that the precise date of occurrence is not or cannot be known. In these circumstances, the hearing ought to be able to require the reporter to arrange a review hearing after the occurrence of the event rather than on or before a specified date. A common example might be when a child is required to reside with a person who does not have parental responsibilities and parental rights over the child but who has applied to the court for a residence order. The children's hearing may take the view that compulsory measures of supervision are required in order to secure the child's placement with that person, but for no other reason. If they are aware that the residence order has been applied for it would be proper to require a review at such time as the application for a residence order has been dealt with by the court.[39] Or a review could be required once an adoption order over the child has been made, even although the children's hearing do not know the precise date of the court hearing.[40] However, the event that triggers the review probably ought to be one that is reasonably certain to happen, and this provision should not be used as a means of imposing conditions on people. A review could not be required, say, in the event of a mother failing to attend a course in mothering skills, or failing to cure herself of a drug addiction, or if a father is sent to prison, or if the child fails to attend school. In these situations, if it is appropriate for an early review a date should be specified by the children's hearing. A review, in other words, can be specified to be due "*when* X occurs", but not "*if* X occurs".

It would be good practice for hearings intending to use this power to take advice from the reporter as to the practicality of arranging a review within the time specified.

### Making an Antisocial Behaviour Order

If an ASBO or an interim ASBO has been made under the Antisocial Behaviour etc (Scotland) Act 2004, in respect of a child who is currently subject to a supervision requirement, the reporter may be required by the sheriff making the ASBO to refer the case to a children's hearing, and if so he or she must arrange a children's hearing to review the requirement that the child is currently under.[41] The grounds upon which a sheriff can make an ASBO over a child are given above.[42]

### New grounds of referral

It often happens that the reporter decides to refer to a children's hearing on the basis of new grounds a child who is presently subject to a

---

[39] There might be practical difficulties in ensuring the reporter is kept informed of the happening of the event, but normally the social worker will be able to pass on the appropriate information. Alternatively, the requirement could be that a review be arranged when the reporter becomes aware of the happening of the event.

[40] Remembering that the adoption court itself can terminate the supervision requirement: Adoption (Scotland) Act 1978 s.12(9) and s.18(9).

[41] s.73(8)(aa), as inserted by s.12(5) of the Antisocial Behaviour etc Act 2004.

[42] At p.155.

supervision requirement, without waiting for a review of that require-ment to be called or to fall due. This might be, for example, because new grounds come to the attention of the reporter which he or she considers are pointing to a deteriorating situation or are indicating that the existing measures of supervision are not, or are no longer, appropriate. If new grounds were established under the Social Work (Scotland) Act 1968 in respect of a child already under supervision, the child could find him or herself subject to two supervision requirements, for there was no provision requiring the original supervision requirement to be reviewed when new grounds were accepted or established and that would only be done if a review were due or had been called by a person able to call for it, and was arranged for the same time as the new referral. The Children (Scotland) Act 1995 very sensibly alters that position by providing that whenever the reporter makes a referral to the children's hearing in respect of a child who is already subject to compulsory measures of supervision, the existing supervision requirement must be reviewed before disposing of the new referral.[43] This includes referrals that the reporter is obliged to make because the child's case is remitted to the hearing from a criminal court under s.49 of the Criminal Procedure (Scotland) Act 1995.

The statute is ambiguous as to whether it is the referral by the reporter that triggers the need for a review, or the acceptance or establishment of new grounds of referral. There is no practical difficulty when the grounds are accepted, for the children's hearing at which the grounds were put can then move straight on to a combined consideration of the new grounds and review of the existing supervision requirement. Nor is there difficulty when the grounds have been established in earlier court proceedings.[44] But there is a difficulty when the grounds are required to be put to the child and relevant person and are denied. The opening words of s.65(3), "Where a referral is made in respect of a child who is subject to a supervision requirement . . . " suggests that it is the referral itself that triggers the review; but the obligation is stated to be to review the requirement "before disposing of the referral in accordance with s.69(1)", which can only happen after the grounds have been accepted or established. The question, in other words, is whether the review of the existing supervision requirement should (or even can) take place at the children's hearing at which the new grounds are explained to the child and relevant person in order to determine whether they are accepted or not or, if different (due to a denial of the grounds or lack of understanding thereof), at the children's hearing at which the dispositive decision will be made. Since the primary aim of the provision is to avoid the untidiness of a child being subject to two different supervision requirements, it is submitted that the latter interpretation is to be preferred, with the result that the requirement to hold a review is triggered by the *establishment* of new grounds (by whatever means) rather than by the referral of the child by the reporter to the children's hearing. There will seldom be any point in the children's hearing

---

[43] s.65(3).

[44] Such as under s.54 of the Children (Scotland) Act 1995 or s.48 or s.49 of the Criminal Procedure (Scotland) Act 1995.

reviewing the current supervision requirement if the new grounds are denied or not understood and are sent to the sheriff for proof, and it will nearly always be better for the child if all the facts relevant to his or her case are considered and disposed of together. And if the new, denied, grounds are discharged rather than sent for proof, the need for a review of the existing supervision requirement falls since there are no new established grounds. Even if this interpretation is wrong, and the statute requires the hearing that puts the new grounds to the child and relevant person to review the existing supervision requirement, it will nearly always be in the interests of the child that the review be continued until the sheriff has made his decision.[45]

If it is the establishment of the grounds that triggers the review, it follows that if after hearing the s.68 application to establish the new grounds the sheriff finds the grounds not established and discharges the referral in respect of the new grounds,[46] the requirement to hold a review under s.65(3) lapses, and the normal review provisions govern when the existing supervision requirement is to be reviewed. If the sheriff finds the new grounds established, the children's hearing arranged thereafter to consider these new grounds can combine a consideration of the new grounds with a review of the existing supervision requirement.

Though the statute expressly requires that the review take place before the disposal of the new referral, it will in most cases be both convenient for the hearing and in the interests of the child to do both together, for that will allow the children's hearing to look at the child's case as a whole, reviewing the effectiveness of the existing supervision requirement as an integral part of their consideration of the new grounds and how to respond to them. The existence of the new grounds[47] may itself justify either the continuation or variation of an existing supervision requirement, and that outcome amounts, it is submitted, to a disposal of the combined referral and review. It might be technically competent for the children's hearing to deal with the review quite separately from the consideration of the new grounds, but there is no point in doing so, and there would be great awkwardness in a children's hearing coming to different conclusions for each of the two parts of the process. The existing supervision requirement should not be continued while a new one is imposed in respect of the new grounds, and it may indeed be incompetent to do so. There would be no point in terminating the existing supervision requirement while imposing a new one in respect of the new grounds: if the existing requirement is no longer appropriate the correct approach if the child remains in need of compulsory measures of supervision, evidenced by the new grounds, is to vary the existing requirement. Nor should the children's hearing discharge the new referral while continuing the existing supervision requirement, for that would prevent them thereafter taking the new grounds into account. On the other hand, it would be competent to terminate the existing supervision requirement[48] and to discharge the new referral.[49] But the

---

[45] As always, it is to be remembered that too many hearings stress the child.
[46] Under s.68(9).
[47] Which the children's hearing are required to consider under s.69(1).
[48] Under the terms of s.73(9)(b).
[49] Under the terms of s.69(12).

better approach in all cases, it is submitted, is for children's hearings to consider the new grounds as an integral part of the review of the whole of the child's case and to use that consideration as part of the reasoning towards the outcome of that review.

### Transfer of child in case of necessity

Where a child is in terms of his or her present supervision requirement required to reside in a specified residential establishment or other accommodation, but has had to be transferred, on direction from the chief social work officer of the relevant local authority, from that establishment or accommodation in his or her own interests or in the interests of other children there,[50] the child's case must be reviewed within seven days of that transfer[51] and the reporter must arrange a children's hearing within that time to do so.[52] This covers the situation of the child's placement at a residential establishment breaking down for some reason to such an extent that the child will not or cannot remain where he or she is required to reside, and removal to another place was done as a matter of urgent necessity. The children's hearing will normally be requested to remove the current residential requirement and to replace it by naming another place of residence (if a suitable place has been identified). It would seem that if a review is not timeously held, the local authority lose their power to keep the child in any place. Usually the hearing which is held within seven days is arranged on an emergency basis which does not allow panel members to have sufficient time to digest the reports and usually, therefore, the hearing will be continued: the purpose of the hearing held within seven days is to ensure the child's safety in the meantime.

### Return of fugitive child

A child who is subject to a supervision requirement and who absconds from a place of safety in which he or she was being kept under any provision in the 1995 Act, or from a residential establishment in which he or she was required to reside in terms of the supervision requirement, or from a person who has control over him or her while he or she was being taken to, is awaiting being taken to, or is temporarily taken from a place of safety or residential establishment, or from a person who has control over him or her in terms of a supervision requirement, may be arrested without warrant in any part of the United Kingdom and taken back to the place of safety or residential establishment from which he or she absconded.[53] If, however, the person in charge of the place of safety or residential establishment, or the person who had control of the child, is unwilling or unable to take the child back, that circumstance must be

---

[50] s.72(1).

[51] s.72(2).

[52] s.73(8)(a)(iii).

[53] s.82(1) and (3). A child who at the end of a period of leave from a place of safety or residential establishment fails to return there shall, for these purposes, be taken to have absconded: s.82(2). It is the duty of the local authority to ensure that the child is conveyed back to the place or person he or she absconded from: Children's Hearings (Transmission of Information etc.) (Scotland) Regulations 1996, reg.5.

intimated to the reporter[54] and the child may be kept in a place of safety until he or she can be brought before a children's hearing for a review of the supervision requirement.[55] It is implicit in this provision (though surprisingly not stated) that the reporter is obliged to arrange a review hearing and to make any arrangements incidental to that review. Nor (even more surprisingly) is it laid down how long the child can be kept in a place of safety under this provision,[56] though the reporter ought probably to arrange a review as soon as is practicable: it is to be noted that the child must be kept in a place of safety until the review has been held and there is no authority to release the child before then.

**Child in secure accommodation**

If a child is liable to be kept in secure accommodation[57] then a review hearing must be held within three months of the children's hearing deciding that the child should be so liable or of a subsequent children's hearing which renewed the authorisation under s.70(9) to keep the child there.[58] If no such review is held the authorisation ceases to have effect. If the child has been liable to be kept in secure accommodation for more than six weeks but has not at any time during these six weeks been placed in secure accommodation, either the child or the relevant person may require the reporter, in writing, to arrange a review hearing, which must be held within 21 days of the receipt by the reporter of the notice.[59]

**Placing of child for adoption by adoption society**

When a child who is subject to a supervision requirement is being placed for adoption by an approved adoption society, that society is obliged to refer the case of the child to the reporter, who is then obliged to arrange a children's hearing for the purpose of reviewing the supervision requirement.[60] The children's hearing arranged under this provision is obliged both to review the supervision requirement and to draw up a report under s.73(13) of the Children (Scotland) Act 1995 as to the appropriateness of the proposed placing for adoption, for any court which may subsequently require to come to a decision as to an application under s.12 or s.18 of the Adoption (Scotland) Act 1978.[61] This provision is to all intents and purposes the same as that relating to local authority placement of children for adoption.[62]

**Review by the adoption court**

The court that makes an adoption order or an order freeing a child for adoption has the power to terminate any supervision requirement the

---

[54] s.82(4).
[55] s.82(5)(a).
[56] *cf.* the detailed time-limits when the child is kept in a place of safety under any of the warrants discussed in Chap.13.
[57] See above at pp.142–146.
[58] Secure Accommodation (Scotland) Regulations 1996, reg.11.
[59] Secure Accommodation (Scotland) Regulations 1996, reg.12.
[60] Adoption (Scotland) Act 1978, s.22A(1) and (2).
[61] See below at pp.172–173.
[62] See above at p.160.

child is under if satisfied that, as a consequence of the making of the adoption or freeing order, compulsory measures of supervision are no longer necessary.[63] Though technically this is not a review, such a court must, in order to come to its decision on this point, consider the same matters as a children's hearing would in reviewing a supervision requirement and, it is submitted, sheriffs and judges ought to conduct the proceedings in a manner as like a review by a children's hearing as possible. Since a decision by an adoption or freeing court on the supervision requirement is "a decision relating to the adoption of a child", s.6 of the Adoption (Scotland) Act 1978 governs the decision. That section provides that the court must regard the need to safeguard and promote the welfare of the child concerned throughout his or her life as the paramount consideration and must have regard, so far as practicable, (i) to the child's views (if he or she wishes to express them) taking account of his or her age and maturity and (ii) to the child's religious persuasion, racial origin, and cultural and linguistic background.

## POWERS AND DUTIES OF THE CHILDREN'S HEARING ON REVIEW

At a review hearing there is no need to have accepted or established the existence of any grounds of referral and the hearing can, once the introductions and other preliminaries have been carried out, move straight on to a consideration of the child's case.[64] The original grounds of referral may retain some relevance and will sometimes require reconsideration, but the further back in time they occurred the less likely they are to be relevant to the child's present situation and future needs and there is, indeed, no statutory obligation on a review hearing to give any fresh consideration to the grounds of referral.[65] There is usually little point in going over old grounds, though occasionally this must be done. If the original ground was that the child was a member of the same household as a Sch.1 offender, the ground may well require examination in order to determine whether the child's living arrangements still pose a risk to the child. On the other hand, the fact that the child committed a single criminal offence well over a year previously will seldom be relevant to a consideration of what is best for the child now. A review hearing should conduct a wide-ranging discussion into the child's present circumstances in order to determine whether the child still requires compulsory measures of supervision. A consideration of how successful the current supervision requirement has been in tackling the problems facing the child is inevitable. If a review has been specifically requested (*i.e.* it is not the annual review) it will be sensible for the person or body

---

[63] Adoption (Scotland) Act 1978, s.12(9) and s.18(9), as added by Children (Scotland) Act 1995, Sch.2, paras 7 and 11.

[64] The statute is inconsistent in the terminology it uses: some provisions, such as s.72(2), require a review of the child's case, while others, such as s.73(9), require a review of the supervision requirement. This change in terminology makes no difference in practice since the supervision requirement cannot properly be reviewed without a consideration of the child's case.

[65] Unlike the hearing which originally imposed the supervision requirement: s.69(1).

who requested the review to be asked why he or she did so. With these specialties, the actual discussion will follow much the same lines as a discussion at an original hearing.[66] At the end of the discussion the options available to the review hearing as a decision are as follows.

First, where the children's hearing are satisfied that in order to complete the review of the supervision requirement it is necessary to have a further investigation of the child's case, they may continue the review to a subsequent hearing.[67] This is the proper decision to come to when the hearing feel that they need more information before they will be in a position to make a dispositive decision. If the review hearing is continued, the hearing will have the same powers to require the child to undergo investigative assessment and to be kept in a place of safety as when a hearing at which established grounds of referral are being considered is continued.[68] At some point during the review hearing the children's hearing must consider whether it is necessary to appoint a person to safeguard the interests of the child in the hearing, and if they do so consider they must make such an appointment on such terms and conditions as appear to them to be appropriate.[69] They may make an appointment only at a review hearing if the decision is to continue the review (*i.e.* the case is not disposed of) because the appointment is designed to assist the hearing in making the appropriate dispositive decision. Likewise, the appointment of a legal representative must be considered if the circumstances are such that such an appointment would be open at the initial hearing.

Secondly, the children's hearing may terminate the supervision requirement that the child is currently subject to.[70] This will normally be appropriate if the requirement has achieved its aim, or if the child's problems have otherwise been resolved.[71] No child shall continue to be subject to a supervision requirement for any period longer than is necessary in the interests of promoting or safeguarding his or her welfare.[72] The effect of this provision is not to bring the supervision requirement automatically to an end when the child's interests are best served by the termination of the requirement, but rather to indicate to the local authority when they ought to require a review under s.73(4)(a), as well as to indicate to the children's hearing the paramount consideration to which they must direct their minds in determining whether or not a supervision requirement should be terminated.

Thirdly, the supervision requirement can be continued without any variation in its terms or conditions.[73] This would be appropriate if the

---

[66] See above at pp.114–120. Rule 20 of the 1996 Rules applies to review hearings as it does to the original consideration of the case: r.20(1). Curiously, in its terms, the rule applies only to reviews under s.73(8) and not to reviews under the various other provisions discussed in the text. It would, however, be sensible to follow the procedures in r.20 whenever appropriate.

[67] s.73(9)(a).

[68] s.73(10): see above at pp.129–130.

[69] s.41(1).

[70] s.73(9)(b).

[71] If, for example, the child's problem was nothing other than school attendance and he or she has now reached the school-leaving age it may be appropriate to terminate the supervision requirement even when it failed to achieve its purpose of returning the child to school.

[72] s.73(1).

[73] s.73(9)(e).

child still needs compulsory measures of supervision and the supervision requirement in its present form remains the best way forward for the child.

Fourthly, the supervision requirement can be continued but with a variation in its terms and conditions.[74] Any condition that could have been imposed when the supervision requirement was originally made may be inserted into the continued requirement.[75] A decision to vary the supervision requirement might be appropriate if the child's circumstances have changed, for the better or for the worse, and a different form of supervision is now required to address the difficulties that the child continues to face. If the variation is to the effect that the child is required to reside in any specified place or places, the hearing may also order that such place or places shall not be disclosed to any person or class of persons specified in the requirement.[76]

Fifthly, where it appears to the children's hearing that the relevant local authority are in breach of a duty imposed on them by the supervision requirement, the hearing may direct the reporter to give the local authority notice of an intended application to the sheriff principal for an order requiring the local authority to fulfil that duty.[77] Such notice requires to be written and it must set out the respects in which the relevant local authority are in breach of their duties, together with a warning that if, within 21 days, the duties are not fulfilled an application to the sheriff principal may be made.[78] The children's hearing giving such a direction to the reporter must also require a further review to take place on or as soon as is reasonably practicable after the expiry of a period of 28 days after the notice was given (*i.e.* a week after the expiry of the 21 days the local authority have to fulfil their duties).[79] If at this further review it appears to the children's hearing that the local authority remain in breach, they may authorise the reporter to make an application to the sheriff principal.[80]

The decision which of the above options to adopt at a review hearing is one to which the three overarching principles in s.16 apply[81]: so the children's hearing must regard the welfare of the child as their paramount consideration, they must have regard so far as practicable to the views, if he or she wishes to express them, of the child concerned, and they may continue the supervision requirement only when they consider that to do so would be better than having no supervision requirement at all.[82] And as at the initial hearing the terms of the continued supervision

---

[74] s.73(9)(c) and (e).

[75] s.73(9)(d).

[76] s.73(11), reflecting the power of the children's hearing under s.70(6) when the supervision requirement is originally made. It would seem that this power is not available to review hearings continuing without variation a supervision requirement made by an original children's hearing which did not make a non-disclosure order.

[77] s.70(7A), as inserted by the Antisocial Behaviour etc (Scotland) Act 2004, s.136(1). Copies of this notice must be sent to the child, the relevant persons, and any safeguarder: s.70(7B), as so inserted.

[78] s.70(7C), as so inserted.

[79] s.70(7D), as so inserted.

[80] s.70(7E), as so inserted.

[81] See above at pp.121–123.

[82] The minimum intervention principle does not mean minimum intervention with orders that currently exist, but minimum intervention in the child's life.

requirement and its conditions, if any, must consist with the ECHR principle of proportionality.[83]

**Other powers**

The Children (Scotland) Act 1995 specifically gives to a children's hearing who make a supervision requirement under s.70 a number of powers and duties, which are not expressly mentioned in s.73 in relation to review hearings. For example, it is specified that when a children's hearing "make" a supervision requirement they must consider whether to regulate contact between the child and any other person,[84] they may require that the supervision requirement they make shall be reviewed at such time during the duration of the requirement as they determine,[85] and they may specify in the supervision requirement that the child shall be liable to be placed and kept in secure accommodation if certain conditions are satisfied.[86] There is no reason why any of these powers and duties should apply to children's hearings who make a supervision requirement but not to children's hearings who continue such requirements at a review. However, the provisions all refer expressly to the making and not the continuing or varying of supervision requirements and it is worthy of note that other provisions, such as that allowing a children's hearing who make a supervision requirement to require that the child's address be kept secret[87] and that allowing the keeping of a child in a place of safety when the hearing is continued for further investigation, are expressly repeated or referred to for review hearings,[88] which might be taken to indicate that powers and duties other than those do not apply to review hearings. This interpretation of the Act must be avoided, though how this can be done is not immediately apparent. The provision allowing review hearings to "insert in the [supervision] requirement any requirement which could have been imposed by them under s.70(3)"[89] might be used to grant the extra powers and duties, but that would mean interpreting these powers and duties as "conditions" in the requirement. This is clearly inept. A duty to consider whether to impose a condition of contact is clearly not a condition itself, and neither secure accommodation authorisation nor a requirement that the supervision requirement be reviewed at a specified time can properly be described as a condition on the child. Alternatively, it might be possible to interpret "make a supervision requirement" to mean "make, continue or vary" a supervision requirement, though only at the cost of some violence to the actual terms of the statute. Such violence is, it is submitted, necessary if the intention of Parliament is not to be frustrated. The review hearing, like the original hearing, is designed to have maximum flexibility in determining what is best for the child, and the complete lack of any reason why the duties and powers mentioned above should be limited to

---

[83] See above at pp.4–5.
[84] s.70(2). See pp.137–140.
[85] s.70(7). See above at p.142.
[86] s.70(9). See pp.142–146.
[87] s.70(6).
[88] s.73(10) and (11).
[89] s.73(9)(d).

original hearings and denied to review hearings suggests that the word "make" where it appears in s.70(2), (7) and (9) should be interpreted, for the benefit of children, to include "continue" and "vary".[90] Confirmation that this is so can be obtained from s.65(3) of the Adoption (Scotland) Act 1978, which provides that the making of a supervision requirement under which the child is required to reside at a specified place is not to be regarded as a "placement" for adoption.[91] It would simply be ludicrous to suggest that this important provision is limited to original hearings and does not also apply to review hearings.

### Reports to the Court

As was seen above,[92] one of the situations in which a review must be called is when the local authority or an adoption society intend to place the child for adoption or the local authority intend to apply for an order freeing the child for adoption or to apply for a parental responsibilities order, or they become aware that someone intends to apply to adopt the child. When a children's hearing is arranged for any of these reasons they are obliged to draw up a report to provide advice to the court in respect of that matter.[93] They must do so irrespective of what the outcome of the review of the supervision requirement is, that is to say whether it is continued, varied or terminated. Before deciding upon the advice to give, the children's hearing must consider the reference from the local authority or adoption society, any supervision requirement to which the child is subject, a social background report, and any other relevant document or information available to them; they must discuss the case with the child and afford the child, relevant person, safeguarder and legal or non-legal representative (if attending) an opportunity of participating in the discussion and of being heard on the case; and they must take steps to obtain the views of the child, relevant person, safeguarder and representative on what arrangements with respect to the child would be in the best interests of the child.[94] The children's hearing must then determine what advice they will give the court, local authority or adoption society[95] and they shall inform the child, relevant person, safeguarder and representative of that advice.[96] As soon as reasonably practicable after they determine what advice to give, the chairman must make or cause to be made a report in writing providing the advice, including a statement of the reasons for that advice; and the chairman of the hearing must sign the report and the statement.[97]

This report should be wider than the statement of reasons for the decision, which is limited to justifying the decision made in respect of the supervision requirement. Rather, the report should take the form of the

---

[90] The Social Work (Scotland) Act 1968 gives statutory (though express) precedent, for s.47(1) refers to the varying of supervision requirements as the making of supervision requirements.

[91] See further, above at pp.118–120.

[92] Above at pp.160, 167–168.

[93] s.73(13).

[94] 1996 Rules, r.22(3).

[95] *ibid.*

[96] 1996 Rules, r.22(5).

[97] 1996 Rules, r.22(6).

hearing's opinion as to the appropriateness of the order that the court is being asked to make or the proposed placing for adoption. Since the court making an adoption order or freeing order also has the power to terminate the supervision requirement[98] it will often be appropriate for the advice to include a recommendation as to whether or not the court should exercise that power. Within seven days following the determination by the children's hearing, the reporter must send a copy of the report to the court, local authority or adoption society, and to the child, relevant person and safeguarder.[99] The court is then obliged to consider this report before coming to any decision on an application under s.86 of the 1995 Act (parental responsibilities order) or s.12 or s.18 of the Adoption (Scotland) Act 1978 (adoption order or freeing order respectively).[1] The court will already have before it many different reports which it must consider in an application for an adoption order and there will seldom be any issue of fact that can come out of a children's hearing's report which the court will not otherwise be aware of. Nevertheless, the provision will have some use if the children's hearing are convinced that the adoption plans are quite wrong for the particular child since it provides them with a direct line to the court through which they can communicate their doubts.

It would seem that reports have to be drawn up at all stages, that is to say, placing, freeing and applying for the adoption order itself, and if these events are relatively close in time, the children's hearing may feel that they have little to add to their previous reports. Their obligation to draw up a report under s.73(13) is absolute, but it would be competent, if the child's circumstances have not changed since a previous report was drawn up, for the report simply to repeat advice previously given or even to do no more than refer to advice given in a previously drawn up report.

---

[98] Adoption (Scotland) Act 1978, s.12(9) and s.18(9).
[99] 1996 Rules, r.22(7).
[1] s.73(14).

## CHAPTER TWELVE

# REVIEW OF THE ESTABLISHMENT OF THE GROUNDS OF REFERRAL

## INTRODUCTION

Though the Social Work (Scotland) Act 1968 attempted to create a unified and comprehensive code for dealing with children who may be in need of compulsory measures of care, the very novelty of the system it set up meant that certain gaps and omissions were inevitable. Some of these gaps were filled by amending legislation[1]; and some were left to the imagination of the Court of Session. One omission concerned what was to happen when new evidence came to light some time after the sheriff had found grounds of referral to exist, which raised serious doubts as to the accuracy of that original finding. There was no provision in the 1968 Act permitting the reopening of the question of whether grounds of referral existed or not, and the children's hearing were (and are) obliged to accept as fact any finding made by the sheriff; nor could the emergence of new evidence found an appeal since appeal from a sheriff's decision was (and is) available on a point of law or procedural irregularity only. Yet, to deny a remedy because none had been statutorily provided for could lead to results which were perceived as unjust, as was clearly shown in two cases decided within two months of each other. In *R, Petitioner*[2] parents of a child subject to a supervision requirement, who had all along disputed the grounds of referral found established by the sheriff, petitioned the *nobile officium* of the Court of Session for an order requiring the sheriff to consider anew whether or not the grounds of referral had been made out, in the light of new evidence which had since come to light (taking the form, in this case, of a retraction by the child of her original allegations against her father of sexual abuse). The First Division held that such a petition was incompetent since to reopen the question of the existence of grounds of referral after their establishment would amount to a judicial supplement to the statutory procedure laid down in the 1968 Act.[3] However, in *L, Petitioners*[4] a similar petition to the *nobile officium* was granted. The petitioners in that case alleged that new expert evidence was available

---

[1] Such as the provisions introduced by the Children Act 1975 relating to safeguarders, and the addition of a new ground of referral by the Solvent Abuse (Scotland) Act 1983.

[2] 1993 S.L.T. 910.

[3] See also *H, Petitioners*, 1997 S.L.T. 3, where the same conclusion was reached on very similar facts.

[4] 1993 S.L.T. 1310 and 1342.

which cast considerable doubt on the original expert evidence upon which the sheriff had based his findings that serious child abuse had occurred, and that there was currently a much greater awareness since the Clyde Report[5] of the need to be especially careful in interviewing children alleged to be the victims of abuse, which awareness had not been shown in the present case. The First Division accepted that this justified them exercising the *nobile officium* to order the sheriff to examine again the question of whether or not the grounds of referral existed, but the procedure under which this rehearing took place and the effect it had on the extant supervision requirements had to be determined by the Court of Session without any statutory guidance.

The effect of these two cases (which are probably irreconcilable[6]) was to leave the law in a state of considerable doubt. The level of evidence required to persuade the court to exercise the *nobile officium*, the effect on supervision requirements, the role of the Court of Session, the issue of title to sue, the possibility of appeal to the House of Lords, and many other questions were left open. A whole new procedure was therefore introduced by s.85 of the Children (Scotland) Act 1995, which is designed to put the process for reviewing the grounds of referral onto a statutory basis, to clarify the grounds upon which such reviews can take place, and to specify what is to happen to any supervision requirement that had been made on the basis of a ground of referral which is subsequently found not to have been made out. The complex provisions about to be described have not been applied in any reported case since the 1995 Act came into force.

### CIRCUMSTANCES IN WHICH ESTABLISHED GROUNDS OF REFERRAL CAN BE REVIEWED

While there are a number of different ways in which the grounds of referral can be established, the procedure in s.85 for a re-examination of the existence of the grounds can be utilised only when they have been established by a positive finding of the sheriff on an application for proof made under s.65(7) or (9), that is to say on an application made by the reporter because the child or relevant person denied the grounds or because the child was found by the children's hearing to be too young to understand the grounds. The review permitted by s.85 is a review of the sheriff's findings made under s.68(10) that the grounds of referral exist[7] and the existence of grounds of referral cannot be reopened if they had been established in any other way (such as, for example, by the child and relevant person accepting them under s.65(5),[8] or by the court holding the grounds established in relevant proceedings under s.54[9]). It would be

---

[5] *Report of the Inquiry into the Removal of Children from Orkney in February* 1991: H.C. Papers 1992-1993, No.195.

[6] See Norrie, "Children's Hearings, New Evidence and the *Nobile Officium*", 1994 S.L.G. 4.

[7] Which can include findings on the basis of evidence heard or when the hearing of evidence was dispensed with and the ground deemed to be established: Children (Scotland) Act 1995, s.68(10).

[8] See above at pp.85–87.

[9] See above at pp.44–45. This position is a little anomalous. Grounds found by a sheriff to be established in divorce proceedings cannot be challenged under s.85 while grounds found by a sheriff to be established in s.68 proceedings can be.

incompetent to use this procedure to challenge the sheriff's finding that no grounds of referral exist[10]: if new evidence suggests that a ground can now be proved and the reporter wants to take the matter further, he or she must state new grounds.

Section 85 places no limitation on when an application for review can be made, except implicitly that it must be after the sheriff has made his finding that grounds of referral are established. But the application might be made either before a children's hearing have imposed a supervision requirement over the child, or after (even, as in *L, Petitioners*, some years after), or, indeed, after a children's hearing have decided that no supervision requirement is justified in the circumstances of the case or have decided to discharge a previously made supervision requirement. It would be rare to make a s.85 application when there is no extant supervision requirement, but an application might be made in these circumstances as a means of clearing a person's name, unjustly impugned by the original sheriff's finding,[11] or as a means of preventing the establishment of grounds of referral in respect of other children (*e.g.* those in the same household as the originally referred child).

### TITLE TO SEEK REVIEW

Title to seek a review of the establishment of the grounds of referral on the basis of new evidence inheres only in the child and in each of the relevant persons.[12] No other person can challenge a finding of the sheriff that grounds of referral in relation to the child exist. Another person may feel that they have an interest to do so, for example to clear their name from an imputation contained in the original finding, but s.85 is not designed to correct any injustice except that to the child. It is only the child and the relevant person who have the right to accept or deny the grounds of referral put to them at the children's hearing, and it is only they who have title to challenge a finding made by the sheriff after their denial.[13] The statute does not make clear whether the person must be a relevant person at the time of the original s.68 application or at the time of the s.85 application, but since the purpose is to remedy the child's present position it is submitted that title inheres in anyone who, at the date of the present application, is a relevant person in relation to the child. Nor does the statute say whether "the child" must still be a child at the date of the s.85 application. It is submitted that there is no age limitation on title to make an application under s.85. The statute nowhere requires that there be an extant supervision requirement before a s.85 application can be made, and an adult clearly retains an interest in

---

[10] s.85(2).

[11] It is to be remembered that a discharge of a referral based on a finding that the child committed an offence subjects the child to the provisions of the Rehabilitation of Offenders Act 1974: see above, at pp.131–132.

[12] s.85(4).

[13] Though a challenge to a different child's ground of referral may be implicit in an application under s.85. For example, a child referred on the ground of membership of the same household as a victim of a Sch.1 offence who wishes that ground to be reviewed might do so by challenging the validity of the victim's ground of referral.

a finding that he or she had, while a child, committed a criminal offence: such an interest gives him or her title to challenge that finding under s.85 and there is no reason why such title should be limited to offence-based cases.

THE CONDITIONS FOR MAKING THE APPLICATION

The applicant for a review of the establishment of the grounds of referral must claim and, if the application is to be successful, must establish each of the following three conditions.[14]

(a) That the applicant has evidence that was not considered by the sheriff on the original application, being evidence the existence or significance of which might materially have affected the determination of the original application. This new evidence might include evidence which the sheriff did not hear because he dispensed with hearing the evidence under s.68(8). The evidence must be such as to cast doubt on the validity of the original finding. So it might be, for example, a retraction by the child of an allegation of abuse when the child's own previous evidence was the major determinant of the finding,[15] or other evidence that shows that the original evidence founded upon by the sheriff in making the original finding was in some way flawed and is now unreliable, or entirely new evidence which casts a different light on the child's circumstances at the time of the original finding. In exceptional cases the new evidence might be the quashing of a conviction of an alleged Sch.1 offender but it is always to be remembered that the quashing of a criminal conviction, because proof is not established beyond reasonable doubt, is not in itself conclusive that proof on the balance of probabilities similarly ought not to have been established. This matter was given some consideration in England after the Court of Appeal quashed a mother's conviction for murdering her children due to the discrediting of scientific evidence.[16] Shortly thereafter a number of challenges were made to child care proceedings which had previously been activated on similar scientific evidence. The Court of Appeal rejected these challenges and indicated that reliance on cases from the criminal courts was unsound.[17] *And:*

(b) That such evidence (i) is likely to be credible and reliable and (ii) would have been admissible in relation to the ground of referral which was found to be established on the original application. *And:*

---

[14] s.85(3).

[15] *cf. R, Petitioner,* 1993 S.L.T. 910; *H, Petitioners,* 1997 S.L.T. 3. Both these cases held that retraction was not sufficient to justify exercising the *nobile officium.* The test under s.85 is not so strict and the child's evidence that he or she lied before can, it is submitted, be properly regarded as new evidence.

[16] *R v Canning* [2004] EWCA (Crim) 1.

[17] *Re LU (A Child) and LB (A Child)* [2004] EWCA (Civ) 567, discussed in Norrie "Identity Crisis" (2004) 49 J.L.S.S. 7/27.

(c) That there is a reasonable explanation for the failure to lead such evidence on the original application. The onus will be on the applicant to provide an explanation. This is a lesser test than the Court of Session required for an application under the *nobile officium*, for in *L, Petitioners* it was held that evidence could be heard only if the circumstances which had arisen were "exceptional and unforeseen". A reasonable explanation might include the non-availability of the evidence, for whatever reason (so long as that reason is not directly attributable to the applicant), or because of new understandings which have developed since the original finding.[18] If evidence was available at the original proof but for some reason was not led, there will be a heavy onus in providing a reasonable explanation for that failure.

**Procedure**

An application under s.85 must contain the name and address of the applicant and his or her representative (if any),[19] the reporter, any safeguarder,[20] and any other party to the application. It must include the date and finding made under s.68 and the name of the sheriff who made the finding, the grounds for making the application, specification of the nature of the new evidence, the explanation for the failure to lead such evidence in the s.68 application, and any reports, affidavits and productions upon which the applicant intends to rely.[21]

The sheriff must hear the parties and may allow such further procedure as he thinks fit before determining whether these claims have been made out[22]: he makes his determination on the basis of argument put before him. If any of these claims is not established to the satisfaction of the sheriff, he must dismiss the application.[23] If the three claims are established to the sheriff's satisfaction, the application for a review of the original finding will be granted, and the sheriff must then move on to consider the evidence which the applicant claims to have.[24] He may fix a further hearing for that purpose.[25] The consideration of the

---

[18] As in *L, Petitioners*, 1993 S.L.T. 1310 and 1342.

[19] The applicant can be represented by an advocate or solicitor or any other person who can satisfy the sheriff that he or she is a suitable person to represent the applicant and that he or she is authorised to do so: Act of Sederunt (Child Care and Maintenance Rules) 1997, r.3.21.

[20] It will be a rare case indeed in which a safeguarder is still in office when an application under s.85 is made. It might be that this provision refers to any safeguarder who previously acted as such, either at the s.68 hearing or when the children's hearing subsequently disposed of the case.

[21] AS 1997, r.3.62.

[22] AS 1997, r.3.63(3).

[23] s.85(5).

[24] s.85(6). This provision requires that the sheriff consider "the evidence". It is unclear whether this refers only to the new evidence referred to in s.85(3), but it is submitted that such a limitation should not be read into s.85(6). There may well be cases (particularly if the s.68 application was some years previously) in which the sheriff will be able to determine whether the grounds of referral are established only by hearing the new evidence and rehearing previously heard evidence. In most cases, however, the focus of the proof should be clearly on the new evidence.

[25] AS 1997, r.3.63(3).

evidence will take the same form as a consideration of evidence at an original hearing to establish grounds of referral under s.68,[26] except that there is no power, as there is under s.68(8), to dispense with the hearing of the evidence. A safeguarder may be appointed.[27] Somewhat surprisingly (in the light of the requirement on the child to attend the hearing in a s.68 application)[28] there is no requirement that the child attend the hearing in a s.85 application. However, the Rules require that the sheriff hear the parties to the application[29] and the child should, it is submitted, always be regarded as one of the parties. It is open to argument that the rules on attendance and procedure in applications under s.68 are implicitly applicable to applications under s.85, but there is no indication in the statute or the Rules that this is so. Nevertheless the s.68 model should, in the absence of any other statutory guidance, be followed.

Having examined the evidence and heard such parties as wish to make representations to the sheriff, the sheriff will then give his decision orally at the conclusion of the hearing.[30] He may, when giving his decision or within seven days thereafter, issue a note of the reasons for his decision and if he does so the sheriff clerk must forthwith send a copy of such a note to the child, the relevant persons, any safeguarder appointed by the sheriff, and the reporter.[31]

## FINDING THAT ONE OR MORE OF THE ORIGINAL GROUNDS IS ESTABLISHED

If the sheriff is satisfied on the evidence presented to him that any one or more of the original grounds of referral has again been established he may remit the case under s.68(10) to the reporter to arrange a children's hearing.[32] The use of the permissive "may" in this provision can be compared with the wording in s.68(10), where it is stated that the sheriff "shall" remit the case to the reporter on a finding that grounds of referral have been established. If the child is currently subject to a supervision requirement as a result of the grounds found once again to exist, a remit to the reporter will normally be redundant, but it might be appropriate if the evidence presented to the sheriff satisfies him that the requirement ought to be reviewed (*e.g.* because only some of the original grounds of referral are found established).[33] If the child is not currently under a supervision requirement in respect of the grounds found again to be established because a hearing has not yet been arranged then it would normally be pointless for the sheriff to remit the case to the reporter if the reporter is already in the process of arranging a children's

---

[26] See above at pp.104–110.
[27] s.41.
[28] s.68(4).
[29] AS 1997, r.3.63(3).
[30] AS 1997, r.3.64 and r.3.51.
[31] *ibid.*
[32] s.85(6)(b).
[33] Technically, it would appear that such a hearing would not be a review, as governed by s.73 (under which there is no obligation on the reporter to arrange a review when the sheriff finds grounds established under s.86), though in practice it will be treated as such.

hearing. The sheriff ought therefore to inquire of the reporter during the rehearing as to the situation in this respect before making his decision whether to remit the case to the reporter. If the child is not under a supervision requirement because the children's hearing have previously discharged the referral in respect of the grounds now confirmed (but challenged, say, because of its effects on the referrals of other children) the sheriff should normally decide not to remit the case to the reporter to arrange a children's hearing; but he may decide to do so if the circumstances have changed sufficiently, or if new circumstances have come to light in the course of the rehearing, to justify the hearing looking at the matter afresh.

## FINDING THAT NONE OF THE ORIGINAL GROUNDS IS ESTABLISHED

If the sheriff is satisfied that none of the original grounds of referral is established he must discharge the referral.[34] If the application has been made before any supervision requirement has been imposed by a children's hearing then none can be imposed thereafter in respect of these grounds. However, if the child is currently subject to a supervision requirement, imposed in respect of the grounds now found not to be established, the sheriff must terminate the supervision requirement, though he may do so either immediately or on a date he may specify.[35] It is not within the discretion of the sheriff to do anything else, such as continuing the supervision requirement. It is nowhere stated, but an inevitable consequence of discharging the referral in a case based on s.52(2)(i) (that is that the child has committed an offence) is that the provisions of the Rehabilitation of Offenders Act 1974 no longer apply and the child is freed from the obligation to reveal offences.

### Postponement of termination of supervision requirement

The decision to postpone the termination of the supervision require-ment[36] must be made on the basis of the welfare of the child.[37] This was one of the aspects of the Inner House's decision in *L, Petitioners,*[38] where it was considered to be against the children's interests to be returned home immediately since they had been separated from their parents for a very long time, and this is likely to be the typical sort of reason why a termination will not be ordered immediately it is found that there are no grounds of referral. Such a postponement does not necessarily infringe the ECHR: the European Court has accepted that "after a considerable period of time has passed since the child was originally taken into public care, the interests of the child not to have his or her *de facto* family situation changed again may override the interests of the parents to have their family reunited".[39] It is difficult to visualise a situation in which the

---

[34] s.85(6)(a).
[35] s.85(7)(a).
[36] Under s.85(7)(a)(ii).
[37] s.16(1).
[38] 1993 S.L.T. 1310 and 1342.
[39] *KA v Finland* January 14, 2003 at para.138.

child's interests would require that a supervision requirement that does not contain a condition of residence should not be terminated immediately, and the power to postpone termination is one which sheriffs should use very sparingly indeed. Apart from anything else, there is much that is left unsaid in the statute when termination is postponed. There is, for example, no limit specified on how long the sheriff can postpone the termination of the supervision requirement for. It is submitted that it would be inconsistent with the provisions determining the duration of supervision requirements[40] to allow the sheriff to specify a date beyond the time at which a children's hearing must sit in order to review that requirement under s.73(2) or (3).[41] Otherwise the sheriff would be prolonging an order which was made upon the basis of false information beyond its natural life. If the child's interests require further compulsory measures of supervision then new grounds justifying these measures must be formulated by the reporter, and if none can be so formulated the child must be returned home no later than the date of that review. Again, the statute does not say whether anyone can call for a review before the annual review during the period of postponement. It is, however, likely to be considered incompetent to call for such a review, for any variation or termination of the supervision requirement by the children's hearing would be inconsistent with the sheriff's order to postpone termination and would therefore subvert this whole provision.

If the sheriff is satisfied that none of the original grounds of referral is established but has decided, in the child's best interests, to postpone the termination of the supervision requirement, he may vary that requirement in any way he thinks fit (being guided again by the child's welfare), or vary any condition attached to it, or any requirement to keep the child's address secret, or any determination by the children's hearing as to when the supervision requirement is to be reviewed.[42] In other words, once the sheriff has determined that a supervision requirement has to be terminated because none of the grounds of referral in the original application has been established, but that the termination ought to be postponed, every aspect of that requirement comes under the control of, and open to variation by, the sheriff. Surprisingly, in deciding whether to postpone the termination of a supervision requirement, and if so whether to vary any of its terms or conditions, the sheriff is not obliged (in terms of s.16(2)[43]) to take account of the views of the child. Good practice, however, suggests that the sheriff should take such account of the child's views as a children's hearing would in reviewing a supervision requirement.

### Non-compulsory supervision or guidance

If a supervision requirement is to be terminated because none of the original grounds is found established (whether that termination is

---

[40] s.73.

[41] *i.e.*the annual review or review before the child's 18th birthday.

[42] s.85(8). This determination must be varied if the sheriff wishes to postpone termination until some date after the children's hearing have required a review. A review during the period of postponement would be pointless and it is entirely unclear what, if any, powers such a review hearing would have in the face of the sheriff's order.

[43] Which is limited to the circumstances listed in s.16(4).

immediate or on a later specified date) the sheriff must go on to consider whether the child still requires supervision or guidance.[44] If so, he must direct the local authority to provide it. Such a direction may be given not only to the local authority who is presently responsible for implementing the supervision requirement but also to any local authority specified by the sheriff. The local authority directed to provide supervision or guidance under this provision must do so, unless the child is unwilling to accept the supervision or guidance offered and he or she is of sufficient age and maturity to understand what is being offered.[45]

### Finding that another ground of referral exists

In a s.68 application it is not open to the sheriff to find that the grounds which the reporter seeks to establish have not been made out but that, nevertheless, other grounds have been.[46] This is for the very good reason that those denying the grounds must be given fair notice of what they are to deny. This important principle of natural justice is disregarded in relation to s.85 applications, which may therefore be vulnerable to due process challenges under Art.6 of the ECHR. If the sheriff determines that the grounds of referral which are being reviewed have not been made out, but that the evidence establishes that other grounds of referral do exist which were not stated in the original application, then as well as discharging the original referral[47] he may also remit the case under s.68(10) to the reporter to arrange a children's hearing for the consideration of the case based on these new established grounds.[48] But a finding to this effect would be consistent with Art.6, it is submitted, only if the child and relevant persons were given due notice and the opportunity to challenge the allegations upon which the sheriff is making his finding. If the sheriff does decide to remit the case to the reporter he cannot terminate the supervision requirement based on the grounds of referral found not to be established, for in listing the sheriff's options when he finds that none of the original grounds of referral is established, s.85(7) allows him *either* to terminate any existing supervision requirement (with or without postponement) *or,* if another ground is established instead, to remit the case to the reporter. If the child is subject to a supervision requirement and the sheriff has now found grounds of referral to exist which are different from the original grounds, then that amounts to a finding that the basis for the original supervision requirement was false and that requirement therefore stands in need of urgent review. If the child is, for whatever reason, not currently under a supervision requirement[49] but new grounds are established then the question arises as to

---

[44] s.85(9).

[45] s.85(10).

[46] The rule that the sheriff can find one offence established when the reporter has sought to prove another offence (AS 1997, r.3.50) does not detract from this since the ground of referral, that the child has committed an offence, remains the same.

[47] Which he must do under s.85(6)(a)—though this does not affect any supervision requirement.

[48] s.85(7)(b). The sheriff cannot find new grounds to exist *in addition* to old grounds reconfirmed under s.85(6)(b), because s.85(7) is activated only when none of the grounds of referral in the original application is established: s.85(6)(a).

[49] Whether none was imposed or it has subsequently been terminated.

whether compulsory measures of supervision are required[50]: in that circumstance the sheriff should always remit the case to the reporter for him or her to arrange a children's hearing, just as such a finding in an application under s.68 would oblige the sheriff to do so.[51]

## APPEALS

An appeal from any decision of the sheriff under s.85 can be made in terms of s.51(11) to the sheriff principal or the Court of Session.[52]

---

[50] s.52(1).
[51] s.68(10).
[52] See further, Chap.14.

## CHAPTER THIRTEEN

# WARRANTS AND ORDERS TO APPREHEND AND DETAIN CHILD

## INTRODUCTION

There are a number of different provisions in the Children (Scotland) Act 1995 which give the children's hearing power to issue or grant warrants to remove a child to, and detain him or her in, a place of safety before they have made a dispositive decision on the referral. The power to grant warrants is conferred in order to ensure that the process towards the dispositive decision is not frustrated by lack of co-operation, and also to ensure that there is no hiatus in the protection that can be afforded children in the period after the emergency protection provisions[1] have been exhausted but before a dispositive decision has been made. Though each provision concerning warrants is designed to deal with an essentially separate stage in the process, the wording of the Act does not make this clear and, on a superficial reading, there are large areas of overlap in which the hearing appears to have a choice of which provision to found upon in granting a warrant. So, for example, if it seems likely that a child will not attend the children's hearing, a warrant can be granted. But this is stated to be one of the grounds for granting a warrant in s.45(5), in order to allow the reporter to fulfil his or her responsibility of securing the child's attendance; in s.66(1), whenever a hearing are unable to dispose of the case; and in s.69(7), when a case has been continued to a subsequent hearing. Each of these provisions has different time limits: s.45 warrants last for seven days, s.66 warrants last for 22 days and can be continued for up to a total of 66 days, and s.69 warrants last for 22 days and can be granted an unlimited number of times. It would be contrary both to natural justice and the intention of Parliament to allow the stricter time-limits in one provision to be avoided by utilising another provision which seems, in its words, to cover the same point but which is, in fact, intended to deal with a quite separate situation. The layout of the Act can be used to help in the interpretation of the limitations in availability of each provision, and it is submitted that the Act should be read as a whole and interpreted in such a way that, when a warrant is to be granted, the children's hearing are never presented with a choice of two of more alternative provisions under which they can act.

### Types of warrants

Section 69 warrants are the easiest to delimit, for the power to grant warrants under that section is expressly limited to cases which have, after

---

[1] Discussed in Chap.15.

consideration, been continued for further investigation and the use of s.69 would be inept by any other hearing than one who so continue the case. The limits on s.66 warrants are less clearly defined. The power to grant a warrant under s.66 is expressly without prejudice to any other power to grant a warrant under any other section in Part II of the 1995 Act: this means, it is submitted, that wherever there seems to be a choice of which section to grant a warrant under, the power in s.66 must give way to the power in the other section, for only then can s.66 be kept within manageable limits. Section 66 warrants are stated to be available whenever the hearing are "unable to dispose of the case".[2] A case is disposed of when the children's hearing make a dispositive decision, that is to say a decision to impose a supervision requirement or to discharge the referral or, on review, to continue or vary or terminate an existing supervision requirement. If they are unable to make such a decision then they are "unable to dispose of the case" and s.66 appears to be activated. This might occur, for example, when, after a consideration of the case, the children's hearing feel that they do not have enough information to make an informed decision. But that is precisely the situation covered by s.69, which should be used whenever a case is continued to a subsequent hearing (otherwise the strict time-limits in s.69 would be "prejudiced" by being bypassed through the utilisation of s.66). Again, a children's hearing may consider themselves unable to dispose of a case because the child breaches his or her obligation to attend and the hearing consider that attendance necessary for a proper consideration of the case. However, a warrant, which can last a maximum of seven days, can be granted under s.45(5) for this reason and it is that provision which should be used in these circumstances rather than s.66 with its 22–day limit and possibility of extension. It follows that a warrant under s.66 is available not in all cases in which a children's hearing are unable to dispose of the case, but only when they are unable to do so for reasons other than that the case has been continued or that the child has failed to attend. The major (but not only) situation in which the hearing will be "unable to dispose of the case" within the meaning of s.66 is where the grounds have been denied or they have not been understood and the hearing direct the reporter to make an application to the sheriff under s.68. It is in these circumstances that the power to grant a warrant under s.66 is activated.[3] The layout of the surrounding sections provides some confirmation of this limited interpretation to the apparent breadth of s.66: s.65 deals with putting the grounds of referral to the child and relevant person, s.67 with the sheriff's renewal of a s.66 warrant, and s.68 with applications to the sheriff for proof if the grounds are denied or not understood. Also, while 66 days or more may sometimes be needed before the sheriff court hearing is completed, there will never be needed to be more than seven days before a children's hearing can be arranged to hear the case of a child who failed to attend a previously arranged hearing but is now being detained under a warrant.

---

[2] Children (Scotland) Act 1995, s.66(1)(b).

[3] s.66 might also be used in other circumstances in which s.69 or s.45 is not appropriate, such as, for example, if the case is continued not for further investigation but because a relevant person has failed to attend or because a relevant person did not receive reports timeously.

Section 45 deals with the child's right and duty to attend at all stages of the children's hearing and warrants under s.45(5) are available in all cases in which the child has failed to attend a hearing. If the child is considered likely to fail to attend a hearing in the future, then a choice of provisions seems to be offered, but only one can be used in any one type of hearing. When the case is being continued after consideration, s.69 is the appropriate provision; when the case is being sent to the sheriff for proof, it is s.66 that should be used; in all other cases s.45(4) can be used.

EFFECT OF WARRANTS

Warrants, issued or granted under any provision in the Children (Scotland) Act 1995, provide authority to apprehend the child subject to the warrant and detain him or her in a place of safety and they may be implemented as if they were warrants for the apprehension of an accused person issued by a court of summary jurisdiction; and any enactment or rule of law applying to such a warrant shall apply in like manner to a warrant under the 1995 Act.[4] A child who absconds from a place of safety may be arrested without further warrant in any part of the United Kingdom and taken back to the place of safety; and a court which is satisfied that there are reasonable grounds for believing that the child is within any premises may, where the child is liable to such arrest, grant a warrant authorising a constable to enter those premises and search for the child using reasonable force if necessary.[5] A child who at the end of a period of leave from a place of safety fails to return there shall be taken to have absconded for these purposes.[6] It is an offence for any person knowingly to assist or induce, or persistently attempt to induce, a child to abscond from a place of safety, to harbour or conceal a child who has so absconded, or to prevent a child from returning to a place of safety.[7] However, a local authority are not "harbouring" a child where the child appears to them to be at risk of harm and at the child's request they provide him with a refuge in a residential establishment or arrange for refuge to be provided in an approved household.[8]

If a child has been taken to a place of safety which is a residential establishment under a warrant or order and subsequent to its issue the chief social work officer of the relevant local authority and the person in charge of the residential establishment are satisfied that the criteria for the granting of secure accommodation authorisation are fulfilled, the child may be placed and kept in secure accommodation. The reporter and relevant person must be informed forthwith.[9] A children's hearing must be arranged within 72 hours if the warrant is granted under s.66, s.68, or s.69, and if granted by a sheriff under s.67 an application to the sheriff must be made within 72 hours.[10]

---

[4] s.84.
[5] s.82(1).
[6] s.82(2).
[7] s.83.
[8] s.38(1).
[9] Secure Accommodation (Scotland) Regulations 1996, reg.9(1).
[10] *ibid.,* reg.9(2). The 72 hours are counted excluding public holidays (reg.2.2)

## Definition of "place of safety"

"Place of safety" is defined as follows:

"(a)  a residential or other establishment provided by a local author-
       ity;
 (b)  a community house within the meaning of section 53 of the
       Children Act 1989;
 (c)  a police station[11]; or
 (d)  a hospital, surgery or other suitable place, the occupier of which
       is willing temporarily to receive the child".[12]

In paragraph (d) of this definition the words "other suitable place" need
not, it is submitted, be interpreted *ejusdem generis* with "hospital or
surgery". It might include, for example, a relative's house, so allowing a
child removed, say, from parents to go to stay with grandparents. Such
an interpretation is clearly sensible as a means of minimising the
inevitable trauma caused to a child who is removed from his or her
home. A place is suitable if the child's safety, from the risk that justified
the granting of the warrant, can be secured there.

## Procedure relating to warrants

A children's hearing at which a decision has to be made about whether
to grant or continue a warrant is subject to the same general procedural
provisions as other children's hearings. In addition, the Rules provide[13]
that in warrant hearings, the children's hearing must, before making a
decision, take appropriate steps to obtain the views of the child, and
endeavour to obtain the views of any relevant person and of any
safeguarder of what arrangements would be in the best interests of the
child. If a warrant is granted or continued, the reporter must send a copy
of the warrant or continuation and a copy of the statement of reasons for
the decision as soon as reasonably practicable to the child, any relevant
person and any safeguarder, together with notice of the right of the child
and relevant person to appeal against the decision to the sheriff.[14] It is
not an interference with the child's right to a fair trial under Art.6 of the
European Convention on Human Rights, nor an interference with the
child's right to take proceedings by which the lawfulness of detention can
be decided speedily under Art.5(4), for a warrant to be issued with an
authorisation of secure accommodation even if a legal representative has
not yet been appointed.[15] Warrants are often granted in circumstances of
emergency and the right to appeal against a warrant within three days, at
which a legal representative may be present, is sufficient protection of
European Convention rights.

---

[11] It is to be noted that where, further to emergency protection measures, a child is
taken to a police station as a place of safety, he or she must be moved to another type of
place of safety as soon as reasonably practicable: Emergency Child Protection Measures
(Scotland) Regulations 1996, reg.15.

[12] s.93(1).

[13] Children's Hearings (Scotland) Rules 1996, r.15 and r.26(1).

[14] 1996 Rules, r.26(2).

[15] *Martin v N,* 2004 S.L.T. 249.

**Conditions**

Conditions can be attached to warrants granted by a children's hearing under s.63, s.66 or s.69, but not under s.45.

**Appeals**

A children's hearing's decision to issue or grant a warrant is an appealable decision,[16] and any appeal must be disposed of within three days of having been lodged, failing which the warrant will cease to have effect.[17]

WARRANT TO SECURE CHILD'S ATTENDANCE (SECTION 45)

As was seen in Chapter 5, a child referred to a children's hearing has a right and also a duty to attend at all stages of the hearing,[18] though the child can be released from that duty in certain circumstances.[19] In relation to the hearing at which grounds of referral are to be put to the child and relevant person, the purpose of the child's attendance is primarily to give him or her the opportunity to accept or deny the grounds. In relation to all other hearings the purpose of the child's attendance is primarily to protect the child's right, conferred by s.16(2) and fleshed out by r.15 of the 1996 Rules, to be given an opportunity to express views on the matter at hand (though it is also in the child's interests that he or she be kept aware of what is happening to him or her). It should not be forgotten that the child has a duty as well as a right to attend hearings, and it may sometimes be appropriate to enforce that duty by issuing a warrant to bring the child before a children's hearing. Such a warrant can be either prospective (under s.45(4)) or retrospective (under s.45(5)). In determining whether to issue a warrant under either of these subsections, the welfare of the child shall be the children's hearing's paramount consideration.[20] The obligation to take account of the child's views does not apply to s.45(5) since the child is not present to give views. Though the minimum intervention principle, which applies to warrants granted under s.66 and s.69, does not apply to s.45 warrants,[21] the equivalent principle from ECHR jurisprudence, that of proportionality,[22] suggests that warrants should be granted only if this is the way of achieving the child's attendance that is least invasive of his or her rights to private and family life.

**Prospective warrants**

It is the reporter who has the responsibility for securing the attendance of the child at the hearing of his or her case by a children's hearing[23] and

---

[16] See further, below at p.211.
[17] s.51(8).
[18] s.45(1).
[19] s.45(2). See above at pp.64–67.
[20] s.16(1).
[21] Or to s.63 warrants.
[22] See above at pp.4–5.
[23] s.45(3).

this responsibility is usually fulfilled by notifying the child of the date, time and place of the hearing and, if required, arranging with the local authority to provide transport to the place where the hearing is to take place. Sometimes, however, the reporter will have cause to believe that for some reason the child is unlikely to attend the hearing. In these circumstances the reporter may apply to a children's hearing, requesting them to issue a warrant to find the child, keep him or her in a place of safety, and bring him or her to a hearing.[24] Though this provision is not worded in terms of likelihood that the child will fail to attend,[25] that is its effect since the warrant can be issued only when the reporter shows cause why it is necessary to do so for the purpose of fulfilling his or her responsibility for securing the attendance of the child. It might, for example, be that the child has a history of non-attendance at previous hearings, or that the child is at risk of being spirited away before the hearing, or that a parent has expressed the intention of preventing the child from attending. A warrant under this subsection is not available to protect the child's interests or to ensure his or her safety in circumstances in which there is no suggestion of the child failing to attend,[26] but can be used only for the purposes of securing the child's attendance. The hearing must be satisfied that it is "necessary" to issue the warrant. "Necessity" has its usual double meaning: in domestic law it indicates that the hearing must be persuaded that the child is unlikely to attend a hearing unless a warrant to bring him or her to a hearing is issued, and in ECHR law it indicates that the granting of a warrant is a proportionate response to the child's predicted non-attendance.

If the children's hearing have considered the child's case but continue it for further investigation, a warrant for the purpose of ensuring the child's attendance can be granted under s.69[27]; if the hearing put the grounds of referral but then sent them to the sheriff for proof, a warrant for this purpose can be granted under s.66.[28] Section 45(4) is limited to other hearings, and the most likely circumstances in which this sort of warrant will be needed is to ensure the child's attendance at a review hearing or at the hearing at which grounds of referral are to be put. Since the warrant under this provision will be issued before the child is due to attend a children's hearing, the hearing that issues the warrant will not be the hearing that was due to review the child's case or to put the grounds of referral to the child and relevant person, but will be one arranged for some other purpose or solely for the purpose of issuing the warrant. As a consequence, the hearing who are considering the issuing of a warrant will usually not have had access to full reports on the circumstances of the child or the background of the case, and the decision will often have to be made on the basis of information verbally provided by the reporter. And though, *ex hypothesi*, the child will not be

---

[24] s.45(4). If the reporter does not, or refuses to, make such an application, it would be incompetent for the children's hearing to issue a warrant under this provision.

[25] *cf.* s.66(2)(a) and s.69(7)(b).

[26] If there is a danger to the child before any children's hearing has been held, the emergency procedures discussed in Chap.15 can be utilised. These procedures cannot be bypassed by persuading the reporter to apply for a warrant from a children's hearing.

[27] See below at pp.197–198.

[28] See below at p.192.

present and so unable to argue against the issuing of the warrant this is not in itself contrary to the child's right to a fair trial or right to argue against detention,[29] which is protected by the right to appeal against the warrant.[30]

### Retrospective warrants

If a hearing has been arranged at which the child was obliged to attend, but the child has failed to attend, then that children's hearing may issue a warrant to find the child, keep him or her in a place of safety, and bring him or her to a subsequent hearing.[31] From the wording of the statute, it would appear incompetent for a hearing other than the one at which the child failed to attend to issue a warrant under this provision. Since this is the only provision in the Act dealing with a child who has *failed,* rather than is *likely to fail* to attend, warrants can be issued under it by any type of hearing at which a child has failed to attend.[32] The children's hearing can issue this sort of warrant on their own motion, as well as on the application of the reporter (unlike with prospective warrants, which can be issued only on the application of the reporter). A warrant ought not to be issued unless there is a fear that the non-attendance will be repeated at the next hearing and any known reason for non-attendance may serve to indicate how realistic that fear is. Both the reason for the child's failure to attend and the likelihood of that failure recurring are relevant to whether the issuing of a warrant is a proportionate response to the non-attendance. While a s.45(4) warrant may only be issued by a hearing "if satisfied . . . that it is necessary", these words do not appear in s.45(5). Nevertheless, a substantially similar limitation is imported into s.45(5) by the ECHR principle of proportionality. A warrant under this provision would be appropriate when the child has deliberately and for no good reason breached his or her obligation to attend, and when the fear is realistic that the child will not attend in the future without the issuing of a warrant. The more urgent the case is, the more likely it is that the children's hearing will consider it appropriate to issue a warrant in the face of non-attendance. Many hearings decide to give a non-attending child another chance to attend without a warrant being issued, on the basis that it may be against the interests of the child to be removed to a place of safety by the police and a disproportionate response to the child's failure to attend; but it is always against the interests of a child for whom compulsory measures of supervision may be necessary to allow him or her to evade a children's hearing and in many cases the issuing of a warrant will eventually become necessary.

A children's hearing cannot, it is submitted, issue a warrant under s.45(5) if a child has failed to attend a hearing from which he or she has previously been relieved of the obligation to attend.[33] If the hearing

---

[29] *Martin v N,* 2004 S.L.T. 249.

[30] See p.211. below.

[31] s.45(5).

[32] Except, for obvious reasons, a hearing who make a dispositive decision in the child's absence.

[33] Under s.45(2). *cf.* s.68(6), under which the sheriff can grant an order to find and keep the child who has failed to attend the hearing of a s.68 application: this power is expressly limited to situations in which the child has not been relieved of the obligation to attend.

wishes to see the child in that circumstance,[34] they must either withdraw the release previously given and continue the hearing for the child to attend at some later date or, if they are persuaded that the child will not attend at the later hearing even if the legal obligation to do so is reimposed, issue a prospective warrant under s.45(4). This latter option is available only when the reporter is willing to make application for a warrant under that subsection.

**Effect of a section 45 warrant**

A warrant issued under either s.45(4) or s.45(5) will normally be executed by the police, and it will be authority for them to search for the child, to take the child to a place of safety and keep him or her there, and to bring him or her before a children's hearing. If the child surrenders to the warrant before it has been executed there may be no need to take him or her to a place of safety until a hearing sits and the warrant can be withdrawn. If, however, the child has been removed to a place of safety in pursuance of a s.45 warrant, the authority to keep the child there lasts for only a limited period of time, and will terminate either on the expiry of seven days[35] from the day the child was first taken to the place of safety or, if earlier, the day on which a children's hearing first sit to consider the child's case.[36] The seven-day period begins to run on the day the child is taken to a place of safety, and will expire on midnight of the seventh day.[37] However, in most cases in which a child has been taken to a place of safety under a warrant issued under s.45 a children's hearing will be able to sit at some time before the expiry of the seven days. If the child cannot be brought to a children's hearing immediately on being found in pursuance of a s.45 warrant, then the reporter must, whenever practicable, arrange a children's hearing to sit on the first working day after the child was so found[38] and it is then that the warrant will cease to have effect.[39] It may be impossible to bring a child before a children's hearing immediately because of the lateness of the hour, because it is not a working day, or because the relevant persons have to travel some distance. Due to the requirement in the Rules that the hearing members must usually have seven days notice of the hearing and be in possession of the papers three days before the hearing,[40] in order to allow them time to give proper consideration to any reports submitted, a children's hearing arranged under this provision will normally have to be continued.[41] All that this hearing will be able to do is

---

[34] For example, because they are not convinced that the child will not understand the grounds of referral, or because they believe that the child's views will be an essential part of their consideration of the case.

[35] Notice, not working days.

[36] s.45(6).

[37] So, for example, if a child is taken to a place of safety on a Monday evening, the period expires at midnight on the following Sunday.

[38] s.45(7).

[39] A warrant issued under s.45 cannot be continued, though the hearing are able to grant a s.66 warrant after grounds have been put, or a s.69 warrant after they have continued the hearing.

[40] 1996 Rules, r.5(1).

[41] In terms of s.69(2).

(i) to put any grounds of referral to the child and the relevant person and (ii) to consider whether to grant a warrant to detain the child under s.66 or s.69 until the next hearing.

## WARRANT GRANTED WITH DIRECTION TO REPORTER TO APPLY TO SHERIFF (SECTION 66)

Where a children's hearing has been arranged but they are unable to dispose of the case because the grounds of referral have been denied or have not been understood and they have not felt it appropriate to discharge the referral,[42] they may grant a warrant, if certain conditions are met, which will be authority to keep the child in a place of safety and to bring the child to a children's hearing in the event of the sheriff finding the grounds established.[43] The hearing may[44] grant such warrant either *ex proprio motu* or on the motion of the reporter, though the matter is always one for their discretion, in the exercise of which they must apply the three overarching principles in s.16.[45]

**Grounds for granting the warrant**

The grounds upon which a warrant may be granted under s.66 are contained in s.66(2); but since there is overlap with other provisions in the statute it has to be remembered that these grounds must exist in the context of the relevant stage in the process, that is to say primarily the hearing at which the grounds of referral are denied or not understood and are sent to the sheriff for proof.[46] That hearing can grant a warrant if any one of the following three circumstances exists.

(a) There is reason to believe that the child may not attend at any hearing of his or her case.[47] Reason to believe that the child may not attend at that hearing might be shown by, for example, a previous history of non-attendance, or a parent's threat to refuse to bring the child back to another hearing.

(b) There is reason to believe that the child may fail to comply with a requirement to attend, or reside at any clinic, hospital, or other establishment for the purposes of further investigation to allow a children's hearing to complete their investigation of the child's case.[48] This is a prospective warrant to deal with the situation of when it is likely that the child will fail to attend for further investigation.[49] If, as will be normal, the children's

---

[42] As explained above at p.185, s.66 might be used in other circumstances, but this is likely to be the most common one.

[43] s.66.

[44] One assumes—*cf.* s.45(5) where the point is made clear.

[45] That is to say, the paramountcy of the child's welfare, the requirement to take appropriate account of the child's views, and the minimum intervention principle (as understood to include the ECHR principle of proportionality).

[46] See above at pp.184–185.

[47] s.66(2)(a)(i).

[48] s.66(2)(a)(ii).

[49] *cf.* s.69(4) under which a warrant can be granted after the child has *failed* so to attend.

hearing who grant a warrant under s.66 are doing so in the context of referring the case to the sheriff for proof, they will be unable to make any requirement that the child attends for further investigation.[50] So in order to grant a warrant under this provision the hearing will have to be convinced that a future hearing will continue the case for further investigation, that the future hearing will require the child to attend for such investigation, and that the child may fail to comply with that requirement. It is difficult to imagine a situation where the hearing at which grounds of referral are denied or not understood will be able to predict these events. It is only in other circumstances in which s.66 might be used (say, if the children's hearing are unable to dispose of the case because the relevant person has failed to attend) that a requirement that the child attends for further investigation can be made. But if further investigation is required then that, rather than non-attendance by a relevant person, is the real reason why the children's hearing are unable to dispose of the case, in which case s.69 is more appropriate than s.66. But s.69 does not permit a warrant to be granted when the child is likely to fail to attend for further investigation, while s.66(2)(a) does so permit, but only if, fortuitously, some reason in addition to the need for further investigation can be found which prevents the hearing from disposing of the case.

(c) It is necessary that the child should be kept in a place of safety in order to safeguard or promote his or her welfare.[51] This is the most common ground upon which a s.66 warrant will be granted. There is inevitably a delay between a children's hearing sending denied grounds of referral to the sheriff for proof, and the sheriff's decision as to whether or not the grounds are established, and if it appears that the child's welfare will suffer by remaining where he or she is during that time, the hearing are entitled to grant a warrant to secure the child's protection. It is, however, always to be remembered that at this stage in the process no grounds of referral have been established and the hearing must therefore be convinced on the information they have that removal to a place of safety is necessary. This is one of the most difficult decisions that children's hearings are faced with, since the decision must be made purely on the basis of as yet unproven allegations.[52] In making their decision it should be borne in mind that children are always damaged by summary removal from familiar surroundings, and warrants under this provision are justified only when the hearing are persuaded that the likely harm to the child in remaining where he or she is will be greater than the

---

[50] Since that requirement can only be made under s.69(3) after the hearing have considered the case under s.69(1) and decided to continue the case under s.69(2).

[51] s.66(2)(b).

[52] But they are, nevertheless, entitled to make their decision on that basis: see *McGregor v K*, 1982 S.L.T. 293.

certain harm of removal. This consideration will also satisfy the ECHR principle of proportionality. On the slightly different wording in s.37(4) of the Social Work (Scotland) Act 1968[53] the First Division said this[54]: "Detention of a child in a place of safety may be in the child's 'own interest' in a variety of circumstances and for a variety of reasons. In our view it is quite undesirable to attempt to define in advance what circumstances and reasons may be relevant for the purposes of the subsection. The question in any case must simply be whether, in all the circumstances, it would be better for the child to remain in a place of safety than to be left to his own unprotected devices while the investigation is taking place". It was held that a risk that the child might make his position worse by committing further offences was sufficient to satisfy this test, and it is submitted that the same conclusion can be reached in relation to the wording contained in s.66(2)(b). A child's welfare is threatened rather than safeguarded if there is a real risk that, left to his or her own unprotected devices, he or she will commit criminal offences. However, it would be a mistake to strike the balance of what is "better" for a child too finely. The European Court has on numerous occasions held that childcare mechanisms are not justified because a child would be "better off" living away from his or her parents[55] and it would similarly (it is submitted) be illegitimate to justify a warrant merely because it would be "better" for the child to be kept in a place of safety. Rather, as always, the proportionality test requires the identification of a legitimate aim for granting the warrant as well as a consideration of whether this is the only way to achieve that aim, or the one that does so with the least detriment to the child's (and relevant person's) family life. The warrant must be "necessary" (in the proportionate sense) rather than merely "better" before it can be justified.

### Effect of a section 66 warrant

The warrant granted under s.66(1) may require any person named in the warrant (a) to find and to keep or, as the case may be, to keep the child in a place of safety; and (b) to bring the child before a children's hearing at such times as may be specified in the warrant.[56] The child cannot be kept in a place of safety for longer than 22 days.[57] The time specified in the warrant for the bringing of the child to a children's hearing may be after the 22 days in which he or she was kept in a place of safety, though in practical terms the hearing will usually be arranged during the child's

---

[53] Under which a warrant could be granted if this were "necessary in [the child's] own interests".

[54] *Humphries v S*, 1986 S.L.T. 683 at 684K, *per* Lord President Emslie.

[55] *Olsson v Sweden (No. 2)* (1994) 17 E.H.R.R. 134 at para.72; *KA v Finland* Jan 14, 2003 at para.92.

[56] s.66(3).

[57] s.66(3)(a). The warrant can, however, be continued under s.66(5): see below at p.196.

residence in a place of safety. It is to be noted that the 22 days commence when the warrant is granted[58] and not when the child is found or first kept in a place of safety.[59] So if a child is not found until the 21st day after the warrant is granted, he or she can be kept only for one day (during which time, as will be seen below, the warrant may be continued under s.66(5)).

The warrant may contain such conditions as the children's hearing think necessary or expedient.[60] Secifically, the warrant may require the child to submit to any medical or other examination or treatment, and it may regulate the contact that the child is to have with any other person while the child is being kept in the place of safety. A condition that the child submit to medical or other examination or treatment is expressly made subject to s.90 of the Children (Scotland) Act 1995,[61] which provides that the child's capacity to consent to any medical procedure or treatment remains to be determined by s.2(4) of the Age of Legal Capacity (Scotland) Act 1991 and that any condition contained in a warrant granted under s.66 or s.69 may only be carried out if a child who has capacity under the 1991 Act consents. In other words, a child who is old enough to understand (in the opinion of the medical practitioner) the nature and consequences of the examination or treatment required by the condition in the warrant may refuse to submit to such examination or treatment, and any that is carried out in the face of such refusal will be an assault against the child. Hearings ought therefore to protect a child's right to refuse medical or other examination or treatment (even when that refusal is not in the interests of the child) by inquiring of the child whether he or she is willing to accept the proposed examination or treatment, and attaching no condition to the warrant when the child indicates that he or she will not co-operate. For the hearing to attach a condition in the face of known refusal will breach the minimum intervention principle,[62] since the condition can be of no effect when the child refuses consent. If the child does not have capacity to consent or refuse under the 1991 Act, then a condition in a s.66 warrant does not provide the authority required for the examination or treatment to go ahead: power to give that authority still rests with those who have parental responsibilities and parental rights, and a requirement that the child "submits" to medical treatment does not replace that power. A condition of medical examination or treatment ought not to be attached to a s.66 warrant in an attempt to acquire evidence that will assist the reporter in proving the grounds of referral before the sheriff, for the reporter ought to have all the evidence he or she needs at the hearing at which the grounds are put to the child and relevant person.[63] Rather, such a condition would be appropriate to ensure that the child receives

---

[58] The day of granting not counting towards the 22 days: *cf. B v Kennedy,* 1992 S.L.T. 870.

[59] s.66(3)(a).

[60] s.66(4).

[61] s.66(4)(a).

[62] s.16(3), applied to warrants granted under s.66 by s.16(4)(a)(ii).

[63] It would be very bad practice for a reporter to bring a case to a hearing before he or she is in a position to prove grounds of referral, in the hope that the need for proving the case will be avoided by appropriate acceptances.

necessary medical attention which he or she might not receive (for whatever reason) otherwise.

### Continuation of a section 66 warrant

A warrant granted by a children's hearing under s.66(1) allows a child to be kept in a place of safety for a maximum period of 22 days, though there is no reason why the hearing should not specify a shorter period, if this is appropriate in the child's interests. It very frequently happens, however, that the sheriff court hearing to establish the grounds of referral takes place at some time after 22 days from the date of the original children's hearing.[64] If the risk to the child that justified the warrant remains, the warrant may be continued.[65] A children's hearing must be arranged by the reporter,[66] at which he or she must show cause why the warrant should be continued, and if the hearing are satisfied that it is necessary to do so they may continue the warrant for a period not exceeding 22 days, with or without a variation of its terms. "Necessity", as always, is to be understood in its dual sense of being better for the child than not continuing the warrant, and a proportionate response to the risk facing the child that the warrant is designed to avoid. The cause that must be shown is that the original or new grounds for concern still exist; in addition, an explanation of why the case has not advanced ought to be given by the reporter. If the hearing which has been arranged do not continue the warrant, it comes to an end, even if 22 days from its granting have not yet elapsed at the date of the hearing. There is no limit to the number of times that the warrant can be continued, but the total length of time during which the child can be kept in a place of safety under a warrant granted and continued under s.66 is 66 days.[67] It does not, however, follow from this that a child must always be released from a place of safety after having been kept there for a period of 66 days. Rather, all s.66(8) does is to limit the power of the children's hearing to keep a child in a place of safety for 66 days. Thereafter, the reporter may apply to the sheriff for a warrant to keep the child for longer.[68]

### Secure accommodation authorisation

In cases in which the children's hearing who grant a s.66 warrant are satisfied that one of the conditions for authorising the child to be kept in secure accommodation[69] is satisfied, and it is necessary to do so, the hearing may authorise the child to be kept there, pending the disposal of his or her case.[70] As under s.70(9),[71] the children's hearing do not order that the child be kept in secure accommodation: rather they merely

---

[64] It is, indeed, to be noted that the statute provides for the sheriff hearing the application within 28 days of the reporter lodging the application: s.68(2).

[65] s.66(5).

[66] At any time before the expiry of the 22 days and not necessarily on the 22nd day.

[67] s.66(8).

[68] s.67. See below at pp.202–203.

[69] s.70(10).

[70] s.66(6), as amended by the Antisocial Behaviour etc (Scotland) Act 2004, Sch.4.

[71] Under which such authorisation can be attached to a supervision requirement.

authorise that this can be done if, in addition, the chief social work officer of the relevant local authority considers it necessary. The authorisation under this subsection cannot stand alone and it must be given in connection with a warrant under s.66(1): this is implicit from the wording of s.66(8) which provides that a child may not be kept in a place of safety or in secure accommodation by virtue of s.66 for more than 66 days after being taken to a place of safety under a warrant granted under s.66(1). It follows that the secure authorisation is open to review (and can be withdrawn) at the same time as the warrant is being continued, and that the authorisation cannot be continued if the warrant is discontinued. The presence of a legal representative at a hearing granting a warrant is not in all cases required before a secure accommodation authorisation can be made.[72]

### Non-disclosure of child's whereabouts

The children's hearing who grant or continue a warrant under s.66 can order that the place of safety at which the child is to be kept shall not be disclosed to any person or class of persons specified in the order. This important power[73] is designed as a protective measure for the child and a children's hearing ought not to make a non-disclosure order unless they are satisfied that there is a real need for it, that is to say that there is a realistic threat to the child's well-being from the named person or class of persons. Since, however, such an order has the potential to interfere with the family life of the named person, the order must be a proportionate response to a real and identified danger facing the child.

WARRANT ON CONTINUATION OF HEARING (SECTION 69)

After having considered the child's case in accordance with s.69(1), the children's hearing may come to the view that they are unable to make a dispositive decision and that it is necessary to continue the case in order to have a further investigation.[74] If this is the decision, the children's hearing who continue the case may grant a warrant requiring that the child be taken to and kept in a place of safety until the next hearing.[75] The decision to grant a warrant under s.69 is governed by all three overarching principles in s.16,[76] as well as the proportionality principle. The hearing may grant a warrant under s.69(7) if either of the following two circumstances exists.

(a) Keeping the child in a place of safety is necessary in the interests of safeguarding or promoting the welfare of the child.

---

[72] *Martin v N,* 2004 S.L.T. 249.
[73] Also to be found in s.69(10), s.70(6) and s.73(11).
[74] s.69(2). Continuation is also appropriate when a proper consideration of the child's case has not been possible, for example when the child is brought to a hearing under a s.45 warrant and the hearing have not had sufficient time to digest all the reports.
[75] s.69(7).
[76] That is to say, the paramountcy of the child's welfare, the requirement to take appropriate account of the child's views, and the minimum intervention principle.

Some factor indicating a threat to the child's welfare were he or she not to be kept in a place of safety ought to be shown. This might be, for example, the child's continued troubled behaviour, or the parent's current inability to care for the child properly, or, it may be, a likelihood that the child will breach a requirement made under s.69(3) to attend or reside at a clinic or hospital for further investigation. Or,

(b) There is reason to believe that the child may not attend the subsequent hearing of his or her case. A history of non-attendance will be sufficient as might, for example, a threat by a parent not to bring the child back to the continued hearing.

A warrant granted under s.69(7) will be authority to take the child to and to keep him or her in a place of safety,[77] and it ceases to have effect at the end of 22 days after it was granted or, if earlier, on the day a hearing convenes to consider the continued case.[78] There is no provision for the renewal of a warrant granted under s.69(7),[79] which is designed to ensure that a continued hearing takes place within as short a period of time as possible. However, the continued hearing may decide again to continue the case on the ground that the investigations are not yet complete or that further investigations are required, and the granting of another warrant under s.69(7) is competent. Indeed, there is no limit to the number of times the children's hearing can continue the case and grant a warrant. However, it is not in a child's interests to be kept indefinitely in a place of safety without a substantive decision being made as to his or her future; and the longer a child is kept in limbo the less likely it is that that keeping will be regarded as a proportionate response to the child's vulnerabilities.

**Warrant to enforce assessment requirement**

If the case has been continued for further investigation, the children's hearing may, for the purposes of that investigation, require the child to attend, or to reside at, any clinic, hospital or other establishment.[80] If the child thereafter fails to attend or reside for investigation as required, a warrant may be granted, with or without an application to that effect by the reporter.[81] The effect of this warrant is to give authority (a) to find the child, (b) to remove the child to a place of safety and keep him or her there, and (c) where the place of safety is not the clinic, hospital or other establishment referred to in the requirement to attend, to take the child from the place of safety to that named place for the purposes of the investigation.[82] The warrant under this provision can, however, only be granted retrospectively, that is after the child has failed to fulfil the requirement, and it cannot be granted on the basis that the child is likely to fail to fulfil the requirement. It follows that the hearing who require

---

[77] For the meaning of place of safety, see s.93(1) and discussion above at p.187.
[78] s.69(8).
[79] cf. the renewal provisions concerning warrants granted under s.66, above at p.196.
[80] s.69(3). See further, above at pp.129–130.
[81] s.69(4).
[82] s.69(5).

the child to attend at a hospital or clinic for investigation cannot grant a warrant under this provision.[83] It will be the subsequent hearing, who will again have to continue the case, who grant the warrant.[84]

A warrant granted under s.69(4) cannot authorise the keeping of a child in a place of safety for any more than 22 days after the granting of the warrant or after the beginning of the subsequent hearing, whichever is earlier.[85] It is also to be remembered that the requirement to attend or reside at a clinic or hospital cannot exceed 22 days,[86] and the warrant to enforce that requirement cannot last beyond the requirement itself.

### Effect of section 69 warrants

A warrant granted under either s.69(4) or (7) may contain such conditions as appear to the children's hearing to be necessary or expedient, and can in particular require the child to submit to any medical or other examination or treatment and can regulate contact between the child and any specified person or class of persons.[87]

The children's hearing who grant a warrant under s.69(4) or (7) can order that the place of safety at which the child is to be kept shall not be disclosed to any person or class of persons specified in the order.[88]

In cases in which a children's hearing who grant a s.69 warrant are satisfied that one of the conditions for authorising the child to be kept in secure accommodation[89] is satisfied, and it is necessary to do so, the hearing may authorise the child to be kept there while the warrant remains in effect.[90] It is to be remembered that this section is applicable only when the case has been continued, and the authorisation to keep the child in secure accommodation will not last beyond 22 days or, if earlier, the commencement of the continued hearing. The authorisation can, of course, be renewed if the continued hearing again continues the case to a subsequent hearing, or makes a supervision requirement in terms of which the child is required to reside in a residential establishment.[91] It is difficult, though not impossible, to imagine the scenario in which a warrant under s.69(4) (*i.e.* to enforce an assessment requirement) would appropriately also include secure accommodation authorisation—both that and a warrant under s.69(7) need to be a proportionate response to the child's needs.

### WARRANT AFTER CHILD ARRESTED BY POLICE (SECTION 63)

A child may come to the attention of the reporter as being potentially in need of compulsory measures of supervision by the reporter being

---

[83] *cf.* s.66(1) and (2)(a)(ii) and comments thereupon above at pp.192–193.

[84] There would, however, be nothing to stop the hearing who continue the case under s.69(2) and make a requirement to attend for investigation under s.69(3) from granting a warrant under s.69(7) on the basis of the child's interests. The place where the child is required to attend may well be a place of safety itself.

[85] s.69(6).

[86] See above, at pp.129–130.

[87] s.69(9). The same considerations apply here as apply to conditions attached to warrants granted under s.66(1), and reference should be made to the comments thereupon above at p.195.

[88] s.69(10). In relation to this power with s.66 warrants, see comments above at p.197.

[89] s.70(10).

[90] s.69(11), as amended by the Antisocial Behaviour etc (Scotland) Act 2004, Sch.4.

[91] s.70(9).

informed that the child has been apprehended by the police and is being detained in a place of safety in terms of s.43(5) of the Criminal Procedure (Scotland) Act 1995. In such circumstances, the reporter must, unless he or she considers that compulsory measures of supervision are not required in relation to the child, arrange a children's hearing to which he or she shall refer the case.[92] The child may be kept in the place of safety until the commencement of the hearing. That hearing, which must begin not later than the third day after the reporter received the information,[93] must do two things. First, they must consider whether to grant a warrant to keep the child in a place of safety,[94] and secondly they may direct the reporter to arrange a children's hearing in order to put grounds of referral to the child.[95] The children's hearing may decide to do neither, or to do both, or to give a direction but not grant a warrant; but they cannot grant a warrant without giving a direction. Nor, it is submitted, can the hearing do anything else, such as seeking acceptance of any grounds of referral which the reporter has been able to draw up.[96]

### Granting the warrant

The warrant granted under this provision has similar effect to one granted under s.66 (that is, one granted when the case is referred to the sheriff for proof of the grounds of referral), and the grounds upon which a s.63 warrant can be granted are identical to the grounds upon which a s.66 warrant is granted.[97] These are (i) that there is reason to believe that the child may not attend any hearing of his or her case or may fail to comply with a requirement to undergo investigation, or (ii) that it is necessary to safeguard or promote his or her welfare that the child be kept in a place of safety.[98] The effect of a s.63 warrant, and the terms and conditions on which it can be granted, are the same as with a s.66 warrant,[99] which includes its time-limits, conditions, continuations, secure accommodation authorisations and non-disclosure of child's whereabouts.[1] There are, however, two differences between a s.63 warrant and a s.66 warrant. First, the termination of a warrant granted under s.63 by the expiry of 66 days does not activate the sheriff's power to grant an additional warrant under s.67, as he may do on the termination of a warrant granted and continued under s.66.[2] Secondly, a child is not to be kept in a place of safety in accordance with a warrant granted under s.63(5) where the reporter, having regard to the welfare of the child, considers that, whether as a result of a change in the circumstances of the case or of further information relating to the case

---

[92] s.63(1).
[93] s.63(2). *i.e.* not later than a Thursday if information is received on a Monday.
[94] s.63(5)(a).
[95] s.63(5)(b).
[96] In practice, the time-scale for giving notice of hearings will prevent grounds of referral being put in any case.
[97] s.63(5)(a), referring to the conditions in s.66(2).
[98] For a discussion of these grounds in respect of s.66 warrants, see above at pp.192–194.
[99] s.63(5), referring to s.66(3)—(8).
[1] See above at pp.194–197.
[2] s.67(1) expressly refers to s.66 warrants only.

having been received, either the conditions for the granting of the warrant no longer exist or the child is not in need of compulsory measures of supervision.[3] The reporter has no such power during the currency of a s.66 warrant.

### Directing the reporter

If the warrant is granted, the children's hearing must (and if they decide not to grant a warrant they may) also direct the reporter to arrange a children's hearing as under s.65(1) (*i.e.* to put grounds of referral to the child and parent).[4] In cases in which they have a discretion, the hearing should so direct the reporter only when satisfied both that grounds of referral have been established and that the child is in need of compulsory measures of supervision. The fact that the child has been arrested will indicate that the child may have committed an offence, and it would be appropriate for the hearing not to direct the reporter to arrange a children's hearing only when satisfied that, even if the ground is accepted or established, no compulsory measures of supervision will be required.

While it can be assumed that a reporter directed by a children's hearing to arrange a children's hearing must do so[5] (though the Act does not actually say this), it is left unclear from the terms of the statute whether the children's hearing (who decide not to grant a warrant) are permitted expressly to direct the reporter not to arrange a children's hearing and whether the reporter can, in the absence of any direction to do so, nevertheless arrange a children's hearing. The discretion of the reporter has long been seen as an important element in the whole children's hearing system and it is submitted that the terms of s.63(5)(b) should be interpreted to limit that discretion only in so far as is absolutely necessary to give effect to its terms. It follows (i) that the reporter retains a discretion to arrange a children's hearing even if the hearing arranged under this section do not direct him to do so, and (ii) that the hearing have no power expressly to direct the reporter not to arrange a children's hearing. The hearing's power under this paragraph is limited to directing the reporter to arrange a hearing (which they must do if they grant a warrant) or leaving the matter to the discretion of the reporter.

WARRANTS AND ORDERS TO DETAIN GRANTED BY SHERIFF

### Warrants for further detention

If a child has been kept in a place of safety by means of a warrant granted under s.66 (that is to say granted when the children's hearing

---

[3] s.63(6). When the reporter comes to this conclusion he or she must give notice to that effect to the person who is keeping the child in the place of safety in accordance with the warrant.

[4] s.63(5)(b).

[5] Unless the reporter has released the child from a place of safety under s.63(6) because a change of circumstances or further information has persuaded him or her that compulsory measures of supervision are not necessary: any direction granted under s.63(5)(b) is granted "subject to" s.63(6) which means that a direction falls if s.63(6) is used.

have been unable to dispose of the case because they have directed the reporter to make an application for proof of a ground of referral to the sheriff) the reporter can apply to the sheriff for a warrant to keep the child where he or she is after the warrant granted and continued by the children's hearing has expired.[6] A warrant granted under this section must specify the date on which it will expire[7] and though there is no requirement in either the statute or the Rules that the date specified be no more than 22 days hence, it would consist with the other statutory time-limits, as well as the proportionality principle, for such a practice to be adopted. The sheriff must hear the parties and allow such other procedure as he thinks fit before granting or refusing the application for a warrant.[8] The reporter can apply to the sheriff for another warrant whenever a previous warrant granted by the sheriff under this section is about to expire. There is a noticeable lack of any provision[9] that the sheriff can renew the warrant (or grant another warrant) "on one occasion only", and it would appear therefore that the sheriff can grant as many successive warrants as he thinks fit. This prevents the necessity (which sometimes arose under the Social Work (Scotland) Act 1968) to apply to the *nobile officium* for authority to keep the child in a place of safety longer than the statutory scheme permitted.[10] Reference should, however, be made to s.16(1), under which the child's welfare must be the sheriff's paramount consideration—it will seldom be in the child's interests to be kept in a place of safety, waiting to be brought to a children's hearing, for even as long as 66 days. Parliament's intention in setting time-limits must be taken to be that referrals be disposed of without unnecessary delay.[11] In addition, the other two overarching principles in s.16[12] also apply to the sheriff's decision whether to grant a warrant under this subsection,[13] as does the ECHR principle of proportionality.[14]

If the application to the sheriff is determined by the sheriff finding grounds of referral established, the reporter will arrange a children's hearing to consider the child's case, but it might sometimes remain necessary to keep the child in a place of safety after the sheriff's decision until the hearing sits (due, for example, to a continued risk to the child's wellbeing). If that is so, the reporter can apply to the sheriff for a warrant under this section in the same proceedings as those in which the ground of referral is sought to be proved.[15] In this situation, the reporter

---

[6] s.67(1) and Act of Sederunt (Child Care and Maintenance Rules) 1997, rr.3.41–3.43.

[7] s.67(2)(a).

[8] AS 1997, r.3.43.

[9] Such as appeared in s.40(8B) of the Social Work (Scotland) Act 1968.

[10] See *Humphries, Petitioner,* 1982 S.L.T. 481, in which Lord President Emslie stated, at p.83, that it was Parliament's intention that a child who has been referred to a children's hearing may be kept in a place of safety pending the final disposal of the referral. See also *Ferguson v P,* 1989 S.L.T. 681.

[11] *per* Lord President Emslie in *Humphries, Petitioner,* 1982 S.L.T. 481 at 482.

[12] That is to say the requirement to take appropriate account of the child's views and the minimum intervention principle.

[13] s.16(4)(b)(iii). The procedure where the child wishes to express a view is set out in AS 1997, r.3.5.

[14] See above at pp.4–5.

[15] s.67(4).

can bypass the children's hearing and seek a warrant from a sheriff even before the power of the children's hearing under s.66 to grant or continue a warrant has been exhausted.[16]

A reporter can apply to the sheriff for a warrant under this provision only when the child is currently in a place of safety (for otherwise the requirement in s.67(1) has not been satisfied), and it follows that a child who has been at home until the sheriff court hearing cannot be removed to a place of safety thereafter under this provision.[17]

### Grounds for granting the warrant

The reporter must show cause why a warrant ought to be granted by the sheriff under this section.[18] Though the statute does not say so, it is submitted that an essential part of that cause must be the continued satisfaction of the conditions listed in s.66(2)[19] for the granting of a warrant under s.66(1), for it is only after a warrant granted under that provision has ceased to have effect that s.67 comes into operation. Because the sheriff is obliged to regard the child's welfare as his paramount consideration it must be shown to his satisfaction that it is less detrimental to the child to be kept waiting for this length of time than to be released home. In addition, the reporter is probably also obliged to explain to the sheriff why the case has not advanced sufficiently after 66 days to allow the child to be brought before the sheriff to consider whether grounds of referral are established or not.

### Conditions attached to the warrant

The sheriff's warrant granted under s.67 may contain any such requirement or condition as could have been contained in a warrant granted by the children's hearing under s.66.[20] So a warrant may contain such conditions as appear to be necessary or expedient, and in particular may require the child to submit to medical or other examination or treatment and may regulate contact between the child and any other persons[21]; it may contain an order that the child be liable to be placed and kept in secure accommodation[22]; and it may contain an order that the place of safety at which the child is to be kept shall not be disclosed to any person or class of persons specified in the order.[23]

### Orders to detain in relation to section 68 applications

When the reporter makes an application to the sheriff under s.68 for a finding as to whether any of the grounds of referral are established, the

---

[16] Normally, however, it would be bad practice for reporters to seek a sheriff's warrant under s.67 when a children's hearing's warrant under s.66 is still available for continuation by the hearing themselves.

[17] The appropriate provision to deal with that situation is s.68(10)(b). See below at p. 175.

[18] s.67(2).

[19] See above at pp.192–194.

[20] s.67(2)(b).

[21] See s.66(4), and comments thereupon above at pp.195–196.

[22] s.67(3) and s.66(6).

[23] s.67(3) and s.66(7).

child has a right and a duty to attend at the hearing of that application.[24] Where the child fails to attend, and his or her obligation to attend has not previously been dispensed with, the sheriff may grant an order to find and keep the child in a place of safety until the sheriff can hear the application, and to bring the child before the sheriff for that purpose.[25] The child cannot be kept in a place of safety by virtue of an order granted under this provision after the expiry of 14 days after the child is found or, if earlier, the disposal of the application by the sheriff.[26] There is no provision for the renewal of this order, which is designed to ensure that the hearing of the evidence takes place as soon after the child has been found as possible. The purpose of the sheriff court hearing is to establish facts, and no order should be granted by the sheriff under this provision unless the child's presence is likely to assist the sheriff in the fact-finding process: any other approach runs the risk of being regarded as a disproportionate response to the child's non-attendance and so contrary to the child's ECHR rights.

Once the s.68 application has been disposed of, if the sheriff finds that grounds of referral have been established, he may issue an order to detain the child in a place of safety until the children's hearing sit.[27] Such an order can be issued on one of two grounds: (i) that the sheriff is satisfied that keeping the child in a place of safety is necessary in the child's best interests, or (ii) that he is satisfied that there is reason to believe that the child will run away before the children's hearing sit to consider the case. The reference in s.68(10)(b)(ii) to the child running away rather than failing to attend suggests that an order under this provision cannot be issued if the risk is that the child will be prevented from attending the children's hearing by the parent spiriting the child away or refusing to bring the child to a hearing,[28] but it is submitted that it would be against the welfare of the child to be prevented from exercising his or her right to attend a children's hearing, with the result that an order can be issued under s.68(10)(b)(i) in these circumstances. An order issued under s.68(10) ceases to have effect on the expiry of three days[29] or, if earlier, the consideration of the child's case by a children's hearing.[30] The reason this time period is so short is that it is not for the sheriff to determine that the child needs to be kept in a place of safety until the children's hearing dispose of the case,[31] but for the children's hearing themselves: the order issued by the sheriff under this provision is designed solely to keep the child safe until a children's hearing can be convened to consider that matter or to ensure the child's attendance, and it is that children's hearing who can grant a longer-lasting warrant under s.69(7) to keep the child safe until the case is

---

[24] s.68(4), discussed above at pp.98–100.

[25] s.68(6). This warrant must be signed by the sheriff himself: AS 1997, r.3.52.

[26] s.68(7).

[27] s.68(10)(b).

[28] *cf.* s.66(2)(a)(i), and s.69(7)(b), which both refer to the risk that the child "may not attend".

[29] The day the child is first brought to a place of safety being the first day: *cf. S, Appellants,* 1979 S.L.T. (Sh. Ct.) 37.

[30] s.68(12).

[31] See *P v Kennedy,* 1995 S.L.T. 476.

finally disposed of. If the sheriff is satisfied that one of the conditions for authorising the child to be kept in secure accommodation is fulfilled, and it is necessary to do so, he may provide that the child shall be liable to be placed and kept in secure accommodation within a residential establishment.[32] This authorisation ceases to have effect when the order to which it is attached ceases to have effect, but the children's hearing themselves are then able to grant such authorisation.[33]

Under neither of the provisions in s.68 does the sheriff have the power to require that the place of safety where the child is required to reside be not disclosed to any person or class of persons.[34]

---

[32] s.68(11), as amended by the Antisocial Behaviour etc. (Scotland) Act 2004, Sch.4.
[33] Either under s.69(11) if the case is continued or s.70(9) if a supervision requirement is imposed.
[34] *cf.* s.66(7), s.67(3), s.69(10), s.70(6) and s.73(11).

CHAPTER FOURTEEN

# APPEALS

## INTRODUCTION

All decisions of the children's hearing have legal effect, and are sometimes far-reaching for the child and his or her family. It is essential, therefore, that these decisions be open to review and it is no exaggeration to say that the integrity of the whole system, and its consistency with the due process requirements of (in particular) Art.6 of the European Convention on Human Rights, is dependent to a large extent on the appeal mechanisms that are laid down in the Children (Scotland) Act 1995 and the associated rules and regulations. The Act allows decisions of the children's hearing to be appealed against to the sheriff. Decisions of the sheriff, whether on appeal from the children's hearing or on an application for finding established a ground of referral, can be appealed against either to the sheriff principal or direct to the Court of Session. Decisions of the sheriff principal can be appealed against, with leave of the sheriff principal, to the Court of Session. No appeal from the Court of Session to the House of Lords can be taken, and the decision of the Court of Session is final.[1]

## APPEALS FROM CHILDREN'S HEARINGS: GENERAL

### Title

In keeping with the essentially private nature of the children's hearing system, title to appeal against a decision of the hearing inheres only in certain specified individuals, that is to say the child and the relevant person.[2] The child can appeal on his or her own behalf if possessed of legal capacity to do so. A person under the age of 16 years has legal capacity to instruct a solicitor and to sue or to defend in any civil proceedings (which includes, it is submitted, appeals from decisions of children's hearings) where that person has a general understanding of what it means to do so; and without prejudice to that generality a person 12 years of age or more will be presumed to be of sufficient age and maturity.[3] If a safeguarder has been appointed by the children's hearing

---

[1] Children (Scotland) Act 1995, s.51(11)(b).

[2] s.51(1). Either may be represented by a solicitor or advocate or such other person who can satisfy the sheriff that he or she is a suitable person to represent the child or relevant person and that he or she is authorised to do so: Act of Sederunt (Child Care and Maintenance Rules) 1997 (hereinafter AS 1997), r.3.21.

[3] Age of Legal Capacity (Scotland) Act 1991, s.2(4A) and (4B).

he or she may sign the appeal on the child's behalf,[4] effectively acting for this purpose as the child's legal representative; since this is done on behalf of the child, a safeguarder may not appeal if the child is old enough to do so him or herself but decides not to do so. There is no incompetency in the safeguarder appearing as a respondent in an appeal.[5] The relevant person[6] with title to appeal is the person who has the right and obligation to attend the children's hearing and to dispute the grounds of referral. The right of appeal inheres in this person even when he or she did not attend the hearing against whose decision the appeal is being taken. The person must be a relevant person at the time of the hearing from whose decision the appeal is being taken, and a person does not acquire title to appeal on becoming a relevant person at some later date.[7] The reporter, of course, has no title or interest in appealing a decision of the hearing, whether in relation to the disposal of the case or the granting of a warrant, but is the contradictor in any appeal made to the sheriff. The reporter would seem to have no title or interest in appealing a decision to refuse to grant a warrant which he or she has applied for.[8] The appeal must be dismissed if made by a person with no title.[9]

**Time-scale**

Appeals to the sheriff must be made within a period of three weeks beginning with the date of the hearing's decision.[10] There is no provision in the statute requiring the sheriff to dispose of the appeal within a specified time-scale,[11] except in relation to appeals against the issuing (or granting) of warrants, in which case the appeal must be disposed of within three days of being lodged, failing which the warrant shall cease to have effect.[12] The days here are calendar days.[13] On the question of when these periods begin to run there is an apparent conflict in the reported decisions. In *S, Appellants,*[14] which concerned the rule that the appeal has to be lodged within three weeks,[15] the sheriff held that the day the decision being appealed against was made counted as the first

---

[4] AS 1997, r.3.53(3). See, for example, *Catto v Pearson,* 1990 S.L.T. (Sh. Ct.) 77.

[5] *R v Grant,* 2000 S.L.T. 372 at 374C.

[6] Defined in s.93(2)(b). See above at pp.14–17.

[7] *Kennedy v H,* 1988 S.L.T. 586. This case was decided under the previous legislation (which referred to "guardian") and though the wording has changed under the Children (Scotland) Act 1995, the principle remains sound. The rule does, however, sit rather uneasily with the rule that changes in the child's circumstances since the decision can be a ground of appeal against the decision: see below at pp.215–216.

[8] It would be competent for the child or relevant person to appeal against such a decision, though it is difficult to conceive of a situation in which either would want to do so.

[9] *Kennedy v H,* 1988 S.L.T. 586; *Catto v Pearson,* 1990 S.L.T. (Sh. Ct.) 77. See also *B v Kennedy,* 1992 S.L.T. 870.

[10] s.51(1)(a).

[11] Though the Rules require that the sheriff clerk assign a date for the appeal hearing no later than 28 days after the lodging of the appeal: AS 1997, r.3.54(5).

[12] s.51(8).

[13] *B v Kennedy,* 1992 S.L.T. 870.

[14] 1979 S.L.T. (Sh. Ct.) 37.

[15] Under s.49(1) of the Social Work (Scotland) Act 1968, the terms of which are not significantly different from s.51(1) of the 1995 Act.

day and that the appeal therefore had to be lodged on or before the 21st day. On the other hand, in *B v Kennedy*,[16] which concerned the rule that an appeal against a warrant has to be disposed of within three days of being lodged, the Second Division held that there was nothing in the statutory provisions[17] to suggest a departure from the general rule[18] that the day from which time was to run fell to be excluded from the computation of the period, so that the first day was the day after the granting of the warrant and the end of the period was the end of the third day. *S, Appellants* was not referred to in *B v Kennedy,* and it is possible to distinguish the two cases. Section 51(1) (at issue in *S, Applicants)* says that an appeal may be lodged "within a period of three weeks *beginning with the date of any decision*"; s.51(8) (at issue in *B v Kennedy*) says that an appeal against a warrant must be disposed of "within three days of the lodging of the appeal" but does *not* say when the period begins. Thus, consistently with *B v Kennedy*, s.51(8) contains nothing to indicate a departure from the general rule that the period runs from the day after the event (the lodging of the appeal) while the words in s.51(1) italicised above do indicate just such a departure. Following *B v Kennedy*, the sheriff in *J v Caldwell*[19] held that there was no compelling reason why the day of decision should be included in the computation of the period, and the sheriff rejected as too subtle any distinction between statutory wording requiring a period to be computed "beginning with" a particular date and "from" a particular date. He rejected the approach in *S, Appellants.*[20] On the other hand, in *M, Appellant*[21] the sheriff held that the plain words of s.51(1) required that the day of the hearing was the first day of the three-week period, and he followed the approach in *S, Appellants*. It is suggested that, though unfortunate, different statutory formulae may well give different methods of computing time periods and that the plain meaning of words should be given unless there is compelling reason to depart from them: this involves following *S, Appellant* and *M, Appellant* rather than *J v Caldwell*. If this is correct, then when a children's hearing makes a decision on, say June 1, the three-week period for appeal ends at midnight on June 21. At the same time, the three-day period in s.51(8) from the lodging of an appeal against a warrant granted on July 1, ends at midnight on July 4.

After the appeal is lodged, the date assigned for the hearing must be no later than 28 days after the lodging of the appeal.[22]

### Procedure

The appeal, in appropriate form, must be lodged with the sheriff clerk, having been signed by the appellant or his or her representative; an

---

[16] 1992 S.L.T. 870.

[17] s.49(7) of the Social Work (Scotland) Act 1968, the terms of which are not significantly different from s.51(8) of the 1995 Act.

[18] Authorities for which are collected in *Stair Memorial Encyclopaedia of the Laws of Scotland,* vol.22, para.822.

[19] 2001 S.L.T. (Sh. Ct.) 164.

[20] Sheriff Kearney, *Children's Hearings and the Sheriff Court* (2nd ed., 2000) at para.50.09 also expresses reservations about *S, Appellants*.

[21] 2003 S.L.T. (Sh. Ct.) 112.

[22] AS 1997, r.3.54(5): *i.e.* if the appeal is lodged on August 1, the date assigned may be up to August 29, but not thereafter.

appeal by the child may be signed on his or her behalf by any safeguarder appointed by the children's hearing.[23] Thereafter, the sheriff clerk will assign a date for the hearing and intimate it, together with a copy of the appeal to (a) the reporter, (b) if not the appellant, the child (unless the sheriff dispenses with intimation where he considers this appropriate), (c) if not the appellant, the relevant person, (d) any safeguarder appointed by the sheriff for the purposes of the appeal, or appointed by the children's hearing and (e) any other person the sheriff thinks necessary.[24] Any person on whom service of the appeal has been made may lodge answers to the appeal not later than seven days before the diet fixed for the hearing of the appeal.[25] It is the responsibility of the reporter to ensure that there is lodged with the sheriff clerk all the appropriate documentation relevant to the appeal,[26] which includes all reports available to the hearing, reports of the proceedings at all the hearings[27] and the statement of reasons for the decision which has been made or been caused to have been made by the chairman under r.10(5) of the 1996 Rules.

As soon as reasonably practicable after an appeal has been lodged, the sheriff must consider whether it is necessary to appoint a safeguarder in the appeal and he may indeed appoint a safeguarder at any later stage of the appeal.[28] The safeguarder, on appointment, will have all the powers and duties at common law of a curator *ad litem* in respect of the child[29] and will be entitled to receive from the sheriff clerk a copy of the appeal and any answers.[30] The safeguarder must without delay intimate in writing to the sheriff clerk whether or not he or she intends to become a party to the proceedings, and if he or she does become a party may appear personally or instruct an advocate or solicitor to appear on his or her behalf.[31] If the safeguarder intimates that he or she does not intend to become a party, he or she must report in writing on the extent of his or her inquiries and his or her conclusion as to the interests of the child; he or she may subsequently seek leave to become a party.[32] Where an appeal has been heard in part and a safeguarder thereafter becomes a party to the appeal, the sheriff may order the hearing of the appeal to commence of new.[33]

In hearing an appeal from a decision of the children's hearing the sheriff must first hear the appellant or his or her representative and any party to the appeal (that is the child, the relevant person, the reporter and, if appropriate, any safeguarder).[34] Thereafter, he is permitted to

---

[23] AS 1997, r.3.53.

[24] AS 1997, r.3.54.

[25] AS 1997, r.3.55(1). A copy of these answers must be intimated to any person on whom service of the appeal has been made: r.3.55(2).

[26] s.51(2).

[27] Which the reporter is obliged to keep in terms of the Rules: Children's Hearings (Scotland) Rules 1996, r.31.

[28] s.41(1) and AS 1997, r.3.7(1).

[29] AS 1997, r.3.8.

[30] AS 1997, r.3.54 and r.3.55.

[31] AS 1997, r.3.8 and r.3.9.

[32] AS 1997, r.3.10.

[33] AS 1997, r.3.56(7).

[34] s.51(1)(b) and AS 1997 r.3.56(1). Procedure for obtaining the views of the child is specified in r.3.5.

hear evidence from or on behalf of the parties to the appeal[35] and in addition he may examine the reporter and the compilers of any reports he has received.[36] It is in the discretion of the sheriff whom he wants to examine and he may call for any further report which he considers may assist him in deciding the appeal, such as an updated social background report, educational report, medical report, safeguarder's report, or any other report that was not available to the children's hearing.[37] It has been suggested[38] that these powers indicate that the sheriff should take a more inquisitorial role in appeals from children's hearings than would normally be appropriate in the sheriff court. The sheriff may hear evidence as to any alleged irregularity if that is the ground of appeal, and in any other case he may hear evidence when he considers it appropriate to do so.[39] The evidence must be kept strictly within the bounds of the appeal, that is to say directed towards the question of whether the hearing's decision was justified in all the circumstances of the case. It would be incompetent to lead evidence directed to other questions, for example whether accepted grounds of referral are in fact accurate.[40] The sheriff may, on the motion of any party or on his own motion, adjourn the hearing of the appeal for such reasonable time and for such purposes as may in the circumstances be appropriate.[41]

The child may be excluded from the hearing by the sheriff where he is satisfied that the nature of the appeal or of any evidence is such that it is in the child's interests not to be present, though in that event any safeguarder and the relevant person or[42] representative of the child shall be permitted to remain during the absence of the child.[43] Likewise, the relevant person and/or his or her representative can be excluded from the hearing where the sheriff considers it is necessary in the interests of any child[44] where he is satisfied that (a) he must do so in order to obtain the views of the child in relation to the hearing or (b) the presence of the person in question is causing or is likely to cause significant distress to the child; where the relevant person has been excluded the sheriff shall, after that exclusion has ended, explain the substance of what took place

---

[35] Under the pre-1995 legislation the right to hear evidence was limited to appeals on the basis of procedural irregularity: AS Social Work (Sheriff Court Procedure Rules) 1971 (SI 1971/92). Presumably this was because irregularity was regarded as a matter of fact which would require to be proved, but the present provisions recognise that there may be other factual bases to the appeal.

[36] s.51(3). The difference between hearing evidence and examining the compilers of reports is that the former but not the latter is done on oath and subject to cross-examination.

[37] s.51(3)(c). On receipt of such further reports, the sheriff must direct the reporter to send a copy thereof to every party to the appeal: AS 1997, r.3.56(2).

[38] Kearney, *Children's Hearings and the Sheriff Court* (2nd ed., 2000) at Chap.35.

[39] AS 1997, r.3.56(3).

[40] Established (but not accepted) grounds of referral can be challenged under s.85: see above at Chap.12.

[41] AS 1997, r.3.57.

[42] The use of the word "or" suggests that the child's representative cannot remain if the relevant person insists on remaining. Since appeals are heard in chambers, however, the sheriff will have a discretion and unless there is good reason why the representative should not remain, in most cases it will be appropriate for the sheriff to allow him or her to do so.

[43] AS 1997, r.3.56(4).

[44] Not just the referred child.

in his or her absence and shall give him or her an opportunity to respond to any evidence given by the child by leading evidence or otherwise.[45]

Appeals are heard by the sheriff in chambers[46] and it will be an offence for any person to publish any matter in respect of proceedings on appeal[47] which is intended to, or is likely to, identify any child concerned in or connected in any way with the appeal[48] or any address or school as being that of any such child.[49]

## APPEALABLE DECISIONS

The statute is not as clear as it might be on which decisions of the children's hearing can be appealed against. Though s.51(1)(a) talks of appeals to the sheriff from "any decision of the children's hearing", it is not, in fact, any decision that a hearing reaches at any stage in the proceedings that can be appealed against. Section 51(15) expressly precludes appeals against decisions of the children's hearing to continue a child protection order[50] and it might be argued that by specifying such decisions as unappealable the Act is indicating that all other decisions made by a children's hearing are appealable. It is submitted, however, that this argument (*expressio unius est exclusio alterius*) is not good since the same wording is used in s.51(1)(a) as appeared in the 1968 Act[51] and there is no indication other than s.51(15) that the words are to be given a meaning different from that gleaned by the courts since 1968. Section 51(15) deals exclusively with decisions relating to child protection orders,[52] and has been enacted for the avoidance of any doubt that the child protection order provisions in ss.57–62 constitute a self-contained procedure with its own review mechanisms, which are not susceptible to appeal under any other provision of the 1995 Act. It follows that the sort of decisions that were not appealable under the 1968 Act remain not appealable under the current legislation. The case law under the earlier statute established that appeals can be taken only against (i) dispositive decisions of the children's hearing (that is to say decisions discharging referrals or imposing, varying, continuing or terminating[53] supervision requirements)[54] and (ii) decisions granting, varying, or renewing warrants.[55] Confirmation that this remains the law can be found in

---

[45] AS 1997, r.3.56(5) and (6).

[46] s.93(5).

[47] Whether to the sheriff, the sheriff principal or the Court of Session.

[48] Which might not necessarily be the child referred to the children's hearing: see *McArdle v Orr*, 1994 S.L.T. 463.

[49] s.44(1). See further, above at pp.78–80.

[50] Made under s.59(4): see below at pp.237–239.

[51] Social Work (Scotland) Act 1968, s.49(1).

[52] For the details of which, see Chap.15.

[53] An appeal against the termination of a supervision requirement would be extremely rare, but is competent: see for example *Thomson, Petitioner*, 1998 S.L.T. 1066 (where in the event the appeal was refused).

[54] *H v McGregor*, 1973 S.L.T. 110.

[55] The competency of appealing against a warrant is confirmed by s.51(5)(a). There are few reported instances, but examples can be found in *McGregor v K*, 1982 S.L.T. 293 and *Humphries v S*, 1986 S.L.T. 683.

s.51(5)(c)(iii)[56] which allows a sheriff, after a successful appeal, to substitute his own disposal for that of the hearing—but that disposal must be one permitted by s.70, which deals only with final dispositive decisions. Any part of such a decision, such as to attach a condition to a supervision requirement, is in itself appealable. So, for example, a requirement to reside in a particular place is appealable without challenging the decision that the child requires compulsory measures of supervision.[57] Decisions which are merely procedural steps in the process towards the making of a dispositive decision, such as decisions to direct the reporter to apply to the sheriff for a finding as to whether the grounds of referral are established, are not appealable, for that would delay unduly the process towards the disposing of the referral.[58] Into the category of unappealable decisions will also fall decisions to transfer the case to a children's hearing in another local government area,[59] decisions to exclude journalists or relevant persons or representatives from part or all of the hearing,[60] decisions to relieve the child from his or her obligation to attend the hearing,[61] decisions to allow other persons to be present at the hearing,[62] decisions to continue the case to a subsequent hearing,[63] and decisions to require the child to reside or attend at a hospital or clinic for investigation.[64] A decision to appoint (or indeed not to appoint) a safeguarder, being a means of allowing the hearing to be in a position to make a properly informed decision, is procedural for that reason and is, therefore, unappealable. A decision to appoint a legal representative to a child is likewise not appealable, but there is a strong due process argument, missing in the case of safeguarders, that a refusal to appoint a legal representative is appealable. The Legal Representation Rules are silent on the matter and authoritative guidance is awaited.[65] Decisions such as that the child's address should be kept secret or that the child be liable to be kept in secure accommodation can be regarded as part of the terms of the supervision requirement or warrant to which they are attached and are therefore appealable. A determination under s.70(7) that a supervision requirement be reviewed at some point during its currency might be regarded as one of the terms of the requirement, but it is difficult to see who would have any interest in appealing it, since it puts the child and the relevant person in a better

---

[56] See further, below at pp.217–219.

[57] See *e.g. D v Sinclair,* 1973 S.L.T. (Sh. Ct.) 47 and *K v Finlayson,* 1974 S.L.T. (Sh. Ct.) 51 in which decisions to require the child to reside in residential establishments were successfully challenged; *A v Children's Hearing for Tayside Region,* 1987 S.L.T. (Sh. Ct.) 126 and *M v Children's Hearing for Strathclyde Region,* 1988 S.C.L.R. 592 (challenges to denial of contact by parents).

[58] *H v McGregor,* 1973 S.L.T. 110; *Sloan v B,* 1991 S.L.T. 530 at 545L; *M v Kennedy,* 1995 S.L.T. 123 at 125L.

[59] Made under s.48.

[60] Made under s.43(4) or s.46(1) respectively.

[61] Made under s.45(2). Such a decision does not deny the child the right to attend: see above at pp.65–66.

[62] Made under s.43(1).

[63] Made under s.69(1)(a).

[64] Made under s.69(3). A warrant granted under s.69(4) when this requirement has not been complied with is, however, appealable.

[65] See Norrie, "Legal Representation at Children's Hearings: The Interim Scheme" (2002) 7 S.L.P.Q. 131.

position than they would otherwise be in. Any advice given at an advice hearing[66] is not appealable since this is not dispositive, but any dispositive decision, such as in relation to contact, that is made at an advice hearing is appealable in the normal way.[67]

It should be remembered, however, that although procedural decisions are not in themselves directly appealable, irregularities in making these decisions can amount to a ground of appeal against the dispositive decision that follows.[68]

## GROUNDS OF APPEAL

The grounds of appeal to the sheriff are not expressly laid down in the 1995 Act except for the rule in s.51(5) (which applies, it may be assumed, both to appeals against dispositive decisions and appeals against the granting of warrants) that the sheriff shall allow the appeal if the decision of the children's hearing is "not justified in all the circumstances of the case". These words do not permit the sheriff to allow the appeal merely because he has a difference of opinion with the hearing as to the correct disposal of the case or as to whether a warrant ought to have been granted. It is perfectly conceivable that two different, even opposing, disposals are justifiable in the circumstances of a single case. It follows from this, it has been held,[69] "that the task facing a sheriff to whom an appeal has been taken is not to reconsider the evidence which was before the hearing with a view to making his own decision on that evidence. Instead, the sheriff's task is to see if there has been some procedural irregularity in the conduct of the case; to see whether the hearing has failed to give proper, or any consideration to a relevant factor in the case; and in general to consider whether the decision reached by the hearing can be characterised as one which could not, upon any reasonable view, be regarded as being justified in all the circumstances of the case". Irregularity in the conduct of the case is a ground of appeal from the sheriff to the sheriff principal or to the Court of Session under s.51(11), from which it can be inferred that irregularity in the conduct of the case is also among the grounds on which a decision of the children's hearing may be appealed to the sheriff under s.51(1).[70] The irregularity alleged in the case cited was that the children's hearing had proceeded on the assumption that the grounds of referral had been accepted when, in fact, they had not been. Other irregularities might be failing to consider contact (as required by s.70(2)), requiring the child to live with foster carers although the procedures in the Fostering of Children (Scotland) Regulations 1996 had not been carried out, excluding a relevant person from the children's hearing for no good reason, purporting to grant a warrant under one provision in the Act when in the

---

[66] See Chap. 10 above.

[67] *H v Stark* 1999 Greens Fam LB 40/4.

[68] *H v McGregor*, 1973 S.L.T. 110, *per* Lord Avonside at 116; *M v Kennedy*, 1995 S.L.T. 123, *per* Lord President Hope at 126F-1.

[69] *Per* Sheriff Principal Nicholson in *W v Schaffer* 2001 S.L.T. (Sh. Ct.) 86 at 87K–88A.

[70] *M v Kennedy*, 1995 S.L.T. 123, *per* Lord President Hope at 126E. That this is a ground of appeal is assumed in the rules: see AS 1997, r.3.56(3)(a).

circumstances only another provision could be used, failing to convene timeously, purporting to make a decision without giving appropriate opportunity to the child, relevant person, safeguarder or representative to express views,[71] taking into account allegations which have been expressly found by the sheriff not to be proved,[72] or failing to give consideration to the appointment of a legal representative when the circumstances required the hearing to do so. However, before the appeal can be upheld, the irregularity must be such that it has a material effect on the conduct of or outcome of the case, or such that it materially prejudices the child or relevant person. A failure, for example, on the part of the chairman to check a toddler's age is unlikely to render the decision "not justified in all the circumstances of the case". In *McGregor v A*[73] the irregularity was constituted by the statement of the grounds of referral mentioning the wrong statute: there was held to be no prejudice and therefore the decision of the children's hearing was upheld. The Court of Session, in the context of an appeal against a decision of a sheriff, has held that for an irregularity to found a successful appeal, it is necessary that the occurrence was damaging to the justice of the proceedings,[74] and this is likely to be true also in relation to proceedings before a children's hearing.

It is clear that procedural irregularity is not the only ground of appeal.[75] Error of law, if different from procedural irregularity, will also be a ground of appeal. This might be constituted, for example, by a misinterpretation of a statutory provision, such as the circumstances in which a warrant can be granted or in which secure accommodation can be authorised. Likewise, unfairness in the determination of the parties' civil rights (if, again, different from procedural irregularity) is a ground of appeal,[76] as is any other breach of a party's ECHR rights. In addition, a lack of clarity in the decision, such as to the effect of conditions attached to a supervision requirement, has been a successful ground of appeal.[77] Lack of clarity in the stated reasons for decision, which the chairman makes or causes to be made,[78] may be a ground of appeal in the sense that if the reasons are stated ambiguously it may be impossible for the sheriff to determine whether or not the decision is justified in all the circumstances of the case: if the sheriff cannot so determine, the decision, it is submitted, cannot stand.[79] The European Court has

---

[71] *cf. Kennedy, Petitioner*, 1988 S.C.L.R. 149 in which the sheriff held that there was a procedural irregularity when one member of the children's hearing stated his decision before the conclusion of the consideration of the case—some two and a half hours into the hearing!

[72] *M v Kennedy*, 1993 S.L.T. 431.

[73] 1982 S.L.T. 45.

[74] *C v Miller*, 2003 S.L.T. 1379.

[75] In *M v Kennedy*, 1995 S.L.T. 123 Lord President Hope described irregularity as being "among the grounds on which that decision may be appealed against".

[76] *Per* Sheriff Ross in *M v Caldwell* 2001 S.L.T. (Sh. Ct.) 106 at para.15.

[77] *D v Strathclyde Regional Council*, 1991 S.C.L.R. 185. In this case, access was stated "to be at the discretion of the local authority" and the evidence showed that the intention had been to terminate access completely.

[78] Children's Hearings (Scotland) Rules 1996, r.10(5).

[79] *K v Finlayson*, 1974 S.L.T. (Sh. Ct.) 51 (overruled on another point in *O v Rae*, 1993 S.L.T. 570). See also *Kennedy v M*, 1995 S.L.T. 717 in which Lord President Hope held that the sheriff's criticism of the children's hearing's statement of reasons was unjustified and that the reasons were not so ambiguous as to be open to challenge.

frequently found an infringement of Art.6 (right to a fair trial) when reasons for decision are insufficient to allow a party the know-how to structure an appeal.[80] More generally, it is open to the sheriff to uphold an appeal on the basis that the decision made by the children's hearing was entirely inappropriate, though this will be so only where the decision is one that no reasonable children's hearing would have reached on the information which was properly before them.[81] This might be because the hearing have founded their decision on irrelevant considerations, or have failed to take into account relevant considerations,[82] or have not been made aware of relevant considerations.[83] A decision might not be justified in all the circumstances of the case if it proceeds upon the basis of information which, in the event, turns out to be factually inaccurate. This is unlikely to eventuate in children's hearings who initially impose supervision requirements (for these hearings are entitled to act upon the grounds of referral accepted or established and an appeal cannot be used to reopen grounds of referral[84]) but it might arise at a review hearing if inaccurate reports, written or verbal, are given to the hearing.[85] This is an important check against a children's hearing relying too heavily on unsubstantiated allegations which have not been made grounds of referral. In *O v Rae,*[86] had the decision to remove the children from their mother's care been made primarily or exclusively on the basis that the father had sexually abused another sibling, and that allegation been shown by evidence led on appeal to be false, the decision would not have been justified and the appeal would have been sustained.[87]

There is sheriff court authority to suggest that a decision might be held to be "not justified in all the circumstances of the case" on the basis that in the time between the decision of the children's hearing and the hearing of the appeal the child's circumstances have changed.[88] The argument is that "all the circumstances of the case" means all the circumstances presently relevant to the child's welfare rather than all the circumstances relevant at the time the children's hearing made their decision. Some support, though tentative, for this is to be found in the use of the present tense in s.51(5), under which the sheriff must allow

---

[80] *Hadjianastassiou v Greece* (1992) 16 E.H.R.R. 219; *H v Belgium* (1987) 10 E.H.R.R. 339.

[81] *O v Rae,* 1993 S.L.T. 570, *per* Lord President Hope at 575I.

[82] As in *D v Sinclair,* 1973 S.L.T. (Sh. Ct.) 47 where the hearing had failed to consider an up-to-date social background report.

[83] Which the sheriff can discover by exercising his power under s.51(3)(c) to call for further reports.

[84] The procedure to do that is contained in s.85: see Chap.12.

[85] Such inaccuracy can be established before the sheriff on appeal since evidence can be led and the sheriff is entitled to examine the authors or compilers of reports or statements: s.51(3).

[86] 1993 S.L.T. 570.

[87] In the event, the appeal in that case was unsuccessful since the allegation was not the primary basis of the decision and there were various other grounds upon which the decision could be justified. It is to be remembered that an appeal will be successful only when the decision is shown to be not justified "in all the circumstances of the case".

[88] In *D v Sinclair,* 1973 S.L.T. (Sh. Ct.) 47 the sheriff allowed an appeal on the ground that the child's circumstances had changed sufficiently since the last hearing (five weeks previously) to justify the hearing looking at the matter again. See also *Kennedy v B,* 1973 S.L.T. 38.

the appeal when the decision "is not justified" rather than "was not, at the date of the decision, justified". To uphold an appeal on this basis would be to allow an appeal against a decision which was *ex hypothesi* correct at the time it was made, in order to ensure that the decision be looked at again in the light of subsequent developments. However, given the strict time-limits within which appeals must be lodged this is unlikely to be a common ground of appeal.

DISPOSAL OF THE APPEAL

Having heard the parties and considered any evidence tendered and reports submitted, the sheriff must then decide whether to reject or to allow the appeal. He must give his decision orally either at the conclusion of the appeal or on such day as he shall appoint.[89] He may issue a note of the reasons for his decision, and must do so if, on allowing the appeal, he decides to remit the case back to the hearing for reconsideration or to substitute his own disposal for that of the children's hearing[90]; any such note must be issued at the time the sheriff gives his decision or within seven days thereafter.[91]

### Appeal rejected

If the sheriff is not satisfied that the decision of the children's hearing is not justified in all the circumstances of the case, the appeal fails and the decision of the hearing is confirmed without variation.[92] It is to be assumed that any previously granted suspension of a supervision requirement[93] will be lifted on the rejection of the appeal.

### Appeal allowed

If the sheriff is satisfied that the decision of the children's hearing is not justified in all the circumstances of the case, he must allow the appeal and then proceed according to one of the three options listed in s.51(5)(c). The sheriff must regard the child's welfare throughout his or her childhood as the paramount consideration in determining which of the three options to choose.[94] If the successful appeal is against a warrant to find or keep a child in a place of safety, the sheriff is obliged to recall the warrant.[95] And if the supervision requirement contained a movement restriction condition[96] under s.70(3)(b) or an authorisation under s.70(9) to keep the child in secure accommodation, he is obliged to direct that that condition or authorisation shall cease to have effect[97] (though he will be entitled to grant such condition or authorisation himself under

---

[89] AS 1997, r.3.58(1).
[90] See below at pp.187–188.
[91] AS 1997, r.3.58(2) and (3).
[92] s.51(4).
[93] Granted under s.51(9): see below at pp.219–221.
[94] s.16(1).
[95] s.51(5)(a).
[96] See pp.141–142 above.
[97] s.51(5)(b).

s.51(5)(c)(iii), which allows him to do anything that the hearing can do under s.70). The three options open to the sheriff are as follows:

*(i) To remit the case back to the hearing for reconsideration of their decision*[98]

When the sheriff does this, he must give reasons for his decision, but he is not entitled to give any directions as to how the hearing should proceed with the case or dispose of it: such matters lie solely in the hands of the children's hearing.[99] His statement of reasons must, therefore, be limited to a statement of why he has found the decision appealed against to be not justified in all the circumstances of the case. The hearing are obliged to reconsider their decision in light of these reasons, but are not obliged to change it.[1]

*(ii) To discharge the child from any further hearing or proceedings in respect of the grounds which led to the hearing whose decision is being appealed against*[2]

When this option is considered appropriate, any supervision requirement imposed in respect of these grounds will be terminated, together with any order attached thereto. This option should be chosen by the sheriff only when he considers that it is not appropriate in all the circumstances of the case for the child to be or to remain subject to compulsory measures of supervision; a procedural irregularity will seldom in itself lead to this conclusion. After discharge, the child cannot then be brought back to a children's hearing by the reporter founding upon the grounds of referral previously established, for that would amount to seeking a review by the children's hearing of the sheriff's decision.[3] The sheriff's discharge of the child has the same effect as a children's hearing's discharge under s.69(12), except that it will not take effect until the time for appealing against it has passed.[4]

*(iii) To substitute for the disposal of the children's hearing any requirement that could have been imposed by them in terms of section 70 on whatever terms and conditions permitted by that section the sheriff considers appropriate*[5]

Since s.70 does not permit the children's hearing to grant, vary or continue any warrant, this option is available only in relation to appeals

---

[98] s.51(5)(c)(i).

[99] *Kennedy v A*, 1986 S.L.T. 358. Nor may the sheriff give procedural directions as to, for example, the makeup of the children's hearing. That function lies with the Chairman of the appropriate Children's Panel and there is no statutory authority for a sheriff giving directions to the Chairman. It follows that the sheriff's decision which led to the case *Kennedy, Petitioner,* 1988 S.C.L.R. 149, that the hearing to which a case was remitted after appeal be composed of panel members other than those who made the decision appealed against, was incompetent.

[1] It might be, for example, that the hearing should simply specify better or clearer reasons for their original decision: see, for example, *D v Strathclyde Regional Council,* 1991 S.C.L.R. 185 in which the appeal was allowed in order that the children's hearing make clear what their decision actually was.

[2] s.51(5)(c)(ii).

[3] The reporter is able to appeal from the sheriff's decision under s.51(11): see below at pp.221–225.

[4] *Stirling v D,* 1995 S.L.T. 1089: see below at p.225.

[5] s.51(5)(c)(iii).

against decisions of the children's hearing disposing of a referral or a review. Appeals against discharge of a referral or against termination of a supervision requirement are extreme rarities,[6] and the overwhelming majority of appeals in which this option is available will concern cases in which a supervision requirement has been imposed, varied or continued. If the sheriff, having upheld the appeal, does not consider it appropriate to discharge the child from any further proceedings (option (ii) above) then what this provision allows is effectively a variation in the terms and conditions of the existing supervision requirement[7] (for example removing, or imposing, a requirement that the child resides at a specified place, or varying a direction regulating contact between the child and another person). Appeals against discharge of a referral or termination of a supervision requirement, though rare, are not incompetent,[8] and on such appeals the sheriff can impose a supervision requirement on such terms and conditions as are available to the hearing under s.70. Though technically all the disposals open to the children's hearing are open to the sheriff, he will in practice be unable to adopt the very disposal previously adopted by the children's hearing themselves, for that would amount to an acceptance by the sheriff that that disposal was justifiable—in which case he must reject the appeal and allow the hearing's decision to stand.[9] Whenever the sheriff exercises his power under this provision to substitute his own disposal for that of the children's hearing he is obliged, so far as practicable, to give the child an opportunity to indicate whether he or she wishes to express his or her views; if the child does so wish, to give him or her the opportunity to express them; and to have regard to such views as the child may express.[10] The child is entitled to express views in any way that the sheriff in his discretion may permit, and may be orally or in writing, or through a legal representative, a safeguarder, a curator *ad litem* or by any other person (either orally or in writing) provided that the sheriff is satisfied that the person is a suitable representative and is clearly authorised to represent the child.[11] Indeed, no order may be made by the sheriff where the child has indicated his or her wish to express views unless an opportunity has been given for these views to be obtained and heard.[12] In addition, the sheriff must not make any requirement or order unless he considers that it would be better for the child that the requirement or order be made than that none should be made at all.[13] A supervision requirement substituted or imposed by the sheriff under this provision will be treated as a disposal of the children's hearing in relation to effect, duration, review and termination.[14] Its date of making will be the date of

---

[6] But they might be appropriate where the child is seeking the protection of a supervision requirement, or the parent is seeking to exercise parental control with the assistance of a supervision requirement.

[7] Though technically the existing supervision requirement is replaced by the new one imposed by the sheriff.

[8] See, for example, *Thomson, Petitioner,* 1998 S.L.T. 1066.

[9] s.51(4).

[10] s.16(2) and (4)(b)(iv).

[11] AS 1997, r.3.5(2). The sheriff may direct that any written views of the child be kept confidential, in accordance with the procedure laid down in r.3.5(4).

[12] AS 1997, r.3.5(1)(b).

[13] s.16(3) and (4)(b)(iv).

[14] s.51(6).

the sheriff's decision.

Adopting this option permits the sheriff to trespass into the role which, prior to the coming into effect of the 1995 Act, rested exclusively with the children's hearing. Perhaps because they recognise that the children's hearing is always the most appropriate forum for determining what compulsory measures of supervision will best meet the child's needs[15] and that it is in every child's interests to have their case determined by the most appropriate forum, sheriffs have since acquiring this power been slow to use it. It is suggested that they are right to show reticence and that the power under this provision should be exercised only when it is clear that there is only one possible option that will serve the child's interests and when, therefore, it would be a procedural waste of time to send the matter back to the children's hearing for disposal.

### FRIVOLOUS APPEALS

Where a sheriff has rejected an appeal against a decision of the children's hearing at a review of a supervision requirement and he is satisfied that the appeal was "frivolous", he may prohibit for a period of 12 months any subsequent appeal against a subsequent decision to continue (with or without variation) the supervision requirement in respect of which the appeal was made.[16] In other words, if the supervision requirement continued by a decision frivolously appealed against is reviewed at any time within 12 months of the sheriff's order, any decision at that review is not appealable until these 12 months have elapsed. An order under this provision will prevent an appeal by anyone, even by those who did not join in the frivolous appeal, though it can be made only in the context of an appeal from a decision of a children's hearing reviewing a supervision requirement and not from the decision which initially imposes it or from a decision to grant, vary or continue a warrant. It may well, however, be contrary to Art.6 of the ECHR (and therefore not open to the sheriff) to prevent another person from appealing. In any case, this power is used only exceedingly rarely. The Act does not define what a frivolous appeal is, but the aims of the provision are clear: (i) to ensure that the courts are not cluttered by appeals which have no chance of success or which seek review when no change whatsoever has occurred in the child's circumstances since the last review and which are being brought by the child or relevant person simply in order to prolong the procedure, and (ii) to protect the child from the needless uncertainty caused by such appeals.

### SUSPENSION OF SUPERVISION REQUIREMENT PENDING APPEAL

It is a general rule in appeals that any order appealed against does not need to be executed until the appeal has been determined.[17] This rule,

---

[15] That proposition is the very foundation of the whole children's hearing system.
[16] s.51(7).
[17] *Macleay v Macdonald*, 1928 S.C. 776.

however, applies only when there is no statutory provision to the contrary. Supervision requirements are to be enforced immediately they are made, even when an appeal is lodged, for the statute provides that the child or relevant person who appeals against a decision of the children's hearing imposing, continuing or varying a supervision requirement can apply to the hearing for the suspension of the requirement until the appeal has been heard.[18] It is implicit in this provision that the supervision requirement remains effective unless and until such an application has been successfully made.[19] The local authority's duties to give effect to the supervision requirement[20] therefore come into effect immediately and are not suspended by the lodging of an appeal.

An application to suspend the effect of a supervision requirement can be made immediately the appeal is lodged, but not before,[21] so the hearing against whose decision the appeal is being taken cannot deal with an application to suspend the requirement they have just made or continued. The application must be in writing.[22] It is the responsibility of the reporter to arrange forthwith (*i.e.* as soon as practically possible) a children's hearing to consider the application for suspension[23] and he or she must give separate written notice to the child and relevant person of the date, time and place of the hearing at which the application will be considered.[24] If the applicant fails to attend at that hearing, the application shall be treated as abandoned.[25] It is not possible to suspend a condition in a supervision requirement without also suspending the requirement itself.[26]

There is no indication as to what criteria the hearing should use to determine such applications (which are very uncommon in practice), but the decision is clearly one governed by the welfare of the child as the paramount consideration.[27] In addition, the applicant and his or her representative and any safeguarder must be given an opportunity of being heard.[28] Though neither s.16(2) nor the Rules oblige them to do so, good practice suggests that the children's hearing should take account of any views expressed by the child even when the child is not the applicant. Suspension will not be appropriate when the children's hearing are of the view that the child is in need of immediate care and protection or is likely to continue with the behaviour that founded the

---

[18] s.51(9). A child will have legal capacity to seek a suspension whenever he or she has capacity to require a review of a supervision requirement: on that matter see above at p.161.

[19] It is different with appeals from the sheriff to the sheriff principal or to the Court of Session for, in the absence of any statutory provision analogous to s.51(9), the general rule applies: *Kennedy v M*, 1995 S.L.T. 717, *per* Lord President Hope at 720K–721B.

[20] See above at pp.20–22.

[21] 1996 Rules, r.23(6).

[22] 1996 Rules, r.23(1).

[23] s.51(10).

[24] 1996 Rules, r.23(2).

[25] 1996 Rules, r.23(5). It is presumably open to the reporter to rearrange a hearing if, on receipt of the notice, the applicant indicates that he or she cannot attend on the date selected.

[26] *S v Proudfoot*, 2002 S.L.T. 743.

[27] s.16(1).

[28] 1996 Rules, r.23(3).

grounds of referral; it might be in the interests of the child to suspend the operation of the supervision requirement pending an appeal when little or no work can in fact be done with the child in the interim (*e.g.* when there is no place yet available at a day care unit, or group work, or other resource which has been identified as appropriate for the child) or when, in the light of further information, the hearing believe that an appeal is likely to be successful.[29] It is difficult to imagine a situation in which suspension of a supervision requirement continued without variation will be appropriate, especially if it involves a continuing plan of work with the child. Suspension is rather more likely to be appropriate when the child was not subject to a supervision requirement before the hearing.

When the decision has been reached, the chairman of the hearing shall inform the applicant of the decision and the reasons for it.[30] The decision on suspension is itself unlikely to be appealable, but it would seem that it is open to judicial review.[31]

Suspension lasts until the appeal has been disposed of by the sheriff. Since the supervision requirement is not "in force" during the period of suspension, that period will not count towards the year before which the supervision requirement must be reviewed,[32] but it would seem not to interrupt the running of the three-month period after which the child or relevant person can call for a review.[33]

### Suspension of warrants?

Section 51(9) does not permit the child or relevant person to seek the suspension of a warrant pending an appeal against its granting, which might be taken to suggest that a warrant cannot be given effect to until the time for an appeal has passed (*i.e.* three weeks).[34] However, the urgency inherent in the need for warrants, taken with the very strict time-limits within which appeals against warrants must be disposed of,[35] militates against this conclusion. It is submitted that warrants, once granted, are immediately effective and remain so during the appeal process until recalled under s.51(5)(a) on a successful appeal.[36]

### APPEALS FROM THE SHERIFF

Appeals can be taken from decisions of the sheriff, both in determining an appeal from any decision of the children's hearing under s.51(1)

---

[29] The hearing arranged under s.51(10) has no power to review the supervision requirement itself.

[30] 1996 Rules, r.23(4).

[31] See *S v Proudfoot*, 2002 S.L.T. 743. This procedure would bring a case to the Outer House, which is entirely outwith the remit, or interest, of Part II of the Children (Scotland) Act 1995. By this route, children's hearings cases might conceivably end up in the House of Lords.

[32] s.73(2): "No supervision requirement shall remain in force for a period longer than one year".

[33] s.73(6): "A child or relevant person may require a review . . . at any time at least three months after—(a) the date on which the requirement is made". This does not require that the requirement be in force for three months before a review can be called for.

[34] *cf. Stirling v D*, 1995 S.L.T. 1089.

[35] See above at pp.207–208.

[36] Or, if the appeal is unsuccessful, until their natural termination in terms of the statutory provisions under which they were granted.

(whether in relation to a disposal or to a warrant) and in determining whether grounds of referral have been established (whether on the initial application under s.68 or at a review of the evidence under s.85).[37] Since the Act expressly specifies only these decisions as being subject to appeal from the sheriff, it would appear that no appeal lies from any other decision that the sheriff makes under the Act, such as decisions to grant warrants or orders to find the child and keep him or her in a place of safety. Decisions on appeal from children's hearings' decisions to grant or issue such warrants are appeals under s.51(1) and would appear, therefore, to be themselves appealable[38] but in practice an appeal to the sheriff principal or Court of Session will never be heard before the warrant ceases to have effect in any case.[39] Title to appeal inheres in the child, the safeguarder on the child's behalf, all relevant persons,[40] and the reporter.[41] The reporter may appeal against a finding that the grounds of referral have not been established, but has no interest in appealing against a decision that the grounds are established, unless the sheriff's decision is that only some of the stated grounds are established, since a finding that others are not will prohibit the children's hearing from considering what the reporter believes to be the whole case. In relation to sheriffs' decisions on appeal from decisions of the children's hearing, since the reporter appeals "on behalf of the children's hearing",[42] he or she can appeal against the sheriff's finding that the hearing's decision was not justified, but not against a confirmation of the hearing's decision.

### The court appealed to

The appeal can be taken either to the sheriff principal of the sheriffdom in which the sheriff, from whose decision the appeal is being taken, sits[43] or direct to the Court of Session[44]; and if the appeal is taken to the sheriff principal there is a further appeal from him to the Court of Session (though only with leave of the sheriff principal).[45] It is a matter for the appellant to decide which court to appeal to. It is to be expected that appeals direct to the Court of Session will occur when the point of law is particularly difficult or contentious, or raises an important matter of principle or statutory interpretation. Leave is not required to appeal from the sheriff to the sheriff principal nor direct from the sheriff to the Court of Session, but if an appeal has already been taken from the sheriff to the sheriff principal a further appeal to the Court of Session will require the leave of the sheriff principal. No guidance is given to the sheriff principal as to the circumstances in which it would be appropriate

---

[37] s.51(11).

[38] See, *e.g. McGregor v K*, 1982 S.L.T. 293; *Humphries v S*, 1986 S.L.T. 683.

[39] Notice that there is no provision analogous to s.51(8) whereby an appeal against the granting of a warrant must be disposed of within three days of being lodged.

[40] s.51(12)(a).

[41] s.51(12)(b).

[42] *ibid.*

[43] s.51(11)(a). See, as examples, *G v Templeton*, 1998 S.C.L.R. 180; *W v Schaffer*, 2001 S.L.T. (Sh. Ct.) 86.

[44] s.51(11)(b).

[45] *ibid.*

to grant or to withhold leave to appeal, but the aim of the requirement for leave is to ensure that appeal to the sheriff principal is not used simply as a delaying tactic. Leave ought to be refused, it is submitted, when an appeal to the sheriff principal has failed and it is his view that the ground of appeal put forward was not arguable. Leave ought to be granted without hesitation if appeal to the Court of Session is necessary to resolve a difference which has arisen between sheriffs principal[46]; and, it is submitted, in the generality of cases unless there is good reason to deny leave it should be granted. The system has benefited immensely over the years by the clarifications provided by the Court of Session in appeal cases.

There is no appeal from the Court of Session to the House of Lords.[47] Decisions of the sheriff in relation to child protection orders are not appealable[48] since they have their own review mechanisms.[49]

**Grounds of appeal**

The appeal can be taken either on a point of law or in respect of any irregularity in the conduct of the case.[50] A point of law might, for example, concern the sheriff's interpretation of one of the grounds of referral in s.52,[51] or his failure to take account of the whole facts of the case,[52] or his interpretation of when he could grant or recall a warrant,[53] or his adopting the wrong standard of proof,[54] or his misapplying the rules of evidence,[55] or his paying insufficient regard to ECHR jurisprudence.[56] Irregularity in the conduct of the children's hearing is a ground of appeal to the sheriff, and the sheriff's decision on whether or not there is any irregularity is appealable; likewise irregularity in the proceedings before the sheriff amounts to a ground of appeal.[57] Kearney,[58] in a passage approved by the Inner House,[59] said this: "for an appeal based on such grounds to succeed, however, it would seem that the defect must be 'material' in the sense of causing real prejudice to the person affected by the irregularity or, presumably, to the interests of the child". Such an irregularity may, for example, be when the sheriff refuses to hear one or other of the parties to an appeal, or wrongly excludes a relevant person from the hearing of a s.68 application,[60] or has purported

---

[46] As in, for example, *K & F, Applicants*, 2002 S.L.T. (Sh. Ct.) 38.

[47] s.51(11)(b).

[48] s.51(15)(a).

[49] See below at pp.236–243.

[50] s.51(11).

[51] See, for example, *McGregor v L*, 1981 S.L.T. 194; *McGregor v H*, 1983 S.L.T. 626; *B v Harris*, 1990 S.L.T. 208; *D v Kelly*, 1995 S.L.T. 1220; *S v Kennedy*, 1996 S.C.L.R. 34.

[52] As in *M v McGregor*, 1982 S.L.T. 41.

[53] As in *McGregor v K*, 1982 S.L.T. 293 and *Humphries v S*, 1986 S.L.T. 683.

[54] As in *Harris v F*, 1991 S.L.T. 242.

[55] As in *F v Kennedy (No. 1)*, 1993 S.L.T. 1277; *Ferguson v S*, 1993 S.C.L.R. 712; *T v Watson*, 1995 S.L.T. 1062.

[56] *W v Schaffer*, 2001 S.L.T. (Sh.Ct.) 86.

[57] As in *H v Mearns*, 1974 S.L.T. 184 when the statutory timetable for what are now s.68 applications was not adhered to.

[58] *Children's Hearings and the Sheriff Court* (2nd ed., 2000) at para.49.07.

[59] *C v Miller*, 2003 S.L.T. 1379 at para.71.

[60] As in *C v Kennedy*, 1991 S.L.T. 755 and *S v N*, 2002 S.L.T. 589.

to make a disposal which is not open to him (such as affirming the hearing's decision and at the same time varying the supervision requirement), or has given directions he is not permitted to give,[61] or has heard an appeal from parties with no title to appeal,[62] or has given inadequate reasons for his decision.[63] The irregularity may lie in the actions of the reporter rather than the sheriff.[64] It is not for the appeal court to conduct a rehearing or reconsideration of the decision taken by the sheriff.[65]

**Procedure**

An appeal from a decision of the sheriff or the sheriff principal is by way of stated case[66] and the application to state a case must be made within a period of 28 days from the date of the sheriff's or the sheriff principal's decision,[67] otherwise the right of appeal is lost.[68] Within 14 days of the lodging of a note of appeal against a decision of the sheriff, the sheriff must issue a draft stated case.[69] Within seven days of issuing the draft stated case the appellant or any party to whom intimation has been made[70] may lodge with the sheriff clerk a note of any adjustments which he or she seeks to make and may state any point of law which he or she wishes to raise in the appeal; a note of such adjustment or point of law must be intimated to the appellant and the other parties.[71] The sheriff may allow a hearing on adjustments of the stated case, and must do so where he proposes to reject any proposed adjustments.[72] Within 14 days after the latest date on which a note of adjustments has been or may be lodged, or after the hearing on adjustments, the sheriff must, after considering such note and any representations made to him at the hearing, state and sign the case.[73] The stated case must include, as the case may be, (a) questions of law, framed by the sheriff, arising from the points of law stated by the parties and such other questions of law as he may consider appropriate, (b) any proposed adjustments which were rejected by him, and (c) a note of the irregularity in the conduct of the case averred by the parties and any questions of law or other issues which he considers arise therefrom.[74] The procedure on appeals must be followed strictly in accordance with these rules.[75]

No new evidence can be placed before the appeal court, since that would not bear upon any irregularity in the conduct of the case or assist the court in determining a point of law.[76] An appeal under s.51(11)

---

[61] As in *Kennedy v A*, 1986 S.L.T. 358.
[62] As in *Kennedy v H*, 1988 S.L.T. 586.
[63] *C v Miller* ,2003 S.L.T. 1379 at para.71.
[64] *ibid.*
[65] *W v Schaffer*, 2001 S.L.T. (Sh.Ct.) 86.
[66] s.51(11) and AS 1997, r.3.59.
[67] With the day of the decision counting as the first day: see comments above at pp.207–208.
[68] s.51(13).
[69] AS 1997, r.3.59(3).
[70] In terms of AS 1997, r.3.59(2).
[71] AS 1997, r.3.59(4).
[72] AS 1997, r.3.59(5).
[73] AS 1997, r.3.59(6).
[74] AS 1997, r.3.59(7).
[75] *Kennedy v A*, 1986 S.L.T. at p.361A and *Sloan v B*, 1991 S.L.T. at p.544J—L.
[76] *Stirling v R*, 1996 S.C.L.R. 191 (Notes).

cannot involve a general review of the decisions of fact made by the sheriff: the only matters of fact that can properly be raised are those associated with the alleged error of law.[77] There is no provision similar to that under s.51(9) under which the child or relevant person can apply to have the supervision requirement suspended pending the outcome of the appeal.[78] However, if an appeal from an order made by the sheriff is lodged, the order itself does not need to be complied with: so if the sheriff remits the case back to a children's hearing for reconsideration under s.51(5)(c)(i) the reporter is not obliged to arrange a children's hearing if the sheriff's decision is being appealed against,[79] and if the sheriff discharges the referral under s.51(5)(c)(ii) the child remains subject to a supervision requirement while the appeal from the sheriff is pending[80] (and the supervision requirement must be reviewed and continued at the appropriate point before the appeal has been heard if it is not to lapse under s.73(2)[81]). It would also follow from these authorities that if the sheriff makes his own disposal under s.51(5)(c)(iii) and that disposal is appealed against, it is the original terms of the supervision requirement made or continued by the children's hearing rather than the terms substituted by the sheriff that should be complied with until the appeal from the sheriff has been disposed of.

Once the appeal has been determined the sheriff principal or the Court of Session must remit the case back to the sheriff for disposal in accordance with such directions as the court may give.[82] The breadth of this provision allows the court on appeal from a sheriff to go further than the sheriff on appeal from the hearing could go, for a sheriff cannot give the hearing directions as to how to dispose of the case: the sheriff principal or the Court of Session can so direct the sheriff.

---

[77] *C v Miller,* 2003 S.L.T. 1379 at para.79.

[78] See above at pp.219–221. A suspension lapses on the sheriff's decision and cannot continue even after an appeal from the sheriff's decision has been lodged.

[79] *Kennedy v M,* 1995 S.L.T. 717.

[80] *Stirling v D,* 1995 S.L.T. 1089. It was also stated in this case that a consequence of this rule is that such a discharge is inoperative in all cases until the time for appeals has passed, otherwise the right to appeal would be negated.

[81] *ibid.* As the commentator to this case points out, the delays in hearing appeals may mean that a child remains subject to a supervision requirement for many months after the sheriff has discharged the referral.

[82] s.51(14). If an appeal is being taken from the sheriff principal to the Court of Session the remit to the sheriff will itself not need to be given effect to.

## CHAPTER FIFTEEN

# EMERGENCY PROTECTION OF CHILDREN

## INTRODUCTION

It sometimes happens that a child's circumstances give rise to the belief that protective measures need to be taken immediately, without the delay necessarily inherent in a referral to the reporter and thence to a children's hearing.[1] This might arise, for example, if social workers or teachers or health care workers notice apparently non-accidental physical injuries on a child, or if the child's home is discovered to be in a grossly unhygienic state, or if the child discloses continuing sexual abuse. Prior to the coming into force of the Children (Scotland) Act 1995, emergency protective measures which could not wait until a children's hearing was convened took the form of a place of safety order, granted by a court or justice of the peace under s.37 of the Social Work (Scotland) Act 1968, which authorised the removal of a child to a place of safety. Though the rules in that section were straightforward, there were a number of criticisms that could be, and were, made of the operation of the provision. For one thing, while the grounds upon which a place of safety order could be made were relatively clear, they were not directed to the needs of the particular child for immediate protection. It would not, for example, have been appropriate to remove a child from his or her parent every time the child was a victim of a scheduled offence, though in every such case it would have been competent to do so under s.37(2)(a) of the 1968 Act. Another criticism was that the provisions were too inflexible since they authorised only the removal of the child to a place of safety and could not authorise any other, less traumatic, action which might in some cases have provided sufficient protection. Again, there was no provision for the court to regulate the contact that the child was to have with any other person, and the matter was left entirely in the hands of those in charge of the place of safety to which the child was taken. Also, there was no means by which the granting of the order could be challenged before the matter came into the hands of the children's hearing: the system made no provision for the family who were willing to attend a children's hearing (perhaps confident that they would be able to rebut any allegations made) but who wanted their child back home in the meantime. All these criticisms were brought

---

[1] The reporter has certain investigative and preparatory functions to carry out before arranging a children's hearing and, generally speaking, once arranged, the hearing members require at least three days' notice. See Children's Hearings (Scotland) Rules 1996, r.5(1).

to the public attention in the Orkney Case, which led to the public inquiry and the publication of the Clyde Report.[2]

The whole system of emergency protection of children was redesigned in the light of these criticisms, and the present rules are contained in ss.57–61 of the Children (Scotland) Act 1995, which govern the granting and the effect of the new form of order, known as a child protection order (hereinafter CPO). The provisions are fairly complicated and the time-scale short in which the CPO is granted, reviewed and terminated. The basic aim is to separate the procedure relating to child protection orders from the children's hearing system, though that system will usually take over when the CPO comes to an end, and to ensure that the grounds for its granting are clearly directed towards the needs of the particular child for protection. The order itself can last only until the eighth working day after it has been implemented, and there will always be one, and sometimes two, reviews to determine whether it is or was necessary to remove the child and whether it remains necessary to keep the child away from home. The diagram in Appendix 1 illustrates the procedure that is to be followed.

## The Grounds for Granting a CPO

A CPO can be applied for under one of two separate subsections, and the application must, of course, specify which is being founded upon.

### Section 57(1): reasonable grounds for believing harm

Under s.57(1), any person, whether a local authority, a reporter, a parent, a constable, or even the child him or herself can apply to the sheriff for a CPO, which can be granted if the following conditions are satisfied:

"(a) there are reasonable grounds to believe that a child[3] —

    (i) is being so treated (or neglected) that he is suffering significant harm; or

    (ii) will suffer such harm if he is not removed to and kept in a place of safety, or if he does not remain in the place where he is then being accommodated (whether or not he is resident there); and

(b) an order under this section is necessary to protect that child from such harm (or such further harm)."

Both paragraphs must be fulfilled. Under paragraph (a) the sheriff must be satisfied that there is evidence sufficient to ground a reasonable belief

---

[2] *Report of the Inquiry into the Removal of Children From Orkney in February 1991* (H.C. Papers 1992–1993, No. 195).

[3] "Child" does not include an unborn child. There is conflicting authority as to whether the parents of an unborn child can lodge a caveat for notice of any application by the local authority which intends to apply for a CPO as soon as the child is born: compare *C, Petitioner,* 2002 Fam. L.R. 42. with *K & F, Applicants,* 2002 S.L.T. (Sh. Ct.) 38.

that the child is being or will be significantly harmed. Subparagraph (i) concerns the way that some other person is presently acting towards the child and it covers, for example, the child who is being assaulted or who is not being fed or washed. "Is being treated" suggests a continuing state of affairs brought about by someone other than the child and it does not cover either significant harm caused by the child's own acts or omissions, or harm caused to the child in the past. It cannot be said, it is submitted, of a child who was beaten some time in the past that he or she "is being treated" unless, perhaps, the injuries are still being suffered from.[4] Subparagraph (ii) concerns future harm and is capable of covering both significant harm that another person will cause to the child in the future and harm which is being or will be caused by the child him or herself. Harm inflicted upon the child in the past (whether by the child or some other person) may well provide reasonable grounds for believing that it will be repeated, particularly if it is continuing. So a parent who has beaten a child will give reasonable grounds for believing that the child "will suffer" harm, but only if it is reasonable to believe that the beating is likely to be repeated. A child may be presently harming him or herself, say, by abusing alcohol or drugs, or by associating with thieves or prostitutes: such actions clearly can give reasonable ground to believe that the child will suffer significant harm if not removed to a place of safety and kept there.

In relation to either subparagraph, the harm that the child must be suffering or threatened with is "significant" harm, that is to say harm of a not minor, transient or superficial nature. It may be physical or emotional or, perhaps, social (for a child who is anti-social does him or herself harm).[5] "The categories of harm are never closed".[6] The subjecting of the child to any sexual activity is likely always to be considered significant, as is any physical assault consisting of a blow to the head, shaking or the use of an implement.[7] There is, however, no necessary connection between "significant harm" and harm that would lead to a criminal charge against the perpetrator: the latter does not have to be "significant" and the test is not that the child is a victim of an offence. Emotional harm will be significant when it can properly be described as trauma; distress and upset will not usually be sufficient. Harm will always be significant when it is clearly more serious than the potential trauma that removal from home will cause almost every child.

Under paragraph (b), the sheriff must be satisfied that the making of a CPO is "necessary" to protect the child from the actual or threatened significant harm. If the harm is not such as to require, in the eyes of the reasonable person, immediate action to protect the child from any continuation of the harm, then the making of the order cannot be said to

---

[4] But even then, since the purpose of the CPO is to provide necessary protection from immediate harm, the words should not be interpreted to cover harm that has already occurred.

[5] The English Children Act 1989 defines "harm" to mean "ill-treatment or the impairment of health or development": s.31(9). There is no definition of "harm" in the Scottish statute but would, it is submitted, include developmental impairment.

[6] Freeman, *Children, their Families and the Law* (1992) at p.93.

[7] These sorts of assault are never "justifiable" as the parental right of chastisement: Criminal Justice (Scotland) Act 2003, s.51(3).

be necessary. This does not mean that the CPO must be shown to be the only possible way in which the child can be protected. Rather the word "necessary" has, it is submitted, a somewhat looser meaning, and this condition is fulfilled when the CPO is shown to be either the only, or the most efficacious, or in the circumstances the most appropriate, means of protecting the child. Necessity must be interpreted in the light of a continuing risk to the child, for the whole point of the order is to give immediate protection to the child from risk. So even when significant harm has been unquestionably caused, a CPO will not be necessary unless there is a likelihood of the harm continuing or being repeated. A parent may admittedly injure his or her child but suffer real remorse and contrition: the question of whether compulsory measures of supervision are necessary always arises but if the event is unique and the contrition genuine the granting of a CPO is unlikely to be considered "necessary". It will certainly not be necessary if the source of the harm has been removed from the child's home and taken, say, into police custody. "Necessity", in this context as in others, also imports the ECHR proportionality test. In *KA v Finland*[8] the European Court held that with emergency orders the proportionality test is satisfied if (i) there are relevant and sufficient reasons for making the order and (ii) the parent had the opportunity to participate adequately in the decision making. The more draconian the measure, the greater must be the risk facing the child before the proportionality test is satisfied. In *P, C & S v United Kingdom*[9] the European Court said this: "the taking of a new-born baby into public care at the moment of its birth is an extraordinarily harsh measure. There must be extraordinarily compelling reasons before a baby can be physically removed from its mother, against her will, immediately after birth".

### Section 57(2): frustration of enquiries

A CPO might be sought under s.57(2) rather than under s.57(1). The effect of the order, if granted, is the same whichever subsection is used to base the application, as are the matters it may authorise and the procedures that its implementation activates. The difference lies in (i) the fact that only a local authority can apply for an order under s.57(2)[10] (because only the local authority has the investigative duties the frustration of which will justify the order[11]) and (ii) the fact that the grounds upon which the order can be granted are different. The grounds under s.57(2) are as follows:

"(a) That [the local authority] have reasonable grounds to suspect that a child is being or will be so treated (or neglected) that he is suffering or will suffer significant harm;
(b) that they are making or causing to be made enquiries to allow them to decide whether they should take any action to safeguard the welfare of the child; and

---

[8] Jan 14, 2003 at paras 103–104.
[9] (2002) 35 E.H.R.R. 31 at para.116.
[10] This is expressly stated in s.57(2) to be "without prejudice to subsection (1)", so that a local authority can choose which subsection to use.
[11] See above at pp.40–41.

(c) that those enquiries are being frustrated by access to the child being unreasonably denied, the authority having reasonable cause to believe that such access is required as a matter of urgency".

The enquiries must be rendered wholly ineffectual in allowing the local authority to determine whether or not their suspicions are justified, because of the denial of access for no good cause, by the person with control over who has contact with the child. Merely hampering or making more difficult these enquiries will not be sufficient. Due to the local authority's various duties in relation to children it would appear that the onus of proving reasonable cause lies with those denying the local authority access (though the onus of proving reasonable grounds for suspicion will lie with the applicant local authority).

**The sheriff's decision**

On receipt of an application for a CPO, the sheriff, having considered the grounds for the application, the supporting evidence and, within reason,[12] any interested party, must forthwith grant or refuse it.[13] He cannot adjourn and give his decision at a later date. The sheriff is not entitled to appoint a safeguarder at this stage in the proceedings in order to assist him or to safeguard the interests of the child,[14] for that would inevitably require an adjournment until a safeguarder could be contacted. Sheriff Kearney[15] describes the process as follows:

"The hearing before the sheriff is not a 'proof'. The strict rules of evidence do not apply. The sheriff is entitled to have regard to hearsay evidence and will consider the whole *information* which has been presented and draw such inferences as common sense may suggest. The sheriff has to be 'satisfied'".

Even when the grounds in either s.57(1) or s.57(2) are satisfied, the sheriff retains a discretion and he is not obliged to grant the order sought. He is guided in the exercise of that discretion by s.16(1), under which the welfare of the child must be his paramount consideration. This may well indicate that no order should be made if, for example, it appears that the making of an order is likely to do more harm (perhaps psychological) to the child than good. Welfare, as always, is to be given broad scope and is not limited to the immediate circumstances which would otherwise justify the granting of a CPO. The granting of a CPO can quite conceivably be both necessary to protect a child from significant harm and at the same time be against the welfare of the child. The removal of a child from familiar surroundings might sometimes be so traumatic and cause such distress to the child as to be a greater, psychological, injury than the physical harm it is designed to bring a stop

---

[12] See *C, Petitioner*, 2002 Fam. L.R. 42.
[13] Act of Sederunt (Child Care and Maintenance Rules) 1997 (hereinafter AS 1997), r.3.31.
[14] s.41(2).
[15] *Children's Hearings and the Sheriff Court* (2nd ed., 2000) at para.6.06.

to. It is common experience for children to express a preference to remain in a highly unsatisfactory home than to be summarily removed to the alien environment most children would regard a residential establishment (or even a foster home) to be, and their opinions are not to be dismissed lightly on that matter. This is not, of course, to deny that in many cases the child's welfare will indeed require immediate removal of the child from a source of risk. The other overarching principles in s.16 (*i.e.* having regard to the views of the child and the minimum intervention principle) do not apply to the making of a child protection order (though curiously they do apply to the varying and discharging thereof[16]). This is probably because in an emergency situation there will seldom be time to allow the child the opportunity to express views, and because both the minimum intervention principle, with its requirement that any intervention be shown to be "better" than no intervention, and the ECHR principle of proportionality, would be tautologous in light of the "necessity" requirement in s.57.

MATTERS AUTHORISED

A child protection order is designed to be much more flexible than the old place of safety order, and it may not only authorise the removal of the child to a place of safety but may require, authorise or provide any one or more of the actions listed in s.57(4), as follows.

The CPO may:

"(a) require any person in a position to do so to produce the child to the applicant;
(b) authorise the removal of the child by the applicant to a place of safety, and the keeping of the child at that place;
(c) authorise the prevention of the removal of the child from any place where he is being accommodated;
(d) provide that the location of any place of safety in which the child is being kept should not be disclosed to any person or class of person specified in the order".[17]

It is likely that most CPOs will authorise the action in either paragraphs (b) or (c). An order under paragraph (b) authorises the taking by the applicant of the child to a place of safety[18] and the keeping of the child there; in other words the effect will be the same as with the old place of safety order.[19] The wording of this paragraph, with its reference to removal, suggests that it cannot be used when the child is already in a place of safety, but is to be used only to take a child to a place of safety and keep him or her there. An order under paragraph (d), since it refers to the child being kept in a place of safety, can be made only in

---

[16] s.16(4)(b)(ii).
[17] s.57(4).
[18] Defined in s.93(1): see above at p.187.
[19] If the place of safety is provided by a local authority, that authority will have duties towards the child as specified in s.17: s.57(7).

conjunction with an order under paragraphs (b) or (c); it is less clear whether an order under paragraph (a) can stand alone, but it is submitted that it should usually be made in conjunction with paragraph (b) if the applicant is the local authority unless the mere production of the child is sufficient to lay their suspicions to rest. If the applicant is some other person, such as the parent, the order under paragraph (a) may well, in some circumstances, properly stand alone.[20] The order under paragraph (c), preventing the removal of the child from the place where he or she is being accommodated will cover (but is not limited to) the situation of the child already in a place of safety,[21] but its wording initially suggests that it cannot be used to detain the child there against his or her will: the word "removal" indicates that the order is designed to prevent someone else from taking the child away but does not authorise the prevention of the child leaving a place on his or her own volition. However, paragraph (b) deals only with a child taken to a place of safety and not a child already there and a strict interpretation would mean that a child already in a place of safety could not be protected under that paragraph. The Act must be interpreted in such a way as does not frustrate the intention to protect all children in need of protection and the word "removal" in paragraph (c) should therefore be taken to include removal of the child by the child him or herself from the place of safety.

Once made, the applicant must, as soon as practicable, inform both the local authority and the reporter of the making of the child protection order,[22] and serve a copy of the order and notice that it has been made on the child and any other person named in the application.[23] A CPO must not be enforced automatically and unthinkingly, and the applicant is authorised to act only when he reasonably believes that it is necessary to safeguard or promote the welfare of the child to do so.[24] If the applicant acts without this belief then he is acting without statutory authority and can be subject to liability therefor. Though it is likely to be difficult to establish lack of reasonable belief that the implementation of a CPO is unnecessary when a sheriff has granted it on the basis that it is necessary, this is not impossible, such as, for example, when the original source of danger to the child has died or been removed to police custody since the granting of the order.

### DIRECTIONS ATTACHED TO CPOs

Section 37 of the 1968 Act authorised the removal of a child to a place of safety and nothing more. In particular, it contained no provisions in

---

[20] The CPO procedure might be used by a parent seeking to recover a child from grandparents who are refusing to return the child and who pose some threat to the child. While this might be quicker than a common law action of recovery, it would have the consequence that a children's hearing will require to be held unless the reporter decides that this is not necessary.

[21] Perhaps having been taken there under the provisions of s.61 (justice of the peace authorisations and police officer removals: see below at pp.247–251).

[22] s.57(5).

[23] AS 1997, r.3.32.

[24] s.57(6).

relation to the contact that was to be permitted between a parent or guardian and a child removed to a place of safety and the matter remained in the hands of the local authority, until such time as a children's hearing was convened and made any provision therefor. This was regarded as one of the flaws in the system and s.58(1) of the 1995 Act therefore imposes upon the sheriff an obligation to give consideration in all cases in which a CPO is made to the question of whether he should give any direction as to contact between the child and any specified person or class of persons. In addition, the sheriff may also give directions in relation to the exercise of parental responsibilities or parental rights, including directions as to medical examination, assessment and treatment of the child.[25]

### Directions as to contact

It should be noted that the terminology in s.58(1) is significantly different from that in s.11 of the Children (Scotland) Act 1995, where the court can make an order "regulating contact" between the child and any other person. The direction under s.58(1) does not regulate contact but is in the nature of a direction to the applicant to allow contact between the child and another person (typically but not necessarily the parent). A direction cannot be given here to a person who is not an applicant and if the applicant is not the person who will be looking after the child then a direction under this section will seldom be appropriate. So it would serve no purpose to give a direction to a police officer who is the applicant when the child is to be taken to an establishment under the management of a local authority. Whenever the local authority is the applicant, they will be deemed to be "looking after" the child[26] even when the place of safety to which the child is taken is not an establishment run by the local authority. So a direction might be appropriate even when the child is removed, say, to a grandparent's house, since even in that situation the applicant local authority will have responsibilities towards the child, including determining with whom the child is to have contact.

The sheriff is obliged to consider the matter of contact, whether requested to do so or not but, rather surprisingly, he is not obliged to give a direction, even when he considers that the direction is "necessary".[27] This is designed to ensure flexibility in the child's interests. The words "necessary" and "necessity" as they appear in s.58(1) should be given a strict construction and the direction ought not to be given simply because the sheriff wants everything to remain within judicial control. The philosophy here, as in other parts of the Act, is that the court should get involved in directing children's lives only when not to do so would be against the child's interests. Necessity might arise, for example, when the applicant is minded not to allow contact and the sheriff thinks that contact would be in the child's interests, or when the applicant cannot come to an agreement with a person who is seeking to have contact with

---

[25] s.58(4) and (5).

[26] s.17(6)(c).

[27] s.58(1) says that the sheriff "shall" consider whether a direction as to contact is necessary, and when he considers that it is necessary he "may" give the direction.

the child. When the applicant is the person who will be looking after the child it is good practice for sheriffs to inquire of the applicant what arrangements for contact they would be minded to make in the absence of any direction. It will be "necessary" to give a direction only when the proposed arrangements are not, in the sheriff's opinion, satisfactory and the child's interest requires that better arrangements be made.

The direction given by the sheriff may require that contact be permitted between the child and another person, or may prohibit it, or may subject it to such conditions as the sheriff considers appropriate.[28] So the sheriff may direct that contact always be supervised, or he may direct where it is to take place or how often, or he may direct that any specified person or class of persons is not to have any contact at all. Different arrangements can be made for different people[29] so that, for example, it may be required that the mother's contact with the child be supervised at all times and that the father have no contact at all. The sheriff's discretion is wide, and the statute does not require that, having decided that a direction is necessary, the sheriff must prescribe all the terms and conditions under which contact will take place, relating to time, place, frequency, duration and supervision. Such prescription might in some cases be appropriate, and in others not.

**Directions as to parental responsibilities and parental rights**

It is important to note that a CPO does not transfer parental responsibilities and parental rights to the applicant, even for the short period of its operation, and these remain with whomsoever had them before the making of the order.[30] Nevertheless, the applicant can, at the same time as applying for the CPO itself, apply to the sheriff for a direction as to the exercise or fulfilment of any parental responsibility or parental right.[31] It would seem that the sheriff cannot give any such direction *ex proprio motu*, as he can with a direction as to contact, but must be asked to give it. (Nevertheless, it would be open to a sheriff to suggest in the course of the application for the CPO that the applicant also apply for such a direction, though his hands will be tied if the applicant declines to follow his suggestion). Usually the applicant will not be a person with parental responsibilities or parental rights and so any direction given will not be directed towards the applicant (as is the case with a direction as to contact), but towards the person whose exercise or fulfilment of parental responsibilities or parental rights is to be regulated. The

---

[28] s.58(2).

[29] s.58(3).

[30] But see Kearney, *Children's Hearings and the Sheriff Court* (2nd ed., 2000) at para.5.07, who suggests that the order, if combined with directions as to parental responsibilities and parental rights, does indeed effect such a transfer. It is difficult to see how this can be so. A child subject to a child protection order is, admittedly, a "looked after" child (s.17(6)) and many of the responsibilities this imposes on a local authority will be similar to those held by parents. But being "looked after" does not in itself transfer the whole gamut of parental responsibilities and parental rights and it is reading too much into s.58(4) to say that a direction applied for by an applicant in respect to the exercise of parental responsibilities and parental rights amounts to a transfer, to the applicant, of all parental responsibilities and parental rights.

[31] s.58(4).

purpose is to provide directions as to how these responsibilities and rights should be carried out. The statute lays down no sanction for failure to follow the directions given, though such a failure could be regarded as contempt of court.

The applicant may request the sheriff to give any direction in relation to the fulfilment or exercise of any parental responsibilities or parental rights, such as, for example, prohibiting the parent from removing the child to another part of Scotland or furth of the jurisdiction, or directing the parent as to the education that is to be made available to the child. It is provided that the directions may in particular be in relation to medical examination, assessment or treatment[32] and this is likely to prove the most useful form of direction under this section. It should be noted that the power to give directions here does not allow the sheriff to authorise examination, assessment or treatment, nor can he authorise the applicant to carry it out.[33] Rather, the sheriff can simply direct the parent or guardian to exercise their parental responsibilities and parental rights in a particular manner. This may include a direction that the parent, say, provides consent to the child's medical examination, assessment or treatment, but that would be competent only when the parent or guardian retains the right to provide such consent. Such a direction will not, therefore, be competent in relation to many older children, for s.90 of the 1995 Act preserves the child's capacity to consent or refuse consent under s.2(4) of the Age of Legal Capacity (Scotland) Act 1991, and s.15(5)(b) of the 1995 Act ensures that a person with parental responsibilities and parental rights can consent only when the child cannot consent or refuse on his or her own behalf.[34] It follows that a direction as to medical examination, assessment or treatment would be competent only when the child is too young to consent to that examination or treatment himself or herself, for only then does the question of the exercise of parental responsibilities or parental rights arise.

Any direction to those with parental responsibilities and parental rights as to how they should exercise these responsibilities and rights is to be given only when the sheriff considers that such a direction is necessary to safeguard or promote the welfare of the child.[35] Such a direction might be necessary, for example, in order to ensure that a parent maintains beneficial contact with the child, or when a parent refuses to consent to an examination of the physical or mental state of the child and this is considered essential to allow for the proper identification of the child's needs. The direction may be granted subject to such conditions as the sheriff thinks appropriate, and in particular he must bear in mind in coming to his decision the duration of the order[36]: a CPO is designed to last only for the shortest possible period of time, and it follows that directions made in connection with it should not,

---

[32] s.58(5).
[33] For child assessment orders, see s.55.
[34] That the rule in s.15(5) applies to consent to medical treatment is explained in Norrie, *Children (Scotland) Act 1995* (2nd ed., 2004), at pp. 48-49.
[35] s.58(6)
[36] *ibid.*

except in cases of immediate necessity, deal irrevocably with matters of long-term significance. In all cases it will be for the applicant to show the existence of such a necessity.

### Duration of directions

The direction, whether relating to contact or to parental responsibilities or parental rights, cannot survive without the CPO to which it is attached and the direction will cease to have effect whenever the order ceases to have effect, for whatever reason.[37] So any direction given, like the CPO itself, can last for a maximum of eight working days, and will come to an end earlier if the order is terminated earlier. In addition, the sheriff may withdraw a direction while continuing the CPO at a review under s.60(7), and an initial hearing may vary it under s.59(4). These provisions are considered in the immediately following section.

REVIEW OF A CPO

A CPO can be granted by a sheriff even before the child and his or her parents have been given a chance to oppose it, or to attempt to state reasons why the order ought not to be granted. Indeed, the first that the parents may know about the granting of a CPO could be when an attempt is made to implement it by removing the child from their care. Even when they are given notice of the application being made, the time-scale may not give them sufficient time to prepare any proper arguments against its granting. For these reasons the statute requires that, once the CPO has been implemented (having authorised either (i) the removal of a child from his or her home and the keeping of the child in a place of safety, or (ii) the prevention of the removal of the child from any specified place) that order must be reviewed not later than on the second working day after its implementation.[38] That review can be undertaken either by the sheriff on application under s.60(7) or, if no such application has been made, by an initial children's hearing under s.59 convened solely for the purpose of determining whether the CPO should be continued.[39] Such an initial hearing must be held on the second working day after the CPO has been implemented; the application to the sheriff may be made at any time before the commencement of the initial hearing, and if it is made it obviates the need for the initial hearing.[40] In addition, if an initial hearing has been held and the CPO is continued, an application to the sheriff can be made within two working days of that continuation,[41] giving thereby a second review and it would be good practice, it is submitted, for an initial hearing which continue the order to advise the family of their right to make a subsequent application to the sheriff.

---

[37] s.58(7).

[38] On the meaning of "implementation", see below at p.244.

[39] In deciding whether to make an application to the sheriff or to allow a children's hearing to review the CPO, it may be relevant to remember that legal representation (and legal aid) will be available at the former but not the latter.

[40] s.59(1)(c).

[41] s.60(8)(b).

**Review by an initial hearing**

If a child has been taken to a place of safety or is prevented from being removed, and remains there on the second working day after having been taken there then, so long as the reporter has not received intimation that an application has been made to the sheriff to have the order set aside or varied, a children's hearing must be arranged by the reporter to conduct an initial hearing into the question of whether the CPO should be continued.[42] That hearing must sit on the second working day[43] after the order was implemented[44] and the terms of that requirement are such that it would be incompetent to hold the hearing on any other day, such as the day before, even when that is practicable. Failure to hold a hearing on the second working day will bring the CPO to an end, for the order can survive beyond that day only if an initial hearing continues it under s.59(4).[45] It is not open to the initial hearing to continue the hearing for further information beyond the second working day: the Act does not say this but the time-scale is such that it is implicit that the CPO will either be terminated or continued on the second working day. It follows that a legal representative cannot be appointed to the child for the purposes of the initial hearing. However, the initial hearing is a "children's hearing"[46] and there is nothing in the Legal Representation rules limiting the type of children's hearing at which a legal representative can be appointed. It may well follow that, if the initial hearing considers that it is likely (or even possible) that the child will not be able to participate at the eighth working day hearing, or that that hearing will have secure accommodation under active consideration, then the initial hearing may appoint a legal representative to attend at the eighth working day hearing.

The initial hearing is subject to the same rules of constitution and procedure as a substantive hearing, except that their role is more limited. They can make no dispositive decision, nor review any supervision requirement that the child is already under.[47] Rather, the initial hearing is limited to considering two questions. First, they must decide whether they are satisfied that the conditions for the making of the CPO, set out in s.57(1) or (2), exist or not.[48] This is a matter of fact, which leaves no room for discretion, though there is room for the exercise of judgment as to whether the fact exists or not (and that judgment may well be different from the sheriff's). It is not made clear whether the hearing have to determine that the conditions are established as at the time of

---

[42] s.59(1).

[43] "Working day" is defined in s.93(1) to be every day except Saturdays and Sundays, December 25 and 26, and January 1 and 2. All other public holidays count as working days. It follows that if a CPO is implemented on a Monday, the initial hearing must sit on the immediately following Wednesday; if the CPO is implemented on a Friday, the initial hearing must sit on the following Tuesday.

[44] s.59(3).

[45] s.60(6)(a).

[46] It is referred to as such in s.59.

[47] The provision in s.65(3) requiring a review of a supervision requirement when a child is referred under new grounds does not apply to the initial hearing since it has no power to "dispose" of the case.

[48] s.59(4).

the granting of the order, or as at the time they are looking at the matter, though the latter interpretation is probably to be preferred.[49] Given the shortness of time between the making of the order and the initial hearing it is unlikely that there will be any significant change in circumstances, but extreme cases (such as death of the source of danger) are not beyond the realms of possibility. If the conditions are found to be not satisfied then the initial hearing have no authority to continue the CPO,[50] and the failure to continue it will bring the order to an end.[51]

If the conditions for the granting of a CPO are found to be established by the initial hearing, they must then move on to their second question, which is whether to continue the order, with or without a variation in its terms. This is a matter within their discretion: the hearing "may" continue the order when the conditions for its granting are satisfied,[52] but they do not have to. The welfare of the child is their paramount consideration in the exercise of this discretion[53] and in most cases, when the conditions for the granting of a CPO are held by the hearing to remain satisfied the welfare of the child is likely to require the continuation of the order. This is not, however, an invariable conclusion and it may be that the trauma caused to the child by implementing the CPO has proved so detrimental as to outweigh any harm he or she might suffer by being returned home, or it has become apparent that keeping a child from home is a disproportionate response to the risk facing him or her. In these circumstances the initial hearing may well decide not to continue the order, even when it remains "necessary to protect the child from such harm" (the condition in s.57(1)).

While the initial hearing may vary the terms of the order, and the terms of any direction the sheriff makes under s.58 (which includes withdrawing the direction), the wording of s.59(4) does not permit the hearing to impose a direction in the absence of any made by the sheriff. Though some may regard this as an unnecessary limitation on the powers of the initial hearing it can be justified by the limited purpose of the hearing, which is to examine the appropriateness of the order made by the sheriff. If the order is not appropriate the hearing can refuse to continue it or can vary it. It is to be remembered that the CPO is a very short-term emergency provision and that long-term decisions as to, for example, contact, lie with the children's hearing who finally dispose of the case.

The initial hearing remains a children's hearing and this requires the attendance and participation of all those who would be required to attend and be given the opportunity to participate at any other children's hearing. In addition, it is provided in the Rules[54] that the children's

---

[49] Even if this is wrong, the fact that the conditions are no longer satisfied will invariably result in the CPO not being continued. *cf. Kennedy v B,* 1973 S.L.T. 38 in which it was held that a sheriff in determining whether grounds of referral are established must look at the facts that exist on the day he sits and not at the time of the original hearing.

[50] For they can continue it only when satisfied that the conditions are established: s.59(4).

[51] s.60(6)(a).

[52] s.59(4).

[53] s.16(1).

[54] 1996 Rules, r.26(1).

hearing must, before making their decision, take appropriate steps to obtain the views of the child[55] and endeavour to obtain the views of any relevant person and any safeguarder[56] on what arrangements would be in the best interests of the child (*i.e.* on whether the CPO should be continued). Also, at some point during the proceedings, the hearing must consider whether it is necessary to appoint a person to safeguard the interests of the child and, if so, they must make such an appointment.[57] It will, however, seldom be appropriate for the initial hearing to appoint a safeguarder. The proper children's hearing which will usually follow on the eighth working day after the granting of a CPO will be in possession of much more information upon which to judge the necessity of appointing a safeguarder and, since that hearing will usually be continued in any case, no time is lost by postponing appointment until then. However, a safeguarder is entitled to adopt an advisory role in relation to the child and appointment by an initial hearing would be appropriate in order to ensure that the child receives independent advice at the eighth working day hearing.

After the decision has been made the reporter must send a copy of the continuation (if that is the decision) plus a copy of the statement of the reasons as soon as reasonably practicable to the child, any relevant person and any safeguarder.[58]

### Review by a sheriff before the initial hearing

If an application to the sheriff to set aside or vary the CPO has been made before the sitting of the initial hearing (which must otherwise sit on the second working day after the order was implemented) then no initial hearing may take place,[59] and the review will be conducted by the sheriff. There is nothing to prevent the review being conducted by the same sheriff as who made the original order: this is unlikely to be incompatible with Art.6 ECHR since the process is not an appeal but a review. The applicant can be either one or more of the following, that is to say:

(a) the child to whom the order or direction relates;
(b) a person having parental rights over the child;
(c) a relevant person;
(d) any person to whom notice of the application for the order was given by virtue of the rules;[60] or
(e) the applicant for the CPO itself.[61]

---

[55] Under r.15.

[56] It would be highly unusual for a safeguarder to be in place when an initial hearing under s.59(4) sits (particularly since the sheriff making the order cannot appoint a safeguarder) but it might happen when a CPO is made over a child already referred but whose case has not yet been disposed of before the emergency arises.

[57] s.41(1).

[58] 1996 Rules, r.26(2)(a). Rule 26(2)(b) requires additionally notice of the right to appeal to be sent, but that must apply only to the other orders covered by r.26 since there is no right to appeal against a decision of the initial hearing to continue a child protection order: 1995 Act, s.51(15)(b).

[59] s.59(1)(c).

[60] AS 1997, r.3.12.

[61] s.60(7). The applicant must lodge a copy of the CPO with the application to vary or set it aside: AS 1997, r.3.33(2).

No-one else can make an application to the sheriff, even when they appear to have an interest in doing so, such as a stranger seeking to clear his or her name of an allegation of abuse against the child. If the application to set aside or vary the order is made by the child, then he or she will require the application to be made on his or her behalf if he or she has no capacity (determined by the Age of Legal Capacity (Scotland) Act 1991, s.2(4A) and (4B)) to conduct civil proceedings, or when he or she does have that capacity but consents to be represented in proceedings by someone who used to be his or her legal representative.[62] "Relevant person" is defined in s.93(2)(b), and since it includes any person having parental rights over the child s.60(7)(b) above is entirely otiose.

If the application to the sheriff is not made within the strict time-limits laid down in s.60(8) then it cannot be made thereafter. The application must be made *either* before the commencement of an initial hearing *or,* if it was not made before then, within two working days of the continuation of the order by the initial hearing.[63] In either situation, the sheriff must determine the application within three working days of its being made.[64] If he has not determined the application by then, the CPO ceases to have effect[65]: generally, however, the sheriff ought to be able to make his decision on the day the application is made.[66]

The applicant is required to send notice of the application to the reporter,[67] since if notice is not given to the reporter of an application to the sheriff to set aside or vary the CPO within two working days of its implementation, the reporter is obliged to arrange an initial hearing in terms of s.59.

The sheriff must hear the parties to the application and, if he or she wishes to make representations, the reporter.[68] The "parties to the application" are the child,[69] the parties who make the application to set aside or vary the CPO, and the person who originally sought and obtained the CPO, together, it is submitted, with any person who opposed its making. In addition, any person on whom service of the order is made may appear or be represented at the hearing of the application.[70] The sheriff would appear entitled to appoint a safeguarder in order to safeguard the interests of the child in the proceedings.[71] However, it will seldom be practicable to do so since appointing a safeguarder will inevitably require the hearing to be adjourned but it

---

[62] Children (Scotland) Act 1995, s.15(6).

[63] For which, see further, above at pp.237–239.

[64] So if the application is made, for example, on a Friday he must determine it by the following Wednesday.

[65] s.60(2).

[66] *cf.* the making of a CPO: AS 1997, r.3.31 requires the sheriff to decide whether to grant or refuse the application "forthwith".

[67] s.60(9).

[68] s.60(11) and AS 1997, r.3.33(4).

[69] The child's views must be taken into account in any case: s.16(2), as applied to these applications by s.16(4)(b)(ii). The procedure where the child wishes to express views is set out in AS 1997, r.3.5.

[70] AS 1997, r.3.33(3).

[71] s.41(1). The exclusion of safeguarders in s.41(2) is limited to s.57 proceedings, *i.e.* the original application for a CPO.

does not interrupt the running of the three working days within which the application must be determined.[72]

After hearing the parties to the action and having allowed such further procedure as he thinks fit, the sheriff must make his decision[73] and, where the sheriff so directs, intimation of that decision must be given by the applicant to such persons as the sheriff directs.[74] The decision to be made is whether or not "the conditions for the making of a child protection order under s. 57" are satisfied or, where the application relates only to the variation or cancellation of a s.58 direction, whether that direction should be varied or cancelled.[75] The sheriff's decision must be made within three working days of the application, otherwise the CPO loses effect.[76] Where the sheriff finds that the conditions in s.57 are satisfied, he "may" do any of the acts listed in s.60(12). These are as follows:

(a) confirm or vary the order, or any term or condition on which it was granted;
(b) confirm or vary any direction given, in relation to the order, under s.58;
(c) give a new direction under s.58; or
(d) continue in force the order and any such direction until the commencement of the children's hearing on the eighth working day.[77]

The extent of the sheriff's discretion permitted by the Act is a matter of some doubt. On the one hand it may be that he is limited to doing one or other of the acts listed above, and he has no power to do anything not listed: the wording of s.60(12) suggests this. On the other hand, the words "he may" in s.60(12) might be interpreted to permit him to do one or other of the acts listed, or none or them, or something not listed at all (such as, for example, recalling the order). Probably the latter interpretation is to be preferred, for three reasons. First, there is no doubt that an initial hearing, on finding the conditions for the granting of a CPO are satisfied, do have the power not to continue the order (otherwise the words "may continue" in s.59(4) would have to mean "shall continue") and it is unlikely that the statute intended to give the sheriff a lesser discretion than the hearing. Secondly, the sheriff's decision is governed by the welfare of the child, which requires that his discretion should not be fettered except by clear statutory provision. And thirdly the ECHR proportionality test probably requires that the sheriff has the power to bring the order to an end when he considers that it is not or is no longer proportionate to the risk the child faces. For these reasons, the sheriff ought to be permitted to recall the CPO, even when the conditions for its granting remain satisfied, in the same sort of

---

[72] s.60(8).
[73] AS 1997, r.3.33(4).
[74] AS 1997, r.3.33(6).
[75] s.60(11).
[76] s.60(8).
[77] s.60(12).

circumstances[78] in which an initial hearing might refuse to continue the order even when the conditions for its granting remain satisfied.

Where the sheriff finds that the conditions in s.57 are not satisfied he "shall" recall the CPO and cancel any direction given.[79] Again there is some doubt as to the extent of the sheriff's discretion. The doubt revolves around the words in s.60(11)(a), "the conditions for the making of a child protection order under s. 57". The phrase might, on the one hand, refer only to the conditions listed in s.57(1) or s.57(2) before the CPO can be granted; or it might, on the other hand, refer to all the conditions in s.57, including conditions as to its form such as are contained in s.57(3). The latter interpretation is, it is submitted, a more natural reading since s.60(11)(a) does not limit itself to "the conditions in s. 57(1) or (2)". However, this would mean that the sheriff would seem to be obliged, in terms of s.60(13), to recall the CPO if any procedural or formal condition is not satisfied. That obligation must, however, be read in the light of s.16, which provides that the three overarching principles apply when "the sheriff is considering . . . whether to . . . discharge a child protection order'":[80] these words have the effect, if they have any effect at all, of conferring a discretion onto the sheriff's decision. If the sheriff finds that all of the conditions in s.57 have not been satisfied it can be assumed that in the vast majority of cases it will be for the child's welfare to recall the order, but this would not be so if the condition not satisfied were a mere procedural or formal condition (such as that in s.57(3)) while the ground upon which the order was made (as listed in s.57(1) or s.57(2)) clearly does still exist. In these circumstances the sheriff can, it is submitted, rely on s.16(1) to refuse to recall the order. The views of the child must be taken into account[81] but will never determine the issue and could not, it is submitted, subvert the apparent obligation to recall the order. The minimum intervention principle applies[82] and means, as always, minimum intervention by the state in the life of the child, rather than minimum interference with orders already granted with the result, in this case, that there is a presumption in favour of recalling the order.

### Review by sheriff after initial hearing

An application to the sheriff can also be made within two working days after the initial hearing have continued the CPO under s.59(4), effectively giving a second review. If this is done, then the same rules and procedure apply as when the application to the sheriff is made before the sitting of the initial hearing, except that the sheriff will have at his disposal the reasons why the initial hearing considered it appropriate to continue the order, and for that reason it will seldom, if ever, be appropriate for the reporter to arrange an advice hearing under s.60(10).

### Advice hearings

Section 60(10) introduces a wholly new type of advice hearing. The reporter is given the discretion to arrange a children's hearing (to which

---

[78] Described above at pp.237–238.
[79] s.60(13).
[80] s.16(4)(b)(ii).
[81] s.16(2) and s.16(4)(b)(ii) and AS 1997, r.3.5.
[82] s.16(3) and s.16(4)(b)(ii).

the normal rules of attendance and procedure apply) after an application has been made to the sheriff, but before the sheriff has determined the application, for variation or setting aside of a CPO, in order that the hearing may provide the sheriff with advice to assist him in his decision. Such an advice hearing can be held either when the application to the sheriff is before an initial hearing or when it is made after the initial hearing has continued the CPO. In the latter case, however, there will usually be little point in holding an advice hearing since the initial hearing will have stated reasons for their decision and these reasons will be available to advise the sheriff if an application is made to him thereafter. An advice hearing will be more useful when an application is made to the sheriff before any initial hearing have sat. The nature of the advice given is entirely for the children's hearing themselves to decide, but it should, of course, be directed towards the question of whether it remains in the child's best interests for the CPO to be continued (if the application is to set aside the order) or whether its terms and conditions are appropriate (if the application is to vary the order or any directions given in connection with it). Any advice the hearing gives must have regard to the welfare of the child as the paramount consideration,[83] and must be given after the hearing have offered the child an opportunity to express views and having had regard so far as practicable to these views taking account of the child's age and maturity.[84] The sheriff is not, of course, obliged to accept the advice, but it is implicit that he must take it into account in reaching his decision. The statute gives no guidance to the reporter as to how and when to exercise his or her discretion to arrange this advice hearing, and often the matter will be determined by the availability of time: the arranging of this hearing does not interrupt the running of the three working days within which the sheriff must determine the application and on that time-scale it will seldom be possible for a children's hearing to give sufficiently deep consideration to the child's circumstances to be able to say anything very useful.

## Termination of a CPO

### The eighth working day hearing

The CPO is designed to be used as an emergency short-term procedure, providing immediate protection to the child when this is necessary for the protection or enhancement of his or her welfare. It will nearly always lead in to a children's hearing, which will have to examine the question of whether more long-term measures of supervision or protection are required, but that system is effectively quite separate. In no circumstance can a CPO ever remain effective beyond the eighth working day after it was implemented, and on the eighth working day there must be held a children's hearing[85] at which grounds of referral will be put to the child and relevant person for acceptance or denial. At that hearing, if it is felt

---

[83] s.16(1).
[84] s.16(2), as applied to advice hearings by s.16(4)(a)(iii).
[85] s.65(2).

that the child should remain in the place of safety in which he or she was detained under the CPO, the children's hearing may grant a warrant under either s.66(1) or s.69(7). It follows that as soon as the CPO has been granted, the reporter must carry out those investigative duties that he or she has under s.56, must prepare a statement of the grounds of referral, and not less than three days before the date of the eighth working day hearing give a copy of the statement of grounds to the child and to each relevant person whose whereabouts are known.[86] The eighth working day hearing cannot make a supervision requirement unless the reporter has made available to them a report from the local authority on the child and his or her social background.[87]

### Non-implementation of the order

In order to obtain a CPO, the applicant must have been able to persuade the sheriff that the order is immediately necessary for the protection of the child. If, however, the applicant delays in attempting to implement it after it has been granted, it can be assumed that such immediate necessity to act no longer exists and the order, therefore, ought to fall. The rule is, therefore, that the CPO will cease to have effect unless an attempt to implement it is made within 24 hours of making the order.[88] Implementation occurs on the day the child is removed to a place of safety, if that is what the CPO authorises,[89] and on the day the CPO is made when it authorises the prevention of the removal of the child from the place where he or she is being accommodated.[90] It is difficult to see how the applicant can attempt to implement the keeping secret of the child's whereabouts if no-one attempts to find this out and it is submitted that here too implementation occurs on the day that the order is made. The applicant can be said to make an attempt to implement the order when he takes necessary steps directed to that end, and the nature of the attempt will of course vary with the nature of the order. The attempt might not be successful until after the 24 hours have passed, but that does not bring the order to an end so long as the attempt commences before then. So, for example, if the CPO authorises the removal of a child to a place of safety the order ceases if the applicant does nothing for more than 24 hours, but it does not cease if the applicant attempts to obtain the child but the attempt is frustrated by the parents of the child spiriting him or her away or the child running away.

### Non-continuation or recall

The CPO will also come to an end if, after it has been reviewed, it is not continued by the initial hearing,[91] or, implicitly, if the initial hearing that

---

[86] 1996 Rules, r.18(1) and (3).

[87] 1996 Rules, r.24. The practical result of this rule is that even when grounds of referral are accepted and the hearing can move on to a consideration of the case, a dispositive decision may not be made since the social background report may not have been drawn up within the timescale allowed. It will be more likely if the child is already known to the local authority.

[88] s.60(1).

[89] s.59(5)(a).

[90] s.59(5)(b).

[91] s.60(6)(a).

ought to have been held to review the order has not been held on the second working day. The order comes to an end in the former case at the conclusion of the initial hearing and in the latter case at the end of the second working day. If an application has been made to the sheriff to review the CPO, either before or after an initial hearing, the order comes to an end if the sheriff fails to determine that application within three working days of it having been made[92] or if he recalls the CPO having found that the conditions for its granting are not (or are no longer) satisfied.[93]

### Release from a place of safety by reporter

When a child is kept in a place of safety, or is prevented from being removed from the place where he or she is being accommodated, or is subjected to any term or condition, the reporter is obliged to keep a continual eye on the situation, and the CPO will not justify that keeping or prevention or subjection when the reporter considers that the conditions for the granting of the CPO or the giving of the directions are no longer satisfied. Where the reporter so considers, and notifies the person who implemented the order that he or she so considers, the authority to keep the child or prevent the child's removal ceases and the direction is terminated.[94] It follows that the child must be returned home or freed, unless some other statutory authority[95] to keep the child can be invoked; and conditions attached to the CPO similarly cease to have effect. The reporter can reach the view that the child should be released either because he or she has received further information relating to the case or because of a change in the circumstances of the case; the reporter cannot release a child simply because he or she disagrees with the sheriff who granted the order. The further information that comes to the attention of the reporter might suggest either that the conditions are no longer satisfied or, implicitly, that they never were, in fact, satisfied. Evidence that the child's welfare is suffering due to the implementation of the CPO will be a persuasive (and usually sufficient) change in circumstances. Similarly the removal of the source of danger[96] will be a material change in circumstances. The reporter must notify the person who implements the order, and it is this notification that takes away that person's authority to keep the child.

When a child is released from a CPO under this provision, the CPO ceases to have effect,[97] with the result that there is no longer an

---

[92] s.60(2).

[93] s.60(13).

[94] s.60(3). Whenever such notice is given, the reporter must also notify the sheriff: s.60(5).

[95] Such as a warrant granted by a children's hearing under s.45(4). It might sometimes be appropriate for a reporter to seek such a warrant even when of the view that a CPO is not necessary, for the purpose of the warrant under that subsection will be to secure the child's attendance rather than to protect him or her from harm, but in practice reporters may well be inclined to let a CPO run, particularly since the time-scale for the holding of a children's hearing after a s.45(4) warrant has been granted is even tighter than the timetable for holding a hearing after a CPO.

[96] Perhaps by the implementation of an exclusion order under s.76.

[97] s.60(6)(d).

obligation on the reporter to arrange a children's hearing on the eighth working day under s.65(2). It does, however, remain open to the reporter to arrange a hearing under s.65(1) (*i.e.* not necessarily on the eighth working day after the CPO was implemented), for s.60(3) and s.60(6)(d) are directed solely to the question of whether the child should be kept in a place of safety and not whether a children's hearing should be arranged to consider his or her case.

The aim of s.60(3) is to allow the reporter to react speedily to sudden changes in circumstances. The effect of that provision is, however, limited by s.60(4), which provides that the reporter cannot arrange for the return or release of the child after the commencement of any initial hearing that is held under s.59 or the commencement of any application to the sheriff to set aside or vary the order. This means that the reporter's power under s.60(3) to arrange for the release of the child lasts only until the end of the second working day after the implementation of the CPO and he or she cannot arrange for the child's release thereafter, however much the circumstances change or whatever the nature of the new evidence he or she acquires. If an initial hearing has been held, it will be open to the reporter, up to two working days thereafter, to apply to the sheriff to set aside or vary the CPO.[98] If, however, there was no initial hearing because the application had been made immediately to the sheriff, the reporter's hands will be tied for up to six working days. The child, however, can be released at any time if the reporter decides not to arrange a children's hearing under s.65(2).[99] This might not appear to cover the situation where the reporter believes that compulsory measures of supervision are necessary but that there is no need for the child to be kept away from home, but it is open to argument that a decision not to arrange a children's hearing under s.65(2) does not prevent the reporter arranging a children's hearing under s.65(1). The advantage of accepting that argument is that the reporter will then be able to release the child from a place of safety in the light of information required after the second working day and still arrange a children's hearing; the disadvantage is that the basis of the decision not to arrange a children's hearing will be that compulsory measures of supervision are not necessary and it is anomalous to say that they are necessary under s.65(1) but not necessary under s.65(2). However, it is suggested that reporters should not be deprived of an important element of their discretionary powers and that children should not be deprived of the possibility of release from a place of safety after the second working day even when the question of whether compulsory measures of supervision are necessary clearly arises. This is achieved by holding that reporters are free to arrange a hearing under s.65(1) even when they decide not to arrange a hearing under s.65(2): the release of a child from an unnecessary place of safety is sufficient ground for the exercise by the reporter of the power under s.60(6)(c). Releasing a child from a place of safety but arranging a children's hearing thereafter may well be a more proportionate response to the circumstances than requiring the child to remain unnecessarily in a place of safety solely in

---

[98] s.60(7)(d) and s.57(5).
[99] s.60(6)(c).

order to ensure that a children's hearing can be arranged: if so an interpretation of the provisions that allows this may be mandated by Art.8 of the ECHR.

## EMERGENCY PROTECTION IN THE ABSENCE OF A SHERIFF

It will sometimes happen that either a sheriff is not available to grant a CPO or it appears that a child's safety can be secured only by his or her immediate and summary removal from a source of danger. In these circumstances a CPO, though designed to be granted quickly, might not be available quite quickly enough. Section 61 attempts to resolve that problem by permitting a justice of the peace to grant authorisations to do certain of the acts that could be authorised by a CPO, and by permitting police officers to remove a child from an immediate source of danger. The provisions in s.61 are simpler than those relating to CPOs and have no reviews or appeals, nor indeed any requirement to refer the case to a children's hearing thereafter, but they are designed to be holding measures only, until a CPO can be sought (which does, of course, involve such a requirement). The expectation is that an application for a CPO will be made during the period in which the authorisation granted under s.61 lasts. As early as is consistent with the protection and welfare of the child, after these measures have been taken the child must (taking account of his or her age and maturity) be informed of the reason why emergency measures have been taken and given an opportunity to express views.[1] The applicant must allow reasonable contact, if in accordance with the welfare of the child, between the child and any relevant person or any person with whom the child was living immediately before the taking of emergency protection measures, and contact may be allowed with any other person.[2]

### Justice of the peace authorisations

When the conditions specified in either s.57(1)[3] or s.57(2)[4] for the granting of a CPO are satisfied, but it is not practicable to obtain such an order from a sheriff, then, so long as the justice of the peace is satisfied that had a CPO been granted it is probable that it would have contained either an authorisation to remove the child to a place of safety and to

---

[1] Emergency Child Protection Measures (Scotland) Regulations 1996, reg.13.

[2] *ibid.*, reg.16.

[3] *i.e.* that (a) there are reasonable grounds to believe that a child (i) is being so treated (or neglected) that he or she is suffering significant harm; or (ii) will suffer such harm if he or she is not removed to and kept in a place of safety or if he or she does not remain in the place where he or she is then being accommodated (whether or not he or she is resident there); and (b) an order under s.57 is necessary to protect the child from such harm (or such further harm).

[4] *i.e.* (a) that the local authority applicant have reasonable grounds to suspect that a child is being or will be so treated (or neglected) that he or she is suffering or will suffer significant harm; (b) that they are making or causing to be made enquiries to allow them to decide whether they should take any action to safeguard the welfare of the child; and (c) that those enquiries are being frustrated by access to the child being unreasonably denied, the authority having reasonable cause to believe that such access is required as a matter of urgency.

keep the child there or an authorisation to prevent the removal of a child from any place where he or she is being accommodated, the justice of the peace may grant an authorisation which may:

"(a) require any person in a position to do so to produce the child to the applicant;

(b) prevent any person from removing a child from a place where he is then being accommodated; [or]

(c) authorise the applicant to remove the child to a place of safety and to keep him there until the expiration of the authorisation".[5]

These acts are the same as those authorised by a CPO itself,[6] except for the power in s.57(4)(d), to order that the location of any place of safety in which the child is being kept should not be disclosed to any person. However, under the Rules[7] the applicant may withhold this information from the relevant person or any other person with whom the child was residing immediately before the authorisation of the justice of the peace, if the applicant considers it necessary to do so in order to safeguard the welfare of the child. As with CPOs, there is no limitation on who may apply for an authorisation under s.61: the applicant can be "any person", though normally it will be a local authority. The only situation in which it would be not practicable to obtain a CPO from a sheriff is when no sheriff is, for whatever reason, available in sufficient time to deal with the particular emergency that has arisen. This eventuality is unlikely to occur in large urban areas such as Glasgow or Edinburgh in which there are many sheriffs, but it may occur more frequently in rural areas such as the Western or the Northern Isles. It will often remain practicable to approach a sheriff even when it is easier and quicker to approach a justice of the peace: the test, it is to be remembered, is practicality rather than convenience.

In deciding whether to grant the authorisation the justice of the peace will be governed by the obligation to regard the welfare of the child as paramount[8] but, not being a sheriff, his decision is not governed by the requirement to have regard to the views of the child or by the minimum intervention principle. He is, however, a public authority under the Human Rights Act 1998[9] with the result that the proportionality principle applies, as does his obligation to involve the child and family in the decision-making process if at all possible. The very emergency that gives a justice of the peace authority in this context is likely, in many cases, to make such involvement impossible.

---

[5] s.61(3).

[6] See s.57(4).

[7] Emergency Child Protection Measures (Scotland) Regulations 1996, reg.10.

[8] s.16(1). Sheriff Kearney points out in *Children's Hearings and the Sheriff Court* (2nd ed., 2000) at para.11.07 that a justice of the peace is not a "court" and so not directly governed by s.16(1). However, he suggests that given that the justice of the peace must be satisfied that a sheriff would grant a CPO, the welfare test is equally applicable.

[9] Human Rights Act 1998, s.6.

The act or acts authorised must be performed within 12 hours of the authorisation having been granted, otherwise the authorisation falls[10] and in any case the authorisation must be implemented as soon as reasonably practicable.[11] The authorisation itself ceases to have effect 24 hours after having been granted (note, not after having been given effect to) or on the disposal of an application for a CPO, whichever of these two alternatives occurs earlier.[12] There is no requirement to seek a CPO after the obtaining of an authorisation under this section, but that will be the only way in which a child can be kept in a place of safety for longer than the periods provided here, and it is expected that this is what will normally happen.

As soon as reasonably practicable after taking the steps authorised, the applicant must take such steps as are reasonably practicable to inform (a) any relevant person, (b) any person with whom the child was residing, (c) where not the applicant the local authority in whose area the child was residing, (d) where not the applicant the local authority in whose area the child is ordinarily resident, (e) where not the applicant the local authority in whose area the child was residing immediately before the grant of the authorisation, and (f) the reporter of the following matters: (i) the grant of the authorisation and the steps taken to implement it, (ii) the place of safety where the child is being kept, (iii) the reasons for the granting of the authorisation, and (iv) any other step the applicant takes to safeguard the child's welfare.[13] The address of the place of safety and details of other steps taken can be withheld from the relevant person and persons with whom the child was residing if to do so is necessary to safeguard the welfare of the child.[14]

**Emergency protection by a constable**

A child can be removed from, or kept away from, a source of immediate danger without any involvement of a sheriff or a justice of the peace by a police officer who has reasonable cause to believe that the conditions in s.57(1)[15] for the granting of a CPO exist but it is not practicable in the circumstances for him or her to obtain a CPO.[16] But he or she can remove or keep a child only when to do so is necessary to protect the child from significant harm. The necessity must be immediate, otherwise the provisions concerning authorisations by a justice of the peace can be adopted, or a CPO itself can be sought, and removal must be a proportionate response. A police officer can, for example, step in and remove a child to a place of safety if he or she witnesses the child being

---

[10] s.61(4)(a). The applicant must thereafter inform various people: Emergency Child Protection Measures (Scotland) Regulations 1996, reg.11.

[11] Emergency Child Protection Measures (Scotland) Regulations 1996, reg.7.

[12] s.61(4)(b).

[13] Emergency Child Protection Measures (Scotland) Regulations 1996, regs.8 and 9.

[14] *ibid.*, reg.10.

[15] *i.e.* that (a) there are reasonable grounds to believe that a child (i) is being so treated (or neglected) that he or she is suffering significant harm; or (ii) will suffer such harm if he or she is not removed to and kept in a place of safety, or if he or she does not remain in the place where he or she is then being accommodated (whether or not he or she is resident there); and (b) an order is necessary to protect the child from such harm (or such further harm).

[16] s.61(5).

beaten up by his or her parents, or if a child is brought to a female and child unit at a police station in a distressed state, or if the police officer comes across a child who has been expelled from the family home in conditions that create a risk of significant harm. It should be noted that where, further to emergency protection measures, a child is taken to a police station as a place of safety, the constable keeping him or her there must as soon as reasonably practicable take the child to another type of place of safety and keep the child in that other place.[17]

If a child is taken to or kept in a place of safety by a police officer under the terms of s.61(5), he or she can be kept there only for a maximum period of 24 hours after first being removed or kept from the source of danger.[18] If the child is to be kept for any longer period than that, a CPO must be sought and obtained: if obtained the authority to keep the child comes from that order rather than from s.61(5), and if an application for a CPO is made but fails the authorisation under s.61(5) comes to an end.[19]

As soon as reasonably practicable after a child has been removed to a place of safety under this provision, the constable must take such steps as are reasonably practicable to inform (a) any relevant person, (b) any person other than a relevant person with whom the child was residing, (c) the local authority in whose area the place of safety is situated, (d) the local authority in whose area the child is ordinarily resident, (e) the local authority in whose area the child was residing immediately before being removed to a place of safety, and (f) the reporter of the following matters: (i) the removal of the child to a place of safety, (ii) the place of safety where the child is being kept, (iii) the reasons for the removal to a place of safety and (iv) any other steps taken to safeguard the child's welfare.[20] The address of the place of safety and details of other steps taken can be withheld from the relevant person and persons with whom the child was residing if to do so is necessary in order to safeguard the welfare of the child.[21] The child may be kept in a place of safety only so long as the conditions for activating s.61(5) remain satisfied.[22]

### Release by reporter

As with CPOs, the reporter has ultimate control over whether a child is kept in a place of safety, and the child cannot be kept in a place of safety or prevented from being removed from a place by any provision in s.61 if the reporter is of the view either (i) in cases of authorisation by a justice of the peace that the conditions for its granting in s.61(1) are not satisfied, or (ii) in cases of emergency removal and keeping by a constable that the conditions specified in s.61(5) for the exercise of that power of removal are not satisfied, or (iii) in either case that it is no longer in the best interests of the child that he or she be kept in a place of safety or prevented from being removed from the place where he or

---

[17] Emergency Child Protection Measures (Scotland) Regulations 1996, reg.15.
[18] s.61(6).
[19] s.61(7).
[20] Emergency Child Protection Measures (Scotland) Regulations 1996, regs.3 and 4.
[21] *ibid.,* reg.5.
[22] *ibid.,* reg.6.

she is being accommodated.[23] It remains open to the reporter to refer the case of a child released to a children's hearing under s.65(1).[24]

It is expressly provided that there is no appeal to the sheriff principal or the Court of Session from any decision of the sheriff in granting or refusing to grant a CPO, nor any appeal to the sheriff from the decision of an initial children's hearing continuing a CPO.[25] It is surprising that there is no reference at all in the Act to an appeal against a sheriff's decision to continue or to vary or to recall a CPO under s.60. The issue is unlikely to arise in practice in relation to continuation or variation, since the time-scale is such that the CPO will come to an end in any case very shortly after the sheriff's decision, though that consideration applies equally to decisions of the initial hearing, for which express, negative, provision is made.[26] More plausible is an appeal against a sheriff's decision to recall a child protection order that has already been granted, though the only interest in an appeal against such a decision would lie with those seeking to protect the child and that protection is probably better (and more quickly) provided by other means (such as arranging a children's hearing under s.65(1)); nevertheless it is odd that the right of appeal against recall of a CPO by a sheriff is not either expressly excluded or expressly provided for. It is open to argument that, not being expressly excluded, a right of appeal against the sheriff's decision to vary or recall a CPO remains, on general principles, open on a point of law, but in relation to the particular child any such point of law would be entirely moot by the time an appeal was heard since the CPO, even had it been continued, would long since have come to an end. For this reason any such appeal is likely to be considered incompetent. Alternatively, it might be argued that appeal is excluded by the terms of s.51(15)(a) if "a decision of the sheriff on an application under s. 57" is interpreted to mean the whole process instigated by s.57 and not just the initial application. This argument is, it is submitted, persuasive.

It is an offence, making the offender liable on summary conviction to a fine not exceeding level three on the standard scale, for any person intentionally to obstruct a person who is acting either under a CPO or under an authorisation by a justice of the peace under s.61(1) or s.61(2) or to obstruct a constable removing a child to a place of safety under s.61(5).[27] It is also an offence for any person knowingly to assist or

---

[23] s.61(8).
[24] And indeed release by the reporter does not prevent any person seeking a CPO under s.57.
[25] s.51(15).
[26] s.51(15)(b).
[27] s.81.

induce, or persistently attempt to induce, a child to abscond from a place of safety, to harbour or conceal a child who has so absconded, or to prevent a child from returning to a place of safety.[28] However, a local authority are not "harbouring" a child where the child appears to them to be at risk of harm and at the child's request they provide him with a refuge in a residential establishment or arrange for refuge to be provided in an approved household.[29]

---

[28] s.83.
[29] s.38.

# APPENDIX 1

## Child Protection Order Flowchart

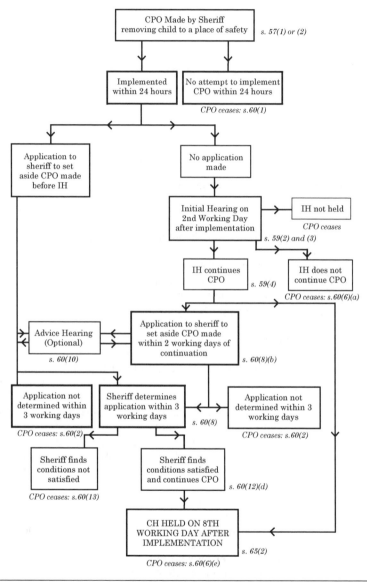

CPO : child protection order
CH : children's hearing
IH : initial hearing

**N.B.:** **s.60(6)(c):** CPO ceases to have effect when reporter decides not to arrange a children's hearing
**s.60(6)(d):** CPO ceases to have effect when reporter considers that the conditions for its granting are no longer satisfied.

## Children (Scotland) Act 1995

### (c.36)

· · ·

PART II

PROMOTION OF CHILDREN'S WELFARE BY LOCAL AUTHORITIES AND BY
CHILDREN'S HEARINGS ETC.

CHAPTER 1

SUPPORT FOR CHILDREN AND THEIR FAMILIES

*Introductory*

**Welfare of child and consideration of his views**

**16.**—(1) Where under or by virtue of this Part of this Act, a children's hearing decide, or a court determines, any matter with respect to a child the welfare of that child throughout his childhood shall be their or its paramount consideration.

(2) In the circumstances mentioned in subsection (4) below, a children's hearing or as the case may be the sheriff, taking account of the age and maturity of the child concerned, shall so far as practicable—

(a) give him an opportunity to indicate whether he wishes to express his views;

(b) if he does so wish, give him an opportunity to express them; and

(c) have regard to such views as he may express;

and without prejudice to the generality of this subsection a child twelve years of age or more shall be presumed to be of sufficient age and maturity to form a view.

(3) In the circumstances mentioned in subsection (4)(a)(i) or (ii) or (b) of this section, no requirement or order so mentioned shall be made with respect to the child concerned unless the children's hearing consider, or as the case may be the sheriff considers, that it would be better for the child that the requirement or order be made than that none should be made at all.

(4) The circumstances to which subsection (2) above refers are that—

(a) the children's hearing—

(i) are considering whether to make, or are reviewing, a supervision requirement;

(ii) are considering whether to grant a warrant under subsection (1) of section 66, or subsection (4) or (7) of section 69, of this Act or to provide under subsection (5) of the said section 66 for the continuation of a warrant;

(iii) are engaged in providing advice under section 60(10) of this Act; or

(iv) are drawing up a report under section 73(13) of this Act;

(b) the sheriff is considering—

(i) whether to make, vary or discharge a parental responsibilities order, a child assessment order or an exclusion order;

(ii) whether to vary or discharge a child protection order;

(iii) whether to grant a warrant under section 67 of this Act; or

(iv) on appeal, whether to make such substitution as is mentioned in section 51(5)(c)(iii) of this Act; or

(c) the sheriff is otherwise disposing of an appeal against a decision of a children's hearing.

(5) If, for the purpose of protecting members of the public from serious harm (whether or not physical harm)—

(a) a children's hearing consider it necessary to make a decision under or by virtue of this Part of this Act which (but for this paragraph) would not be consistent with their affording paramountcy to the consideration mentioned in subsection (1) above, they may make that decision; or

(b) a court considers it necessary to make a determination under or by virtue of Chapters 1 to 3 of this Part of this Act which (but for this paragraph) would not be consistent with its affording such paramountcy, it may make that determination.

. . .

CHAPTER 2

CHILDREN'S HEARINGS

*Constitution of children's hearings*

**Formation of children's panel and children's hearings**

**39.**—(1) For every local government area there shall be a children's panel for the purposes of this Act, and any other enactment conferring powers on a children's hearing (or on such a panel).

(2) Schedule 1 to this Act shall have effect with respect to the recruitment, appointment, training and expenses of members of a children's panel and the establishment of Children's Panel Advisory Committees and joint advisory committees.

(3) Sittings of members of the children's panel (to be known as "children's hearings") shall be constituted from the panel in accordance with subsection (5) below.

(4) A children's hearing shall be constituted for the performance of the functions given to such a hearing by or by virtue of—

(a) this Act; or

(b) any other enactment conferring powers on a children's hearing.

(5) A children's hearing shall consist of three members, one of whom shall act as chairman; and shall not consist solely of male, or solely of female, members.

*Qualifications, employment and duties of reporters*

**Qualification and employment of reporters**

**40.**—(1) The qualifications of a reporter shall be such as the Secretary of State may prescribe.

(2) A reporter shall not, without the consent of the Scottish Children's Reporter Administration, be employed by a local authority.

(3) The Secretary of State may make regulations in relation to the functions of any reporter under this Act and the Criminal Procedure (Scotland) Act 1975.

[1](4) The Secretary of State may—

(a) by regulations empower a reporter, whether or not he is an advocate or solicitor, to conduct before a sheriff any proceedings which under this Chapter or Chapter 3 of this Part of this Act are heard by the sheriff;

(b) prescribe such requirements as they think fit as to qualifications, training or experience necessary for a reporter to be so empowered. (5) In this section, "reporter" means—

(a) the Principal Reporter; or

(b) any officer of the Scottish Children's Reporter Administration to whom there is delegated, under section 131(1) of the Local Government etc. (Scotland) Act 1994, any of the functions which the Principal Reporter has under this or any other enactment.

NOTE

1. As amended by the Scotland Act 1998 (Consequential Modifications) No. 1 Order 1999 (SI 1999/1042), Art.4, Sch.2, para.10 (effective May 20, 1999).

*Safeguards for children*

### Safeguarding child's interests in proceedings

**41.**—(1) Subject to subsection (2) below, in any proceedings under this Chapter or Chapter 3 of this Part of this Act either at a children's hearing or before the sheriff, the hearing or, as the case may be, the sheriff—

(a) shall consider if it is necessary to appoint a person to safeguard the interests of the child in the proceedings; and

(b) if they, or he, so consider, shall make such an appointment, on such terms and conditions as appear appropriate.

(2) Subsection (1) above shall not apply in relation to proceedings under section 57 of this Act.

(3) Where a children's hearing make an appointment under subsection (1)(b) above, they shall state the reasons for their decision to make that appointment.

(4) The expenses of a person appointed under subsection (1) above shall—

(a) in so far as reasonably incurred by him in safeguarding the interests of the child in the proceedings, and

(b) except in so far as otherwise defrayed in terms of regulations made under section 101 of this Act,

be borne by the local authority—

(i) for whose area the children's panel from which the relevant children's hearing has been constituted is formed;

(ii) where there is no relevant children's hearing, within whose area the child resides.

(5) For the purposes of subsection (4) above, "relevant children's hearing" means, in the case of proceedings—

(a) at a children's hearing, that hearing;

(b) under section 68 of this Act, the children's hearing who have directed the application;

(c) on an appeal under section 51 of this Act, the children's hearing whose decision is being appealed against.

*Conduct of proceedings at and in connection with children's hearing*

## Power of Secretary of State to make rules governing procedure at children's hearing etc.

**42.**—(1) Subject to the following provisions of this Act, the Secretary of State may make rules for constituting and arranging children's hearings and other meetings of members of the children's panel and for regulating their procedure.

(2) Without prejudice to the generality of subsection (1) above, rules under that subsection may make provision with respect to—

(a) the conduct of, and matters which shall or may be determined by, a business meeting arranged under section 64 of this Act;

(b) notification of the time and place of a children's hearing to the child and any relevant person in relation to the child and to such other persons as may be prescribed;

(c) how the grounds for referring the case to a children's hearing under section 65(1) of this Act are to be stated, and the right of the child and any such relevant person to dispute those grounds;

(d) the making available by the Principal Reporter, subject to such conditions as may be specified in the rules, of reports or information received by him to—

(i) members of the children's hearing; (ii) the child concerned;

(iii) any relevant person; and

(iv) any other person or class of persons so specified;

(e) the procedure in relation to the disposal of matters arising under section 41(1) of this Act;

(f) the functions of any person appointed by a children's hearing under section 41(1) of this Act and any right of that person to information relating to the proceedings in question;

(g) the recording in writing of any statement given under section 41(3) of this Act;

(h) the right to appeal to the sheriff under section 51(1)(a) of this Act against a decision of the children's hearing and notification to such persons as may be prescribed of the proceedings before him;

(i) the right of the child and of any such relevant person to be represented at a children's hearing;

(j) the entitlement of the child, of any such relevant person and of any person who acts as the representative of the child or of any such relevant person to the refund of such expenses, incurred by the child or as the case may be the person or representative, as may be prescribed in connection with a children's hearing and with any proceedings arising from the hearing;

(k) persons whose presence shall be permitted at a children's hearing.

## Privacy of proceedings at and right to attend children's hearing

**43.**—(1) Subject to subsection (3) below, a children's hearing shall be conducted in private, and, subject to any rules made under section 42 of this Act, no person other than a person whose presence is necessary for the proper consideration of the case which is being heard, or whose presence is permitted by the chairman, shall be present.

(2) The chairman shall take all reasonable steps to ensure that the number of persons present at a children's hearing at any one time is kept to a minimum.

(3) The following persons have the right to attend a children's hearing—

(a) a member of the Council on Tribunals, or of the Scottish Committee of that Council, in his capacity as such; and

(b) subject to subsection (4) below, a bona fide representative of a newspaper or news agency.

(4) A children's hearing may exclude a person described in subsection (3)(b) above from any part or parts of the hearing where, and for so long as, they are satisfied that—

(a) it is necessary to do so, in the interests of the child, in order to obtain the child's views in relation to the case before the hearing; or

(b) the presence of that person is causing, or is likely to cause, significant distress to the child.

(5) Where a children's hearing have exercised the power conferred by subsection (4) above to exclude a person, the chairman may, after that exclusion has ended, explain to the person the substance of what has taken place in his absence.

### Prohibition of publication of proceedings at children's hearing

**44.**—[1](1) No person shall publish any matter in respect of a case about which the principal reporter has from any source received information any matter or in respect of proceedings at a children's hearing, or before a sheriff on an application under section 57, section 60(7), section 65(7) or (9), section 76(1) or section 85(1) of this Act, or on any appeal under this Part of this Act, which is intended to, or is likely to, identify—

[1](a) the child concerned in, or any other child connected (in any way) with the case, proceedings or appeal; or

(b) an address or school as being that of any such child.

(2) Any person who contravenes subsection (1) above shall be guilty of an offence and shall be liable on summary conviction to a fine not exceeding level 4 on the standard scale in respect of each such contravention.

(3) It shall be a defence in proceedings for an offence under this section for the accused to prove that he did not know, and had no reason to suspect, that the published matter was intended, or was likely, to identify the child or, as the case may be, the address or school.

(4) In this section "to publish" includes, without prejudice to the generality of that expression,—

(a) to publish matter in a programme service, as defined by section 201 of the Broadcasting Act 1990 (definition of programme service); and

(b) to cause matter to be published.

(5) The requirements of subsection (1) above may, in the interests of justice, be dispensed with by—

(a) the sheriff in any proceedings before him;

(b) the Court of Session in any appeal under section 51(11) of this Act; or

(c) the Secretary of State in relation to any proceedings at a children's hearing,

to such extent as the sheriff, the Court or the Secretary of State as the case may be considers appropriate.

NOTE
1. As amended by Criminal Justice (Scotland) Act 2003 (asp 7), s.52.

### Attendance of child and relevant person at children's hearing

**45.**—(1) Where a child has been notified in accordance with rules made under subsection (1) of section 42 of this Act by virtue of subsection (2)(b) of that section that his case has been referred to a children's hearing, he shall—

(a) have the right to attend at all stages of the hearing; and

(b) subject to subsection (2) below, be under an obligation to attend those stages in accordance with the notice.

(2) Without prejudice to subsection (1)(a) above and section 65(4) of this Act, where a children's hearing are satisfied—

[1](a) in a case concerned with an offence mentioned in Schedule 1 to the Criminal Procedure (Scotland) Act 1995, that the attendance of the child is not necessary for the just hearing of that case; or

(b) in any case, that it would be detrimental to the interests of the child for him to be present at the hearing of his case, they may release the child from the obligation imposed by subsection (1)(b) above.

(3) Subject to subsection (2) above, the Principal Reporter shall be responsible for securing the attendance of the child at the hearing of his case by a children's hearing (and at any subsequent hearing to which the case is continued under section 69(1)(a) of this Act).

(4) On the application of the Principal Reporter, a children's hearing, if satisfied on cause shown that it is necessary for them to do so, may issue, for the purposes of subsection (3) above, a warrant under this subsection to find the child, to keep him in a place of safety and to bring him before a children's hearing.

(5) Where a child has failed to attend a children's hearing in accordance with such notice as is mentioned in subsection (1) above, they may, either on the application of the Principal Reporter or of their own motion, issue a warrant under this subsection, which shall have the same effect as a warrant under subsection (4) above.

(6) A child who has been taken to a place of safety under a warrant granted under this section shall not be kept there after whichever is the earlier of—

(a) the expiry of seven days beginning on the day he was first so taken there; or

(b) the day on which a children's hearing first sit to consider his case in accordance with subsection (7) below.

(7) Where a child has been found in pursuance of a warrant under this section and he cannot immediately be brought before a children's hearing, the Principal Reporter shall, wherever practicable, arrange a children's hearing to sit on the first working day after the child was so found.

(8) Subject to section 46 of this Act, a person who is a relevant person as respects a child shall, where a children's hearing are considering the case of the child—

(a) have the right to attend at all stages of the hearing; and

(b) be obliged to attend at all stages of the hearing unless the hearing are satisfied that it would be unreasonable to require his attendance or that his attendance is unnecessary for the proper consideration of the case.

(9) Any person who fails to attend a hearing which, under subsection (8)(b) above, he is obliged to attend shall be guilty of an offence and shall be liable on summary conviction to a fine not exceeding level 3 on the standard scale.

NOTE
1. As amended by the Criminal Procedure (Consequential Provisions) (Scotland) Act 1995, c.40, s.3 and Sch.3, para.97.

### Power to exclude relevant person from children's hearing

**46.**—(1) Where a children's hearing are considering the case of a child in respect of whom a person is a relevant person, they may exclude that person, or that person and any representative of his, or any such representative, from any part or parts of the hearing for so long as is necessary in the interests of the child, where they are satisfied that—

(a) they must do so in order to obtain the views of the child in relation to the case before the hearing; or

(b) the presence of the person or persons in question is causing, or is likely to cause, significant distress to the child.

(2) Where a children's hearing exercise the power conferred by subsection (1) above, the chairman of the hearing shall, after that exclusion has ended, explain to any person who was so excluded the substance of what has taken place in his absence.

### Presumption and determination of age

**47.**—(1) Where a children's hearing has been arranged in respect of any person, the hearing—

(a) shall, at the commencement of the proceedings, make inquiry as to his age and shall proceed with the hearing only if he declares that he is a child or they so determine; and

(b) may, at any time before the conclusion of the proceedings, accept a declaration by the child, or make a fresh determination, as to his age.

(2) The age declared to, or determined by, a children's hearing to be the age of a person brought before them shall, for the purposes of this Part of this Act, be deemed to be the true age of that person.

(3) No decision reached, order continued, warrant granted or requirement imposed by a children's hearing shall be invalidated by any subsequent proof that the age of a person brought before them had not been correctly declared to the hearing or determined by them.

*Transfer etc. of cases*

### Transfer of case to another children's hearing

**48.**—(1) Where a children's hearing are satisfied, in relation to a case which they are hearing, that it could be better considered by a children's hearing constituted from a children's panel for a different local government area, they may at any time during the course of the hearing request the Principal Reporter to arrange for such other children's hearing to dispose of the case.

(2) Where a case has been transferred in pursuance of subsection (1) above, the grounds of referral accepted or established for the case shall not require to be further accepted or established for the purposes of the children's hearing to which the case has been transferred.

**Referral or remission to children's hearing where child guilty of an offence**

**49.** *[Repealed by the Criminal Procedure (Consequential Provisions) (Scotland) Act 1995 (c.40), s.6 and Sch.5.]*

**Treatment of child's case on remission by court**

[1]**50.**—(1) Where a court has, under section 49 of the Criminal Procedure (Scotland) Act 1995, remitted a case to a children's hearing for disposal, a certificate signed by the clerk of the court stating that the child or person concerned has pled guilty to, or has been found guilty of, the offence to which the remit relates shall be conclusive evidence for the purposes of the remit that the offence has been committed by the child or person.

(2) Where a court has under subsection (7) of the said section 49 remitted a case to a children's hearing for disposal, the provisions of this Act shall apply to the person concerned as if he were a child.

NOTE
1. As amended by the Criminal Procedure (Consequential Provisions) (Scotland) Act 1995, c.40, s.3 and Sch.3, para.97.

*Appeals*

**Appeal against decision of children's hearing or sheriff**

**51.**—(1) Subject to subsection (15) below, a child or a relevant person (or relevant persons) or both (or all)—

(a) may, within a period of three weeks beginning with the date of any decision of a children's hearing, appeal to the sheriff against that decision; and

(b) where such an appeal is made, shall be heard by the sheriff.

(2) The Principal Reporter shall, in respect of any appeal under subsection (1) above, ensure that all reports and statements available to the hearing, along with the reports of their proceedings and the reasons for the decision, are lodged with the sheriff clerk.

(3) The sheriff may, on appeal under subsection (1) above, hear evidence from, or on behalf of, the parties in relation to the decision; and, without prejudice to that generality, the sheriff may—

(a) examine the Principal Reporter;

(b) examine the authors or compilers of any reports or statements; and

(c) call for any further report which he considers may assist him in deciding the appeal.

(4) Where the sheriff decides that an appeal under this section has failed, he shall confirm the decision of the children's hearing.

(5) Where the sheriff is satisfied that the decision of the children's hearing is not justified in all the circumstances of the case he shall allow the appeal, and—

(a) where the appeal is against a warrant to find and keep or, as the case may be, to keep a child in a place of safety, he shall recall the warrant;

¹(b) where the child is subject to a supervision requirement containing a movement restriction condition imposed under subsection (3)(b) of section 70 of this Act or a condition imposed under subsection (9) of that section of this Act, he shall direct that the condition shall cease to have effect; and

(c) in any case, he may, as he thinks fit—

　(i) remit the case with reasons for his decision to the children's hearing for reconsideration of their decision; or

　(ii) discharge the child from any further hearing or other proceedings in relation to the grounds for the referral of the case; or

　(iii) substitute for the disposal by the children's hearing any requirement which could be imposed by them under section 70 of this Act.

(6) Where a sheriff imposes a requirement under subsection (5)(c)(iii) above, that requirement shall for the purposes of this Act, except of this section, be treated as a disposal by the children's hearing.

(7) Where the sheriff is satisfied that an appeal under subsection (1) above against the decision of a children's hearing arranged under section 73(8) of this Act is frivolous, he may order that no subsequent appeal against a decision to continue (whether with or without any variation) the supervision requirement in question shall lie until the expiration of twelve months beginning with the date of the order.

(8) An appeal under subsection (1) above in respect of the issue of a warrant by a children's hearing shall be disposed of within three days of the lodging of the appeal; and failing such disposal the warrant shall cease to have effect at the end of that period.

(9) Where a child or a relevant person appeals under subsection (1) above against a decision of a children's hearing in relation to a supervision requirement, the child or the relevant person may make application to a children's hearing for the suspension of the requirement appealed against.

(10) It shall be the duty of the Principal Reporter forthwith to arrange a children's hearing to consider the application under subsection (9) above, and that hearing may grant or refuse the application.

(11) Subject to subsections (13) and (15) below, an appeal shall lie by way of stated case either on a point of law or in respect of any irregularity in the conduct of the case—

(a) to the sheriff principal from any decision of the sheriff—

　(i) on an appeal under subsection (1) of this section;

　(ii) on an application made under section 65(7) or (9) of this Act; or

　(iii) on an application made under section 85(1) of this Act; and

(b) to the Court of Session from any decision of the sheriff such as is mentioned in sub-paragraphs (i) to (iii) of paragraph (a) above and, with leave of the sheriff principal, from any decision of the sheriff principal on an appeal under that paragraph; and the decision of the Court of Session in the matter shall be final.

(12) An appeal under subsection (11) above may be made at the instance of—

(a) the child or any relevant person, either alone or together; or

(b) the Principal Reporter on behalf of the children's hearing.

(13) An application to the sheriff, or as the case may be the sheriff principal, to state a case for the purposes of an appeal under subsection (11)(a) or (b) above shall be made within a period of twenty-eight days beginning with the date of the decision appealed against.

(14) On deciding an appeal under subsection (11) above the sheriff principal or as the case may be the Court of Session shall remit the case to the sheriff for disposal in accordance with such directions as the court may give.

(15) No appeal shall lie under this section in respect of—

(a) a decision of the sheriff on an application under section 57 of this Act; or

(b) a decision of a children's hearing continuing a child protection order under section 59(4) of this Act.

NOTE
1. As amended by the Antisocial Behaviour etc. (Scotland) Act 2004 (asp.8), Sch.4, para.4.

CHAPTER 3

PROTECTION AND SUPERVISION OF CHILDREN

*Children requiring compulsory measures of supervision*

**Children requiring compulsory measures of supervision**

**52.**—(1) The question of whether compulsory measures of supervision are necessary in respect of a child arises if at least one of the conditions mentioned in subsection (2) below is satisfied with respect to him.

(2) The conditions referred to in subsection (1) above are that the child—

(a) is beyond the control of any relevant person;

(b) is falling into bad associations or is exposed to moral danger; (c) is likely—

    (i)   to suffer unnecessarily; or

    (ii)  be impaired seriously in his health or development, due to a lack of parental care;

¹(d) is a child in respect of whom any of the offences mentioned in Schedule 1 to the Criminal Procedure (Scotland) Act 1995 (offences against children to which special provisions apply) has been committed;

(e) is, or is likely to become, a member of the same household as a child in respect of whom any of the offences referred to in paragraph (d) above has been committed;

(f) is, or is likely to become, a member of the same household as a person who has committed any of the offences referred in paragraph (d) above;

¹(g) is, or is likely to become, a member of the same household as a person in respect of whom an offence under sections 1 to 3 of the

Criminal Law (Consolidation) (Scotland) Act 1995 (incest and intercourse with a child by step-parent or person in position of trust) has been committed by a member of that household;

(h) has failed to attend school regularly without reasonable excuse;

(i) has committed an offence;

(j) has misused alcohol or any drug, whether or not a controlled drug within the meaning of the Misuse of Drugs Act 1971;

(k) has misused a volatile substance by deliberately inhaling its vapour, other than for medicinal purposes;

(l) is being provided with accommodation by a local authority under section 25, or is the subject of a parental responsibilities order obtained under section 86, of this Act and, in either case, his behaviour is such that special measures are necessary for his adequate supervision in his interest or the interest of others.

[2](m) is a child to whom subsection (2A) below applies.

[2](2A) This subsection applies to a child where—

(a) a requirement is made of the Principal Reporter under section 12(1) of the Antisocial Behaviour etc. (Scotland) Act 2004 (asp 8) (power of sheriff to require Principal Reporter to refer case to children's hearing) in respect of the child's case; and

(b) the child is not subject to a supervision requirement.

(3) In this Part of this Act, "supervision" in relation to compulsory measures of supervision may include measures taken for the protection, guidance, treatment or control of the child.

NOTES
1. As amended by the Criminal Procedure (Consequential Provisions) (Scotland) Act 1995, (c.40), s.3 and Sch.3, para.97.
2. Inserted by the Antisocial Behaviour etc. (Scotland) Act 2004 (asp.8), s.12.

*Preliminary and investigatory measures*

### Provision of information to the Principal Reporter

**53.**—(1) Where information is received by a local authority which suggests that compulsory measures of supervision may be necessary in respect of a child, they shall—

(a) cause inquiries to be made into the case unless they are satisfied that such inquiries are unnecessary; and

(b) if it appears to them after such inquiries, or after being satisfied that such inquiries are unnecessary, that such measures may be required in respect of the child, give to the Principal Reporter such information about the child as they have been able to discover.

(2) A person, other than a local authority, who has reasonable cause to believe that compulsory measures of supervision may be necessary in respect of a child—

(a) shall, if he is a constable, give to the Principal Reporter such information about the child as he has been able to discover;

(b) in any other case, may give the Principal Reporter that information.

(3) A constable shall make any report required to be made under paragraph (b) of section 17(1) of the Police (Scotland) Act 1967 (duty to

make reports in relation to commission of offences) in relation to a child to the Principal Reporter as well as to the appropriate prosecutor.

(4) Where an application has been made to the sheriff—

(a) by the Principal Reporter in accordance with a direction given by a children's hearing under section 65(7) or (9) of this Act; or

(b) by any person entitled to make an application under section 85 of this Act,

the Principal Reporter may request any prosecutor to supply him with any evidence lawfully obtained in the course of, and held by the prosecutor in connection with, the investigation of a crime or suspected crime, being evidence which may assist the sheriff in determining the application; and, subject to subsection (5) below, it shall be the duty of the prosecutor to comply with such a request.

(5) A prosecutor may refuse to comply with a request issued under subsection (4) above where he reasonably believes that it is necessary to retain the evidence for the purposes of any proceedings in respect of a crime, whether the proceedings have been commenced or are to be commenced by him.

(6) The Lord Advocate may direct that in any specified case or class of cases any evidence lawfully obtained in the course of an investigation of a crime or suspected crime shall be supplied, without the need for a request under subsection (4) above, to the Principal Reporter.

[1](7) In subsections (3), (4) and (5) above "crime" and "prosecutor" have the same meanings respectively given by section 307 of the Criminal Procedure (Scotland) Act 1995.

NOTE
1. As amended by the Criminal Procedure (Consequential Provisions) (Scotland) Act 1995, c.40, s.3 and Sch.3, para.97.


### Reference to the Principal Reporter by court

**54.**—(1) Where in any relevant proceedings it appears to the court that any of the conditions in section 52(2)(a) to (h), (j), (k) or (l) of this Act is satisfied with respect to a child, it may refer the matter to the Principal Reporter, specifying the condition.

(2) In this section "relevant proceedings" means—

(a) an action for divorce or judicial separation or for declarator of marriage, nullity of marriage, parentage or non-parentage;

(b) proceedings relating to parental responsibilities or parental rights within the meaning of Part I of this Act;

(c) proceedings for an adoption order under the Adoption (Scotland) Act 1978 or for an order under section 18 of that Act declaring a child free for adoption; and

(d) proceedings for an offence against section 35 (failure by parent to secure regular attendance by his child at a public school), 41 (failure to comply with attendance order) or 42(3) (failure to permit examination of child) of the Education (Scotland) Act 1980.

(3) Where the court has referred a matter to the Principal Reporter under subsection (1) above, he shall—

(a) make such investigation as he thinks appropriate; and

(b) if he considers that compulsory measures of supervision are necessary,

arrange a children's hearing to consider the case of the child under section 69 of this Act; and subsection (1) of that section shall apply as if the condition specified by the court under subsection (1) above were a ground of referral established in accordance with section 68 of this Act.

### Child assessment orders

**55.**—(1) A sheriff may grant an order under this section for an assessment of the state of a child's health or development, or of the way in which he has been treated (to be known as a "child assessment order"), on the application of a local authority if he is satisfied that—

(a) the local authority have reasonable cause to suspect that the child in respect of whom the order is sought is being so treated (or neglected) that he is suffering, or is likely to suffer, significant harm;

(b) such assessment of the child is required in order to establish whether or not there is reasonable cause to believe that the child is so treated (or neglected); and

(c) such assessment is unlikely to be carried out, or be carried out satisfactorily, unless the order is granted.

(2) Where—

(a) an application has been made under subsection (1) above; and

(b) the sheriff considers that the conditions for making a child protection order under section 57 of this Act are satisfied,

he shall make such an order under that section as if the application had been duly made by the local authority under that section rather than this section.

(3) A child assessment order shall—

(a) specify the date on which the assessment is to begin;

(b) have effect for such period as is specified in the order, not exceeding seven days beginning with the date specified by virtue of paragraph (a) above;

(c) require any person in a position to produce the child to—

(i) produce him to any authorised person;

(ii) permit that person or any other authorised person to carry out an assessment in accordance with the order; and

(iii) comply with any other conditions of the order; and

(d) be carried out by an authorised person in accordance with the terms of the order.

(4) A child assessment order may—

(a) where necessary, permit the taking of the child concerned to any place for the purposes of the assessment; and

(b) authorise the child to be kept at that place, or any other place, for such period of time as may be specified in the order.

(5) Where a child assessment order makes provision under subsection (4) above, it shall contain such directions as the sheriff considers appropriate as to the contact which the child shall be allowed to have with any other person while the child is in any place to which he has been taken or in which he is being kept under a child assessment order.

(6) In this section "authorised person" means any officer of the local authority, and any person authorised by the local authority to perform the assessment, or perform any part of it.

**Initial investigation by the Principal Reporter**

**56.**—(1) Where the Principal Reporter receives information from any source about a case which may require a children's hearing to be arranged he shall, after making such initial investigation as he thinks necessary, proceed with the case in accordance with subsection (4) or (6) below.

(2) For the purposes of making any initial investigation under subsection (1) above, the Principal Reporter may request from the local authority a report on the child and on such circumstances concerning the child as appear to him to be relevant; and the local authority shall supply the report which may contain such information, from any person whomsoever, as the Principal Reporter thinks, or the local authority think, fit.

(3) A report requested under subsection (2) above may contain information additional to that given by the local authority under section 53 of this Act.

(4) The Principal Reporter may decide, after an initial investigation under subsection (1) above, that a children's hearing does not require to be arranged; and where he so decides—

(a) he shall inform the child, any relevant person and the person who brought the case to his notice, or any of those persons, that he has so decided; and

(b) he may, if he considers it appropriate, refer the case to a local authority with a view to their making arrangements for the advice, guidance and assistance of the child and his family in accordance with Chapter 1 of this Part of this Act; and

¹(c) he may, where it appears to him that—

(i) an education authority have a duty under section 14(3) of the Education (Scotland) Act 1980 (c.44) in relation to the child; and

(ii) the authority are not complying with that duty,

refer the matter to the Scottish Ministers.

¹(4A) A reference made under subsection (4)(c) above shall be in writing.

¹(4B) A copy of a reference made under subsection (4)(c) above shall be sent by the Principal Reporter to the education authority in respect of which the reference is made.

(5) Where the Principal Reporter has decided under subsection (4) above that a children's hearing does not require to be arranged, he shall not at any other time, on the basis solely of the information obtained during the initial investigation referred to in that subsection, arrange a children's hearing under subsection (6) below.

(6) Where it appears to the Principal Reporter that compulsory measures of supervision are necessary in respect of the child, he shall arrange a children's hearing to which he shall refer the case for consideration and determination.

(7) Where the Principal Reporter has arranged a children's hearing in accordance with subsection (6) above, he—

(a) shall, where he has not previously done so, request a report under subsection (2) above;

(b) may request from the local authority such information, supplementary or additional to a report requested under subsection (2) above, as he thinks fit;

and the local authority shall supply that report, or as the case may be information, and any other information which they consider to be relevant.

NOTE
1. Inserted by the Antisocial Behaviour etc. (Scotland) Act 2004 (asp 8), s.137.

*Measures for the emergency protection of children*

### Child protection orders

**57.**—(1) Where the sheriff, on an application by any person, is satisfied that—
(a) there are reasonable grounds to believe that a child—
  (i) is being so treated (or neglected) that he is suffering significant harm; or
  (ii) will suffer such harm if he is not removed to and kept in a place of safety, or if he does not remain in the place where he is then being accommodated (whether or not he is resident there); and
(b) an order under this section is necessary to protect that child from such harm (or such further harm),
he may make an order under this section (to be known as a "child protection order").

(2) Without prejudice to subsection (1) above, where the sheriff on an application by a local authority is satisfied—
(a) that they have reasonable grounds to suspect that a child is being or will be so treated (or neglected) that he is suffering or will suffer significant harm;
(b) that they are making or causing to be made enquiries to allow them to decide whether they should take any action to safeguard the welfare of the child; and
(c) that those enquiries are being frustrated by access to the child being unreasonably denied, the authority having reasonable cause to believe that such access is required as a matter of urgency,
he may make a child protection order.

(3) Without prejudice to any additional requirement imposed by rules made by virtue of section 91 of this Act, an application for a child protection order shall—
(a) identify—
  (i) the applicant; and
  (ii) in so far as practicable, the child in respect of whom the order is sought;
(b) state the grounds on which the application is made; and
(c) be accompanied by such supporting evidence, whether in documentary form or otherwise, as will enable the sheriff to determine the application.

(4) A child protection order may, subject to such terms and conditions as the sheriff considers appropriate, do any one or more of the following—
(a) require any person in a position to do so to produce the child to the applicant;
(b) authorise the removal of the child by the applicant to a place of safety, and the keeping of the child at that place;

(c) authorise the prevention of the removal of the child from any place where he is being accommodated;

(d) provide that the location of any place of safety in which the child is being kept should not be disclosed to any person or class of person specified in the order.

(5) Notice of the making of a child protection order shall be given forthwith by the applicant to the local authority in whose area the child resides (where that authority is not the applicant) and to the Principal Reporter.

(6) In taking any action required or permitted by a child protection order or by a direction under section 58 of this Act the applicant shall only act where he reasonably believes that to do so is necessary to safeguard or promote the welfare of the child.

(7) Where by virtue of a child protection order a child is removed to a place of safety provided by a local authority, they shall, subject to the terms and conditions of that order and of any direction given under section 58 of this Act, have the like duties in respect of the child as they have under section 17 of this Act in respect of a child looked after by them.

**Directions in relation to contact and exercise of parental responsibilities and parental rights**

**58.**—(1) When the sheriff makes a child protection order, he shall at that time consider whether it is necessary to give a direction to the applicant for the order as to contact with the child for—

(a) any parent of the child;

(b) any person with parental responsibilities in relation to the child; and

(c) any other specified person or class of persons;

and if he determines that there is such a necessity he may give such a direction.

(2) Without prejudice to the generality of subsection (1) above, a direction under that subsection may—

(a) prohibit contact with the child for any person mentioned in paragraphs (a) to (c) of that subsection;

(b) make contact with the child for any person subject to such conditions as the sheriff considers appropriate to safeguard and promote the welfare of the child.

(3) A direction under subsection (1) above may make different provision in relation to different persons or classes of person.

(4) A person applying for a child protection order under section 57(1) or (2) of this Act may at the same time apply to the sheriff for a direction in relation to the exercise or fulfilment of any parental responsibilities or parental rights in respect of the child concerned, if the person considers such a direction necessary to safeguard or promote the welfare of the child.

(5) Without prejudice to the generality of subsection (4) above, a direction under that subsection may be sought in relation to—

(a) any examination as to the physical or mental state of the child;

(b) any other assessment or interview of the child; or

(c) any treatment of the child arising out of such an examination or assessment, which is to be carried out by any person.

(6) The sheriff may give a direction sought under subsection (4) above where he considers there is a necessity such as is mentioned in that subsection; and such a direction may be granted subject to such conditions, if any, as the sheriff (having regard in particular to the duration of the child protection order to which it relates) considers appropriate.

(7) A direction under this section shall cease to have effect when—

(a) the sheriff, on an application under section 60(7) of this Act, directs that it is cancelled; or

(b) the child protection order to which it is related ceases to have effect.

**Initial hearing of case of child subject to child protection order**

**59.**—(1) This section applies where—

(a) a child in respect of whom a child protection order has been made—

(i) has been taken to a place of safety by virtue of section 57(4)(b) of this Act; or

(ii) is prevented from being removed from any place by virtue of section 57(4)(c) of this Act;

(b) the Principal Reporter has not exercised his powers under section 60(3) of this Act to discharge the child from the place of safety; and

(c) the Principal Reporter has not received notice, in accordance with section 60(9) of this Act, of an application under subsection (7) of that section.

(2) Where this section applies, the Principal Reporter shall arrange a children's hearing to conduct an initial hearing of the child's case in order to determine whether they should, in the interests of the child, continue the child protection order under subsection (4) below.

(3) A children's hearing arranged under subsection (2) above shall take place on the second working day after that order is implemented.

(4) Where a children's hearing arranged under subsection (2) above are satisfied that the conditions for the making of a child protection order under section 57 of this Act are established, they may continue the child protection order and any direction given under section 58 of this Act (whether with or without variation of the order or, as the case may be, the direction) until the commencement of a children's hearing in relation to the child arranged in accordance with section 65(2) of this Act.

(5) In subsection (3) above, section 60 and section 65(2) of this Act any reference, in relation to the calculation of any period, to the time at which a child protection order is implemented shall be construed as a reference—

(a) in relation to such an order made under paragraph (b) of subsection (4) of section 57 of this Act, to the day on which the child was removed to a place of safety in accordance with the order; and

(b) in relation to such an order made under paragraph (c) of that subsection, to the day on which the order was made, and "implement" shall be construed accordingly.

**Duration, recall or variation of child protection order**

**60.**—(1) Where, by the end of twenty-four hours of a child protection order being made (other than by virtue of section 57(4)(c) of this Act), the applicant has made no attempt to implement the order it shall cease to have effect.

(2) Where an application made under subsection (7) below has not been determined timeously in accordance with subsection (8) below, the order to which the application relates shall cease to have effect.

(3) A child shall not be—

(a) kept in a place of safety under a child protection order;

(b) prevented from being removed from any place by such an order; or

(c) subject to any term or condition contained in such an order or a direction given under section 58 of this Act,

where the Principal Reporter, having regard to the welfare of the child, considers that, whether as a result of a change in the circumstances of the case or of further information relating to the case having been received by the Principal Reporter, the conditions for the making of a child protection order in respect of the child are no longer satisfied or that the term, condition or direction is no longer appropriate and notifies the person who implemented the order that he so considers.

(4) The Principal Reporter shall not give notice under subsection (3) above where—

(a) proceedings before a children's hearing arranged under section 59(2) of this Act in relation to the child who is subject to the child protection order have commenced; or

(b) the hearing of an application made under subsection (7) of this section has begun.

(5) Where the Principal Reporter has given notice under subsection (3) above, he shall also, in such manner as may be prescribed, notify the sheriff who made the order.

(6) A child protection order shall cease to have effect—

(a) where an initial hearing arranged under section 59(2) of this Act does not continue the order under subsection (4) of that section;

(b) where an application is made to the sheriff under subsection (7) below, on the sheriff recalling such order under subsection (13) below;

(c) on the person who implemented the order receiving notice from the Principal Reporter that he has decided not to refer the case of a child who is subject to the order to a children's hearing arranged in accordance with section 65(2) of this Act;

(d) on the Principal Reporter giving notice in accordance with subsection (3) above in relation to the order that he considers that the conditions for the making of it are no longer satisfied; or

(e) where such order is continued under section 59(4) of this Act or subsection (12)(d) below, on the commencement of a children's hearing arranged under section 65(2) of this Act.

(7) An application to the sheriff to set aside or vary a child protection order made under section 57 of this Act or a direction given under

section 58 of this Act or such an order or direction continued (whether with or without variation) under section 59(4) of this Act, may be made by or on

(a) the child to whom the order or direction relates;

(b) a person having parental rights over the child;

(c) a relevant person;

(d) any person to whom notice of the application for the order was given by virtue of rules; or

(e) the applicant for the order made under section 57 of this Act.

(8) An application under subsection (7) above shall be made—

(a) in relation to a child protection order made under section 57, or a direction given under section 58, of this Act, before the commencement of a children's hearing arranged in accordance with section 59(2) of this Act; and

(b) in relation to such an order or direction continued (whether with or without variation) by virtue of subsection (4) of the said section 59,

within two working days of such continuation,

and any such application shall be determined within three working days of being made.

(9) Where an application has been made under subsection (7) above, the applicant shall forthwith give notice, in a manner and form prescribed by rules, to the Principal Reporter.

(10) At any time which is—

(a) after the giving of the notice required by subsection (9) above; but

(b) before the sheriff has determined the application in accordance with subsection (11) below,

the Principal Reporter may arrange a children's hearing the purpose of which shall be to provide any advice they consider appropriate to assist the sheriff in his determination of the application.

(11) The sheriff shall, after hearing the parties to the application and, if he wishes to make representations, the Principal Reporter, determine whether—

(a) the conditions for the making of a child protection order under section 57 of this Act are satisfied; or

(b) where the application relates only to a direction under section 58 of this Act, the direction should be varied or cancelled.

(12) Where the sheriff determines that the conditions referred to in subsection (11)(a) above are satisfied, he may—

(a) confirm or vary the order, or any term or condition on which it was granted;

(b) confirm or vary any direction given, in relation to the order, under section 58 of this Act;

(c) give a new direction under that section; or

(d) continue in force the order and any such direction until the commencement of a children's hearing arranged in accordance with section 65(2) of this Act.

(13) Where the sheriff determines that the conditions referred to in subsection (11)(a) above are not satisfied he shall recall the order and cancel any direction given under section 58 of this Act.

**Emergency protection of children where child protection order not available**

**61.**—(1) Where, on the application of any person, a justice of the peace is satisfied—

(a) both that the conditions laid down for the making of a child protection order in section 57(1) of this Act are satisfied and that it is probable that any such order, if made, would contain an authorisation in terms of paragraph (b) or (c) of subsection (4) of that section; but

(b) that it is not practicable in the circumstances for an application for such an order to be made to the sheriff or for the sheriff to consider such an application, he may grant to the applicant an authorisation under this section.

(2) Where on the application of a local authority a justice of the peace is satisfied—

(a) both that the conditions laid down for the making of a child protection order in section 57(2) of this Act are satisfied and that it is probable that any such order, if made, would contain an authorisation in terms of paragraph (b) or (c) of subsection (4) of that section; but

(b) that it is not practicable in the circumstances for an application for such an order to be made to the sheriff or for the sheriff to consider such an application,

he may grant an authorisation under this section.

(3) An authorisation under this section may—

(a) require any person in a position to do so to produce the child to the applicant;

(b) prevent any person from removing a child from a place where he is then being accommodated;

(c) authorise the applicant to remove the child to a place of safety and to keep him there until the expiration of the authorisation.

(4) An authorisation under this section shall cease to have effect—

(a) twelve hours after being made, if within that time—
 (i) arrangements have not been made to prevent the child's removal from any place specified in the authorisation; or
 (ii) he has not been, or is not being, taken to a place of safety; or

(b) where such arrangements have been made or he has been so taken when—
 (i) twenty-four hours have expired since it was so given; or
 (ii) an application for a child protection order in respect of the child is disposed of,

whichever is the earlier.

(5) Where a constable has reasonable cause to believe that—

(a) the conditions for the making of a child protection order laid down in section 57(1) are satisfied;

(b) that it is not practicable in the circumstances for him to make an application for such an order to the sheriff or for the sheriff to consider such an application; and

(c) that, in order to protect the child from significant harm (or further such harm), it is necessary for him to remove the child to a place of safety, he may remove the child to such a place and keep him there.

(6) The power conferred by subsection (5) above shall not authorise the keeping of a child in a place of safety for more than twenty-four hours from the time when the child is so removed.

(7) The authority to keep a child in a place of safety conferred by subsection (5) above shall cease on the disposal of an application in relation to the child for a child protection order.

(8) A child shall not be—

(a) kept in a place of safety; or

(b) prevented from being removed from any place,

under this section where the Principal Reporter considers that the conditions for the grant of an authorisation under subsection (1) or (2) above or the exercise of the power conferred by subsection (5) above are not satisfied, or that it is no longer in the best interests of the child that he should be so kept.

**Regulations in respect of emergency child protection measures**

**62.**—(1) The Secretary of State may make regulations concerning the duties in respect of a child of any person removing him to, and keeping him in, a place of safety under section 61 above.

(2) Regulations under this section may make provision requiring—

(a) notification of the removal of a child to be given to a person specified in the regulations;

(b) intimation to be given to any person of the place of safety at which a child is being kept;

(c) notification to be given to any person of the ceasing to have effect, under section 61(4)(a) of this Act, of an authorisation.

*Children arrested by the police*

**Review of case of child arrested by police**

¹**63.**—(1) Where the Principal Reporter has been informed by a constable, in accordance with section 43(5) of the Criminal Procedure (Scotland) Act 1995, that charges are not to be proceeded with against a child who has been detained in a place of safety in accordance with that section, the Principal Reporter shall, unless he considers that compulsory measures of supervision are not required in relation to the child, arrange a children's hearing to which he shall refer the case.

(2) A children's hearing arranged under subsection (1) above shall begin not later than the third day after the Principal Reporter received the information mentioned in that subsection.

(3) Where the Principal Reporter considers that a child of whose detention he has been informed does not require compulsory measures of supervision, he shall direct that the child shall no longer be kept in the place of safety.

(4) Subject to subsection (3) above, a child who has been detained in a place of safety may continue to be kept at that place until the commencement of a children's hearing arranged under subsection (1) above.

(5) Subject to subsection (6) below, a children's hearing arranged under subsection (1) above may—

(a) if they are satisfied that the conditions mentioned in subsection (2) of section 66 of this Act are satisfied, grant a warrant to keep the child in a place of safety; and

(b) direct the Principal Reporter to arrange a children's hearing for the purposes of section 65(1) of this Act, and subsections (3) to (8) of the said section 66 shall apply to a warrant granted under this subsection as they apply to a warrant granted under subsection (1) of the said section 66.

(6) A child shall not be kept in a place of safety in accordance with a warrant granted under subsection (5) above where the Principal Reporter, having regard to the welfare of the child, considers that, whether as a result of a change in the circumstances of the case or of further information relating to the case having been received by the Principal Reporter—

(a) the conditions mentioned in section 66(2) of this Act are no longer satisfied in relation to the child; or

(b) the child is not in need of compulsory measures of supervision,

and where he does so consider he shall give notice to that effect to the person who is keeping the child in that place in accordance with the warrant.

NOTE
1. As amended by the Criminal Procedure (Consequential Provisions) (Scotland) Act 1995, c.40, s.3 and Sch.3, para.97.

*Business meeting preparatory to children's hearing*

**Business meeting preparatory to children's hearing**

**64.**—(1) At any time prior to the commencement of proceedings at the children's hearing, the Principal Reporter may arrange a meeting with members of the children's panel from which the children's hearing is to be constituted under section 39(4) of this Act for those proceedings (any such meeting being, in this Part of this Act referred to as a "business meeting").

(2) Where a business meeting is arranged under subsection (1) above, the Principal Reporter shall give notice to the child in respect of whom the proceedings are to be commenced and any relevant person in relation to the child—

(a) of the arrangement of the meeting and of the matters which may be considered and determined by the meeting;

(b) of their right to make their views on those matters known to the Principal Reporter; and

(c) of the duty of the Principal Reporter to present those views to the meeting.

(3) A business meeting, subject to subsection (4) below—

(a) shall determine such procedural and other matters as may be prescribed by rules under subsection (1) of section 42 of this Act by virtue of subsection (2)(a) of that section; and

(b) may give such direction or guidance to the Principal Reporter in relation to the performance of his functions in relation to the proceedings as they think appropriate.

(4) Before a business meeting makes such a determination or gives such direction or guidance to the Principal Reporter, the Principal Reporter shall present, and they shall consider, any views expressed to him by virtue of subsection (2)(b) above.

(5) Subject to any rules made under section 42(1) of this Act by virtue of subsection (2)(a) of that section and with the exception of sections 44

and, as regards any determination made by the business meeting under subsection (3)(a) above, 51, the provisions of this Act which relate to a children's hearing shall not apply to a business meeting.

*Referral to, and disposal of case by, children's hearing*

**Referral to, and proceedings at, children's hearing**

**65.**—(1) The Principal Reporter shall refer to the children's hearing, for consideration and determination on the merits, the case of any child in respect of whom he is satisfied that—

(a) compulsory measures of supervision are necessary, and

(b) at least one of the grounds specified in section 52(2) of this Act is established;

and he shall state such grounds in accordance with rules made under section 42(1) of this Act by virtue of subsection (2)(c) of that section.

¹(1A) Where the Principal Reporter is satisfied that the ground specified in section 52(2)(m) of this Act is established in respect of any child, he shall be taken to be satisfied as to the matter mentioned in section 65(1)(a) in respect of the child.

(2) Where a referral is made in respect of a child who is subject to a child protection order made under section 57, and that order is continued under section 59(4) or 60(12)(d), of this Act, the Principal Reporter shall arrange for the children's hearing under subsection (1) above to take place on the eighth working day after the order was implemented.

(3) Where a referral is made in respect of a child who is subject to a supervision requirement, the children's hearing shall, before disposing of the referral in accordance with section 69(1)(b) or (c) of this Act, review that requirement in accordance with subsections (9) to (12) of section 73 of this Act.

(4) Subject to subsections (9) and (10) below, it shall be the duty of the chairman of the children's hearing to whom a child's case has been referred under subsection (1) above to explain to the child and the relevant person, at the opening of proceedings on the referral, the grounds stated by the Principal Reporter for the referral in order to ascertain whether these grounds are accepted in whole or in part by them.

(5) Where the chairman has given the explanation required by subsection (4) above and the child and the relevant person accept the grounds for the referral, the children's hearing shall proceed in accordance with section 69 of this Act.

(6) Where the chairman has given the explanation required by subsection (4) above and the child and the relevant person accept the grounds in part, the children's hearing may, if they consider it appropriate to do so, proceed in accordance with section 69 of this Act with respect to those grounds which are accepted.

(7) Where the chairman has given the explanation required under subsection (4) above and either or both of the child and the relevant person—

(a) do not accept the grounds for the referral; or

(b) accept the grounds in part, but the children's hearing do not consider it appropriate to proceed with the case under subsection (6) above, the hearing shall either direct the Principal Reporter to make an application to the sheriff for a finding as to whether such grounds for the referral as are not accepted by the child and the relevant person are established or shall discharge the referral.

(8) Subject to subsection (10) below, it shall be the duty of the chairman to explain to the child and to the relevant person the purpose for which the application to the sheriff is being made and to inform the child that he is under an obligation to attend the hearing before the sheriff.

(9) Where a children's hearing are satisfied that the child—

(a) for any reason will not be capable of understanding the explanation of the grounds for the referral required under subsection (4) above; or

(b) has not understood an explanation given under that subsection,

they shall either direct the Principal Reporter to make an application to the sheriff for a finding as to whether any of the grounds of the referral are established or discharge the referral.

(10) The acceptance by the relevant person of the grounds of the referral shall not be a requirement for a children's hearing proceeding under this section to consider a case where that person is not present.

NOTE
1. Inserted by the Antisocial Behaviour etc. (Scotland) Act 2004 (asp 8), s.12.

**Warrant to keep child where children's hearing unable to dispose of case**

**66.**—(1) Without prejudice to any other power enjoyed by them under this Part of this Act and subject to subsection (5) below, a children's hearing—

(a) arranged to consider a child's case under this Part of this Act; and

(b) unable to dispose of the case,

may, if they are satisfied that one of the conditions mentioned in subsection (2) below is met, grant a warrant under this subsection.

(2) The conditions referred to in subsection (1) above are—

(a) that there is reason to believe that the child may—
   (i) not attend at any hearing of his case; or
   (ii) fail to comply with a requirement under section 69(3) of this Act; or

(b) that it is necessary that the child should be kept in a place of safety in order to safeguard or promote his welfare.

(3) A warrant under subsection (1) above may require any person named in the warrant—

(a) to find and to keep or, as the case may be, to keep the child in a place of safety for a period not exceeding twenty-two days after the warrant is granted;

(b) to bring the child before a children's hearing at such times as may be specified in the warrant.

(4) A warrant under subsection (1) above may contain such conditions as appear to the children's hearing to be necessary or expedient, and without prejudice to that generality may—

(a) subject to section 90 of this Act, require the child to submit to any medical or other examination or treatment; and

(b) regulate the contact with the child of any specified person or class of persons.

(5) Subject to subsection (8) below, at any time prior to its expiry, a warrant granted under this section may, on an application to the children's hearing, on cause shown by the Principal Reporter, be continued in force, whether with or without variation of any condition imposed by virtue of subsection (4) above, by the children's hearing for such further period, not exceeding twenty-two days, as appears to them to be necessary.

[1](6) Where a children's hearing are satisfied

(a) that one of the conditions mentioned in section 70(10) of this Act is met; and

(b) that it is necessary to do so,

they may order that, pending the disposal of his case, the child shall be liable to be placed and kept in secure accommodation within a residential establishment at such times as the person in charge of that establishment, with the agreement of the chief social work officer of the relevant local authority, considers necessary.

(7) Where a children's hearing grant a warrant under subsection (1) above or continue such a warrant under subsection (5) above, they may order that the place of safety at which the child is to be kept shall not be disclosed to any person or class of persons specified in the order.

(8) A child shall not be kept in a place of safety or secure accommodation by virtue of this section for a period exceeding sixty-six days from the day when he was first taken to a place of safety under a warrant granted under subsection (1) above.

NOTE
1. As amended by the Antisocial Behaviour etc. (Scotland) Act 2004 (asp 8), Sch.4, para.4.

**Warrant for further detention of child**

**67.**—(1) Where a child is being kept in a place of safety by virtue of a warrant granted under section 66 of this Act or under this subsection, the Principal Reporter at any time prior to the expiry of that warrant may apply to the sheriff for a warrant to keep the child in that place after the warrant granted under the said section 66 or, as the case may be, this subsection has expired.

(2) A warrant under subsection (1) above shall only be granted on cause shown and—

(a) shall specify the date on which it will expire; and

(b) may contain any such requirement or condition as may be contained in a warrant granted under the said section 66.

(3) Where the sheriff grants a warrant under subsection (1) above, he may also make an order under this subsection in such terms as are mentioned in subsection (6) or (7) of the said section 66; and any order under this subsection shall cease to have effect when the warrant expires.

(4) An application under subsection (1) above may be made at the same time as, or during the hearing of, an application which the Principal Reporter has been directed by a children's hearing to make under section 65(7) or (9) of this Act.

**Application to sheriff to establish grounds of referral**

**68.**—(1) This section applies to applications under subsections (7) and (9) of section 65 of this Act and a reference in this section (except in subsection (8)) to "an application" is a reference to an application under either of those subsections.

(2) An application shall be heard by the sheriff within twenty-eight days of its being lodged.

(3) Where one of the grounds for the referral to which an application relates is the condition referred to in section 52(2)(i)—

(a) the application shall be made to the sheriff who would have jurisdiction if the child were being prosecuted for that offence; and

(b) in hearing the application in relation to that ground, the standard of proof required in criminal proceedings shall apply.

(4) A child shall—

(a) have the right to attend the hearing of an application; and

(b) subject to subsection (5) below, be under an obligation to attend such hearing;

and without prejudice to the right of each of them to be legally represented, the child and the relevant person may be represented by a person other than a legally qualified person at any diet fixed by the sheriff for the hearing of the application.

(5) Without prejudice to subsection (4)(a) above, the sheriff may dispense with the obligation imposed by subsection (4)(b) above where he is satisfied—

(a) in an application in which the ground of referral to be established is a condition mentioned in section 52(2)(d), (e), (f) or (g) of this Act, that the obligation to attend of the child is not necessary for the just hearing of that application; and

(b) in any application, that it would be detrimental to the interests of the child for him to be present at the hearing of the application.

(6) Where the child fails to attend the hearing of an application at which his attendance has not been dispensed with under subsection (5) above, the sheriff may grant an order to find and keep the child; and any order under this subsection shall be authority for bringing the child before the sheriff and, subject to subsection (7) below, for keeping him in a place of safety until the sheriff can hear the application.

(7) The child shall not be kept in a place of safety by virtue of subsection (6) above after whichever is the earlier of—

(a) the expiry of fourteen days beginning with the day on which the child is found; or

(b) the disposal of the application by the sheriff.

(8) Where in the course of the hearing of an application—

(a) under section 65(7) of this Act, the child and the relevant person accept any of the grounds for referral to which the application relates, the sheriff shall; or

(b) under section 65(9) of this Act, the relevant person accepts any of the grounds for referral to which the application relates, the sheriff may, if it appears to him reasonable to do so,

dispense with the hearing of evidence relating to that ground and deem the ground to be established for the purposes of the application, unless he is satisfied that, in all the circumstances of the case, the evidence should be heard.

(9) Where a sheriff decides that none of the grounds for referral in respect of which an application has been made are established, he shall

dismiss the application, discharge the referral to the children's hearing in respect of those grounds and recall, discharge or cancel any order, warrant, or direction under this Chapter of this Act which relates to the child in respect of those grounds.

(10) Where the sheriff, after the hearing of any evidence or on acceptance in accordance with subsection (8) above, finds that any of the grounds for the referral to which the application relates is, or should be deemed to be, established—

(a) he shall remit the case to the Principal Reporter to make arrangements for a children's hearing to consider and determine the case; and

(b) he may if he is satisfied that—

    (i) keeping the child in a place of safety is necessary in the child's best interests; or

    (ii) there is reason to believe that the child will run away before the children's hearing sit to consider the case,

issue an order requiring, subject to subsection (12) below, that the child be kept in a place of safety until the children's hearing so sit.

[1](11) An order issued under subsection (10) above may, if the sheriff is satisfied

(a) that one of the conditions mentioned in section 70(10) of this Act is met; and

(b) that it is necessary for the order to do so,

provide that the child shall be liable to be placed and kept in secure accommodation within a residential establishment at such times as the person in charge of the establishment, with the agreement of the chief social work officer of the relevant local authority, considers necessary.

(12) A child shall not be kept in a place of safety by virtue of subsection (10)(b) above after whichever is the earlier of the following—

(a) the expiry of three days beginning with the day on which he is first so kept; or

(b) the consideration of his case by the children's hearing arranged under subsection (10)(a) above.

NOTE
1. As amended by the Antisocial Behaviour etc. (Scotland) Act 2004 (asp 8), Sch.4, para.4.

**Restrictions on evidence in certain cases involving sexual abuse**

[1]**68A.**—(1) This section applies in relation to—

(a) an application under section 65(7) or (9) of this Act in which the ground of referral to be established is a condition mentioned in—

    (i) paragraph (b) of subsection (2) of section 52 of this Act where that condition is alleged to be satisfied by reference to sexual behaviour engaged in by any person,

    (ii) paragraph (d), (e) or (f) of that subsection where that condition is alleged to be satisfied by reference to a relevant offence, or

    (iii) paragraph (g) of that subsection, or

(b) an application under section 85 of this Act for a review of a finding that any such ground of referral is established.

(2) In hearing the application, the sheriff shall not admit, or allow questioning designed to elicit, evidence which shows or tends to show

that the child who is the subject of the application or any other witness giving evidence at the hearing (such child or other witness being referred to in this section and section 68B of this Act as "the witness")—

    (a) is not of good character (whether in relation to sexual matters or otherwise),

    (b) has, at any time, engaged in sexual behaviour not forming part of the subject matter of the ground of referral,

    (c) has, at any time (other than shortly before, at the same time as or shortly after the acts which form part of the subject matter of the ground of referral), engaged in such behaviour, not being sexual behaviour, as might found the inference that the witness is not a credible or reliable witness, or

    (d) has, at any time, been subject to any such condition or predisposition as might found the inference referred to in paragraph (c) above.

(3) In subsection (1)(a)(ii) above, "relevant offence" means—

    (a) an offence mentioned in paragraph 1 or 4 of Schedule 1 (offences against children under the age of 17 to which special provisions apply) to the Criminal Procedure (Scotland) Act 1995 (c.46), or

    (b) any other offence mentioned in that Schedule where there is a substantial sexual element in the alleged commission of the offence.

(4) In subsection (2)(b) and (c) above—

    (a) "the subject matter of the ground of referral" means—

        (i) in the case of an application in which the ground of referral to be established is the condition referred to in paragraph (a)(i) of subsection (1) above, the sexual behaviour referred to in that paragraph,

        (ii) in the case of any other application, the acts or behaviour constituting the offence by reference to which the ground of referral is alleged to be established, and

    (b) the reference to engaging in sexual behaviour includes a reference to undergoing or being made subject to any experience of a sexual nature.

NOTE
1. Inserted by the Vulnerable Witnesses (Scotland) Act 2004 (asp 3), s.23.

**Exceptions to restrictions under section 68A**

[1]**68B.**—(1) The sheriff hearing an application referred to in subsection (1) of section 68A of this Act may, on an application by any party to the proceedings, admit such evidence or allow such questioning as is referred to in subsection (2) of that section if satisfied that—

    (a) the evidence or questioning will relate only to a specific occurrence or occurrences of sexual or other behaviour or to specific facts demonstrating—

        (i) the character of the witness, or

        (ii) any condition or predisposition to which the witness is or has been subject,

    (b) that occurrence or those occurrences of behaviour or facts are relevant to establishing the ground of referral, and

    (c) the probative value of the evidence sought to be admitted or elicited is significant and is likely to outweigh any risk of prejudice to the proper administration of justice arising from its being admitted or elicited.

(2) In subsection (1) above—

(a) the reference to an occurrence or occurrences of sexual behaviour includes a reference to undergoing or being made subject to any experience of a sexual nature,

(b) "the proper administration of justice" includes-

(i) appropriate protection of the witness's dignity and privacy, and

(ii) ensuring the facts and circumstances of which the sheriff is made aware are relevant to an issue to be put before the sheriff and commensurate with the importance of that issue to the sheriff's decision on the question whether the ground of referral is established.

(3) In this section, "the witness" means the child who is the subject of the application referred to in section 68A(1) or other witness in respect of whom the evidence is sought to be admitted or elicited.

NOTE
1. Inserted by the Vulnerable Witnesses (Scotland) Act 2004 (asp 3), s.23.

**Continuation or disposal of referral by children's hearing**

**69.**—(1) Where the grounds of referral of the child's case stated by the Principal Reporter are accepted or are established in accordance with section 68 or section 85 of this Act, the children's hearing shall consider those grounds, any report obtained under section 56(7) of this Act and any other relevant information available to them and shall—

(a) continue the case to a subsequent hearing in accordance with subsection (2) below;

(b) discharge the referral of the case in accordance with subsection (12) below; or

(c) make a supervision requirement under section 70 of this Act.

(2) The children's hearing may continue the case to a subsequent hearing under this subsection where they are satisfied that, in order to complete their consideration of the case, it is necessary to have a further investigation of the case.

(3) Where a children's hearing continue the case under subsection (2) above, they may, for the purposes of the investigation mentioned by that subsection, require the child to attend, or reside at, any clinic, hospital or other establishment during a period not exceeding twenty-two days.

(4) Where a child fails to fulfil a requirement made under subsection (3) above, the children's hearing may, either on an application by the Principal Reporter or of their own motion, grant a warrant under this subsection.

(5) A warrant under subsection (4) above shall be authority—

(a) to find the child;

(b) to remove the child to a place of safety and keep him there; and

(c) where the place of safety is not the clinic, hospital or other establishment referred to in the requirement made under subsection (3) above, to take the child from the place of safety to such clinic, hospital or other establishment for the purposes of the investigation mentioned in subsection (2) above.

(6) A warrant under subsection (4) above shall be granted for such period as appears to the children's hearing to be appropriate, provided that no warrant shall permit the keeping of a child in a place of safety after whichever is the earlier of—

(a) the expiry of twenty-two days after the warrant is granted; or
(b) the day on which the subsequent hearing of the child's case by a children's hearing begins.

(7) Where a child's case has been continued under subsection (2) above and the children's hearing are satisfied that—

(a) keeping the child in a place of safety is necessary in the interests of safeguarding or promoting the welfare of the child; or
(b) there is reason to believe that the child may not attend the subsequent hearing of his case,

they may grant a warrant requiring that the child be taken to and kept in a place of safety.

(8) A warrant under subsection (7) above shall cease to have effect on whichever is the earlier of—

(a) the expiry of twenty-two days after the warrant is granted; or
(b) the day on which the subsequent hearing of the child's case by a children's hearing begins.

(9) A warrant under subsection (4) or (7) above may contain such conditions as appear to the children's hearing to be necessary or expedient, and without prejudice to that generality may—

(a) subject to section 90 of this Act, require the child to submit to any medical or other examination or treatment;
(b) regulate the contact with the child of any specified person or class of persons.

(10) Where a child is to be kept at a place of safety under a warrant granted under this section or is to attend, or reside at, any place in accordance with a requirement made under subsection (3) above, the children's hearing may order that such place shall not be disclosed to any person or class of persons specified in the order.

[1](11) Where a child is to reside in a residential establishment by virtue of a requirement made or warrant granted under this section, the children's hearing may, if satisfied

(a) that one of the conditions mentioned in section 70(10) of this Act is met; and
(b) that it is necessary for the order to do so,

order that while the requirement or warrant remains in effect he shall be liable to be placed in secure accommodation within that establishment at such times as the person in charge of the establishment, with the agreement of the chief social work officer of the relevant local authority, considers necessary.

(12) Where a children's hearing decide not to make a supervision requirement under section 70 of this Act they shall discharge the referral.

(13) On the discharge of the referral of the child's case any order, direction, or warrant under Chapter 2, or this Chapter, of this Act in respect of the child's case shall cease to have effect.

NOTE
1. As amended by the Antisocial Behaviour etc. (Scotland) Act 2004 (asp 8), Sch.4, para.4.

**Disposal of referral by children's hearing: supervision requirements, including residence in secure accommodation**

**70.**—(1) Where the children's hearing to whom a child's case has been referred under section 65(1) of this Act are satisfied that compulsory measures of supervision are necessary in respect of the child they may make a requirement under this section (to be known as a "supervision requirement").

(2) A children's hearing, where they decide to make such a requirement, shall consider whether to impose any condition such as is described in subsection (5)(b) below.

(3) A supervision requirement may require the child—

(a) to reside at any place or places specified in the requirement; and

(b) to comply with any condition contained in the requirement.

[1](3A) A children's hearing may, for the purpose of enabling a child to comply with a supervision requirement, impose such duties on the relevant local authority as may be specified in the supervision requirement.

[1](3B) The duties imposed under subsection (3A) above may include that of securing or facilitating the provision for the child of services of a kind other than that provided by the relevant local authority.

(4) The place or, as the case may be, places specified in a requirement under subsection (3)(a) above may, without prejudice to the generality of that subsection, be a place or places in England or Wales; and a supervision requirement shall be authority for the person in charge of such a place to restrict the child's liberty to such extent as that person may consider appropriate, having regard to the terms of the requirement.

(5) A condition imposed under subsection (3)(b) above may, without prejudice to the generality of that subsection—

(a) subject to section 90 of this Act, require the child to submit to any medical or other examination or treatment;

(b) regulate the contact with the child of any specified person or class of persons.

(6) A children's hearing may require, when making a supervision requirement, that any place where the child is to reside in accordance with the supervision requirement shall not be disclosed to any person specified in the requirement under this subsection or class of persons so specified.

(7) A children's hearing who make a supervision requirement may determine that the requirement shall be reviewed at such time during the duration of the requirement as they determine.

[1](7A) Where, on a review under subsection (7) above, it appears to the children's hearing that the relevant local authority are in breach of a duty imposed on them under section 71 of this Act, the hearing may direct the Principal Reporter to give the authority notice of an intended application under section 71A(2) of this Act.

[1](7B) The Principal Reporter shall, at the same time as giving the notice of an intended application under section 71A(2) of this Act, send a copy of the notice to—

(a) the child to whom the duty referred to in subsection (7A) above relates;

(b) any person who, in relation to the child, is a relevant person;

(c) any person appointed under section 41 of this Act to safeguard the interests of the child in any proceedings which are taking place when the notice is given.

[1](7C) Notice of an intended application under section 71A(2) of this Act is a written notice—

(a) setting out the respects in which the relevant local authority are in breach of the duty imposed on them under section 71 of this Act; and

(b) stating that if the authority do not comply with that duty within the period of 21 days beginning with the day on which they received the notice, the Principal Reporter may make an application under section 71A(2) of this Act.

[1](7D) Where a children's hearing have made a direction under subsection (7A) above, they shall determine that a further review under subsection (7) above take place on or as soon as is reasonably practicable after the expiry of the period of 28 days beginning with the day on which notice was given in pursuance of that direction.

[1](7E) Where on a further review under subsection (7) above which takes place by virtue of subsection (7D) above, it appears to the children's hearing that the relevant local authority continues to be in breach of the duty referred to in subsection (7A) above, the hearing may authorise the Principal Reporter to make an application under section 71A(2) of this Act.

(8) A supervision requirement shall be in such form as the Secretary of State may prescribe by rules.

[2](9) A children's hearing may exercise a power mentioned in subsection (9A) below in relation to a child if they are satisfied—

(a) that one of the conditions mentioned in subsection (10) below is met; and

(b) that it is necessary to exercise the power concerned.

[3](9A) The powers are—

(a) that the children's hearing may specify in the supervision requirement that the child shall be liable to be placed and kept in secure accommodation in a residential establishment specified, under subsection (3)(a) above, in the requirement, during such period as the person in charge of that establishment, with the agreement of the chief social work officer of the relevant local authority, considers necessary; and

(b) that the children's hearing may impose, under subsection (3)(b) above, a movement restriction condition.

[2](10) The conditions are—

(a) that the child, having previously absconded, is likely to abscond and, if he absconds, it is likely that his physical, mental or moral welfare will be at risk; and

(b) that the child is likely to injure himself or some other person.

[3](11) In this section, "movement restriction condition" means a condition—

(a) restricting the child's movements in such way as may be specified in the supervision requirement; and

(b) requiring the child to comply with such arrangements for monitoring compliance with the restriction mentioned in paragraph (a) above as may be so specified.

[3](12) Where a children's hearing impose a condition such as is mentioned in subsection (9A)(b) above, they shall also impose under subsection (3)(b) above such of the conditions prescribed by the Scottish Ministers for the purposes of this section as they consider necessary in the child's case.

[3](13) The Scottish Ministers may by regulations make provision as to the arrangements mentioned in subsection (11)(b) above.

[3](14) Regulations under subsection (13) above may in particular include provision—

(a) prescribing what method or methods of monitoring compliance with the restriction mentioned in paragraph (a) of subsection (11) above may be specified in a supervision requirement;

(b) specifying the devices which may be used for the purpose of that monitoring;

(c) prescribing the person who may be designated by a children's hearing to carry out that monitoring or the class or description of person from which that person may be drawn;

(d) requiring a children's hearing who have designated a person in pursuance of paragraph (c) above who is no longer within the provision made under that paragraph to vary the designation accordingly and notify the child of the variation.

[3](15) The Scottish Ministers may, by contract or otherwise, secure the services of such persons as they think fit to carry out the monitoring mentioned in subsection (11)(b) above and may do so in a way in which those services are provided differently in relation to different areas or different forms of that monitoring.

[3](16) Nothing in any enactment or rule of law prevents the disclosure to a person providing services in pursuance of subsection (15) above of information relating to a child where the disclosure is made for the purposes only of the full and proper provision of the monitoring mentioned in subsection (11)(b) above.

[3](17) A children's hearing may include in a supervision requirement a movement restriction condition only if the hearing is constituted from the children's panel for a local government area which is prescribed for the purposes of this section by the Scottish Ministers.

NOTES
1. Inserted by the Antisocial Behaviour etc. (Scotland) Act 2004 (asp 8), s.136.
2. Substituted by the Antisocial Behaviour etc. (Scotland) Act 2004 (asp 8), s.135.
3. Inserted by the Antisocial Behaviour etc. (Scotland) Act 2004 (asp 8), s.135.

**Duties of local authority with respect to supervision requirements**

**71.**—(1) The relevant local authority shall, as respects a child subject to a supervision requirement, give effect to the requirement.

[1](1A) Where a supervision requirement imposes, under section 70(3A) of this Act, duties on the relevant local authority, the authority shall perform those duties.

(2) Where a supervision requirement provides that the child shall reside—

(a) in relevant accommodation; or

(b) in any other accommodation not provided by a local authority, the relevant local authority shall from time to time investigate whether, while the child is so resident, any conditions imposed by the supervision requirement are being fulfilled; and may take such steps as they consider reasonable if they find that such conditions are not being fulfilled.

(3) In this section, "relevant accommodation" means accommodation provided by the parents or relatives of the child or by any person associated with them or with the child.

NOTE
1. Inserted by the Antisocial Behaviour etc. (Scotland) Act 2004 (asp 8), s.136.

### Enforcement of local authorities' duties under section 71

[1]**71A.**—(1) The sheriff principal may, on an application under subsection (2) below, make an order requiring a relevant local authority in breach of a duty imposed on them under section 71 of this Act to perform that duty.

(2) The Principal Reporter, having been so authorised by a children's hearing under section 70(7E) of this Act, may apply for an order under subsection (1) above.

(3) No such application shall be competent unless—
(a) the Principal Reporter has, on a direction of the children's hearing made under section 70(7A) of this Act, given the relevant local authority the notice referred to in that provision; and
(b) the authority have failed to comply, within the period stipulated in the notice, with the duty there referred to.

(4) In deciding whether to apply under subsection (2) above, the Principal Reporter shall not take into account any factor relating to the adequacy of the means available to the relevant local authority to enable it to comply with the duty.

(5) An application under subsection (2) above shall be made by summary application.

(6) The sheriff principal having jurisdiction under this section is the sheriff principal of the sheriffdom in which is situated the principal office of the relevant local authority in breach of the duty referred to in subsection (1) above.

(7) An order under subsection (1) above shall be final.

NOTE
1. Inserted by the Antisocial Behaviour etc. (Scotland) Act 2004 (asp 8), s.136.

### Transfer of child subject to supervision requirement in case of necessity

**72.**—(1) In any case of urgent necessity, where it is in the interests of—
(a) a child who is required by a supervision requirement imposed under section 70(3)(a) of this Act to reside in a specific residential establishment or specific other accommodation; or
(b) other children in that establishment or accommodation,
the chief social work officer of the relevant local authority may direct that, notwithstanding that requirement, the child be transferred to another place.

(2) Any child transferred under subsection (1) above shall have his case reviewed, in accordance with section 73(8) of this Act, by a children's hearing within seven days of his transfer.

### Duration and review of supervision requirement

**73.**—(1) No child shall continue to be subject to a supervision requirement for any period longer than is necessary in the interests of promoting or safeguarding his welfare.

(2) Subject to any variation or continuation of a supervision requirement under subsection (9) below, no supervision requirement shall remain in force for a period longer than one year.

(3) A supervision requirement shall cease to have effect in respect of a child not later than on his attaining the age of eighteen years.

(4) A relevant local authority shall refer the case of a child who is subject to a supervision requirement to the Principal Reporter where they are satisfied that—

(a) the requirement in respect of the child ought to cease to have effect or be varied;

(b) a condition contained in the requirement is not being complied with; or

(c) the best interests of the child would be served by their—

    (i) applying under section 86 of this Act for a parental responsibilities order;

    (ii) applying under section 18 of the Adoption (Scotland) Act 1978 for an order freeing the child for adoption; or

    (iii) placing the child for adoption,

and they intend to apply for such an order or so place the child.

(5) Where the relevant local authority are aware that an application has been made and is pending, or is about to be made, under section 12 of the said Act of 1978 for an adoption order in respect of a child who is subject to a supervision requirement, they shall forthwith refer his case to the Principal Reporter.

(6) A child or any relevant person may require a review of a supervision
requirement in respect of the child at any time at least three months after—

(a) the date on which the requirement is made; or

(b) the date of the most recent continuation, or variation, by virtue of this section of the requirement.

(7) Where a child is subject to a supervision requirement and, otherwise than in accordance with that requirement or with an order under section 11 of this Act, a relevant person proposes to take the child to live outwith Scotland, the person shall, not later than twenty-eight days before so taking the child, give notice of that proposal in writing to the Principal Reporter and to the relevant local authority.

[1](8) The Principal Reporter shall—

(a) arrange for a children's hearing to review any supervision requirement in respect of a child where—

    (i) the case has been referred to him under subsection (4) or (5) above;

    (ii) the review has been required under subsection (6) above;

    (iii) the review is required by virtue of section 70(7) or section 72(2) of this Act;

    (iv) he has received in respect of the child such notice as is mentioned in subsection (7) above; or

    (v) in any other case, the supervision requirement will expire within three months;

(aa) where—

    (i) a requirement is made of the Principal Reporter under section 12(1) of the Antisocial Behaviour etc. (Scotland) Act 2004 (asp 8) (power of sheriff to require Principal Reporter to refer case to children's hearing) in respect of the child's case; and

(ii) the child is subject to a supervision requirement,

arrange for a children's hearing to review the supervision requirement; and

(b) make any arrangements incidental to any such review.

(9) Where a supervision requirement is reviewed by a children's hearing arranged under subsection (8) above, they may—

(a) where they are satisfied that in order to complete the review of the supervision requirement it is necessary to have a further investigation of the child's case, continue the review to a subsequent hearing;

(b) terminate the requirement;

(c) vary the requirement;

(d) insert in the requirement any requirement which could have been imposed by them under section 70(3) of this Act; or

(e) continue the requirement, with or without such variation or insertion.

(10) Subsections (3) to (10) of section 69 of this Act shall apply to a continuation under paragraph (a) of subsection (9) above of a review of a supervision requirement as they apply to the continuation of a case under subsection (1)(a) of that section.

(11) Where a children's hearing vary or impose a requirement under subsection (9) above which requires the child to reside in any specified place or places, they may order that such place or places shall not be disclosed to any person or class of persons specified in the requirement.

(12) Where a children's hearing is arranged under subsection (8)(a)(v) above, they shall consider whether, if the supervision requirement is not continued, the child still requires supervision or guidance; and where a children's hearing consider such supervision or guidance is necessary, it shall be the duty of the local authority to provide such supervision or guidance as the child is willing to accept.

(13) Where a children's hearing is arranged by virtue of subsection (4)(c) or (5) above, then irrespective of what the hearing do under subsection (9) above they shall draw up a report which shall provide advice in respect of, as the case may be, the proposed application under section 86 of this Act or under section 18 of the said Act of 1978, or the proposed placing for adoption or the application, or prospective application, under section 12 of that Act, for any court which may subsequently require to come to a decision, in relation to the child concerned, such as is mentioned in subsection (14) below.

(14) A court which is considering whether, in relation to a child, to grant an application under section 86 of this Act or under section 18 or 12 of the said Act of 1978 and which, by virtue of subsection (13) above, receives a report as respects that child, shall consider the report before coming to a decision in the matter.

NOTE
1. As amended by the Antisocial Behaviour etc. (Scotland) Act 2004 (asp 8), s.12.

**Further provision as respects children subject to supervision requirements**

**74.** The Secretary of State may by regulations provide—

   (a) for the transmission of information regarding a child who is subject to a supervision requirement to any person who, by virtue of that requirement, has, or is to have, control over the child;

   (b) for the temporary accommodation, where necessary, of a child so subject; and

   (c) for the conveyance of a child so subject—

      (i) to any place in which, under the supervision requirement, he is to reside;

      (ii) to any place to which he falls to be taken under subsection (1) or (5) of section 82 of this Act; or

      (iii) to any person to whom he falls to be returned under subsection (3) of that section.

**Powers of Secretary of State with respect to secure accommodation**

**75.**—(1) The Secretary of State may by regulations make provision with respect to the placing in secure accommodation of any child—

   (a) who is subject to a requirement imposed under section 70(3)(a) of this Act but not subject to a requirement under subsection (9) of that section; or

   (b) who is not subject to a supervision requirement but who is being looked after by a local authority in pursuance of such enactments as may be specified in the regulations.

(2) Regulations under subsection (1) above may—

   (a) specify the circumstances in which a child may be so placed under the regulations;

   (b) make provision to enable a child who has been so placed or any relevant person to require that the child's case be brought before a children's hearing within a shorter period than would apply under regulations made under subsection (3) below; and

   (c) specify different circumstances for different cases or classes of case.

(3) Subject to subsection (4) below and without prejudice to subsection (2)(b) above, the Secretary of State may prescribe—

   (a) the maximum period during which a child may be kept under this Act in secure accommodation without the authority of a children's hearing or of the sheriff;

   (b) the period within which a children's hearing shall be arranged to consider the case of a child placed in secure accommodation by virtue of regulations made under this section (and different periods may be so prescribed in respect of different cases or classes of case).

(4) Subsection (8) of section 66 of this Act shall apply in respect of a child placed in secure accommodation under regulations made under this section as if such placing took place by virtue of that section.

(5) The Secretary of State may by regulations vary the period within which a review of a condition imposed under section 70(9) of this Act shall be reviewed under section 73 of this Act.

(6) The Secretary of State may by regulations make provision for the procedures to be applied in placing children in secure accommodation; and without prejudice to the generality of this subsection, such regulations may—

(a) specify the duties of the Principal Reporter in relation to the placing of children in secure accommodation;

(b) make provision for the referral of cases to a children's hearing for review; and

(c) make provision for any person with parental responsibilities in relation to the child to be informed of the placing of the child in secure accommodation.

. . .

*Offences in connection with orders etc. for protection of children*

**Offences in connection with orders etc. for protection of children**

**81.** A person who intentionally obstructs—

(a) any person acting under a child protection order;

(b) any person acting under an authorisation granted under section 61(1) or (2) of this Act; or

(c) a constable acting under section 61(5) of this Act,

shall, subject to section 38(3) and (4) of this Act, be guilty of an offence and shall be liable on summary conviction to a fine not exceeding level 3 on the standard scale.

*Fugitive children and harbouring*

**Recovery of certain fugitive children**

**82.**—(1) A child who absconds—

(a) from a place of safety in which he is being kept under or by virtue of this Part of this Act;

(b) from a place (in this section referred to as a "relevant place") which, though not a place of safety such as is mentioned in paragraph (a) above, is a residential establishment in which he is required to reside by virtue of section 70(3)(a) of this Act or a hospital or other institution in which he is temporarily residing while subject to such a requirement; or

(c) from a person who, by virtue of a supervision requirement or of section 74 of this Act, has control over him while he is being taken to, is awaiting being taken to, or (whether or not by reason of being on leave) is temporarily away from, such place of safety or relevant place,

may be arrested without warrant in any part of the United Kingdom and taken to the place of safety or as the case may be the relevant place; and a court which is satisfied that there are reasonable grounds for believing that the child is within any premises may, where there is such power of arrest, grant a warrant authorising a constable to enter those premises and search for the child using reasonable force if necessary.

(2) Without prejudice to the generality of subsection (1) above, a child who at the end of a period of leave from a place of safety or relevant place fails to return there shall, for the purposes of this section, be taken to have absconded.

(3) A child who absconds from a person who, not being a person mentioned in paragraph (c) of subsection (1) above, is a person who has

control over him by virtue of a supervision requirement may, subject to the same provisions as those to which an arrest under that subsection is subject, be arrested as is mentioned in that subsection and returned to that person; and the provision in that subsection for a warrant to be granted shall apply as respects such a child as it applies as respects a child mentioned in that subsection.

(4) If a child—

(a) is taken under subsection (1) above to a place of safety or relevant place; or

(b) is returned under subsection (3) above to a person,

but the occupier of that place of safety or of that relevant place, or as the case may be that person, is unwilling or unable to receive him, that circumstance shall be intimated forthwith to the Principal Reporter.

(5) Where intimation is required by subsection (4) above as respects a child, he shall be kept in a place of safety until—

(a) in a case where he is subject to a supervision requirement, he can be brought before a children's hearing for that requirement to be reviewed; or

(b) in any other case, the Principal Reporter has, in accordance with section 56(6) of this Act, considered whether compulsory measures of supervision are required in respect of him.

**Harbouring**

**83.** A person who—

(a) knowingly assists or induces a child to abscond in circumstances which render the child liable to arrest under subsection (1) or (3) of section 82 of this Act;

(b) knowingly and persistently attempts to induce a child so to abscond;

(c) knowingly harbours or conceals a child who has so absconded; or

(d) knowingly prevents a child from returning—

    (i) to a place mentioned in paragraph (a) or (b) of the said subsection (1);

    (ii) to a person mentioned in paragraph (c) of that subsection, or in the said subsection (3),

shall, subject to section 38(3) and (4) of this Act, to section 51(5) and (6) of the Children Act 1989 and to Article 70(5) and (6) of the Children (Northern Ireland) Order 1995 (analogous provision for England and Wales and for Northern Ireland), be guilty of an offence and liable on summary conviction to a fine not exceeding level 5 on the standard scale or to imprisonment for a term not exceeding six months or to both such fine and such imprisonment.

*Implementation of authorisations etc.*

**Implementation of authorisations etc.**

**84.** Where an order, authorisation or warrant under this Chapter or Chapter 2 of this Part of this Act grants power to find a child and to keep him in a place of safety, such order, authorisation or warrant may be implemented as if it were a warrant for the apprehension of an accused person issued by a court of summary jurisdiction; and any enactment or rule of law applying to such a warrant shall, subject to the provisions of this Act, apply in like manner to the order, authorisation or warrant.

*New evidence: review of establishment of grounds of referral*

**Application for review of establishment of grounds of referral**

**85.**—(1) Subject to subsections (3) and (4) below, where subsection (2) below applies an application may be made to the sheriff for a review of a finding such as is mentioned in section 68(10) of this Act.

(2) This subsection applies where the sheriff, on an application made by virtue of subsection (7) or (9) of section 65 of this Act (in this section referred to as the "original application"), finds that any of the grounds of referral is established.

(3) An application under subsection (1) above may only be made where the applicant claims—

(a) to have evidence which was not considered by the sheriff on the original application, being evidence the existence or significance of which might materially have affected the determination of the original application;

(b) that such evidence—

    (i)   is likely to be credible and reliable; and

    (ii)  would have been admissible in relation to the ground of referral which was found to be established on the original application; and

(c) that there is a reasonable explanation for the failure to lead such evidence on the original application.

(4) An application under subsection (1) above may only be made by—

(a) the child in respect of whom the ground of referral was found to be established; or

(b) any person who is a relevant person in relation to that child.

(5) Where the sheriff on an application under subsection (1) above is not satisfied that any of the claims made in the application are established he shall dismiss the application.

(6) Where the sheriff is satisfied on an application under subsection (1) above that the claims made in the application are established, he shall consider the evidence and if, having considered it, he is satisfied that—

(a) none of the grounds of referral in the original application to which the application relates is established, he shall allow the application, discharge the referral to the children's hearing in respect of those grounds and proceed in accordance with subsection (7) below in relation to any supervision requirement made in respect of the child (whether or not varied under section 73 of this Act) in so far as it relates to any such ground; or

(b) any ground of referral in the original application to which the application relates is established, he may proceed in accordance with section 68(10) of this Act.

(7) Where the sheriff is satisfied as is mentioned in subsection (6)(a) above, he may—

(a) order that any supervision requirement so mentioned shall terminate—

    (i)  immediately; or

    (ii)  on such date as he may specify; or

  (b)  if he is satisfied that there is evidence sufficient to establish any ground of referral, being a ground which was not stated in the original application, find such ground established and proceed in accordance with section 68(10) of this Act in relation to that ground.

(8) Where the sheriff specifies a date for the termination of a supervision requirement in accordance with subsection (7)(a)(ii) above, he may, before such termination, order a variation of that requirement, of any requirement imposed under subsection (6) of section 70 of this Act, or of any determination made under subsection (7) of that section; and such variation may take effect—

  (a)  immediately; or

  (b)  on such date as he may specify.

(9) Where the sheriff orders the termination of a supervision requirement in accordance with subsection (7)(a) above, he shall consider whether, after such termination, the child concerned will still require supervision or guidance; and where he considers that such supervision or guidance will be necessary he shall direct a local authority to provide it in accordance with subsection (10) below.

(10) Where a sheriff has given a direction under subsection (9) above, it shall be the duty of the local authority to comply with that direction; but that duty shall be regarded as discharged where they offer such supervision or guidance to the child and he, being a child of sufficient age and maturity to understand what is being offered, is unwilling to accept it.

· · ·

CHAPTER 4

PARENTAL RESPONSIBILITIES ORDERS, ETC.

*Parental responsibilities orders*

· · ·

*Miscellaneous*

**Consent of child to certain procedures**

**90.** Nothing in this Part of this Act shall prejudice any capacity of a child enjoyed by virtue of section 2(4) of the Age of Legal Capacity (Scotland) Act 1991 (capacity of child with sufficient understanding to consent to surgical, medical or dental procedure or treatment); and without prejudice to that generality, where a condition contained, by virtue of—

  (a)  section 66(4)(a), section 67(2) or section 69(9)(a) of this Act, in a warrant; or

  (b)  section 70(5)(a) of this Act, in a supervision requirement,

requires a child to submit to any examination or treatment but the child has the capacity mentioned in the said section 2(4), the examination or treatment shall only be carried out if the child consents.

. . .

**92.**—For section 29 of the Legal Aid (Scotland) Act 1986 substitute the following section—

**"Legal aid in respect of certain proceedings relating to children**

**29.**—(1) This section applies to legal aid in connection with—

(a) proceedings before the sheriff (including, without prejudice to that generality, proceedings on an appeal to the sheriff principal from a decision of the sheriff) in respect of any matter arising under Chapter 2 or 3 of Part II of the Children (Scotland) Act 1995 (in this section referred to as "the 1995 Act"); or

(b) an appeal to the Court of Session in connection with such proceedings.

(2) Subject to subsections (3) to (5) below, legal aid to which this section applies shall be available to a child and any relevant person in relation to him in connection with—

(a) proceedings before the sheriff on an application for a child protection order or child assessment order, or for the variation or recall of such an order;

(b) an appeal to the sheriff under section 51 of the 1995 Act against—

  (i) a decision of a children's hearing to grant a warrant such as is mentioned in subsection (5)(a) of that subsection; or

  (ii) any other decision of a children's hearing;

(c) an application—

  (i) by virtue of section 65(7) or (9) of the 1995 Act for a finding as to whether the grounds for a referral are established; or

  (ii) under section 85 of the 1995 Act for a review of such a finding;

(d) an appeal to the sheriff principal or to Court of Session under section 51 of the 1995 Act.

(3) Legal aid shall be available under subsection (2)(b)(i) above on an application made to the sheriff without inquiry into the resources of the child or the relevant person.

(4) Legal aid shall be available under subsection (2)(a),(b)(ii) or (c) above on an application made to the sheriff if the sheriff is satisfied—

(a) that it is in the interests of the child that legal aid be made available; and

(b) after consideration of the financial circumstances of the child and any relevant person in relation to him that the expenses of the case cannot be met without undue hardship to the child or to any relevant person in relation to him or the dependants of any of them.

(5) Legal aid shall be available under subsection (2)(d) above on an application made to the Board if it is satisfied—

(a) after consideration of the financial circumstances of the child and any relevant person in relation to him that the expenses of the appeal cannot be met without undue hardship to the child or to any relevant person in relation to him or the dependants of any of them; and

(b) that the child, or as the case may be the relevant person has substantial grounds for making or responding to the appeal and it is reasonable, in the particular circumstances of the case, that legal aid should be made available accordingly.

(6) The Board may require a person receiving legal aid under subsection (2)(d) above or subsection (9) below to comply with such conditions as it considers expedient to enable it to satisfy itself from time to time that it is reasonable for him to continue to receive such legal aid.

(7) Subject to subsection (8) below, legal aid to which this section applies shall be available in connection with proceedings before the sheriff on an application for an exclusion order (or for the variation or recall of such an order) to—

(a) a child;

(b) a relevant person in relation to a child;

(c) a person who is a named person, or will be such a person if the application is granted;

(d) a spouse or partner of a person mentioned in paragraph (c) above; and

(e) a person who is an appropriate person, or will be such a person if the application is granted.

(8) Legal aid shall be available under subsection (7) above on an application to the sheriff if the sheriff is satisfied after consideration of the financial circumstances of the applicant and, where the applicant is a child, of any relevant person or appropriate person in relation to him that the expenses of the case cannot be met without undue hardship to the applicant or any dependant of the applicant.

(9) Legal aid shall be available in connection with any appeal from a decision of the sheriff on an application for an exclusion order or for the variation or recall of such an order to any of the persons mentioned in paragraphs (a) to (e) of subsection (7) above on an application to the Board if it is satisfied—

(a) after consideration of the financial circumstances of the applicant and, where the applicant is a child, of any relevant person or appropriate person in relation to him, that the expenses of the appeal cannot be met without undue hardship to the applicant or any dependant of the applicant; and

(b) that the applicant has substantial grounds for making or responding to the appeal and that it is reasonable, in the particular circumstances of the case, that legal aid should be made available accordingly.

(10) Where in connection with any proceedings—

(a) the sheriff has been satisfied as is mentioned in subsection (4)(b) or subsection (8) above; or

(b) the Board has been satisfied as is mentioned in subsection (5)(a) or subsection (9)(a) above,

and has made legal aid available to any person, it shall not be necessary for the sheriff or, as the case may be, the Board to be so satisfied in respect of an application for legal aid by such a person in connection with any subsequent proceedings arising from such proceedings.

(11) Legal aid to which this section applies shall consist of representation by a solicitor and, where appropriate, by counsel in any proceedings (including any appeal) mentioned in subsection (1) above and shall include all such assistance as is usually given by solicitor or counsel in the steps preliminary or incidental to such proceedings.

(12) In this section—

(a) "child" and "relevant person" have the meanings given by section 93(2)(b) of the 1995 Act;

(b) "child protection order", "child assessment order" and "exclusion order" have the meanings given by section 93(1) of that Act;

(c) "named person" and "appropriate person" have the meanings given by section 76 of that Act; and

(d) "partner" shall be construed in accordance with section 79(4) of that Act.".

*Interpretation of Part II*

### Interpretation of Part II

**93.**—(1) In this Part of this Act, unless the context otherwise requires,—

"accommodation" shall be construed in accordance with section 25(8) of this Act;

"chief social work officer" means an officer appointed under section 3 of the Social Work (Scotland) Act 1968;

"child assessment order" has the meaning given by section 55(1) of this Act;

"child protection order" has the meaning given by section 57(1) of this Act;

"children's hearing" shall be construed in accordance with section 39(3), but does not include a business meeting arranged under section 64, of this Act;

"compulsory measures of supervision" means, in respect of a child, such measures of supervision as may be imposed upon him by a children's hearing;

"constable" means a constable of a police force within the meaning of the Police (Scotland) Act 1967;

"contact order" has the meaning given by section 11(2)(d) of this Act;

"disabled" has the meaning given by section 23(2) of this Act;

[1]"education authority" has the meaning given by section 135(1) of the Education (Scotland) Act 1980 (c.44);

"exclusion order" has the meaning given by section 76(12) of this Act;

"family", in relation to a child, includes—

(a) any person who has parental responsibility for the child; and

(b) any other person with whom the child has been living;

"local authority" means a council constituted under section 2 of the Local Government etc. (Scotland) Act 1994;

"local government area" shall be construed in accordance with section 1 of the said Act of 1994;

"parental responsibilities" has the meaning given by section 1(3) of this Act;

"parental responsibilities order" has the meaning given by section 86(1) of this Act;

"parental rights" has the meaning given by section 2(4) of this Act;

"place of safety", in relation to a child, means—

(a) a residential or other establishment provided by a local authority;

(b) a community home within the meaning of section 53 of the Children Act 1989;

(c) a police station;

[2](d) a hospital, or surgery, the person or body of persons responsible for the management of which is willing temporarily to receive the child;

[3](e) the dwelling-house of a suitable person who is so willing; or

[3](f) any other suitable place the occupier of which is so willing.

"the Principal Reporter" means the Principal Reporter appointed under section 127 of the said Act of 1994 or any officer of the Scottish Children's Reporter Administration to whom there is delegated, under section 131(1) of that Act, any function of the Principal Reporter under this Act;

[4]"relevant local authority", in relation to a child who is subject to a warrant granted under this Part of this Act or to a supervision requirement, means the local authority for whose area there is established the children's panel from which the children's hearing which granted the warrant or imposed the supervision requirement was constituted;

"residence order" has the meaning given by section 11(2)(c) of this Act;

"residential establishment"—

(a) in relation to a place in Scotland, means an establishment (whether managed by a local authority, by a voluntary organisation or by any other person) which provides residential accommodation for children for the purposes of this Act or the Social Work (Scotland) Act 1968;

(b) in relation to a place in England and Wales, means a community home, voluntary home or registered children's home (within the meaning of the Children Act 1989); and

(c) in relation to a place in Northern Ireland, means a home provided under Part VIII of the Children (Northern Ireland) Order 1995, or a voluntary home, or a registered children's home (which have respectively the meanings given by that Order);

"school age" shall be construed in accordance with section 31 of the Education (Scotland) Act 1980;

[5]"secure accommodation" means accommodation provided in a residential establishment, approved by the Scottish Ministers in accordance with regulations made under section 29(9)(a) of the Regulation of Care (Scotland) Act 2001 (asp 8) or by the Secretary of State in accordance with regulations made under paragraph 4(2)(i) of Schedule 4 to the Children Act 1989 for the purpose of restricting the liberty of children;

"supervision requirement" has the meaning given by section 70(1) of this Act, and includes any condition contained in such a requirement or related to it;

"voluntary organisation" means a body (other than a public or local authority) whose activities are not carried on for profit; and "working day" means every day except—

(a) Saturday and Sunday;

(b) December 25th and 26th; and

(c) January 1st and 2nd.

(2) For the purposes of—

[6](a) Chapter 1 and this Chapter (except this section) of this Part and section 44,"child" means a person under the age of eighteen years; and

[3](b) Chapter 2 (except section 44) and Chapter 3 of this Part—
"child" means—
- (i) a child who has not attained the age of sixteen years;
- (ii) a child over the age of sixteen years who has not attained the age of eighteen years and in respect of whom a supervision requirement is in force; or
- (iii) a child whose case has been referred to a children's hearing by virtue of section 33 of this Act;

and for the purposes of the application of those Chapters to a person who has failed to attend school regularly without reasonable excuse includes a person who is over sixteen years of age but is not over school age; and

"relevant person" in relation to a child means—
- (a) any parent enjoying parental responsibilities or parental rights under Part I of this Act;
- (b) any person in whom parental responsibilities or rights are vested by, under or by virtue of this Act; and
- (c) any person who appears to be a person who ordinarily (and other than by reason only of his employment) has charge of, or control over, the child.

(3) Where, in the course of any proceedings under Chapter 2 or 3 of this Part, a child ceases to be a child within the meaning of subsection (2) above, the provisions of those Chapters of this Part and of any statutory instrument made under those provisions shall continue to apply to him as if he had not so ceased to be a child.

(4) Any reference in this Part of this Act to a child—
- (a) being "in need", is to his being in need of care and attention because—
  - (i) he is unlikely to achieve or maintain, or to have the opportunity of achieving or maintaining, a reasonable standard of health or development unless there are provided for him, under or by virtue of this Part, services by a local authority;
  - (ii) his health or development is likely significantly to be impaired, or further impaired, unless such services are so provided;
  - (iii) he is disabled; or
  - (iv) he is affected adversely by the disability of any other person in his family;
- (b) who is "looked after" by a local authority, shall be construed in accordance with section 17(6) of this Act.

(5) Any reference to any proceedings under this Part of this Act, whether on an application or on appeal, being heard by the sheriff, shall be construed as a reference to such proceedings being heard by the sheriff in chambers.

NOTES
1. Inserted by the Antisocial Behaviour etc. (Scotland) Act 2004 (asp 8), s.137.
2. Substituted by the Regulation of Care (Scotland) Act 2001 (asp 8), s.74.
3. Inserted by the Regulation of Care (Scotland) Act 2001 (asp 8), s.74.
4. Amended by the Antisocial Behaviour etc. (Scotland) Act 2004 (asp 8), Sch.4, para.4.

5. Amended by the Regulation of Care (Scotland) Act 2001 (asp 8), s.79 and Sch.3, para.19(4)(a) and brought into force by the Regulation of Care (Scotland) Act 2001 (Commencement No. 2 and Transitional Provisions) Order 2002 (SSI 2002/162), para.2 (effective from April 1, 2002).

6. Amended by the Criminal Justice (Scotland) Act 2003 (asp 7), s.52.

. . .

# APPENDIX 3

## Children's Hearings (Scotland) Rules 1996

### SI 1996/3261 (S.251)

### ARRANGEMENT OF RULES

### PART I

### INTERPRETATION, ETC

### PART II

### CONSTITUTION AND ARRANGEMENTS OF CHILDREN'S HEARINGS

### PART III

### GENERAL PROVISIONS AS TO CHILDREN'S HEARING

### PART IV

### CHILDREN'S HEARINGS ON REFERRAL AND AT REVIEW OF SUPERVISION REQUIREMENTS

# PART I

# INTERPRETATION, ETC

The Secretary of State, in exercise of the powers conferred on him by
section 42(1) of the Children (Scotland) Act 1995, and all other powers
enabling him in that behalf, hereby makes the following Rules:

**Citation and commencement**

**1.** These Rules may be cited as the Children's Hearings (Scotland)
Rules 1996 and shall come into force on 1st April 1997.

**Interpretation**

**2.**—(1) In these Rules, unless the context otherwise requires—
"the Act" means the Children (Scotland) Act 1995;
"the 1978 Act" means the Adoption (Scotland) Act 1978;
"the 1994 Act" means the Local Government etc. (Scotland) Act 1994;
"the 1995 Act" means the Criminal Procedure (Scotland) Act 1995;
"the 1996 Regulations" means the Secure Accommodation (Scotland)
Regulations 1996;
"chairman" means the chairman of a children's hearing;
"child" has the meaning given to that term by section 93(2)(b) of the
Act;
"child protection order" has the meaning given to that term by section
57 of the Act;
"children's hearing" means a children's hearing as defined in section
39(3) of the Act;
"day" means a period of twenty-four hours commencing at midnight;

"enactment" includes any order, regulation or other instrument made under the Act;

"local authority" means the local authority for the area of the children's hearing;

"relevant person" has the meaning given to that term by section 93(2)(b) of the Act;

"Principal Reporter" has the meaning given to that term by section 93(1) of the Act;

"representative" has the meaning given to that term by rule 11(3) below;

"safeguarder" means a person appointed by a children's hearing under section 41(1) of the Act for the purpose of safeguarding the interests of the child in the proceedings;

"Scottish Children's Reporter Administration" has the meaning given to that term by section 128 of the 1994 Act;

"secure accommodation" means accommodation provided in a residential establishment in accordance with the 1996 regulations for the purpose of restricting the liberty of children.

(2) Unless the context otherwise requires, any reference in these Rules to:

(a) a numbered rule or Form shall be construed as a reference to the rule of Form bearing that number in these Rules; and any reference to a specified paragraph or sub-paragraph shall be construed as a reference to that paragraph or sub-paragraph in the rule in which that reference occurs; and

(b) a Form includes a Form substantially to the same effect as that set out in these Rules with such variation as circumstances may require.

## PART II

## CONSTITUTION AND ARRANGEMENTS OF CHILDREN'S HEARINGS

### Recording and transmission of information at beginning of case

**3.**—(1) Where the Principal Reporter receives information from any source of a case which may require a children's hearing to be arranged, he shall keep a record of the name and address where available for the person from whom the information was received.

(2) Where the Principal Reporter decides that no further action on the case is required as mentioned in subsection (4) of section 56 of the Act, or refers the case to the local authority under subsection (4)(b) of that section, or arranges a children's hearing under subsection (6) of that section, he shall—

(a) keep a record of that decision or, as the case may be, that course of action; and

(b) if the information was received from a local authority or an officer of a police force, give notice of that decision, or as the case may be, that course of action to that local authority or, the chief constable of that police force.

### Business meeting preparatory to constitution of children's hearing

**4.**—(1) Where the Principal Reporter arranges a children's hearing, he may, for the purpose of—

(a) determining any procedural matter specified in paragraph (2), and
(b) obtaining any direction or guidance in relation to the performance of his functions in relation to the proceedings,

arrange a meeting (in this rule referred to as a "business meeting") with members of the children's panel from which the children's hearing is to be constituted and with the provisions the same as in section 39(5) of the Act applying to the business meeting.

(2) A business meeting shall determine any of the following procedural matters as may be referred to the meeting by the Principal Reporter—

(a) whether notice of the children's hearing is to be given by the Principal Reporter under rule 7 to a person as a "relevant person" in terms of paragraph (c) of the definition of that term in section 93(2)(b) of the Act (person who appears to be a person who ordinarily (and other than by reason only of his employment) has charge of, or control over, the child);

[1](b) where notice of the children's hearing has been or is to be given by the Principal Reporter to the child under rule 6, whether notice is also to be given that the child is released under section 45(2) of the Act from the obligation to attend the hearing under subsection (1)(b) of that section; and

(c) where notice has been or is to be given by the Principal Reporter to a relevant person under rule 7, whether notice is also to be given that the hearing are satisfied under section 45(8)(b) of the Act that it would be unreasonable to require his attendance or that his attendance is unnecessary for the proper consideration of the case.

(3) Where the Principal Reporter arranges a business meeting under paragraph (1), he shall, not later than 4 working days before the date of the meeting—

(a) give notice in writing to the members of the panel who will attend the meeting of the date, time and place of the meeting;

(b) give notice in writing to the child, any relevant person and any safeguarder that the meeting has been arranged and of the date on which it is to be held;

(c) give to the members of the panel and to the child, any relevant person and any safeguarder—

(i) notice of the matters referred to the business meeting for determination or for direction and guidance;

(ii) a copy of any documents or information relevant to these matters; and

(iii) a copy of the grounds of referral of the case of the child prepared in terms of section 65 of the Act.

(4) The Principal Reporter shall, when giving notice under paragraph (3), advise the child, any relevant person and any safeguarder—

(a) of their entitlement to make their views on the matters to be considered by the business meeting known to the Principal Reporter, and

(b) that any such views shall be presented by him to the meeting.

(5) The Principal Reporter shall record in writing any views given to him other than in writing under paragraph (4), for the purpose of presenting these views to the business meeting for consideration.

(6) The Principal Reporter shall as soon as reasonably practicable after receiving any views give a copy of these views in writing to the members of the children's panel who will attend the business meeting and to the other persons who received notice of the meeting under paragraph (3).

(7) Before making a determination, or giving guidance or directions to the Principal Reporter, the business meeting shall consider any views given to them under paragraph (6).

(8) Where the business meeting has made a determination, or given guidance or directions to the Principal Reporter as to the exercise of his functions, the Principal Reporter shall as soon as reasonably practicable give notice in writing of the determination or, as the case may be, the guidance or direction, to the child, any relevant person and any safeguarder.

NOTE
1. 1995 c.36; s.45(2) was amended by the Criminal Procedure (Consequential Provisions) (Scotland) Act 1995 (c.40), Sch.4, para.97.

**Notification of children's hearings and provision of documents to chairman and members, relevant persons etc.**

**5.**—(1) Subject to the 1996 Regulations, where the Principal Reporter arranges any children's hearing, he shall wherever practicable at least seven days before the date of the hearing notify the chairman and members of the time and place of the hearing and, subject as aforesaid, as soon as reasonably practicable but not later than three days before the date of the hearing, he shall give to each of them a copy of any of the following documents as are relevant to the case of a child to be considered at the hearing:-

   (a) a report of a local authority on the child and his social background;
   (b) the statement of the grounds for the referral of the case to the children's hearing prepared under rule 18;
   (c) any judicial remit or reference or any reference by a local authority;
   (d) any supervision requirement to which the child is subject;
   (e) any report prepared by any safeguarder appointed in the case;
   (f) any views of the child given in writing to the Principal Reporter by virtue of rule 15(4).

(2) If the Principal Reporter has obtained any information (including any views of the child given orally to the Principal Reporter by virtue of rule 15) or any document, other than a document mentioned in paragraph (1) which is material to the consideration of the case of a child at any children's hearing, he shall make that information or copies of that document available to the chairman and members of the children's hearing before the hearing.

(3) Where the Principal Reporter gives a copy of any document to the chairman and members of the children's hearing under paragraph (1), or make available to them information or any document or copy thereof under paragraph (2), he shall at the same time give a copy of the document or, as the case may be, make available the information or a copy of the document, to—

(a) each relevant person in relation to the child, whose case is to be considered at the children's hearing; and

(b) any father of the child whose case is to be considered at the children's hearing who is living with the mother of the child where both the father and the mother are parents of the child as defined in section 15(1) of the Act,

except that where a children's hearing is arranged to continue consideration of the case of the child by virtue section 69(2) of the Act, this obligation of the Principal Reporter shall apply only in respect of any information or document which has not already been made available to the person concerned.

(4) The chairman and members of children's hearings shall keep securely in their custody and documents made available to them under this rule and, except as otherwise provided in rules 20(4) and 22(4), they shall not cause or permit any information contained in the documents or otherwise disclosed during the hearing to be made known to any person.

(5) Immediately after the conclusion of a children's hearing the chairman and members shall return to the Principal Reporter any documents which have been made available to them under this rule.

(6) Any information or document which the Principal Reporter makes available under this rule to the chairman and members of any children's hearing shall also be made available, if requested, to any member of the Scottish Committee of the Council on Tribunals who is attending that hearing and the Council on Tribunals shall be required to return all papers to the Principal Reporter at the end of the hearing.

(7) Any information or document which the Principal Reporter makes available under this rule to the chairman and members of any children's hearing shall also be made available, if requested, to any member of the Children's Panel Advisory Committee or to any member of a sub-committee of the Advisory Committee who has given notice of his intention to attend that hearing as an observer. Any person provided with papers under this rule shall not cause or permit any information contained in the said documents or otherwise disclosed during the hearing to be made known to any person and shall return to the Principal Reporter at the end of the hearing any document which has been made available to him.

### Notification of children's hearings to children

**6.**—(1) Subject to paragraphs (2) and (3), where the Principal Reporter arranges a children's hearing he shall not less than 7 days before the hearing give notice in writing to the child whose case has been referred to the hearing of his right and obligation to attend the hearing and of the date, time and place of the hearing.

(2) Where the Principal Reporter arranges a children's hearing—

(a) to consider under section 45(7), 59(2), 68(10) or by virtue of section 82(5) of the Act the case of a child kept in a place of safety;

(b) to consider under Chapters 2 or 3 of Part II of the Act the case of a child placed in secure accommodation under regulation 7 of the 1996 Regulations;

(c) to review an application under section 51(9) of the Act for the suspension of a supervision requirement; or

(d) to review the case of a child transferred under section 72 of the Act to a place of residence other than that named in the supervision requirement;

he shall as soon as reasonably practicable before the hearing give the notice required under paragraph (1) above in writing; provided that if such notice cannot be given in writing, the Principal Reporter may give notice to the child orally.

(3) Where under section 45(2) of the Act a children's hearing are satisfied either in a case as specified in 45(2) of the Act that the attendance of the child is not necessary or in any case that it would be detrimental to the interests of the child for him to be present at the hearing of his case, the Principal Reporter shall give him notice in writing of his right under section 45(1) of the Act to attend the hearing and of the date, time and place of the hearing.

(4) When giving to a child under this rule notice of a children's hearing to which rule 15 applies, the Principal Reporter shall inform the child—

(a) of the entitlement by virtue of section 16(2) of the Act and these rules to indicate whether he wishes to express his views;

(b) that if he does so wish, he will be given an opportunity to express them; and

(c) that any such views as may be given by the child to the Principal Reporter before the time at which the children's hearing is to be held will be conveyed by the Principal Reporter to the members of the children's hearing, to any relevant person and to any safe-guarder, for the purpose of the hearing.

**Notification of children's hearings to relevant persons and certain parents with right to attend**

7.—(1) Where a relevant person in relation to child whose case is to be considered at a children's hearing, has a right to and is obliged under section 45(8) of the Act to attend at all stages of the hearing, the Principal Reporter shall give him notice in writing, if his whereabouts are known, of the right to and obligation to attend at all stages of the hearing and of the date, time and place of the hearing.

(2) Where under section 45(8) of the Act a children's hearing are satisfied either that it would be unreasonable to require the attendance of a relevant person at a children's hearing or that the attendance of that person would be unnecessary for the proper consideration of the case, the Principal Reporter shall give him notice in writing, if his where-abouts are known, of his right under section 45(8) of the Act to attend at all stages of the hearing and of the date, time and place of the hearing but that for the above reason or reasons he is not obliged to attend.

(3) Where a person has a right by virtue of rule 12(1) to attend at all stages of the children's hearing, the Principal Reporter shall give such notice in writing of his right, if his whereabouts are known.

(4) Any notice under this rule, except a notification to a relevant person of a children's hearing mentioned under rule 6(2), shall be given not later than seven days before the date of the children's hearing to which it relates.

(5) In the case of such a children's hearing mentioned in rule 6(2), the notice to the relevant person under paragraph (1) shall be given as soon

as reasonably practicable in writing before the hearing, and if such notice cannot be given in writing the Principal Reporter may give notice to a relevant person orally.

### Notification of children's hearing to chief social work officer

**8.** Where the Principal Reporter arranges any children's hearing he shall notify the chief social work officer of the local authority for the area in which the children's hearing is to sit of the date, time and place of the hearing, and of the name, date of birth and address, so far as is known of the child whose case is to be considered.

### Withholding of address where disclosure may result in serious harm

**9.** Where in fulfilling his obligations under rules 5, 7 or 8 the Principal Reporter considers that the disclosure of the whereabouts of the child or any relevant person may place that person at risk of serious harm (whether or not physical harm) he may withhold such information as is necessary to prevent such disclosure and indicate the address of the person as that of the Principal Reporter.

### Constitution of children's hearing and functions of chairman of children's hearing

**10.**—(1) The selection of the chairman and the members of any children's hearing from among the member of the children's panel for a local authority area shall be made either directly by the chairman of the children's panel, or in his absence by the deputy chairman, or by the operation of standing arrangements in that behalf made by the chairman of the children's panel after such consulting the Principal Reporter and such members of the panel as he may think fit. Such standing arrangements may provide for the selection of the chairman and members of any hearing to be made by members of the panel appointed for that purpose by the chairman of the panel.

(2) The chairman of the children's panel shall keep under review any standing arrangements which he has made under paragraph (1) and shall from time to time consult the Principal Reporter and such members of the panel as the thinks fit as to the operation of those arrangements.

(3) Except as otherwise provided by these Rules and any other enactment, the procedure at any children's hearing shall be such as the chairman shall in his discretion determine.

(4) Without prejudice to the generality of paragraph (3) and to the power of a children's hearing under the Act to continue a hearing for the further investigation of a case, the chairman of a children's hearing may at any time during the hearing adjourn the hearing provided that any adjournment under this rule shall be such as to enable the children's hearing to sit again on the same days as the adjournment was made.

(5) As soon as reasonably practicable after a children's hearing make—

(a) a decision disposing of the case of a child on a referral or at a review of a supervision requirement or a condition imposed under section 70(9) of the Act with respect to residence in secure accommodation;

(b) a decision to issue a warrant to find a child or for the keeping of a child in a place of safety or to continue a warrant for the the keeping of such a child;

(c) a requirement or warrant, or continuation of a warrant, under section 69 of the Act,

the chairman shall make or cause to be made a report of the decision and a statement in writing of the reasons for the decision, and shall sign the report and statement.

## PART III

## GENERAL PROVISIONS AS TO CHILDREN'S HEARING

**Representation for the purposes of assisting children and relevant persons at children's hearing**

**11.**—(1) Any child whose case comes before a children's hearing and any relevant person who attends that children's hearing may each be accompanied by one person for the purpose of assisting the child, or as the case may be, the relevant person at the hearing.

(2) Any representative attending any children's hearing may assist the person whom he represents in the discussion of the case of the child with the children's hearing.

(3) In these Rules any reference to a representative is a reference to a person who under this rule assists a child or a relevant person or both, and includes, unless the context otherwise requires, a reference both to any representative of a child and any representative of a relevant person.

**General attendance at hearings of certain parents of the child (not relevant persons) and specific limited right of duly authorised officials etc.**

**12.**—(1) A father of the child as described in rule 5(3)(b) shall be entitled to attend at all stages of the children's hearing while the hearing are considering the case of the child but shall be subject to the same provisions as those contained in section 46 of the Act as if those provisions apply to him.

(2) A constable, prison officer or other person duly authorised who has in his lawful custody a person who has to attend a children's hearing shall be entitled to be present at the hearing for the purposes of escorting that person.

**Persons who may attend children's hearings at chairman's discretion**

**13.** Without prejudice to the right of a child and of a relevant person under rule 11 above to be accompanied at a children's hearing by a representative, and subject to subsections (1) to (3) of section 43 of the Act (provisions as to privacy of children's hearings), the persons whose presence at the children's hearing may be permitted by the chairman under the said subsection (1) shall be—

(a) the chairman and members of the Children's Panel Advisory Committee for the local authority area of the children's hearing and the clerk to the Children's Panel Advisory Committee of the local authority;

(b) any members or possible members of children's panels whose attendance is required at children's hearings for the purpose of their training as members of children's hearings, and their instructors;

(c) any student engaged in formal education or training in social work or any person engaged in research relating to children who may be in need of compulsory measures of supervision; and

(d) any other person whose presence at the hearing may in the opinion of the chairman be justified by special circumstances.

### Safeguarders

**14.**—(1) Where a children's hearing appoint a safeguarder under section 41(1) of the Act, the chairman shall state in writing the reasons for their decision to make that appointment.

(2) The Principal Reporter shall give the safeguarder a copy of such statement and also give notice of the date, time and place of the hearing at the same time and in the same manner as giving notice to a relevant person under rule 7.

(3) Any safeguarder appointed by a children's hearing shall be entitled to be present throughout the duration of any hearing of the case until the disposal of the case.

(4) where a safeguarder is appointed by a children's hearing, he shall—

(a) prepare a report in writing one the case of the child; and

(b) prepare any further report in writing on the case as the hearing may require,

and give the report or, as the case maybe, the further report to the Principal Reporter.

(5) Any information or document which the Principal Reporter makes available compliance with rule 5 (under exception of rule (5)(1)(e)) or otherwise to the chairman and members of any children's hearing shall also be made available to any safeguarder regardless of the date his appointment in the proceedings.

(6) A safeguarder—

(a) shall keep securely in his custody any documents made available to him under paragraph (4);

(b) shall not cause or permit any information contained in the documents or otherwise disclosed during the hearing to be made know to any person, other than may be necessary for the performance of his own duties; and

(c) shall return to the Principal Reporter any document which has been made available to him under paragraph (4) above when he has completed with his appointment.

### Views of the Child

**15.**—(1) The Children's hearing, taking account of the age and maturity of the child whose case has been referred to hearing for a purpose mentioned in paragraph (2) shall so far as practicable give the child an opportunity to indicate whether he wishes to express his views.

(2) This rule shall apply where the children's hearing—

(a) are considering whether to make, or are reviewing a supervision requirement;

(b) are considering whether to grant a warrant under subsections (4) or (5) of section 45, subsection (5) of section 63, subsection (1) of section 66, or subsection (4) or (7) of section 69, of the Act or provide under subsection (5) of the said section 66 for the continuation of a warrant;

(c) are considering whether to continue a child protection order under section 59(4) of the Act;

(d) are engaged in providing advice under section 60(10) of the Act; or

(e) are considering whether to make requirement under section 69(3) of the Act;

(f) are drawing up a report under section 73(13) of the Act, and

(g) are considering whether to issue a warrant under 1996 Regulations.

(3) Where he has indicated his wish to express his views—

(a) the children's hearing and the chairman of the hearing may exercise any of their powers under the Act or these Rules as they or, as the case may be, he considers appropriate in order to ascertain the views of the child; and

(b) the Children;'s hearing shall not make any decision or take any action mentioned in paragraph (2) unless an opportunity has been given for the views of the child to be obtained or heard and in terms of section 16(2)(c) of the Act they have had regard to such views as he may have expressed.

(4) Without prejudice to the generality of the Powers mentioned in paragraph (3)(a), the views of the child may be conveyed to the children's hearing—

(a) by the child, or by his representative, individually or together in person;

(b) by the child in writing, on audio or video tape or through an interpreter; or

(c) by any safeguarder appointed by the hearing.

(5) For the purpose of this rule, a child of twelve years of age or more shall be presumed to be of sufficient age and maturity to form a view.

## PART IV

## CHILDREN'S HEARINGS ON REFERRAL AND AT REVIEW OF SUPERVISION REQUIREMENTS

### Application of Part IV

**16.** This Part shall, subject to the provisions thereof, apply to (a) any Children's hearing arranged under Part II of the Act or under the 1996 Regulations either for the purposes of considering and determining on referral the case of any child or for the review of a supervision requirement or a condition imposed by section 70(9) of the Act with respect to residence in secure accommodation; and (b) any children's hearing to which a case is stood referred under section 49(4) of the 1995 Act.

### Statement of grounds of referral

**17.**—(1) The statement of the grounds for the referral of a case to a children's hearing shall be signed by the Principal Reporter and shall specify which one or more of the conditions mentioned in section 52(2) of the Act is or are considered by the Principal Reporter to be satisfied with respect to the child, and the statement shall state the facts on the basis of which it is sought to show that any condition is satisfied.

(2) In the case of a condition mentioned in section 52(2)(i) of the Act, the statement of the facts constituting the offence shall have the same degree of specification as is required by section 138(4) of the 1995 Act in a charge in a complaint and the statement shall also specify the nature of the offence in question.

### Notification of statement of grounds for referral

**18.**—(1) Subject to paragraphs (2) and (3), where the Principal Reporter arranges a children's hearing under section 65(1) of the Act, he shall—

(a) prepare a statement of the grounds for the referral of the case to children's hearing; and

(b) not less than seven days before the date of the hearing give a copy of the statement to the child and to each relevant person whose whereabouts are known.

(2) Notwithstanding paragraph (1), Where before the children's hearing the child is kept in a safe place under the Act, or so kept by virtue of the 1996 Regulations, the provisions of paragraphs (1)(a) and (b) shall apply except that in paragraph (1)(b) the words "as soon as reasonably practicable" shall be substituted for the words " not less than seven days".

(3) Notwithstanding paragraph (1), Where the Principal Reporter arranges a children's hearing under the section 65(2) of the Act, the provisions of paragraphs (1)(a) and (b) shall apply except that in paragraph (1)(b) the words "not less than three days " shall be substituted for the words "not less than seven days ".

(4) Notwithstanding that a children's hearing proceeds in accordance with section 65 of the Act to more than one hearing, nothing in this rule shall require a copy of the statement to be given to any person more than once.

### Notification of application to sheriff for finding as to grounds if they consider it appropriate to do so for referral

**19.** Where a children's hearing have given a direction to the Principal Reporter under section 65 of the Act to apply sheriff for a finding as to whether or not any grounds for the referral of any case to them are satisfied, the Principal Reporter shall give notice of this in writing to the child and to any relevant person.

### Conduct of Children's hearing considering case on referral or at review of supervision requirement

**20.**—(1) This rule applies to children's hearing considering under section 65 of the Act a case on referral or at a review under section 73(8) of the Act of a supervision requirement.

(2) Unless a children's hearing consider the case of a child in the absence of the child, any relevant person and any representative, the chairman shall, before the children's hearing proceeds to consider the case, explain the purpose of the hearing to such persons as are present.

(3) In Proceeding with the case the children's hearing shall—

(a) consider a report of a local authority on the child and his social background, and any relevant information available to them;

(b) consider any report submitted by the manager of any residential establishment in which the child is required to reside;

(c) discuss the case with the child, any relevant person, any safeguarder and representative if attending the hearing;

(d) take steps under rule 15 to obtain the views of the child, and endeavour to obtain the views of any relevant person and of any safeguarder, if attending the hearing, on what arrangements would be in the best interests of the child.

(4) The chairman shall inform the child and any relevant person of the substance of any reports, documents and information mentioned in paragraph (3)(a) and (b) if it appears to him that this is material to the manner in which the case of the child should be disposed of and that its disclosure would not be detrimental to the interests of the child.

(5) After the children's hearing have considered the case of the child and made a decision disposing of the case, but before the conclusion of the hearing at which the decision is made, the chairman shall inform the child, any relevant person, any safeguarder, and any representative, if attending the hearing, of—

(a) the decision of the hearing;

(b) the reasons for the decision;

(c) the right of the child and of the relevant person under section 51(1) of the Act to appeal to the sheriff against the decision and, where the appeal is against a decision relating to a supervision requirement, to apply to the children's hearing for suspension of the requirement appealed against.

(6) The children's hearing shall not dispose of the case by making a supervision requirement under section 70(1) of the Act requiring the child to reside at any place or places specified in the requirement (which for the purposes of this rule is a place or places where he is to be under the charge or control of a person who is not a relevant person) unless—

(a) they have received and considered a report from the local authority for the purposes of paragraph (3)(a), together with recommendations from that authority on—

(i) the needs of a child;

(ii) the suitability to meet those needs of the place or places in which the child is to reside by virtue of the supervision requirement, and of the person or persons who is or are to have charge of or control over the child, and

(b) the local authority have confirmed to the hearing that in compiling the report they have carried out the procedures and gathered the information described in regulation 15 of the Fostering of Children (Scotland) Regulations 1996.

**Notification of decisions, etc on referral or at review of supervision requirement**

**21.**—(1) Subject to sections 70(6) and 73(11) of the Act, as soon as reasonably practicable after a children's hearing have made a decision disposing of the case of a child under this Part of the Rules, the principal Reporter shall send to the child, any relevant person, any safeguarder and the local authority—

   (a) notice of the decision and a copy of any supervision requirement or, as the case may be, any continuation of a supervision requirement;

   (b) a copy of the statement of reasons for the decision; and

   (c) except in the case of a review which continues a supervision requirement, being a review in relation to which an order under section 51(7) of the Act is in force, notice of the right of the child or, as the case may be, a relevant person under section 51 of the Act to appeal to the sheriff against the decision,

and such notice shall be given in writing.

   (2) Where a children's hearing have made a decision disposing of the case of a child, the Principal Reporter shall as soon as reasonably practicable give notice of the decision—

   (a) to any person with whom the child is residing; and

   (b) where the information leading to the investigation of the case of the child was given by an officer of a police force, to the chief constable of the police area.

   (3) Where the decision was—

   (a) to make a supervision requirement in relation to a child who has attained the age of 16 years; or

   (b) to terminate a supervision requirement relating to such a child,

the Principal Reporter shall as soon as reasonably practicable give notice of the decision to the chief constable of the police are and if the child resides outwith the police area, to the chief constable of the police area in which the child resides.

## PART V

## REFERENCES FOR ADVICE AND SUSPENSION OF SUPER-VISION REQUIREMENTS

**Conduct of children's hearing on reference for advice by court, the local authority or approved adoption society**

   **22.**—(1) This rule shall apply to any children's hearing arranged in order to consider the case of a child for the purpose of giving advice to the court, the local authority or the approved adoption society under any of the following provisions:-

     section 73(13) of the Act (advice in relation to placing for adoption, application for adoption order, freeing for adoption order or parental responsibilities order);

     subsection (1)(b) or (6) of section 49 of the 1995 Act (reference by court for advice in case of child not subject to supervision requirement);

     section 49(3) of the 1995 Act (reference by court for advice in case of child subject to supervision requirement);

     section 22A(2) of the 1978 Act (advice in relation to placing a child for adoption).

   (2) Unless the children's hearing consider the case of a child in the absence of the child, a relevant person and any representative, the chairman shall, before the children's hearing proceed to consider the case, explain the purpose of the hearing to such persons as are present.

   (3) The children's hearing shall proceed to consider the case of the child and during such consideration shall—

(a) consider the reference by the court, the local authority or the approved adoption society, any supervision requirement to which the child is subject, a report of a local authority on the child and his social background, and any other relevant document or any relevant information available to them;

(b) discuss the case of the child and afford to the child, any relevant person, any safeguarder and any representative, if attending the hearing, an opportunity of participating in the discussion and of being heard on the case;

(c) take steps on rule 15 to obtain the views of the child, and endeavour to obtain the views of any relevant person, and of any safeguarder if attending the hearing, on what arrangements with respect to the child would be in the best interests of the child;

and the children's hearing shall thereafter determine what advice they will give to the court, the local authority or, as the case may be, the approved adoption society.

(4) The chairman shall inform the child and each relevant person whose whereabouts are known of the substance of any reports, documents and information mentioned in paragraph (3)(a) if it appears to him that this is material to the advice that will be given and that its disclosure would not be detrimental to the interests of the child.

(5) After the children's hearing have considered the case of the child and determined the advice they shall provide, the hearing shall inform the child, any relevant person, any safeguarder and any representative, if attending the hearing of that advice.

(6) As soon as reasonably practicable after the children's hearing determine the advice they shall provide, the chairman shall make or cause to be made a report in writing providing that advice, including a statement of the reasons for that advice, and the chairman of the hearing shall sign the report and statement.

(7) Within 7 days following a determination by the children's hearing, the Principal Reporter shall send a copy of the report prepared under paragraph (6) to the court, the local authority or the approved adoption society, as the case may be, and the child, any relevant person and any safeguarder appointed in the proceedings.

(8) Where the Principal Reporter is obliged under section 73(8)(a)(iv) of the Act to arrange a children's hearing and he is advised by the adoption agency that it has determined that agreement to an application under section 16 or 18 of the 1978 Act is unlikely to be forthcoming, he shall be under an obligation to arrange a hearing to sit within 21 days of that notification from the local authority under section 73(4)(c) of the Act.

**Application for suspension of supervision requirements pending hearing of appeals**

**23.**—(1) An application to a children's hearing by a child or relevant person under section 51(9) of the Act for the suspension of a supervision requirement pending an appeal under section 51(1) of the Act shall be made in writing to the Principal Reporter.

(2) The Principal Reporter shall give notice in writing separately to the child and relevant person of the date, time and place of the children's hearing at which the application will be considered.

(3) The children's hearing shall afford the applicant, and his representative, and any safeguarder if attending the hearing, an opportunity of being heard.

(4) The chairman of the children's hearing shall inform the applicant at the conclusion of the hearing of the decision of the hearing and the reasons for it.

(5) If the applicant fails to attend the hearing, the application shall be treated as abandoned.

(6) An application under this rule shall not be valid unless an appeal under section 51(1) of the Act has already been lodged.

## PART VI

## MISCELLANEOUS AND SUPPLEMENTAL

### Social background report where child in a place of safety

**24.** Subject to the 1996 Regulations, where a children's hearing is arranged under section 65(2) of the Act, the children's hearing shall not proceed in relation to the case of the child in accordance with section 70(1) of the Act unless the Principal Reporter has made available to them a report of local authority on the child and his social background.

### Form of supervision requirement

**25.**—(1) Subject to paragraph (2) below, a supervision requirement under section 70(1) of the Act shall be in the form of Form 1.

(2) A supervision requirement under section 70(1) of the Act with a specification under section 70(9) of the Act (residence in secure accommodation) shall be in the form of Form 2.

(3) Subject to paragraph (4) below, a continuation under section 73(9)(e) of the Act of a supervision requirement (with any variation of the requirement or insertion in the requirement mentioned in paragraph (9)(c) and (d) of that subsection) shall be in the form of Form 3.

(4) A continuation under section 73(9)(e) of the Act of a supervision requirement (with a variation of the requirement or insertion in the requirement as mentioned in relation to a specification as to secure accommodation as described in section 70(9) of the Act) shall be in the form of Form 4.

### Procedure relating to warrants, orders, and to requirements under section 69(3) of the Act

**26.**—(1) Where a children's hearing consider in relation to a child the question whether they should—
  (a) issue or continue a warrant or order under any of the following provisions of the Act:-
  section 45(4) and (5) (warrants to find child, keep in a place of safety and bring before a hearing);
  section 59(4) (continuation of child protection order);
  section 63(5) (warrant to keep child in place of safety following arrest);
  section 66(1) and (5) (warrants where children's hearing unable to dispose of case);

section 69(4) (warrant for fulfilment of requirement to attend or reside at clinic, hospital, etc); and

section 69(7) (warrant to take child to and keep in place of safety while case continued under section 59(4) of the Act).

(b) continue under section 59(4) of the Act any direction given under section 58 (direction as to parental responsibilities or parental rights when child protection order made); or

(c) issue a warrant under the 1996 Regulations;

(d) make a requirement under section 69(3) of the Act (requirement to reside at clinic, etc.),

the children's hearing shall, before they make a decision to issue that warrant or as the case may be that requirement, take steps under rule 15 to obtain the views of the child, and endeavour to obtain the views of any relevant person and of any safeguarder, if attending the hearing, on what arrangements would be in the best interests of the child.

(2) Where a children's hearing have issued or, as the case may be, continued such a warrant, order, discretion or requirement as is mentioned in paragraph (1), the Principal Reporter shall send as soon as reasonably practicable to the child, any relevant person and any safeguarder appointed in the proceedings—

(a) a copy of the warrant, continuation of the warrant, continuation of the order, or requirement and a copy of the statement of the reasons for the decision; and

(b) notice of the right of the child, or, as the case may be, the relevant person under section 51 of the Act to appeal to the sheriff against the decision.

**Forms of warrants and orders for finding and keeping a child in a place of safety**

**27.** The orders or warrants listed and described in the left hand column of the chart below shall be in the form of the Forms (as defined in rule 2(2)(b)) opposite in the right hand column which are in the Schedule to these Rules and references to sections shall be to sections in the Act. The description in the left hand column is for ease of reference and does not reproduce the provisions of the Act in full.

| | *LEFT HAND COLUMN* | *RIGHT HAND COLUMN* |
|---|---|---|
| S45(4) & (5) | Warrant under section 45(4) or 45(5) to find a child, keep him in a place of safety and bring him before a children's hearing | Form 5 |
| S59(4) | Continuation under section 59(4) of a child protection order | Form 6 |
| | Continuation under section 59(4) of a child protection order with first authorisation to remove child and to keep child in place of safety with/ without order of non-disclosure of place of safety | Form 7 |
| S63(5) | Warrant under section 63(5) to keep a child in place of safety with/ without order of non-disclosure of place of safety | Form 8 |

|  | Warrant under section 63(5) with order that child liable to be kept in secure accommodation with/without order of non-disclosure of place of safety | Form 9 |
|---|---|---|
|  | Continuation under section 63(5) of warrant to keep a child in a place of safety | Form 10 |
|  | Continuation under section 63(5) of warrant to keep a child in a place of safety with first authorisation that child liable to be kept in secure accommodation with/without order of non-disclosure of place of safety | Form 11 |
| S66(1) | Warrant under section 66(1) to keep a child in a place of safety when hearing unable to dispose of case | Form 12 |
|  | Warrant under 66(1) to keep a child in a place of safety when hearing unable to dispose of case with order that child liable to be kept in secure accommodation with/without order of non-disclosure of place of safety | Form 13 |
| S66(5) | Continuation under section 66(5) of warrant granted under section 66(1) to keep a child in a place of safety | Form 14 |
|  | Continuation under section 66(5) of warrant granted under section 66(1) to keep a child in a place of safety with first order that child liable to be kept in secure accommodation with/without order of non-disclosure of place of safety | Form 15 |
| S69(4) | Warrant under section 69(4) to find a child and remove to a place of safety when requirement under section 69(3) not fulfilled (where continuation of case) | Form 16 |
|  | Warrant under section 69(4) to find child and remove to place of safety when requirement under section 69(3) not fulfilled with first order that child liable to be kept in secure accommodation with/without order of non-disclosure of place of safety (where continuation of case) | Form 17 |
| S69(7) | Warrant under section 69(7) to keep a child in a place of safety (where continuation of case) | Form 18 |

| | |
|---|---|
| Warrant under section 69(7) to keep a child in a place of safety when there is a continuation of the case by the children's hearing with order to keep child in secure accommodation with/without order of non-disclosure of place of safety (where continuation of case) | Form 19 |

## Miscellaneous Forms

**28.**—(1) A requirement under section 69(3) of the Act shall be in the form of Form 20.

(2) A notification by a Principal Reporter under section 60(3) of the Act shall be in the form of Form 21.

(3) A notification by a Principal Reporter under section 60(5) of the Act shall be in the form of Form 22.

(4) A report of a children's hearing of advice under section 60(10) of the Act shall be in the form of Form 23.

(5) A report of a children's heaving order section 73(13) of the Act shall be in the form of Form 24.

## Authentication of documents

**29.**—(1) A report of any decision, a statement of reasons for a decision or of advice, a warrant or continuation of warrants for finding and keeping a child in a place of safety, or any other writing, authorised or required by Chapter 2 or 3 of the Act or these Rules to be made, given, issued or granted by a children's hearing or by the chairman of a children's hearing shall be sufficiently authenticated if it is signed by the chairman, or, if he is unavailable, by a member of that hearing.

(2) Any document authorised or required by these Rules to be made or executed by the Principal Reporter shall be sufficiently authenticated if it is signed by the Principal Reporter or by a person duly authorised by him.

(3) Any copy of any document authorised or required by these Rules to be given or issued by the Principal Reporter may be certified as a true copy by the Principal Reporter or by a person duly authorised by him.

## Service of notification and other documents

**30.**—(1) Any notice in writing or other document and any oral notification authorised or required under these Rules to be given or issued by the Principal Reporter may be given or issued by the Principal Reporter or by a person duly authorised by him or by any constable.

(2) Any notice in writing or other document authorised or required by these Rules to be given or issued to a child or to a relevant person may be—

(a) delivered to him in person; or

(b) left for him at his dwellinghouse or place of business or where he has no known dwellinghouse or place of business, at any other place in which he may at the time be resident; or

(c) where he is the master of, or a seaman or other person employed in, a vessel, left with a person on board thereof and connected therewith; or

(d) sent by post in a registered or first class service recorded delivery letter to his dwellinghouse or place of business.

(3) Where the Principal Reporter or a person duly authorised by him gives to any relevant person a notification in writing under paragraph (1) of rule 7 above, or an oral notification under that paragraph as read with paragraph (4) of that rule, he shall execute a certificate of notification in the form of Form 25.

(4) Where a notice under rule 6 or 7 or a copy of such a statement as is mentioned in rule 18 is sent by post in accordance with paragraph (2)(d) of this rule, the notification or copy shall be deemed, for the purpose of rule 6, 7 or 18, as the case may be, to have been given the day following the date of posting.

**Reports of proceedings of children's hearing**

**31.**—(1) In relation to the case of any child which comes before a children's hearing, it shall be the duty of the Principal Reporter to keep a report of the proceedings of that hearing and the report—

(a) shall include the information specified in paragraph (2) below; and

(b) may include such other information about the proceedings as the Principal Reporter thinks appropriate.

(2) The information referred to in paragraph (1)(a) above is as follows—

(a) particulars of the place and date of the hearing;

(b) the full name and address of the child and his sex and date of birth;

(c) the full name and address (so far as these can be obtained) of the father, the mother and any other relevant person in relation to the child;

(d) a record as to which (if any) of the persons mentioned in sub-paragraphs (b) and (c) above was present;

(e) the full name and address of any representative attending the hearing;

(f) the full name and address of any safeguarder;

(g) the terms of any decision disposing the case of the child, or of any decision to issue a warrant, made by the children's hearing or any other course of action taken by them with respect to the child; and

(h) in any case where the children's hearing proceed in accordance with section 65 of the Act—

(i) particulars of the grounds of referral which are accepted or, as the case may be, not accepted, and by whom;

(ii) a record of any direction under subsection (7) or (9) of section 65 to make application to the sheriff for a finding under that section; and

(iii) a record of whether the children's hearing proceeded to consider that the case at a hearing.

**Travelling and subsistence expenses**

**32.**—(1) Subject to paragraph (2), the local authority for the area of a children's hearing shall, if a claim is made to them, pay to or in respect of any child, or to any relevant person, or to any one representative of either attending any children's hearing, a sum equal to such travelling expenses and such expenses or subsistence as have, in the opinion of the local authority, been reasonable incurred by or in respect of the child or, as the case may be, by the relevant person or by any representative of either for the purpose of enabling the said child, relevant person or representative to attend that hearing.

(2) A claim under this rule shall be in writing and shall be made before the expiry of the period of one month commencing with the date of the children's hearing to which the claim relates.

**Notification of 16th birthday of child subject to supervision requirement**

**33.** When a child subject to a supervision requirement attains the age of 16 years, the Principal Reporter shall as soon as reasonably practicable give notice of that fact to the chief constable of the police area.

## SCHEDULE

Rule 25(1)

## FORM 1

## SUPERVISION REQUIREMENT

(Place and Date)

A children's hearing for (local authority area), having considered the case of (name and address of child) and in exercise of the powers conferred by section 70 of the Children (Scotland) Act 1995, being satisfied that he/she is in need of compulsory measures of supervision require him/her* [to be under the supervision of the chief social work officer of (name of local authority)]* [to reside in (name of place or places) [to comply with the conditions stated below.]

[The children's hearing order that the place/places* where (name the child) is to reside in accordance with the requirement shall not be disclosed to (person or class of persons)]*

## CONDITIONS REFERRED TO IN THE FOREGOING SUPER-VISION REQUIREMENT

**1.** [ ]

........................................
Chairman of the Children's Hearing

*Delete as appropriate

Rule 25(2)

FORM 2

SUPERVISION REQUIREMENT UNDER SECTION 70(1) OF THE ACT AUTHORISING PLACEMENT IN SECURE ACCOMMODATION

(Place and Date)

A children's hearing for (local authority area) having considered the case of (name and address of child) and in exercise of the powers conferred by sections 70(1), 70(3) and 70(9) of the Children (Scotland) Act 1995 being satisfied (firstly) that the child is in need of compulsory measures of supervision, and (secondly)

[that he/she* has previously absconded and is likely to abscond unless he/she* is kept in secure accommodation, and, that if he/she* absconds, it is likely that his/her* physical, mental or moral welfare will be at risk]*

[that he/she* is likely to injure himself/herself* or some other person unless he/she* is kept in secure accommodation]*,

require him/her* to be under the supervision of the chief social work officer for (name of local authority) and to reside in (name of residential establishment providing secure accommodation subject to the conditions noted below.

[name of the place or places]* (see Note below)

[The children's hearing order that the place where (name of child) is to reside shall not be disclosed to (person or class of person)]*

CONDITIONS REFERRED TO IN THE FOREGOING SUPERVISION REQUIREMENT

**1.** The child is liable to be placed and kept in secure accommodation in (name of residential establishment) at such times as the person in charge of the residential establishment, with the agreement of the chief social work officer of (name of local authority) considers it necessary that the child do so.

..........

Chairman of the Children's Hearing

*Delete as appropriate

*Note:* If the residential establishment providing secure accommodation does not have an open residential facility there will also need to be a reference to some such place.

## FORM 3

## CONTINUATION UNDER SECTION 73(9)(e) OF THE ACT OF SUPERVISION REQUIREMENT

(Place and date)

A children's hearing for (local authority area), considering the case of (name and address of child) and the supervision requirement (a copy of which is attached), and in exercise of its powers under section 73(9)(e) of the Act, continues the said requirement [in force]* [subject to the variations of that requirement noted below]* [with the insertions in the requirement noted below]*

[The children's hearing in [varying]* [imposing]* a requirement order that the place where (name of child) is to reside shall not be disclosed to (person or class of persons)]*

[VARIATION[S] REFERRED TO]*

[INSERTION[S] REFERRED TO]*

..........

Chairman of the Children's Hearing

*Delete as appropriate

Rule 25(4)

## FORM 4

## CONTINUATION UNDER SECTION 73(9)(e) OF THE ACT OF SUPERVISION REQUIREMENT WITH VARIATION AUTHORISING PLACEMENT IN SECURE ACCOMMODATION

(Place and Date)

A children's hearing for (local authority area) having considered the case of (name and address of child) and in exercise of the powers conferred by sections 73(9)(e) of the Children (Scotland) Act 1995 being satisfied (firstly) that the child is in need of compulsory measures of supervision, and (secondly)

[that he/she* has previously absconded and is likely to abscond unless he/she* is kept in secure accommodation, and, that if he/she* absconds, it is likely that his/her* physical, mental or moral welfare will be at risk]*

[that he/she* is likely to injure himself/herself* or some other person unless he/she* is kept in secure accommodation]*,

grant continuation of the supervision requirement dated (ie sent date) a copy of which is attached, subject to the insertion of a requirement on him/her* to be under the supervision of the chief social work officer for (name of local authority) and to reside in (name of residential establishment providing secure accommodation. Subject to the conditions noted below and any other insertions in or variations of the supervision requirement noted below.

[name of place or places]* (see Note below)

[The children's hearing order that the place where (name of child) is to reside shall not be disclosed to (person or class of person)]*

## CONDITIONS VARIATIONS AND INSERTIONS REFERRED TO IN THE SUPERVISION REQUIREMENT

**1.** The child is liable to be placed and kept in secure accommodation in (name of residential establishment) at such times as the person in charge of the residential establishment, with the agreement of the chief social work officer of (name of local authority) considers it necessary that the child do so.

..........

Chairman of the Children's Hearing

*Delete as appropriate

*Note*: If the residential establishment providing secure accommodation does not have an open residential facility there will also need to be a reference to some such place.

Rule 27

## FORM 5

## WARRANT TO FIND A CHILD ETC, UNDER SECTION [45(4)]* [45(5)]* OF THE ACT

(Place and date)

A children's hearing for (local authority area) in respect of the case of (name and address of child)* and exercise of the powers conferred on them by section [45(4)]* [45(5)]* of the Children (Scotland) Act 1995, being satisfied that it is necessary for them to do so, grant warrant to find the child, and keep him/her in a place of safety and to bring him/her before a children's hearing.

..........

Chairman of the Children's Hearing

*Delete as appropriate

Rule 27

## FORM 6

## CONTINUATION UNDER SECTION 59(4) OF THE ACT OF A CHILD PROTECTION ORDER

(Place and date)

A children's hearing for (local authority area), in respect of the case of (name and address of child)* and exercise of the powers conferred on them by section 59(4) of the Children (Scotland) Act 1995, being satisfied that the conditions for the making of a child protection order under section 57 of the Act are established, continue the child protection order dated (insert date of CPO by sheriff, a copy of which is attached) [and the directions made under section 58 of the Act]* until (date) (insert date being date of hearing on eighth working day).

[For the duration of the Order the variation[s] of the [Order]* [and] [direction[s]]* as set out below shall have effect]*

### [VARIATIONS OF [ORDER]* [AND]* [DIRECTIONS]*

**1.** (insert variations)]*

..........

Chairman of the Children's Hearing

*Delete as appropriate

## FORM 7

Rule 27

## CONTINUATION UNDER SECTION 59(4) OF THE ACT OF A CHILD PROTECTION ORDER WITH FIRST AUTHORISATION OF REMOVAL OF CHILD TO PLACE OF SAFETY

(Place and date)

A children's hearing for (local authority area), in respect of the case of (name and address of child)* and in exercise of the powers conferred on them by section 59(4) of the Children (Scotland) Act 1995, being satisfied that the conditions for the making of a child protection order under section 57 of the Act are established, continue the child protection order dated (insert date of CPO by sheriff, a copy of which is attached) [and the directions made under section 58 of the Act]* until (date) (insert date being date of hearing on eighth working day).

[For the duration of the Order the variation[s] of the [Order]* [and] [direction[s]]* as set out below shall have effect]*

### [VARIATIONS OF [ORDER]* [AND]* [DIRECTIONS]*

**1.** The applicant shall be authorised to remove the child to and keep it (name of place or places of safety) subject to the following conditions:

**2.** [The place or plans of safety shall not be disclosed to (person or class of persons)]*

**3.**

Chairman of the Children's Hearing

*Delete as appropriate

Rule 27

## FORM 8

### WARRANT UNDER SECTION 63(5) OF THE ACT FOR KEEPING A CHILD IN A PLACE OF SAFETY

(Place and date)

A children's hearing for (local authority area) in respect of the case of (name and address of child) and in exercise of the powers conferred on them by section 63(5) of the Act, being satisfied [that it is necessary that the child should be kept in a place of safety in order to safeguard or promote his/her welfare]* [there is reason to believe that the child may fail to comply with a requirement that under section 69(3) of the Act]* [there is reason to believe that the child may not attend at any hearing of his/here case]* grant warrant to (insert name and address and where appropriate full designation of applicant) to keep that child in (name of place or places) for a period from (date) to (date) both days inclusive (insert period not exceeding 22 days) [and for the bringing of that child, before a children's hearing at (insert time and/or date)].

[For the duration of this warrant the child should be subject to the conditions

noted below]*

[The children's hearing in granting this warrant order that the place or places where the child is to reside in accordance with the warrant shall not be disclosed to (person or class of persons)]*

[CONDITIONS REFERRED TO IN THE FOREGOING WARRANT

**1.** (insert conditions)]*

............................

Chairman of the Children's Hearing

*Delete as appropriate

FORM 9

WARRANT UNDER SECTION 63(5) OF THE ACT FOR PLACING
AND KEEPING A CHILD IN PLACE OF SAFETY WITH
AUTHORISATION TO KEEP IN SECURE ACCOMMODATION

(Place and date)

A children's hearing for (local authority area), in respect of the case of
(name and address of child) and in exercise of the powers conferred on
them by section 63(5) of the Children (Scotland) Act 1995,

(firstly) being satisfied that [it is necessary that the child should be kept
in a place of safety in order to safeguard or promote his/her* welfare]*
[there is reason to believe that the child may not attend any hearing of
his/her* case]* [there is reason to believe that the child may not comply
with a requirement under section 69(3) of the Act]*

(secondly) being satisfied [that, having previously absconded, he/she* is
likely to abscond unless kept in secure accommodation, and that if he/
she* absconds it is likely that his/her* physical, mental or moral welfare
will be at risk]* [that he/she* is likely to injure himself/herself* or some
other person unless he/she* is kept in such accommodation]*,

grant warrant to (insert name and address and where appropriate full
designation of applicant) to keep the child in (name of residential
establishment providing the secure accommodation) for the period from
(date) to (date) (insert period not exceeding 22 days) both days inclusive
and order that during the duration of the warrant, pending the disposal
of his/her case, the child shall be liable to be placed and kept in secure
accommodation within the said residential establishment at such times as
the person in charge of the residential establishment, with the agreement
of the chief social work officer of (name of local authority), considers
necessary.

[name of place or places]* (see Note below)

[For the duration of this warrant the child should be subject to the
conditions noted below]* [The children's hearing in granting this warrant
order that the place where the child is to reside in accordance with the
warrant shall not be disclosed to (person or class of persons)]*

[CONDITIONS REFERRED TO IN THE FOREGOING WARRANT

**1.** (insert conditions)]*

..........

Chairman of the Children's Hearing

*Delete as appropriate

*Note:* If the residential establishment providing secure accommodation does not have an open residential facility, there will also need to be reference to some such place.

Rule 27

## FORM 10

### CONTINUATION UNDER SECTION 63(5) OF THE ACT OF A WARRANT FOR KEEPING A CHILD IN A PLACE OF SAFETY

(Place and date)

A children's hearing for (local authority area), in respect of the case of (name and address of child) and in exercise of the powers conferred on them by section 63(5) of the Children (Scotland) Act 1995, continues the warrant dated (insert date of warrant), a copy of which is attached, for the keeping of the child in a place of safety for a period from (date) to (date) both days inclusive (insert period not exceeding 22 days) [and for the bringing of that child before a children's hearing at (insert time and/ or date)].

[The continuation of the warrant is subject to the variations]* noted below]*

[VARIATIONS REFERRED TO

**1.** (insert variations)]*

..........

Chairman of the Children's Hearing

*Delete as appropriate

Rule 27

## FORM 11

### CONTINUATION UNDER SECTION 63(5) OF THE ACT OF A WARRANT FOR PLACING AND KEEPING A CHILD IN A PLACE OF SAFETY WITH FIRST AUTHORISATION TO KEEP THE CHILD IN SECURE ACCOMMODATION

(Place and date)

A children's hearing for (local authority area), in respect of the case of (name and address of child) and in exercise of the powers conferred on them by section 63(5) of the Children (Scotland) Act 1995.

(firstly) being satisfied that [it is necessary that the child shall be kept in a place of safety in order to safeguard or promote his/her* welfare]* [there is reason to believe that the child may not attend any hearing or his/her* case]* [there is reason to believe that the child may not comply with a requirement under section 69(3) of the Act]* (secondly) being satisfied [that, having previously absconded he/she* is likely to abscond unless kept in secure accommodation, and that if he/she* absconds it is likely that his/her* physical, mental or moral welfare will be at risk]* [that he/she* is likely to injure himself/herself* or some other person unless he/she* is kept in such accommodation]*,

grant continuation, subject to the variations noted below of the warrant dated (insert date of warrant), a copy of which is attached,

**Variations referred to above**
   **1.** The warrant is varied to read as a warrant to (name and address and where appropriate full designation of applicant) to keep the child in (name of residential establishment providing secure accommodation) for the period from (date) to (date) (insert period not exceeding 22 days) both days inclusive and with an order that during the duration of the warrant pending the disposal of his/her case, the child shall be liable to be placed and kept in secure accommodation within the said residential establishment at such times as the person in charge of the residential establishment, with the agreement of the chief social work officer of (name of local authority), considers necessary.
[name of place or places]* (see Note below)

**2.** etc.

..........

Chairman of the Children's Hearing

*Delete as appropriate

*Note:* If the residential establishment providing secure accommodation does not have an open residential facility there will also need to be a reference to some such place.

Rule 27

FORM 12

WARRANT UNDER SECTION 66(1) OF THE ACT FOR KEEPING A CHILD IN A PLACE OF SAFETY

(Place and date)

A children's hearing for (local authority area) in respect of the case of (name and address of child), being unable to dispose of the case and in exercise of the powers conferred on them by section 63(5) of the Act, being satisfied [that it is necessary that the child should be kept in a place of safety in order to safeguard or promote his/her welfare]* [the child may not attend at any hearing of his/her case]* [there is reason to believe that the child may fail to comply with a requirement that under section 69(3) of the Act]* [there is reason to believe that the child may not attend at any hearing of his/here case]* grant warrant to (insert name and address and where appropriate full designation of applicant) to [find and keep the child in (name of place or places) for a period from (date) to (date) both days inclusive (insert period not exceeding 22 days) [and for the bringing of that child, before a children's hearing at (insert time and/or date)]*.

[For the duration this warrant the child should be subject to the conditions noted below]*

[The children's hearing in granting this warrant order that the place or places where (the child) is to reside in accordance with the warrant shall not be disclosed to (person or class of persons)]*

[CONDITIONS REFERRED TO IN THE FOREGOING WARRANT

**1.** (insert conditions)]*

..........

Chairman of the Children's Hearing

*Delete as appropriate

Rule 27

## FORM 13

### WARRANT UNDER SECTIONS 66(1) AND 66(6) OF THE ACT FOR PLACING AND KEEPING A CHILD IN PLACE OF SAFETY WITH AUTHORISATION TO KEEP IN SECURE ACCOMMODATION

(Place and date)

A children's hearing for (local authority area), in respect of the case of (name and address of child) being unable to dispose of the case and in exercise of the powers conferred on them by section 66(1) and 66(6) of the Children (Scotland) Act 1995,

(firstly) being satisfied that [it is necessary to keep the child in a place of safety in order to safeguard or promote his/her welfare]* [there is reason to believe that the child may not attend any hearing of his/her* case]* [there is reason to believe that the child may fail to comply with a requirement under section 69(3) of that Act]* and

(secondly) being satisfied [that, having previously absconded, he/she* is likely to abscond unless kept in secure accommodation, and that if he/she* absconds it is likely that his/her* physical, mental or moral welfare will be at risk]* [that he/she* is likely to injure himself/herself* or some other person unless he/she* is kept in such accommodation]*,

grant warrant to (insert name and address and where appropriate full designation of applicant) to [find and keep]* [keep]* the child in (name of residential establishment providing the secure accommodation) subject to the conditions noted below for the period from (date) to (date) both days inclusive (insert period not exceeding 22 days) and for the bringing of that child before a children's hearing at (insert time and date).

[name of place or places]* (see Note below)

[The children's hearing in granting this warrant order that the place where the child is to reside in accordance with the warrant shall not be disclosed to (person or class of person)]*

## CONDITIONS REFERRED TO IN THE FOREGOING WARRANT

**1.** The child is liable to be placed and kept in secure accommodation in (name of residential establishment) at such times as the person in charge of the residential establishment, with the agreement of the chief social work officer of (name of local authority), considers it necessary that the child do so.

..........

Chairman of the Children's Hearing

*Delete as appropriate

*Note:* If the residential establishment providing secure accommodation does not have an open residential facility there will also need to be a reference to some such place.

Rule 27

## FORM 14

### CONTINUATION UNDER SECTION 66(5) OF A WARRANT OF THE ACT FOR KEEPING A CHILD IN A PLACE OF SAFETY

(Place and date)

A children's hearing for (local authority area), in respect of the case of (name and address of child), being unable to dispose of the case and in exercise of the powers conferred on them by section 66(5) of the Children (Scotland) Act 1995, being satisfied that (specify cause shown by the Principal Reporter) continue a warrant dated (insert date of warrant), a copy of which is attached, for a period from (date to (date) both days inclusive (insert period not exceeding 22 days) and for the bringing of that child before a children's hearing at (insert time and date).

[The continuation of the warrant is subject to the variations of the warrant [as varied]* noted below]*

[VARIATIONS REFERRED TO IN THE FOREGOING WARRANT

**1.** (insert variations)]*

..........

Chairman of the Children's Hearing

*Delete as appropriate

Rule 27

FORM 15

CONTINUATION UNDER SECTION 66(5) OF THE ACT OF A
WARRANT FOR PLACING AND KEEPING A CHILD IN A
PLACE OF SAFETY WITH FIRST AUTHORISATION TO KEEP
IN SECURE ACCOMMODATION

(Place and date)

A children's hearing for (local authority area), in respect of the case of
(name and address of child) being unable to dispose of the case, in
exercise of the powers conferred on them by section 66(5) and 66(6) of
the Children (Scotland) Act 1995

(firstly) being satisfied that (specify cause shown by the Principal
Reporter,)

(secondly) being satisfied that the child having previously absconded, he/
she* is likely to abscond unless kept in secure accommodation, and that
if he/she* absconds it is likely that his/her* physical, mental or moral
welfare will be at risk]* [that he/she* is likely to injure himself/herself*
or some other person unless he/she* is kept in such accommodation]*,

grant continuation, subject to the variations noted below, of the warrant
dated (insert date of warrant), a copy of which is attached.

[The children's hearing in granting this warrant order that the place
where (name) is to reside in accordance with the warrant shall not be
disclosed (person or class of persons)]*

[VARIATIONS REFERRED TO

**1.** The warrant is varied to read as a warrant to (name and address and
where appropriate full designation of applicant) to keep the child in
(name of residential establishment providing secure accommodation) for
the period from (date) to date (insert period not exceeding 22 days) both
days inclusive and with an order that during the duration of the warrant,
pending disposal of his/her case, the child shall be liable to be placed and
kept in secure accommodation within the said residential establishment
at such times as the person in charge of the residential establishment
with the agreement of the chief social work officer of (name of local
authority), considers necessary.
[name of place or places]* (see Note below)

**2.** ..........

Chairman of the Children's Hearing

*Delete as appropriate

*Note:* If the residential establishment providing secure accommodation does not have an open residential facility there will also need to be a reference to some such place.

Rule 27

## FORM 16

## WARRANT UNDER SECTION 69(4) OF THE ACT FOR APPREHENSION OF CHILD AND REMOVAL TO PLACE OF SAFETY

(Place and date)

A children's hearing for (local authority area) having considered the case of (name and address of child) continue the case and in exercise of the power conferred on them by section 69(4) of the Children (Scotland) Act 1995, being satisfied that (name of child) has failed to fulfil a requirement made under section 69(3) of the Act, grant warrant to (insert name and address and where appropriate full designation of person) to find the child for the purpose of removing him/her* (insert name of place or places of safety) and keeping the child there [and where that place or those places of safety is or are not (insert name of clinic, hospital or establishment named in section 69(3) requirement), to take him/her* from the place of safety to (insert name of clinic, hospital or other establishment) for the purpose of investigation]*

[For the duration of this warrant the child should be subject to the conditions noted

below]*

[The place or places where the child is to reside shall not be disclosed to (person or class of persons)]*

[CONDITIONS REFERRED TO IN THE FOREGOING WARRANT

**1.** (insert conditions)]*

..........

Chairman of the Children's Hearing

*Delete as appropriate

Rule 27

FORM 17

## WARRANT UNDER SECTION 69(4) OF THE ACT TO REMOVE AND KEEP CHILD IN PLACE OF SAFETY WITH AUTHORISATION TO KEEP IN SECURE ACCOMMODATION

(Place and date)

A children's hearing for (local authority area) having considered the case of (name and address of child) continue the case and in exercise of the power conferred on them by section 69(4) of the Children (Scotland) Act 1995, (firstly) being satisfied that the child has failed to fulfil a requirement made under section 69(3) of the Act, grant warrant to (insert name and address and where appropriate full designation of person) to find the child for the purpose of removing him/her* (insert name of place or places of safety) and keeping the child there [and where that place or those places of safety is or are not (insert name of clinic, hospital or establishment named in section 69(3) requirement), to take him/her* (insert name of clinic, hospital or other establishment) for the purpose of investigation]*

(secondly) being satisfied that, the child having previously absconded, he/she* is likely to abscond unless kept in secure accommodation, and that if he/she* absconds it is likely that his/her* physical, mental or moral welfare will be at risk]* [that he/she* is likely to injure himself/herself* or some other person unless he/she* is kept in such accommodation]*, orders that while the warrant or requirement under section 69(3) is in effect the child shall be liable to be placed in secure accommodation within (name of residential establishment providing secure accommodation)* (see Note below) at such times as the person in charge of the establishment, with the agreement of the chief social work officer of (name of local authority) considers necessary.

[For the duration of this warrant the child should be subject to the conditions noted below]*

[The place or places where the child is to reside shall not be disclosed to (person or class of persons)]*

[CONDITIONS REFERRED TO IN THE FOREGOING WARRANT

**1.** (insert conditions)]*

..........

Chairman of the Children's Hearing

*Delete as appropriate

*Note:* If the place of safety does not provide secure accommodation there will also need to be a reference to some such secure accommodation.

Rule 27

## FORM 18

### WARRANT UNDER SECTION 69(7) OF THE ACT FOR KEEPING A CHILD IN A PLACE OF SAFETY

(Place and date)

A children's hearing for (local authority area) having considered the case of (name and address of child) continue the case and in exercise of the powers conferred on them by section 69(7) of the Children (Scotland) Act 1995, being satisfied that [it is necessary that the child should be kept in a place of safety in the interests of safeguarding or promoting his/her* welfare]* [there is reason to believe that (name and address) may not attend the subsequent hearing of his/her* case]* grant warrant to (insert name and address and where appropriate full designation of person) for that child to be taken to and kept in (insert name of place or places of safety)]* [until the day on which the subsequent hearing of the child's case by a children's hearing begins]*

[For the duration of this warrant the child should be subject to the conditions noted below]* [The place or places of safety referred to if this warrant shall not be disclosed to (person or class of person)]*

[CONDITIONS REFERRED TO IN THE FOREGOING WARRANT

**1.** (insert conditions)]*

..........

Chairman of the Children's Hearings

*Delete as appropriate

Rule 27

## FORM 19

### WARRANT UNDER SECTION 69(7) OF THE ACT FOR PLACING AND KEEPING A CHILD IN PLACE OF SAFETY WITH AUTHORISATION TO KEEP IN SECURE ACCOMMODATION

(Place and date)

A children's hearing for (local authority area) having considering the case of (name and address of child) continue the case and in exercise of the powers conferred on them by section 69(4) of the Children (Scotland) Act 1995,

[being satisfied that it is necessary for the child to be kept in a place of safety in the interests of safeguarding or promoting his/her* welfare]* [there is reason to believe that the child may not attend the subsequent hearing of his/her* case]* being satisfied [that, having previously absconded he/she* is likely to abscond unless kept in secure accommodation, and that if he/she* absconds it is likely that his/her* physical, mental or moral welfare will be at risk]* [that he/she* is likely to injure himself/herself* or some other person unless he/she* is kept in such accommodation]*

grant warrant to (insert name and address and where appropriate full designation of person) ordering the taking to and keeping of the said child in (name of residential establishment providing the secure accommodation) [for the period from (date) to (date) both days inclusive (insert period not exceeding 22 days)]* [until the day on which the subsequent hearing of the child's case by a children's hearing begins]* and order that while the warrant is in effect the child shall be liable to be placed in secure accommodation at such times as the person in charge of the residential establishment, with the agreement of the chief social work officer of (name of local authority), considers necessary.

[name of place or places]* (see Note below)

[For the duration of this warrant the child shall be subject to the conditions noted below]*

[The children's hearing in granting this warrant order that the place where (name) is to reside in accordance with the warrant shall not be disclosed to

[CONDITIONS REFERRED TO IN THE FOREGOING WARRANT

**1.** (insert conditions)]*

..........

Chairman of the Children's Hearing

*Delete as appropriate

*Note:* If the residential establishment providing secure accommodation does not have an open residential facility there will also need to be a reference to some such place.

Rule 28

## FORM 20

## REQUIREMENT UNDER SECTION 69(3) OF THE ACT

(Place and Date)

The children's hearing for (name of local authority) in respect of (name and address of child) having considered his/her case and being satisfied that, in order to complete their consideration of the case, it is necessary to have further investigation of the case, continue the case and for the purposes of the said investigation, in exercise of their powers under section 69(3) of the Act, require the child to [attend]* [reside at]* (insert name of clinic, hospital or establishment) during (insert time or period not exceeding twenty-two days).

..........

Chairman of the Children's Hearing

*Delete as appropriate

## FORM 21

### NOTIFICATION BY PRINCIPAL REPORTER UNDER SECTION 60(3) TO PERSON WHO IMPLEMENTED CHILD PROTECTION ORDER THAT CONDITIONS FOR THE MAKING OF THE ORDER ARE NO LONGER SATISFIED

(Date and place)

(To (name and address)

The Principal Reporter, hereby notifies you that having regard to the welfare of (name and address of child) he has decided that, [as a result of a change in the circumstances of his/her* case]* [in the light of further information relating to his/her* case having received by him]* that [the conditions of the making of a child protection order in respect of (name of child) are no longer satisfied]* or [the [term]* [condition]* [direction]* set out below is no longer appropriate]*.

[TERM, CONDITION OR DIRECTION REFERRED TO IN THE FOREGOING NOTIFICATION]

**1.** (Insert term, condition or direction)]*

..........

Principal Reporter

(on behalf of the Principal Reporter)

*Delete as appropriate

## FORM 22

### NOTIFICATION BY PRINCIPAL REPORTER UNDER SECTION 60(3) TO PERSON WHO IMPLEMENTED CHILD PROTECTION ORDER THAT CONDITIONS FOR THE MAKING OF THE ORDER ARE NO LONGER SATISFIED

(Date and place)

(To (name and address)

The Principal Reporter, hereby notifies you that having regard to the welfare of (name and address of child) has decided that, [as a result of a change in the circumstances of his/her* case]* [in the light of further information relating to his/her* case having received by him]* that [the conditions of the making of a child protection order in respect of (name of child) are no longer satisfied]* or [the [term]* [condition]* [direction]* set out below is no longer appropriate]*.

[TERM, CONDITION OR DIRECTION REFERRED TO IN THE FOREGOING NOTIFICATION]

**1.** (Insert term, condition or direction)]*

..........

Principal Reporter

(on behalf of the Principal Reporter)

*Delete as appropriate

Rule 28(4)

FORM 23

FORM OF REPORT BY CHILDREN'S HEARING OF ADVICE
UNDER SECTION 60(10) OF THE ACT FOR CONSIDERATION
BY SHERIFF IN HIS DETERMINATION OF APPLICATION
UNDER SECTION 60(7) OF THE ACT

(Date and place)

To

On (date) a children's hearing for (local authority area), after considering the case of (name of child and address) and the application under section 60(7) to [set aside]* [vary]* [the child protection order]* [a direction under section 58 of the Act]* [the child protection order]* [direction]* continued under section 59(4)]* provide the advice set out below to assist the sheriff in his determination of the application.

ADVICE REFERRED TO IN THE FOREGOING ADVICE
STATEMENT

**1.** (insert advice)

..........

Chairman of the Children's Hearing

*Delete as appropriate

Rule 28(5)

## FORM 24

### FORM OF REPORT BY CHILDREN'S HEARING OF ADVICE UNDER SECTION 73(13) OF THE ACT PROVIDING ADVICE FOR CONSIDERATION BY SHERIFF IN HIS DETERMINATION OF DECISION OF ADOPTION AGENCY

(Date and place)

To

On (date) a children's hearing for (local authority area), after considering the case of (name of child and address) and the [proposed application under section 86 of the Act]* [proposed application under [section 12]* [section 18]* of the Adoption (Scotland) Act 1978]* [the proposed placing for adoption]* provide the advice set out below to assist the sheriff in his determination of the application.

### ADVICE IN RELATION TO THE DECISION OF THE ADOPTION AGENCY

**1.** (insert advice)

..........

Chairman of the Children's Hearing

*Delete as appropriate

Rule 30

## FORM 25

### CHILDREN (SCOTLAND) ACT 1995 CERTIFICATE OF NOTIFICATION OF CHILDREN'S HEARING TO RELEVANT PERSON

(to be subjoined to copy of notification)*

I, ......................... [Principal Reporter/on behalf of Principal Reporter]* of (name of local authority) notified (name of relevant person) by

[speaking to him in person on (date), (time), (place)]*

[delivering a copy of the notification to him in person on (date), (time), (place)]*

[leaving a copy of the notification for him at his [(address), (house), (business), (address of business) or (date)]

[leaving a copy of the notification for him on board (name of vessel) at (place) or (date)]* [sending to him in [a recorded delivery/registered] letter and the post office receipt of said letter accompanies this certificate]*

..........

Principal Reporter to the Children's Hearing

*Delete as appropriate

# APPENDIX 4

## Act of Sederunt (Child Care and Maintenance Rules) 1997

### SI 1997/291 (S.19)

*Coming into force*                    *1st April 1997*

## ARRANGEMENT OF RULES

. . .

## CHAPTER 3:

## CHILDREN (SCOTLAND) ACT 1995

### PART I

### INTERPRETATION

### PART II

### GENERAL RULES

### PROCEDURE IN RESPECT OF CHILDREN

### SAFEGUARDERS

### FIXING OF FIRST HEARING

### SERVICE, CITATION AND NOTICE

## MISCELLANEOUS

## PART III

## CHILD ASSESSMENT ORDERS

## PART IV

## CHILD PROTECTION ORDERS

## PART V

## EXCLUSION ORDERS

## PART VI

## WARRANT FOR FURTHER DETENTION OF A CHILD

## PART VII

## PROCEDURE IN APPLICATIONS UNDER SECTION 65(7) OR (9) OF THE ACT

## PART VIII

## PROCEDURE IN APPEALS UNDER SECTION 51(1) OF THE ACT

## PART IX

## PROCEDURE IN APPEALS UNDER SECTION 51(11) OF THE ACT

## PART X

## APPLICATION FOR REVIEW OF ESTABLISHMENT OF GROUNDS OF REFERRAL—NEW EVIDENCE

. . .

Chapter 3

Children (Scotland) Act 1995

PART I

INTERPRETATION

**Interpretation**

**3.1**—(1) In this Chapter, unless the context otherwise requires—
"the Act" means the Children (Scotland) Act 1995 and expressions used in this Chapter which are also used in that Act shall have the meaning assigned to them for the purposes of Part II of the Act;
"service" includes citation, intimation or the giving of notice as required in terms of this Chapter.

(2) In this Chapter any reference, however expressed, to disputed grounds of referral shall be construed as a reference to grounds of referral which form the subject of an application under section 65(7) or (9) of the Act (application to sheriff).

## PART II

## GENERAL RULES

## PROCEDURE IN RESPECT OF CHILDREN

**Application**

**3.2** Rules 3.3 to 3.5 apply where by virtue of section 16(2) of the Act a child may be given an opportunity to indicate whether he wishes to express his views in relation to an application or proceedings in the circumstances stated in section 16(4)(b) and (c) of the Act.

**Power to dispense with service on child**

**3.3** Where the sheriff is satisfied, taking account of the age and maturity of the child, that it would be inappropriate to order service on the child, he may dispense with—
(a) service on the child; and
(b) the attendance of the child at the hearing of the application.

**Service on child**

**3.4**—(1) Subject to rule 3.3 and to paragraph (2), after the issue of the first order or warrant to cite, as the case may be, the applicant shall forthwith serve a copy of the application and first order or warrant to cite on the child, together with a notice or citation in—
(a) Form 26 in respect of an application for a child assessment order under Part III of this Chapter;
(b) Form 27 in respect of an application to vary or set aside a child protection order in terms of rule 3.33;
(c) Form 28 in respect of an application for an exclusion order in terms of rules 3.34 to 3.39;
(d) Form 29 in respect of an application to vary or recall an exclusion order in terms of rule 3.40;
(e) Form 30 in respect of an application for a warrant to keep a child in a place of safety under Part VI of this Chapter; and
(f) Form 31 in respect of an application under section 65(7) or (9) of the Act made under Part VII of this Chapter.
(2) The sheriff may, on application by the applicant or of his own motion, order that a specified part of the application is not served on the child.

**Procedure where child wishes to express a view**

**3.5**—(1) Where a child has indicated his wish to express his views, the sheriff—
(a) may order such steps to be taken as he considers appropriate to ascertain the views of that child; and
(b) shall not make any order or disposal mentioned in paragraph (b) or (c) of section 16(4) of the Act unless an opportunity has been given for the views of that child to be obtained or heard.
(2) Subject to any order made by the sheriff under paragraph (1)(a) and to any other method as the sheriff in his discretion may permit, the views of the child may be conveyed—

(a) by the child orally or in writing;

(b) by an advocate or solicitor acting on behalf of the child;

(c) by any safeguarder or curator *ad litem* appointed by the court; or

(d) by any other person (either orally or in writing), provided that the sheriff is satisfied that that person is a suitable representative and is duly authorised to represent the child.

(3) Where the views of the child are conveyed orally to the sheriff, the sheriff shall record those views in writing.

(4) The sheriff may direct that any written views given by a child, or any written record of those views, shall—

(a) be sealed in an envelope marked "Views of the child—confidential";

(b) be kept in the court process without being recorded in the inventory of process;

(c) be available to a sheriff only;

(d) not be opened by any person other than a sheriff, and

(e) not form a borrowable part of the process.

## SAFEGUARDERS

### Application

**3.6** Rules 3.7 to 3.10 apply, as regards a safeguarder, to all applications and proceedings to which this Chapter applies except for proceedings under section 57 of the Act for a child protection order.

### Appointment of safeguarder

**3.7**—(1) The sheriff—

(a) shall, as soon as reasonably practicable after the lodging of an application or the commencing of any proceedings, consider whether it is necessary to appoint a safeguarder in the application or proceedings; and

(b) may at that stage, or at any later stage of the application or proceedings, appoint a safeguarder.

(2) Where a safeguarder has been appointed in proceedings before the children's hearing or the sheriff in respect of related proceedings, the appointee shall, unless the sheriff on his own motion or on cause shown by a party directs otherwise, be the same person appointed as safeguarder by the children's hearing or the sheriff.

### Rights, powers and duties of safeguarder on appointment

**3.8** A safeguarder appointed in an application shall—

(a) have the powers and duties at common law of a curator *ad litem* in respect of the child;

(b) be entitled to receive from the Principal Reporter copies of the application, all of the productions in the proceedings and any papers which were before the children's hearing;

(c) subject to rule 3.5(1)(a), determine whether the child wishes to express his views in relation to the application and, if so, where the child so wishes transmit his views to the sheriff;

(d) make such enquiries so far as relevant to the application as he considers appropriate; and

(e) without delay, and in any event before the hearing on the application, intimate in writing to the sheriff clerk whether or not he intends to become a party to the proceedings.

### Provision where safeguarder intimates his intention to become a party to the proceedings

**3.9**—(1) A safeguarder may appear personally in the proceedings or instruct an advocate or solicitor to appear on his behalf.

(2) Where an advocate or a solicitor is appointed to act as a safeguarder, he shall not act also as advocate or solicitor for the child in the proceedings.

### Provision where safeguarder intimates his intention not to become a party to the proceedings

**3.10**—(1) Where a safeguarder intimates that he does not intend to become a party to the proceedings, he shall at the same time report in writing to the sheriff on the extent of his enquiries and his conclusion as to the interests of the child in the proceedings.

(2) The sheriff clerk shall intimate to a safeguarder who has not become a party to the proceedings all interlocutors subsequent to his appointment.

(3) A safeguarder who has intimated his intention not to become a party to the proceedings may subsequently seek leave so to become.

## FIXING OF FIRST HEARING

### Assigning of diet for hearing

**3.11** Except where otherwise provided in these Rules, after the lodging of any application the sheriff clerk shall forthwith assign a diet for the hearing of the application and shall issue a first order or a warrant to cite in Form 32 or Form 33, as the case may be.

## SERVICE, CITATION AND NOTICE

### Service and notice to persons named in application

**3.12**—(1) Subject to the provisions of rule 3.4 (service on child), after the issue of the first order or warrant to cite, as the case may be, the applicant shall forthwith give notice of the application by serving a copy of the application and the first order or warrant to cite together with a notice or citation, as the case may be, on the persons named in the application or, as the case may be, a person who should receive notice of the application (subject to paragraph (2)) in—
- (a) Form 34 in respect of an application for a child assessment order under Part III of this Chapter;
- (b) Form 35 in respect of an application to vary or set aside a child protection order in terms of rule 3.33;
- (c) Form 36 in respect of an application for an exclusion order in terms of rules 3.34 to 3.39;
- (d) Form 37 in respect of an application to vary or recall an exclusion order in terms of rule 3.40;

(e) Form 38 in respect of an application for a warrant to keep a child in a place of safety under Part VI of this Chapter; and

(f) Form 39 in respect of an application under section 65(7) or (9) of the Act made under Part VII of this Chapter.

(2) Notice of the application shall be given in the case of a safeguarder by serving a copy of the application and the first order or warrant to cite together with notice in Form 40.

**Period of notice**

**3.13**—(1) Subject to paragraph (2), citation or notice authorised or required by this Chapter shall be made not later than forty-eight hours, or in the case of postal citation seventy-two hours, before the date of the diet to which the citation or notice relates.

(2) Paragraph (1) shall not apply in relation to citation or notice of the following applications or proceedings—

(a) an appeal against a decision to issue a warrant for the detention of a child;

(b) a hearing in respect of an exclusion order where an interim order has been granted in terms of rule 3.36;

(c) a hearing on an application to vary or set aside a child protection order or any direction given with the order; or

(d) an application for a child assessment order,

in which cases the period of notice and the method of giving notice shall be as directed by the sheriff.

**Citation of witnesses, parties and persons having an interest**

**3.14**—(1) The following shall be warrants for citation of witnesses, parties and havers:—

(a) the warrant for the first diet in an application;

(b) an interlocutor fixing a diet for the continued hearing of an application; and

(c) an interlocutor assigning a diet for a hearing of an appeal or application.

(2) In an application or an appeal, witnesses or havers may be cited in Form 41.

(3) The certificate of execution of citation of witnesses and havers shall be in Form 42.

**Modes of service**

**3.15**—(1) Service authorised or required by this Chapter shall be made by any mode specified in paragraphs (2) and (3).

(2) It shall be deemed legal service to or on any person if such service is—

(a) delivered to him personally;

(b) left for him at his dwelling-house or place of business with some person resident or employed therein;

(c) where it cannot be delivered to him personally and he has no known dwelling-house or place of business, left for him at any other place at which he may at the time be resident;

(d) where he is the master of, or a seaman or other person employed in, a vessel, left with a person on board or connected with the vessel;

(e) sent by first class recorded delivery post, or the nearest equivalent which the available postal service permits, to his dwelling-house or place of business, or if he has no known dwelling-house or place of business to any other place in which he may at the time be resident;

(f) where the person has the facility to receive facsimile or other electronic transmission, by such facsimile or other electronic transmission; or

(g) where the person has a numbered box at a document exchange, given by leaving at the document exchange.

(3) Where service requires to be made and there is not sufficient time to employ any of the methods specified in paragraph (2), service shall be effected orally or in such other manner as the sheriff directs.

### Persons who may effect service

**3.16**—(1) Subject to paragraphs (2) and (3), service shall be effected—

(a) in the case of any of the modes specified in rule 3.15(2), by a sheriff officer;

(b) in the case of any of the modes specified in rule 3.15(2)(e) or (f), by a solicitor, the sheriff clerk, the Principal Reporter or an officer of the local authority; or

(c) in the case of any mode specified by the sheriff in terms of rule 3.15(3), by such person as the sheriff directs.

(2) In relation to the citation of witnesses, parties and havers in terms of rule 3.14 or service of any application, "officer of the local authority" in paragraph (1)(b) includes any officer of a local authority authorised to conduct proceedings under these Rules in terms of rule 3.21 (representation).

(3) The sheriff clerk shall cite the Principal Reporter and the authors or compilers of any reports or statements whom the sheriff may wish to examine under section 51(3) of the Act (appeal against decision of children's hearing or sheriff).

### Production of certificates of execution of service

**3.17**—(1) The production before the sheriff of—

(a) a certificate of execution of service in Form 43; and

(b) additionally in the case of postal service, the post office receipt of the registered or recorded delivery letter,

shall be sufficient evidence that service was duly made.

(2) It shall be sufficient to lodge the execution of service at the hearing, unless the sheriff otherwise directs or on cause shown.

### Power to dispense with service

**3.18** Subject to rule 3.3, the sheriff may, on cause shown, dispense with service on any person named.

## MISCELLANEOUS

### Expenses

**3.19** No expenses shall be awarded in any proceedings to which this Chapter applies.

**Record of proceedings**

**3.20** Proceedings under this Chapter shall be conducted summarily.

**Representation**

**3.21**—(1) In any proceedings any party may be represented by an advocate or a solicitor or, subject to paragraphs (2) and (3), other representative authorised by the party.

(2) Such other representative must throughout the proceedings satisfy the sheriff that he is a suitable person to represent the party and that he is authorised to do so.

(3) Such other representative may in representing a party do all such things for the preparation and conduct of the proceedings as may be done by an individual on his own behalf.

**Applications for evidence of children by television link**

**3.22**—(1) This rule and rule 3.23 shall apply to any proceedings in the sheriff court under Part II of the Act.

(2) An application to the court for the giving of evidence by a child by means of a live television link shall be made in Form 44.

(3) An application referred to in paragraph (2) shall be lodged with the sheriff clerk not later than 14 days before the hearing at which the child is to give evidence (except on special cause shown).

(4) The sheriff shall—

(a) order intimation of the application to be made to the other party or parties to the proceedings; and

(b) hear the application on the earliest practicable date.

**Orders and transfer of cases**

**3.23**—(1) The sheriff who hears an application under rule 3.22 shall, after hearing the parties and allowing such further procedure as the sheriff thinks fit, make an order granting or refusing the application.

(2) Where the sheriff grants the application, he may—

(a) transfer the case to be heard in whole; or

(b) hear the case himself or such part of it as he shall determine, in another sheriff court in the same sheriffdom.

**Exclusion of certain enactments**

**3.24** The enactments specified in column (1) of Schedule 3 to this Act of Sederunt (being enactments relating to matters with respect to which this Chapter is made) shall not, to the extent specified in column (3) of that Schedule, apply to an application or appeal.

# PART III

## CHILD ASSESSMENT ORDERS

**Interpretation**

**3.25** In this Part, "application" means an application for a child assessment order in terms of section 55 of the Act.

**Form of application**

**3.26** An application shall be made in Form 45.

**Orders**

**3.27**—(1) After hearing parties and allowing such further procedure as he thinks fit, the sheriff shall make an order granting or refusing the application.

(2) Where an order is made granting the application, that order shall be made in Form 46 and shall contain the information specified therein.

(3) Where the sheriff, in terms of section 55(2) of the Act, has decided to make a child protection order pursuant to an application, rules 3.31 to 3.33 shall apply.

**Intimation**

**3.28** The local authority shall intimate the grant or refusal of an application to such persons, if any, as the sheriff directs.

## PART IV

## CHILD PROTECTION ORDERS

**Interpretation**

**3.29** In this Part, "application" means, except in rule 3.33, an application for a child protection order in terms of section 57 of the Act.

**Form of application**

**3.30** An application made by a local authority shall be in Form 47 and an application made by any other person shall be in Form 48.

**Determination of application**

**3.31**—(1) On receipt of an application, the sheriff, having considered the grounds of the application and the supporting evidence, shall forthwith grant or refuse it.

(2) Where an order is granted, it shall be in Form 49 and it shall contain any directions made under section 58 of the Act.

**Intimation of making of order**

**3.32** Where an order is granted, the applicant shall forthwith serve a copy of the order on—
(a) the child, along with a notice in Form 50;
(b) any other person named in the application, along with a notice in Form 51.

**Application to vary or set aside a child protection order**

**3.33**—(1) An application under section 60(7) of the Act for the variation or setting aside of a child protection order or a direction given under section 58 of the Act or such an order or direction continued (whether with or without variation) under section 59(4) of the Act shall be made in Form 52.

(2) A person applying under section 60(7) of the Act for the variation or setting aside of a child protection order shall require to lodge with his application a copy of that order.

(3) Without prejudice to rule 3.5, any person on whom service is made may appear or be represented at the hearing of the application.

(4) Subject to section 60(11) of the Act, the sheriff, after hearing parties and allowing such further procedure as he thinks fit, shall grant or refuse the application.

(5) Where an order is made granting the application for variation, that order shall be in Form 53.

(6) Where the sheriff so directs, intimation of the granting or refusing of an application shall be given by the applicant to such person as the sheriff shall direct.

## PART V

## EXCLUSION ORDERS

### Interpretation

**3.34** In this Part, "application" means, except in rule 3.40, an application by a local authority for an exclusion order in terms of sections 76 to 80 of the Act; and "ancillary order" and "interim order" shall be construed accordingly.

### Form of application

**3.35** An application shall be made in Form 54.

### Hearing following interim order

**3.36** Where an interim order is granted under subsection (4) of section 76 of the Act, the hearing under subsection (5) of that section shall take place not later than 3 working days after the granting of the interim order.

### Orders

**3.37**—(1) After hearing parties and allowing such further procedure as he thinks fit, the sheriff shall make an order granting or refusing the application.

(2) Where the sheriff grants an order in terms of paragraph (1), it shall be in Form 55 and shall be served forthwith by the local authority on—

(a) the named person;
(b) the appropriate person;
(c) the relevant child; and
(d) the Principal Reporter.

### Certificates of delivery of documents to chief constable

**3.38**—(1) After the local authority have complied with section 78(4) of the Act, they shall forthwith lodge in process a certificate of delivery in Form 56.

(2) After a person has complied with section 78(5) of the Act, he shall lodge in process a certificate of delivery in Form 56.

**Power to make child protection order in an application for an exclusion order**

**3.39** Where the sheriff, in terms of 76(8) of the Act, has decided to make a child protection order pursuant to an application, rules 3.31 to 3.33 shall apply.

**Variation or recall of an exclusion order**

**3.40**—(1) Any application for the variation or recall of an exclusion order and any warrant, interdict, order or direction granted or made under section 77 of the Act shall be in Form 57.

(2) After hearing parties and allowing such further procedure as he thinks fit, the sheriff shall make an order granting or refusing the application.

(3) Where an order is made granting the application for variation, that order shall be in Form 58.

(4) Intimation of the granting or refusing of an application shall be given by the applicant to such persons as the sheriff shall direct.

## PART VI

## WARRANT FOR FURTHER DETENTION OF A CHILD

**Interpretation**

**3.41** In this Part, "application" means an application for a warrant to keep a child in a place of safety in terms of section 67 of the Act.

**Form of application**

**3.42** An application shall be made in Form 59.

**Orders**

**3.43** After hearing parties and allowing such further procedure as he thinks fit, the sheriff shall make an order granting or refusing the application.

## PART VII

## PROCEDURE IN APPLICATIONS UNDER SECTION 65(7) OR (9) OF THE ACT

**Interpretation**

**3.44** In this Part, "application" means an application under section 65(7) or (9) of the Act (establishment of grounds for referral).

**Lodging of application, etc.**

**3.45**—(1) Within a period of seven days beginning with the date on which the Principal Reporter was directed in terms of section 65 of the Act to make application to the sheriff, he shall lodge with the sheriff clerk an application in Form 60.

(2) Where a safeguarder has been appointed by the chairman at the children's hearing, the Principal Reporter shall intimate such appoint-

ment to the sheriff clerk and shall lodge along with the application any report made by the safeguarder.

### Abandonment of application

**3.46**—(1) At any stage of the proceedings before the application is determined the Principal Reporter may abandon the application, either in whole or in part, by lodging a minute to that effect or by motion at the hearing.

(2) The Principal Reporter shall intimate such abandonment to—

(a) the child, except where service on the child has been dispensed with in terms of rule 3.3;

(b) any relevant person whose whereabouts are known to the Principal Reporter; and

(c) any safeguarder appointed by the sheriff.

(3) In the event of abandonment in whole in terms of paragraph (1), the sheriff shall dismiss the application and discharge the referral.

### Hearing of evidence

**3.47**—(1) In the case of any condition mentioned in section 52(2) of the Act (conditions relative to compulsory measures of supervision), the sheriff shall, in relation to any ground of referral which is in dispute, hear evidence tendered by or on behalf of the Principal Reporter, including evidence given pursuant to an application granted under rule 3.23.

(2) At the close of the evidence led by the Principal Reporter in a case where it is disputed that the condition mentioned in paragraph (i) of section 52(2) of the Act is satisfied, the sheriff shall consider whether sufficient evidence has been led to establish that condition is satisfied and shall give all the parties an opportunity to be heard on the question of sufficiency of evidence.

(3) Where the sheriff is not satisfied that sufficient evidence has been led as mentioned in paragraph (2), he shall make a finding to that effect.

(4) Where the sheriff is satisfied that sufficient evidence has been led as mentioned in paragraph (2), the child, the relevant person and any safeguarder appointed may give evidence and call witnesses with regard to the condition in question.

(5) Where the nature of the case or of any evidence to be given is such that the sheriff is satisfied that it is in the interests of the child that he should not be present at any stage of the proceedings, the sheriff may exclude the child from the hearing during that stage and in that event any safeguarder appointed and the relevant person or representative of the child shall be permitted to remain during the absence of the child.

(6) Subject to paragraph (7), the sheriff may exclude any person, including the relevant person, while any child is giving evidence if the sheriff is satisfied that this is necessary in the interests of the child and that—

(a) he must do so in order to obtain the evidence of the child; or

(b) the presence of the person or persons in question is causing, or is likely to cause, significant distress to the child.

(7) Where the relevant person is not legally represented at the hearing and has been excluded under paragraph (6), the sheriff shall inform that

relevant person of the substance of any evidence given by the child and shall give that relevant person an opportunity to respond by leading evidence or otherwise.

(8) Where evidence in a referral has been heard in part and a safeguarder thereafter becomes a party to proceedings, the sheriff may order the evidence to be reheard in whole or in part.

### Amendment of grounds for referral

**3.48** The sheriff may at any time, on the application of any party or of his own motion, allow amendment of any statement supporting the conditions of the grounds for referral.

### Adjournment for inquiry, etc.

**3.49** Subject to the provisions of section 68(2) of the Act (applications to be heard within twenty-eight days of lodging), the sheriff on the motion of any party or on his own motion may continue the hearing in order to allow time for further inquiry into any application, in consequence of the amendment of any statement under rule 3.48, or for any other necessary cause, for such reasonable time as he may in the circumstances consider necessary.

### Power of sheriff in making findings as to offences

**3.50** Where in a ground of referral it is alleged that an offence has been committed by or against any child, the sheriff may find that any other offence established by the facts has been committed.

### Decision of sheriff

**3.51**—(1) Subject to rule 3.47(3), the sheriff shall give his decision orally at the conclusion of the hearing.

(2) The sheriff clerk shall forthwith send a copy of the interlocutor containing that decision to—

  (a) the child, except where service on the child has been dispensed with in terms of rule 3.3;
  (b) any relevant person whose whereabouts are known;
  (c) any safeguarder appointed by the sheriff; and
  (d) the Principal Reporter.

(3) The sheriff may, when giving his decision in terms of paragraph (1) or within 7 days thereafter, issue a note of the reasons for his decision and the sheriff clerk shall forthwith send a copy of such a note to the persons referred to in paragraph (2).

### Signature of warrants

**3.52** Warrants, other than warrants granted by the sheriff under section 68(6) of the Act where the child has failed to attend a children's hearing, may be signed by the sheriff clerk but any warrant may, and a warrant under the said section 68(6) shall, be signed by the sheriff.

## PART VIII

## PROCEDURE IN APPEALS UNDER SECTION 51(1) OF THE ACT

### Form of appeal

**3.53**—(1) An appeal to the sheriff under section 51(1) of the Act (appeal against decision of children's hearing) shall be in Form 61, 62 or 63 whichever is appropriate and shall be lodged with the sheriff clerk.

(2) Subject to paragraph (3), the appeal shall be signed by the appellant or his representative.

(3) An appeal by a child may be signed on his behalf by any safeguarder appointed by the children's hearing.

**Appointment and intimation of first diet**

**3.54**—(1) On the lodging of the appeal, the sheriff clerk shall forthwith assign a date for the hearing and shall at the same time intimate to the appellant or his representative and, together with a copy of the appeal, to—

(a) the Principal Reporter;
(b) subject to the provisions of paragraph (4), the child (if not the appellant);
(c) the relevant person (if not the appellant);
(d) any safeguarder appointed for the purposes of the appeal by the sheriff or appointed by the chairman of the children's hearing; and
(e) any other person the sheriff thinks necessary.

(2) The sheriff clerk shall endorse on the appeal a certificate of execution of intimation under paragraph (1).

(3) Intimation to a child in terms of paragraph (1)(b) shall be in Form 64.

(4) The sheriff may dispense with intimation to a child in terms of paragraph (1)(b) where he considers that such dispensation is appropriate.

(5) The date assigned for the hearing under paragraph (1) shall be no later than 28 days after the lodging of the appeal.

**Answers**

**3.55**—(1) Except in an appeal under section 51(8) of the Act (appeal against warrant by children's hearing), if any person on whom service of the appeal has been made wishes to lodge answers to the appeal he shall do so not later than 7 days before the diet fixed for the hearing of the appeal.

(2) Any person who has lodged answers shall forthwith intimate a copy thereof to any other person on whom service has been made under rule 3.54(1).

**Procedure at hearing of appeal**

**3.56**—(1) Before proceeding in accordance with section 51(3) of the Act to examine the Principal Reporter and the authors or compilers of any reports or statements, the sheriff shall hear the appellant or his representative and any party to the appeal.

(2) On receipt of a further report called for under section 51(3)(c) of the Act, the sheriff shall direct the Principal Reporter to send a copy of the report to every party to the appeal.

(3) At any appeal the sheriff may hear evidence—

(a) where a ground of the appeal is an alleged irregularity in the conduct of a hearing, as to that irregularity;

(b) in any other circumstances where he considers it appropriate to do so.

(4) Where the nature of the appeal or of any evidence is such that the sheriff is satisfied that it is in the interests of the child that he should not be present at any stage of the appeal, the sheriff may exclude the child from the hearing during that stage and, in that event, any safeguarder appointed and the relevant person or representative of the child shall be permitted to remain during the absence of the child.

(5) Subject to paragraph (6), the sheriff may exclude the relevant person, or that person and any representative of his, or any such representative from any part or parts of the hearing for so long as he considers it is necessary in the interests of any child, where he is satisfied that—

(a) he must do so in order to obtain the views of the child in relation to the hearing; or

(b) the presence of the person or persons in question is causing, or is likely to cause, significant distress to the child.

(6) Where the relevant person has been excluded under paragraph (5) the sheriff shall, after that exclusion has ended, explain to him the substance of what has taken place in his absence and shall give him an opportunity to respond to any evidence given by the child by leading evidence or otherwise.

(7) Where an appeal has been heard in part and a safeguarder thereafter becomes a party to the appeal, the sheriff may order the hearing of the appeal to commence of new.

### Adjournment of appeals

**3.57** The sheriff may, on the motion of any party or on his own motion, adjourn the hearing of the appeal for such reasonable time and for such purpose as may in the circumstances be appropriate.

### Decision of sheriff in appeals

**3.58**—(1) The sheriff shall give his decision orally either at the conclusion of the appeal or on such day as he shall appoint.

(2) The sheriff may issue a note of the reasons for his decision, and shall require to do so where he decides to follow the course of action provided for in sub-paragraph (i) or (iii) of section 51(5)(c) of the Act.

(3) Any note in terms of paragraph (2) shall be issued at the time the sheriff gives his decision or within 7 days thereafter.

(4) The sheriff clerk shall forthwith send a copy of the interlocutor containing the decision of the sheriff, and where appropriate of the note referred to in paragraph (2), to the Principal Reporter, to the appellant (and to the child or the relevant person, if not the appellant) and to any safeguarder appointed by the sheriff, and shall also return to the Principal Reporter any documents lodged by virtue of section 51(2) or (3) of the Act.

## PART IX

## PROCEDURE IN APPEALS UNDER SECTION 51(11) OF THE ACT

### Appeals

**3.59**—(1) An appeal to the sheriff principal under section 51(11) of the Act shall be by note of appeal—

(a) requesting a stated case;

(b) specifying the point of law upon which the appeal is to proceed or the irregularity in the conduct of the case concerned, as the case may be; and

(c) lodged with the sheriff clerk within a period of 14 days beginning with the date of the decision appealed against.

(2) The appellant shall, at the same time as lodging a note of appeal, intimate the lodging of an appeal from the decision of the sheriff—

(a) in the case of an appeal under section 51(1) of the Act, to the parties referred to in rule 3.58(4);

(b) in the case of an application made under section 65(7) or (9) of the Act, to the parties referred to in rule 3.51(2); and

(c) in the case of an application made under section 85(1) of the Act (review of establishment of grounds of referral), to the parties referred to in rule 3.62.

(3) The sheriff shall, within 14 days of the lodging of a note of appeal, issue a draft stated case—

(a) containing findings in fact and law or, where appropriate, a narrative of the proceedings before him;

(b) containing appropriate questions of law or setting out the irregularity concerned; and

(c) containing a note stating the reasons for his decisions in law,

and the sheriff clerk shall send a copy of the draft stated case to the appellant and to parties referred to in paragraph (2).

(4) Within 7 days of the issue of the draft stated case—

(a) the appellant or a party referred to in paragraph (2) may lodge with the sheriff clerk a note of any adjustments which he seeks to make;

(b) the appellant or such a party may state any point of law which he wishes to raise in the appeal; and

(c) the note of adjustment and, where appropriate, point of law shall be intimated to the appellant and the other such parties.

(5) The sheriff may, on the motion of the appellant or a party referred to in paragraph (2) or of his own accord, and shall where he proposes to reject any proposed adjustment, allow a hearing on adjustments and may provide for such further procedure under this rule prior to the hearing of the appeal as he thinks fit.

(6) The sheriff shall, within 14 days after—

(a) the latest date on which a note of adjustments has been or may be lodged; or

(b) where there has been a hearing on adjustments, that hearing,

and after considering such note and any representations made to him at the hearing, state and sign the case.

(7) The stated case signed by the sheriff shall include—

(a) questions of law, framed by him, arising from the points of law stated by the parties and such other questions of law as he may consider appropriate;

(b) any adjustments, proposed under paragraph (4), which are rejected by him;

(c) a note of the irregularity in the conduct of the case averred by the parties and any questions of law or other issue which he considers arise therefrom, as the case may be.

(8) After the sheriff has signed the stated case, the sheriff clerk shall—

(a) place before the sheriff principal all documents and productions in the appeal together with the stated case; and

(b) send to the appellant and the parties referred to in paragraph (2) a copy of the stated case together with a written note of the date, time and place of the hearing of the appeal.

(9) In the hearing of an appeal, a party referred to in paragraph (2) shall not be allowed to raise questions of law or irregularities in the conduct of the case of which notice has not been given except on cause shown and subject to such conditions as the sheriff principal may consider appropriate.

(10) The sheriff may, on an application by any party or of his own motion, reduce any of the periods mentioned in paragraph (3), (4) or (6) to such period or periods as he considers reasonable.

(11) Where the sheriff is temporarily absent from duty for any reason, the sheriff principal may extend any period specified in paragraph (3) or (6) for such period or periods as he considers reasonable.

### Lodging of reports and statements with sheriff

**3.60** Where, in an appeal—

(a) it appears to the sheriff that any report or statement lodged under section 51(2) or (3) of the Act is relevant to any issue which is likely to arise in the stated case; and

(b) the report or statement has been returned to the Principal Reporter,

the sheriff may require the Principal Reporter to lodge the report or statement with the sheriff clerk.

### Hearing

**3.61**—(1) The sheriff principal, on hearing the appeal, may either pronounce his decision or reserve judgement.

(2) Where judgement is so reserved, the sheriff principal shall within 28 days give his decision in writing which shall be intimated by the sheriff clerk to the parties.

## PART X

## APPLICATION FOR REVIEW OF ESTABLISHMENT OF GROUNDS OF REFERRAL—NEW EVIDENCE

### Application

**3.62** An application under section 85 of the Act for a review of a finding made in terms of section 68(10) of the Act (finding that grounds for referral established) shall contain—

(a) the name and address of the applicant and his representative (if any);

(b) the name and address of the Principal Reporter;

(c) the name and address of the safeguarder (if any);

(d) the name and address of any other party to the application;

(e) the date and finding made and the name of the sheriff who made the finding;

(f)  the grounds for the making of the application;
(g)  specification of the nature of evidence in terms of section 85(3) of the Act not considered by the sheriff who made the finding;
(h)  the explanation for the failure to lead such evidence on the original application; and
(i)  any reports, affidavits and productions upon which the applicant intends to rely.

### Hearing on application

**3.63**—(1) After the lodging of the application in terms of rule 3.62, the sheriff clerk shall assign a diet for a hearing of the application and shall issue a warrant to cite in Form 65 which shall require the Principal Reporter to lodge answers if so advised within such time as the sheriff shall appoint.

(2) Subject to the provisions of rule 3.4 (service on child), after the issue of the warrant to cite, the applicant shall forthwith give notice of the application by serving a copy and the warrant on the persons named in rule 3.62.

(3) After hearing parties and allowing such further procedure as he thinks fits, the sheriff shall, if satisfied in terms of section 85(6) of the Act, consider the evidence and may fix a further hearing for that purpose.

### Hearing to consider the evidence

**3.64**—(1) After hearing parties on the evidence and allowing such further procedure as the sheriff thinks fit, he shall make an order as appropriate in terms of section 85(6) and (7) of the Act.

(2) The provisions of rule 3.51 shall apply to any order made under paragraph (1).

# APPENDIX 5

## Secure Accommodation (Scotland) Regulations 1996

### SI 1996/3255 (S.245)

*Coming into force*                    *1st April 1997*

The Secretary of State, in exercise of the powers conferred on him by section 60(1) of the Social Work (Scotland) Act 1968, section 75 of the Children (Scotland) Act 1995, and section 44(5) of the Criminal Procedure (Scotland) Act 1995, and of all other powers enabling him in that behalf, and after consulting the Council on Tribunals, hereby makes the following Regulations:

### Citation and commencement

**1.** These Regulations may be cited as the Secure Accommodation (Scotland) Regulations 1996 and shall come into force on 1st April 1997.

### Interpretation

**2.**—(1) In these Regulations, unless the context otherwise requires—
"the Act" means the Children (Scotland) Act 1995;
"the 1968 Act" means the Social Work (Scotland) Act 1968;
"the 1995 Act" means the Criminal Procedure (Scotland) Act 1995;
[1]"the 1996 Regulations" means the Residential Establishments-Child Care (Scotland) Regulations 1996;
"the appropriate local authority" has the meaning given to that term in section 44(11) of the 1995 Act;
"children's hearing" has the meaning given to that term by section 93(1) of the Act;
"day" includes a part of a day;
[2]"local authority" means a council constituted under section 2 of the Local Government etc. (Scotland) Act 1994;
"managers" means—
  [3](a) in the case of a local authority, those officers having delegated powers under section 56 of the Local Government (Scotland) Act 1973 for the management of the residential establishment providing secure accommodation;
  (b) in any other case those who are responsible for management of the residential establishment providing secure accommodation;
"parent" has the meaning given to that term by section 15(1) of the Act and also includes any person who is not a parent of the child but who has parental responsibilities;
"person in charge" means the person in charge of a residential establishment providing secure accommodation who is responsible to the managers of that establishment;
"Principal Reporter" has the meaning given to that term by section 93(1) of the Act;

"relevant person" has the meaning given to that term by the meaning in section 93(2)(b) of the Act;

"residential establishment" has the meaning given to that term by section 93(1) of the Act;

"secure accommodation" means accommodation provided in a residential establishment for the purpose of restricting the liberty of children;

"supervision requirement" has the meaning given to that term by section 93(1) of the Act.

(2) In the calculation of the periods of 48 hours and 72 hours mentioned in these Regulations, Sundays and public holidays shall be excluded.

(3) In these Regulations any reference to a numbered regulation is to the regulation in these Regulations bearing that number and any reference in a regulation to a numbered paragraph is to the paragraph of that regulation bearing that number.

NOTES:
1. S.I. 1996/3256.
2. (c.39); s.2 was amended by the Environment Act 1995 (c.25), Sch.22, para.232.
3. (c.65); s.56 was amended by the Local Government and Planning (Scotland) Act 1982 (c. 43), s.32, the Abolition of Domestic Rates Etc. (Scotland) Act 1987 (c. 47), s.28, the Local Government Finance Act 1992 (c. 14), Sch.13, para.35, the Local Government etc. (Scotland) Act 1994 (c. 39), Sch.13, para.92, and the Children (Scotland) Act 1995 (c. 36), Sch.4, para.22.

### Approval by the Secretary of State of secure accommodation

**3.** Accommodation shall not be provided and used in residential establishments as secure accommodation unless it has been approved by the Secretary of State, on such terms and conditions as he thinks fit, for such provision and use.

### Welfare of children in secure accommodation

**4.**—(1) Subject to paragraph (2), the managers in consultation with the person in charge shall ensure that the welfare of a child placed and kept in such accommodation is safeguarded and promoted and that the child receives such provision for his education, development and control as is conducive to his best interests.

(2) For the purposes of paragraph (1) the managers and person in charge shall comply with such requirements of Part II of the 1996 Regulations as apply to them and the establishments for which they are responsible.

### Maximum period in secure accommodation under the Act without authority

**5.** Subject to the provisions of regulation 8 the maximum period during which a child may be kept under the Act or the 1995 Act in secure accommodation without the authority of a children's hearing, or, as the case may be, of the sheriff, is an aggregate of 72 hours (whether or not consecutive) in any period of 28 consecutive days.

### Children subject to certain supervision requirements—interim placement

**6.**—(1) A child who is subject to a supervision requirement imposed under section 70 of the Act, but not subject to a condition imposed under subsection (9) of that section that he be liable to be placed and kept in secure accommodation, may not be placed in secure accommodation unless the chief social work officer of the local authority required to give effect to the supervision requirement and the person in charge are satisfied—

    (a) that the criteria specified in paragraph (a) or (b) of section 70(10) of the Act are satisfied with respect to the child; and

    (b) that it is in the child's best interests that he be placed and kept in secure accommodation,

and the chief social work officer shall, in addition, satisfy himself, in relation to the placing of the child in the residential establishment providing the secure accommodation, that the placement in that establishment is appropriate to the child's needs having regard to its statement of functions and objectives.

(2) On a child being placed in secure accommodation under paragraph (1), the chief social work officer of the local authority shall—

    (a) forthwith in writing inform any relevant person in relation to the child and the Principal Reporter accordingly, and shall, in addition, so inform the child (in a manner appropriate to his age and understanding); and

    (b) forthwith, and in any event not later than 24 hours from the time of that placement (whether or not the child is still held in secure accommodation) refer the case to the Principal Reporter and inform him in writing of—

        (i) the details of that placement and any subsequent placement or release;

        (ii) the reasons why at the time of placement the chief social work officer and the person in charge were satisfied with respect to the matters referred to and mentioned in paragraph (1) of this regulation and the reasons why at the time of writing they continue to be so satisfied or otherwise; and

        (iii) the views of the chief social work officer and the person in charge as to the need or otherwise for the child's detention in secure accommodation;

(3) On receipt by the Principal Reporter of the referral and information under paragraph (2)(b), he shall arrange for a review of the child's case by a children's hearing under section 73(8) of the Act which shall apply as if the reference to a transfer under section 72(2) of the Act included a reference to a placement under this regulation.

(4) The review of the child's case referred to in paragraph (3) shall take place no later than 72 hours from the time of the placement of the child in secure accommodation.

**Children looked after by local authority under Part II of the Act—interim placement**

7.—(1) A child who is being looked after by a local authority under chapters 1 or 4 of Part II of the Act may not be placed in secure accommodation unless the chief social work officer of the authority looking after the child and the person in charge are each satisfied with respect to the same matters as to which regulation 6(1) requires them to be satisfied and that the child may be in need of compulsory measures of supervision under Part II of the Act.

(2) On a child being placed in secure accommodation under paragraph (1), the chief social work officer of the local authority shall—

    (a) forthwith, in writing, inform any relevant person in relation to the child and the Principal Reporter accordingly;

    (b) forthwith and in any event not later than 24 hours from the time of that placement (whether or not the child is still held in secure accommodation) refer the child's case to the Principal Reporter and inform him in writing of—

        (i) the details of that placement and any subsequent placement or release;

        (ii) the reasons why at the time of placement the chief social work officer and the person in charge had cause to believe that the child may be in need of compulsory measures of supervision under Part II of the Act and the reasons why at the time of writing they still have such cause or otherwise;

        (iii) the reasons why at the time of placement the chief social work officer and the person in charge were satisfied with respect to the matters referred to and mentioned in regulation 6(1) of these Regulations and the reasons why at the time of writing they continue to be so satisfied or otherwise; and

        (iv) the views of the chief social work officer and the person in charge as to the need or otherwise for the child's detention in secure accommodation.

**8.**—(1) On receipt by the Principal Reporter of the referral and information under regulation 7(2)(b) and within 72 hours of the time of the child's placement in secure accommodation under regulation 7, the Principal Reporter shall consider and proceed, subject to paragraphs (2), (3) and (4), with the child's case in accordance with section 56 of the Act.

(2) Where the Principal Reporter decides under section 56(4) of the Act that a children's hearing does not require to be arranged—

    (a) he shall, within those 72 hours, inform the local authority accordingly and that authority shall thereupon arrange for the child's discharge (if not already discharged) forthwith from secure accommodation and for any relevant person (not already informed) to be informed of his discharge; and

    (b) if he considers that the proper course is to refer the child's case to the local authority with a view to arrangements for advice, guidance and assistance under Chapter 1 of Part II of the Act (support for children and their families), he shall, within these 72 hours, inform the authority accordingly.

(3) Subject to paragraph (4), where under section 56(6) of the Act, it appears to the Principal Reporter that the child is in need of compulsory measures of supervision the Principal Reporter shall arrange for a children's hearing to consider the child's case within 72 hours of the time of the child's placement in secure accommodation under regulation 7, and section 56(6) and (7) shall have effect accordingly.

(4) Notwithstanding the provisions of paragraph (3), the Principal Reporter shall have a further period of 24 hours in addition to the 72 hours referred to in paragraph (3), to fulfil his obligation thereunder if it is not reasonably practicable for him to arrange the hearing to convene

within the 72 hours or for him within the 72 hours to state the grounds for referral.

### Secure accommodation as a place of safety under the Act

**9.**—(1) In cases (other than those in which a children's hearing or court has previously authorised detention in secure accommodation as a condition of a warrant or order) where—

(a) further to a warrant issued or continued by a children's hearing under section 45(4) or (5), 63(5), 66(1) or (5), 69(4) or (7) of the Act or an order or warrant issued by the sheriff under 67(1), 68(6) or 68(10) of the Act, a child is taken to and kept in a place of safety provided by a local authority; and

(b) subsequent to the issue of such a warrant or order the chief social work officer of the local authority and the person in charge are satisfied with respect to the same matters referred to in regulation 6(1),

the child may, subject to the following provisions of this regulation, be placed and kept in secure accommodation; and where the child is so placed, the Principal Reporter and any relevant person shall be informed in writing forthwith of this.

(2) Where a child has been placed in secure accommodation in accordance with paragraph (1), the Principal Reporter shall—

(a) where a warrant in respect of the child has been issued under sections 45(4) or 45(5) of the Act, arrange under section 65 of the Act a children's hearing to consider the child's case;

(b) where a warrant in respect of the child has been issued under sections 63(5) or 66(1) or 66(5) of the Act, arrange under section 66(5) of the Act a children's hearing to consider the child's case within 72 hours of the child being placed in secure accommodation;

(c) where a warrant in respect of the child has been issued under sections 69(4) or 69(7) of the Act, arrange under section 69(1) of the Act a children's hearing to consider the child's case within 72 hours of the child being placed in secure accommodation;

(d) where an order in respect of the child has been granted under sections 68(6) or 68(10) of the Act, arrange under sections 66(1) (notwithstanding a warrant under section 68(6) having been issued previously) or 69(1) respectively of the Act a children's hearing to consider the child's case within 72 hours of the child being placed in secure accommodation; and

(e) where a warrant has been issued in respect of the child under section 67(1) of the Act, apply within 72 hours of the child being placed in secure accommodation to the sheriff for a warrant under section 67(1) in respect of the child.

### Information provided to a children's hearing by a local authority in relation to the use of secure accommodation

**10.** A local authority may submit a report in writing to the children's hearing recommending that a child be placed in a named residential establishment providing secure accommodation subject to a condition or order that he is liable to be kept in secure accommodation only if they are satisfied that the matters referred to in regulation 6(1)(a) and (b) are met.

### Review of supervision requirement

**11.**—(1) Where a children's hearing imposes or continues a condition under section 70(9) of the Act, either on the making of a supervision requirement under section 70(1) of the Act or the continuation of a supervision requirement under section 73(9)(e) of that Act, the Principal Reporter shall arrange a review of the supervision requirement under section 73(8) within 3 months of the condition under section 70(9) being made or continued.

(2) A review held under regulation 12(1) shall be considered a review held for the purposes of paragraph (1).

**12.**—(1) A child subject to a supervision requirement with a condition imposed under section 70(9) of the Act or any relevant person may, in writing, require the Principal Reporter to make arrangements under section 73 of the Act to have the supervision requirement reviewed by a children's hearing if in the preceding 6 weeks the child has not been placed in secure accommodation by virtue of that condition.

(2) Where a notice is given to the Principal Reporter by a child or any relevant person under paragraph (1), the Principal Reporter shall arrange a children's hearing within 21 days of the receipt by him of the notice.

### Child detained under section 44 of Criminal Procedure (Scotland) Act 1995: use of secure accommodation

**13.**—(1) A child who is detained in residential accommodation provided by a local authority in accordance with an order under section 44 of the 1995 Act may be detained in secure accommodation only where the chief social work officer of the appropriate local authority and the person in charge of the residential establishment providing that secure accommodation are satisfied with respect to the same matters as to which regulation 6 requires them to be satisfied.

(2) Where paragraph (1) applies, the child shall be placed and subject to regulation 15 kept in secure accommodation only at such time and for so long as the person in charge with the agreement of the chief social work officer considers necessary.

### Children otherwise dealt with under the Criminal Procedure (Scotland) Act 1995

**14.**—(1) Where a child—

(a) is committed to a local authority under section 51(1)(a)(ii) or 51(4)(b) of the 1995 Act to be detained in a place of safety chosen by the authority, he may not, in pursuance thereof, be placed or detained in secure accommodation as a place of safety under the section;

(b) is to be kept in a place of safety under section 43 of the 1995 Act which is a residential establishment provided by a local authority, he may not, in pursuance thereof, be placed in secure accommodation provided in that establishment; or

(c) is to be detained under section 216(7) of the 1995 Act, in a place chosen by a local authority, he may not, in pursuance thereof, be placed in secure accommodation, unless the chief social work officer of the authority and the person in charge are each satisfied with respect to the same matters as to which regulation 6 requires them to be satisfied in relation to the child.

(2) Where paragraph (1) applies, the child shall be placed and subject to regulation 15 kept in secure accommodation only at such time and for so long as the person in charge with the agreement of the chief social work officer considers necessary.

### Review of the use of secure accommodation

**15.**—(1) The chief social work officer of the appropriate local authority, in consultation with the person in charge, shall ensure that, where a child is detained in secure accommodation by virtue of regulations 13 or 14, arrangements are made by them to review the case of such a child—

(a) within 7 days of the child's placement in secure accommodation (whether or not the child is still held in secure accommodation);

(b) at such times as appear to them necessary or appropriate in the light of the child's progress; and

(c) in any event at intervals of not more than 3 months;

and the child shall be detained in secure accommodation only where, upon such review, the chief social work officer and the person in charge are satisfied that it is in the best interests of the child.

(2) In conducting such a review the chief social work officer and the person in charge shall have regard to all relevant circumstances including—

(a) the matters specified at regulation 6(1); and

(b) where practicable, the views of the child and the opinion of his parents.

(3) In conducting such a review the chief social work officer and the person in charge shall obtain the advice in relation to the detention of the child in secure accommodation of a secure placement review panel, which shall be set up by any local authority responsible for the management of a residential establishment providing secure accommodation (failing which the local authority in whose area the establishment is situated) and consist of at least persons—

(a) none of whom may be the chief social work officer or the person in charge; and

(b) one of whom must be an independent person who is neither an office holder nor an employee of a local authority or the residential establishment.

(4) The chief social work officer and the person in charge shall provide the secure placement review panel with all the relevant facts of the child's case available to them in order that the secure placement review panel can give informed advice.

### Records to be kept in respect of a child in secure accommodation

**16.** The managers, in consultation with the person in charge, shall ensure that a record is kept with respect to the child's placement in such accommodation, which shall include a record of—

(a) the child's full name, sex, and date of birth;

(b) the supervision requirement, order or other provision by reference to which the placement was made;

(c) the date and time of his placement in secure accommodation, the reasons for this, the names of the persons authorising the placement, and the address at which the child was living before the placement;

(d) the name and address of each person to whom notice was given by virtue of these Regulations of the child's placement;

(e) reviews undertaken with respect to the placement by virtue of section 73 of the Act;

(f) the date and time of his discharge, and his place of residence following discharge from secure accommodation, and the names of the persons authorising that discharge.

**Children's Hearings (Transmission of Information etc.) (Scotland) Regulations 1996**

SI 1996/3260 (S.250)

*Coming into force*                                    *1st April 1997*

The Secretary of State, in exercise of the powers conferred on him by sections 17(1), 40(3), 42(1) and 74 of the Children (Scotland) Act 1995 and of all other powers enabling him in that behalf, and after consulting the Council on Tribunals, hereby makes the following Regulations:

**Citation and commencement**

**1.** These Regulations may be cited as the Children's Hearings (Transmission of Information etc.) (Scotland) Regulations 1996 and shall come into force on 1st April 1997.

**Interpretation**

**2.** In these Regulations unless the context otherwise requires—
"the Act" means the Children (Scotland) Act 1995;
"the Children's Hearings Rules" means the Children's Hearings (Scotland) Rules 1996;
"children's hearing" is a children's hearing as defined in section 39(3) of the Act;
"child" has the meaning given to that term by section 93(2)(b) of the Act;
"compulsory measures of supervision" has the meaning given to that term by section 93(1) of the Act;
"place of safety" has the meaning given to that term by section 93(1) of the Act;
"Principal Reporter" has the meaning given to that term by section 93(1) of the Act;
"relevant local authority" has the meaning given to that term by section 93(1) of the Act;
"relevant person" has the meaning given to that term by section 93(2)(b) of the Act;
"residential establishment" has the meaning given to that term by section 93(1) of the Act;
"responsible for" means any person who, by virtue of a supervision requirement, has or is to have control over the child;
"supervision requirement" has the meaning given to that term by section 70(1) of the Act.

**Transmission by relevant local authority of information on child subject to supervision requirement**

**3.**—(1) Where—
(a) in any case a children's hearing have made, continued or varied or inserted a requirement in a supervision requirement in respect of a child; and

(b) a person other than the relevant local authority or a relevant person in relation to the child is responsible for a child under that requirement; and

(c) it appears to the relevant local authority that any report on the child and his social background put to the children's hearing for their consideration of the case would assist that person in the care and supervision of the child,

the relevant local authority shall, as soon as reasonably practicable after they receive notice under rule 21 of the Children's Hearings Rules of the making, continuation or variation or insertion of a requirement in the requirement, give a copy of that report to that person.

(2) Where at any time while a supervision requirement is in force in respect of a child it appears to the relevant local authority that any information they have about the child or his circumstances is relevant to the care of the child, they shall make that information available to any person who is responsible for the care of the child in terms of the supervision requirement.

**Temporary accommodation of child subject to supervision requirement**

4.—(1) Where—

(a) a children's hearing have made, continued or varied or inserted a requirement in a supervision requirement; and

(b) a child is required to reside in a residential establishment or other place specified in the requirement; but

(c) the relevant local authority are unable to make immediate arrangements for his reception in that establishment or place,

the relevant local authority may arrange for the child to be temporarily accommodated in some suitable place, other than that specified in the requirement, for any period not exceeding 22 days commencing on the date of the making, continuation or variation or insertion of a requirement in the requirement.

(2) If it appears to the relevant local authority that they will be unable to make the arrangements mentioned in paragraph (1)(c) above before the expiry of the period of 22 days specified, the authority shall, before that period has expired, refer the case of the child to the Principal Reporter under section 73(4) of the Act on the ground that the supervision requirement ought to be reviewed.

(3) Where the relevant local authority refer the case of a child to the Principal Reporter under paragraph (2) above—

(a) the Principal Reporter shall under section 73(8) of the Act arrange for a children's hearing to review the supervision requirement as soon as is reasonably practicable and in any event within seven days of the date of receipt of the reference by the authority; and

(b) where the date of the sitting of the children's hearing arranged by virtue of sub-paragraph (a) above occurs after the expiry of the period of 22 days mentioned in paragraph (1) above, that period shall be deemed to extend to the date on which the children's hearing sits.

**Conveyance by the relevant local authority of a child to a residential establishment etc**

5. Whenever it is necessary to convey a child—

   (a) to a residential establishment or other place in which he is required to reside by virtue of a supervision requirement;

   (b) to any place to which he falls to be taken under subsection (1) or (5) of section 82 (recovery of certain fugitive children) of the Act; or

   (c) to any person to whom he falls to be returned under subsection (3) of that section,

it shall be the duty of the relevant local authority to ensure that the child is conveyed to that establishment or place or to that person.

# APPENDIX 7

## Emergency Child Protection Measures (Scotland) Regulations 1996

### SI 1996/3258 (S.248)

*Coming into force*                    *April 1, 1997*

The Secretary of State, in exercise of the powers conferred on him by section 62 of the Children (Scotland) Act 1995, and of all other powers enabling him in that behalf, hereby makes the following regulations:

### Citation and commencement

**1.** These Regulations may be cited as the Emergency Child Protection Measures (Scotland) Regulations 1996 and shall come into force on 1st April 1997.

### Interpretation

**2.** In these Regulations, unless the context otherwise requires—
"the Act" means the Children (Scotland) Act 1995;
"applicant" means the person or the local authority who applied to a justice of the peace for an authorisation under subsection (1) or, as the case may be, subsection (2), of section 61 of the Act;
"place of safety" has the meaning given to that term in section 93(1) of the Act;
"Principal Reporter" has the meaning given to that term in section 93(1) of the Act; and
"relevant person" in relation to a child has the meaning given to that term in section 93(2)(b) of the Act.

### Duties of constable where child removed to place of safety

**3.** As soon as reasonably practicable after a child has been removed by a constable to a place of safety under section 61(5) of the Act, a constable shall, subject to regulation 5 below, take such steps as are reasonably practicable to inform the following persons of the matters specified in regulation 4 below:—
(a) any relevant person in relation to the child;
(b) any person, other than a relevant person, with whom the child was residing immediately before being removed to the place of safety;
(c) the local authority for the area in which the place of safety to which the child was removed is situated;
(d) where not falling within paragraph (c) , the local authority for the area in which the child is ordinarily resident;
(e) the local authority for the area in which the child was residing immediately before being removed to a place of safety (where they are not the authority under (c) or (d) of this regulation); and
(f) the Principal Reporter.

**4.** The following matters are specified as matters on which the persons mentioned in regulation 3 above are to be informed:—
(a) the removal of the child by a constable to a place of safety;

(b) the place of safety at which the child is being, or is to be, kept;

(c) the reasons for the removal of the child to a place of safety; and

(d) any other steps which a constable has taken or is taking to safeguard the welfare of the child while in a place of safety.

**5.** Where a constable is informing the persons mentioned in paragraphs (a) and (b) of regulation 3 above, he may, where he considers it necessary to do so in order to safeguard the welfare of the child, withhold from those persons any of the information specified in regulation 4(b) and (d) above.

**6.** Where a child has been removed to a place of safety by a constable under section 61(5) of the Act, a constable keeping him in a place of safety shall, subject to subsections (6) to (8) of that section, continue to so keep him only so long as he has reasonable cause to believe that—

(a) the conditions for the making of a child protection order laid down in section 57(1) of the Act are satisfied; and

(b) it is necessary to keep the child in a place of safety in order to protect him from significant harm (or further such harm).

**Duties where authorisation granted by justice of the peace to protect child**

**7.** Where an authorisation is granted by a justice of the peace under subsection (1) or (2) of section 61 of the Act, the applicant shall implement the authorisation as soon as reasonably practicable.

**8.** Where an authorisation has been granted under section 61 of the Act, as soon as reasonably practicable after steps have been taken to prevent any person from removing the child from a place where he is then being accommodated, or the child has been removed to a place of safety, the applicant shall, subject to regulation 10 below, take such steps as are reasonably practicable to inform the following persons of the matters specified in regulation 9 below—

(a) any relevant person in relation to the child;

(b) any person, other than a relevant person, with whom the child was residing immediately before the grant of the authorisation;

(c) where not the applicant, the local authority for the area in which the place of safety to which the child was or is to be removed is situated;

(d) where not falling within paragraph (c) and where not the applicant, the local authority for the area in which the child is ordinarily resident;

(e) where not the applicant, the local authority for the area in which the child was residing immediately before the grant of the authorisation (where they are not the authority under (c) or (d) of this regulation); and

(f) the Principal Reporter.

**9.** The following matters are specified as matters on which the persons mentioned in regulation 8 above are to be informed:-

(a) the grant of the authorisation and the steps taken to implement it;

(b) the place of safety at which the child is being or is to be kept or, as the case may be, the place at which the child is being accommodated;

(c) the reasons for the grant of the authorisation; and

(d) any other steps which the applicant has taken or is taking to safeguard the welfare of the child while in a place of safety.

**10.** Where an applicant is informing the persons specified in paragraphs (a) and (b) of regulation 8 above, he may, where he considers it necessary to do so in order to safeguard the welfare of the child, withhold from any of those persons any of the information specified in regulation 9(b) and (d) above.

#### Notice where authorisation ceases to have effect

**11.** Where an authorisation granted under subsection (1) or (2) of section 61 of the Act ceases to have effect by virtue of section 61(4)(a) of the Act (authorisation ceasing to have effect where not implemented within 12 hours of being made), the applicant shall immediately notify the justice of the peace who granted the authorisation and as soon as reasonably practicable give notice of this to the persons specified in regulation 8 above.

#### Duties where child subject to emergency protection measures

**12.** In regulations 13 to 16 below—
"emergency protection measures" in relation to a child means—
  (a) further to the grant of an authorisation by a justice of the peace under subsection (1) or (2) of section 61 of the Act, the prevention of the removal of the child by any person from a place where he is then being accommodated or, as the case may be, the removal of the child to a place of safety and keeping him there until the expiry of the authorisation; and
  (b) the removal of a child to a place of safety by a constable under section 61(5) of the Act, and keeping him there;
"specified person" means—
  (a) where an authorisation has been granted by a justice of the peace under subsection (1) or (2) of section 61 of the Act, the applicant for such authorisation; and
  (b) where a child has been removed to a place of safety by a constable under section 61(5) of the Act, a constable keeping him in such a place.

**13.** As early as is consistent with the protection and welfare of the child, the specified person, taking or having taken emergency protection measures, shall taking account of the age and maturity of the child—
  (a) inform the child of the reasons for the emergency protection measures being taken or having been taken, and of any further steps which may be taken with respect to him under the Act or under these Regulations; and
  (b) so far as practicable, give the child an opportunity to express his views, and have regard to any views as may be expressed before continuing with emergency protection measures or taking any such further steps.

**14.** Where emergency protection measures have been taken in relation to a child, the specified person shall do, what is reasonable in all the circumstances for the purpose of safeguarding the welfare of the child (having regard in particular to the length of the period during which the child will be subject to such measures).

**15.** Where further to emergency protection measures a child is taken to a police station as a place of safety, the specified person shall as soon as reasonably practicable take the child to another type of place of safety and keep the child in that other place.

**16.** Where a child is subject to emergency protection measures, the specified person in relation to—

    (a)  any relevant person in relation to the child; and

    (b)  any person with whom the child was living immediately before such measures were taken, shall allow, and

    (c)  any other person, may allow;

such contact (if any) with the child as, in the view of the specified person, is both reasonable and in accordance with the welfare of the child.

# APPENDIX 8

## The Children's Hearings (Legal Representation) (Scotland) Rules 2002

### SSI 2002/63

*Coming into force*             *23rd February 2002*

The Scottish Ministers, in exercise of the powers conferred by sections 42(1) and (2)(a), (b), (d) and (i) and 103(3) of the Children (Scotland) Act 1995, and of all other powers enabling them in that behalf, and after consultation with the Scottish Committee of the Council on Tribunals in accordance with section 8(1) of the Tribunals and Inquiries Act 1992 hereby make the following Rules:

### Citation and commencement

**1.** These Rules may be cited as the Children's Hearings (Legal Representation) (Scotland) Rules 2002 and shall come into force on 23rd February 2002.

### Interpretation

**2.** In these Rules—
>"the Act" means the Children (Scotland) Act 1995;
>"legal representative" means a person appointed under these Rules to act as the legal representative of a child who is the subject of a Children's Hearing;
>"local authority" means the local authority for the area of the Children's Hearing; and
>"the Principal Reporter" means the Principal Reporter appointed under section 127 of the Local Government etc. (Scotland) Act 1994 or any officer of the Scottish Children's Reporter Administration to whom there is delegated under section 131(1) of that Act any functions of the Principal Reporter.

### Legal representation for the purpose of assisting children at a Children's Hearing

**3.—** (1) A business meeting arranged by the Principal Reporter under section 64(1) of the Act may appoint to any child who is due to appear before the Children's Hearing a legal representative if it appears to that business meeting, notwithstanding that an appointment may be made under section 41(1) of the Act, that—
>(a) legal representation is required to allow the child to effectively participate at the Hearing; or
>(b) it may be necessary to make a supervision requirement (or a review of such requirement)

which includes a requirement for the child to reside in a named residential establishment and the child is likely to meet the criteria specified in section 70(10) of the Act and the Secure Accommodation (Scotland) Regulations 1996.

(2) The Children's Hearing may at any time appoint to any child a legal representative if it appears to that Hearing that either of the

circumstances in paragraph (1)(a) or (b) above apply notwithstanding that:

  (a) a business meeting or a previous Children's Hearing has considered the appointment of a legal representative for the child who is the subject of the Hearing; or

  (b) an appointment has been or may be made under section 41(1) of the Act.

(3) When any appointment of a legal representative is made, the business meeting or the Children's Hearing shall direct the Principal Reporter to advise the local authority of that appointment.

### Notification of Children's Hearings and provision of documents to legal representative

**4.**— (1) The Principal Reporter shall make any document, information or copies of any document provided to the Chairman and members of the Children's Hearing available to the legal representative.

(2) Subject to the Children's Hearings (Scotland) Rules 1996, where the Principal Reporter arranges any Children's Hearing, he or she shall, wherever practicable—

  (a) at least seven days before the date of the Hearing, notify the legal representative of the time and place of the Hearing; and

  (b) at least three days before the date of the Hearing, give to the legal representative a copy of the documents which are relevant to the case of a child to be considered at the Hearing.

### Panel of legal representatives

**5.**— (1) Where the business meeting or Children's Hearing appoints a legal representative, the local authority shall make appropriate arrangements for a legal representative to attend the Hearing, who shall be a person who holds a current practising certificate issued by the Law Society of Scotland and who is appointed to one of the following:—

  (a) the panel of persons to safeguard the interests of children established under the Panels of Persons to Safeguard the Interests of Children (Scotland) Regulations 2001 for the local authority area within which the child resides, or if circumstances require, from any other local authority list in Scotland; or

  (b) the panel of curators ad litem and reporting officers established under the Curators ad Litem and Reporting Officers (Panels) (Scotland) Regulations 2001 for the Sheriff Court area within which the child resides or, if circumstances require, any other Sheriff Court district within Scotland.

(2) The local authority shall notify the Principal Reporter of the name of the legal representative.

### Revocations

**6.** The Children's Hearings (Legal Representation) (Scotland) Rules 2001 and the Children's Hearings (Legal Representation) (Scotland) Amendment Rules 2002 are hereby revoked.

# INDEX